Practical Theatre

Editor: Sally Mackey

Stanley Thornes (Publishers) Ltd

Text © Pippa Bound, Tamsin Dodgson, Chris Elwell, Kate Firth, Stephen Leib, Sara Liles, Sally Mackey, Peter Nelson, Aurora Simpson, Janette Smith, Elaine Turner, Vishni Velada Billson, David Wood 1997

Original line illustrations © Stanley Thornes (Publishers) Ltd 1997

Artwork by Phil Ford Design and Illustration

Picture research by Amanda Davidge

Copy-edited by Caroline Arthur

First published in 1997 by:
Stanley Thornes (Publishers) Ltd
Ellenborough House
Wellington Street
CHELTENHAM GL50 1YW
England

00 01 / 10 9 8 7 6 5 4

A catalogue record for this book is available from the British Library.

ISBN 0–7487–2857–0

Typeset by Viners Wood Associates

Printed and bound in Great Britain by Redwood Books, Trowbridge, Wiltshire

Cover photograph: *Tregeagle* – Steve Tanner/Kneehigh Theatre Company

Cover illustration: Setting document for *The Rose Tattoo*, reproduced by permission of Peter Maccoy

Contents

To my parents, with retrospective thanks for pushing me in those earlier years and, particularly, to David, for his ceaseless encouragement and love in the later ones.

Acknowledgements

Editor's note
I would like to thank all the authors of these chapters for their time and patience in writing this book. They have responded to all my queries, nags and deadlines with fortitude and good humour. Particular thanks to Peter Nelson for his help with the minutiae of the GNVQ syllabuses. Additional thanks to Sara Liles, Janette Smith and Peter Nelson who contributed to Chapter 1. Lastly, I would like to thank a friend to many of the authors, Simon Cooper: not a contributor, but always there with a kindly and thoughtful word.

The editor and contributors would like to thank the following people and organisations for their guidance, advice, help, support and/or encouragement in compiling this book:

Ken Albrow and Ray Sinclair-Smith (East Berkshire College), Jackie Alexis (Theatre Centre), Caroline Arthur (Editor), Alan Ayckbourn, Matthew Bailey, Rosemary Beattie (Royal National Theatre), Nick Blackburn and Stephen Hodgson (Ticketmaster), Susan Brooks, Martin Brown (Equity), Lindsey Butcher, Jason Carr, Alison Carter, Tony Castro, Stephen Chappell (Arts Council of England), Chris Cresswell, Rachel Dickinson (Royal National Theatre), the Drama and Education undergraduate students at the Central School of Speech and Drama especially DE97 and DE98, Scilla Dyke, Fergus Early (Green Candle Dance Company), Jackie Eley, Jonathan Firth, Halinka Fraser, Sally Goldsworthy (Lyric Theatre, Hammersmith), David Hamilton-Peters (Royal National Theatre), Dick Hanson, Jeremy Harthill and Alastair Moir (Watford Palace Theatre), Judith Harvey (Stanley Thornes Publishers), Vicky Hebbes, Jack Holloway, Jonathan Holloway, Isobel Horseman and Peter Shepherd (Arts Council of England), Tiffany Hosking, Micky Hunt, Independent Theatre Company, Tony James, Simon Lambros, Mark McDonnell, Catherine Mikic, Musicians Union, Barry Page (Stanley Thornes Publishers), Samantha Pinnel, Dot Queen (Welfare State International), Royal Shakespeare Company, Dr Robert Saxton, David Schaal, Bob Scott, Francis Shaw, Veron Arnold Simpson, the sixth-form students of the Ravensbourne School and Darrick Wood School, Gerard Stephenson, Frances Tilston, Lucy Tragear, Matthew Velada Billson, Gary Yershon.

In particular, we would like to thank all the actors, directors, companies and others who have been interviewed and/or supplied photographs or illustrations.

The authors and publishers are grateful to the following for permission to reproduce copyright photographs:

7.84 Theatre Company Scotland, page 224; AJS Theatre Lighting & Stage Supplies Ltd, pages 291, 294 left, 295, 296; Ancient Art & Architecture Collection, pages 320, 322 top, 323, 325, 326; Simon Annand/Theatre de Complicité, page 95; Brian Aris, page 43; Patrick Baldwin/Pop-Up, page 263, 265; Derek Bierman/Legs on the Wall, pages 128, 129; British Museum, page 322 (middle & bottom); Sheila Burnett, page 81; Stuart Colwill/Black Mime Theatre, page 78; Dee Conway, page 74; Donald Cooper/Photostage, pages 35, 116; Alan Copson, page 330; Johan Cruckshank/The Mask Studio, page 333; Phil Cutts/Rejects Revenge, pages 121, 125; Michael Dalton/Pop-Up, page 251; John Daniell/Greenwich & Lewisham Young Peoples Theatre, page 224; Hannes Flaschberger/Theatre de Complicité, page 96; The Fotomas Index, page 29; Della Grace/Gay Sweatshop, page 231; John Haynes, pages 69, 71; John Haynes/People Show, page 220; Hodder & Stoughton for the picture taken from 'Stages in Design' by Kimber & Wood, page 309; Chris Hoddinott/Scottish Youth Theatre, page 254; Mike Hutson/Redferns, page 367; Coneyl Jay/Faith Wilson Arts Publicity, page 88; Ivan Kyncl, pages 72, 278; Mander & Mitchenson Theatre Collection, pages 28, 228, 230, 234; Jean Mohr/Red Ladder Theatre Company, page 223; Ged Murray/Welfare State International, page 225; Keith Orton, pages 282, 283; Clare Park, page 92; Quintet Publishing Ltd, page 328; The Royal National Theatre, page 348; Justin Slee/Guzelian, page 85; Stephen Speller/Black Mime Theatre, page 76; Steve Tanner, pages 118, 120, 143, 248; Tara Arts, page 91; Theatre Centre, page 241; Allan Titmuss, page 79; Simon Warner, page 87; Werner Forman Archive, pages 319, 321; Mark Wilsher/Trestle Theatre Company, page 343.

The authors and publishers are also grateful to the following, for permission to reproduce other copyright material in this book:

Green Candle Dance Company for the staff structure, page 169; Heinemann Educational Publishers for 'Summer Fires of Mulanje Mountain' from *New Poetry of Africa* (Calder, Mapanje and Pieterse, 1983), page 340; Hodder & Stoughton Educational for the diagram of Maslow's 'Hierarchy of Needs', page 164; *The Independent* for the article 'The Kids Are All Right. Oh No They're Not' (14 December 1994); Peter Maccoy for the setting and running documents, pages 300-301; Keith Orton for the designs, pages 287-9; Palace Theatre, Watford, for the staff structure and balance sheet, pages 353 and 364; Phaidon Press Ltd for the production budget expenditure sheet, page 365; Pop-Up Theatre Ltd/Tim Newton for the extracts from *Iron Dreams*, pages 264-5; Royal Shakespeare Company for the staff structure, page 168; *Time Out* magazine and Times Supplements Limited, 1997 for the reviews of *Iron Dreams*, page 266: Warner/Chappell Music Limited for the extract from *Return to the Forbidden Planet*, page 340 (*Return to the Forbidden Planet* Copyright 1983, 1989 by Bob Carlton. All rights reserved. All enquiries regarding performances should be addressed to Warner/Chappell Music Limited, 129 Park Street, London W1Y 3FA).

Every effort has been made to contact copyright holders. The publishers apologise to any whose rights have been overlooked, and will be happy to rectify any errors or omissions.

List of contributors

Sally Mackey (editor)
Senior Lecturer in the Education Department at the Central School of Speech and Drama; co-author (with Simon Cooper) of *Theatre Studies: An Approach for Advanced Level* (Stanley Thornes, 1995); formerly Head of an Expressive Arts department.

Pippa Bound
Manager of the Tristan Bates Theatre, the Actors' Centre, London.

Tamsin Dodgson
Former teacher; assistant to theatrical agent

Chris Elwell
Artistic Director of the Half Moon Theatre Company, London. Formerly Drama and Education lecturer, teacher and education officer at the English National Ballet and the Royal Shakespeare Company

Kate Firth
Freelance practitioner: actor and voice specialist

Stephen Leib
Freelance practitioner and teacher

Sara Liles
Teacher of drama in Kent

Peter Nelson
Head of Performing Arts at East Berkshire College, Slough

Aurora Simpson
Head of Drama at Pimlico School, London

Janette Smith
Regional Theatre Young Director Scheme bursary winner: trainee director at the Royal Court Theatre, London. Formerly teacher at Beauchamp College, Oadby.

Elaine Turner
Lecturer, Brunel University College and University of Warwick

Vishni Velada Billson
Freelance theatre-in-education practitioner and part-time drama teacher

David Wood
Head of Education Department at the Central School of Speech and Drama; co-author (with Ken Kimber) of *Stages in Design* (Hodder and Stoughton, 1993)

Introduction: How to Use this Book

Practical Theatre is for post-16 students of theatre in schools, colleges, youth groups, higher education colleges and universities.

'Practical' theatre is a broad term used for a number of different activities. Frequently, the implication is that no theory or study is involved. This book seeks to encourage practical work of quality by providing a rigorous framework of knowledge for such activity. For example, if students are engaged in an 'acting' assignment, Chapter 2 offers research into the history of acting, an account of the methods of key 20th-century practitioners who have influenced acting techniques and interviews with professional actors, in addition to guidelines and activities for students' own acting assignments. In this way, students can engage with their own practical theatre work through a greater understanding of the context.

Each chapter (except the first) is divided into two major sections:
- research material and information on the topic of the chapter;
- resource activities, consisting of aims and objectives, background information and a number of tasks. These tasks vary from short exercises to lengthy projects.

There are two methods of using each chapter. Students may choose to read through the first section sequentially and in its entirety, gaining a clear understanding of the topic. Resource activities may be undertaken after this initial study, as appropriate. Alternatively, the student may decide to identify an appropriate resource activity which he or she wishes to undertake. Usually, this activity will require him or her to read certain pages from the research and information section. In this way, the student will read only the information relevant to the activity.

Practical Theatre may be used by students without 'teaching' by a lecturer or facilitator; however, it may also be used as a regular textbook. It is intended to be of use for all post-16 theatre-related courses. In addition, it will be of use to undergraduates and HND students who are engaged in practical drama or theatre courses.

Whilst each chapter has the same framework, the style varies and each author has brought particular areas of interest or a specific focus into his or her chapter.

Where we feel it is useful, we have adopted margin notes to assist in the swift assimilation or revision of the information offered. Occasionally, the style of the chapter does not suit margin notes, as in Chapters 1 and 5.

Each chapter includes an annotated bibliography of books that students may find useful for further research. At the end of the book (p.380), there is a general bibliography of all the books quoted or referred to by the authors.

Guidelines for Using this Book in Post-16 (FE) Courses in the UK

This chart shows the elements of various UK post-16 Performing Arts, Theatre Studies and Drama syllabuses that are covered by the chapters of this book. Chapter 1 is intended as a broad resource for all syllabuses.

Syllabus	Chapter 1	Chapter 2	Chapter 3
GNVQ Advanced, Performing Arts and Entertainment Industries	*See pp.xiii–xiv*		
AEB A-level Theatre Studies	*Paper 1*	*Paper 1 – Individual Skill of Acting*	*Paper 1 – Individual Skill of Directing; Paper 2 – Directing Set Texts; Paper 3 – Commentary and Analysis*
UCLES A-level Performing Arts	*4790 Language of Performing Arts; 4796/7 Student Devised Performance*	*4792 Performance Study: Drama; 4796/7 Student Devised Performance*	*4792 Performance Study: Drama; 4796/7 Student Devised Performance*
BTEC National and First Diplomas in Performing Arts	*Performance Workshop; Production Project; Writing and Devising*	*Acting Techniques I & II; Performance Workshop*	*Production Project; Directing*
International Baccalaureate (Theatre Arts module)	*Part 1 – Performance Skills; Part 4 – Theatre Production*	*Part 1 – Performance Skills; Part 4 – Theatre Production; Part 5 – Individual Study*	*Part 3 – Play Analysis; Part 5 – Individual Study*
ULEAC A-level Drama	*Paper 1 – Performance; Paper 3 – Text in Performance; Paper 4 – Understanding Drama*	*Paper 1–Performance; Paper 3 – Text in Performance*	*Paper 2 – Exploration through Drama*
WJEC A-level Theatre Arts	*Practical work of both projects*	*Objective iv: Presentation of Practical Work; Objective v: Conceptualisation of Practical Work in the Written Work*	
Scottish Certificate (Higher) in Drama	*Investigative Drama*	*Aspects of Theatre: Acting*	

Syllabus	Chapter 4	Chapter 5	Chapter 6	Chapter 7
GNVQ Advanced, Performing Arts and Entertainment Industries	*See pp.xiii–xiv*			
AEB A-level Theatre Studies	*Paper 1 – Group Practical*			
UCLES A-level Performing Arts	*4790 Language of Performing Arts; 4794 The Performer and the Audience; 4795 Contemporary and Historic Art Forms; 4796/7 Student Devised Performance*		*4795 Contemporary and Historic Art Forms; 4794 The Performer and the Audience*	*4794 The Performer and the Audience*
BTEC National and First Diplomas in Performing Arts	*Performance Workshop; Production Project*	*Arts Administration; Arts in Society*	*Arts in Society*	*Arts in Society; Production Project*
International Baccalaureate (Theatre Arts module)	*Part 1 – Performance Skills; Part 4 – Theatre Production*	*Part 4 – Theatre Production*	*Part 2 – Theatre Studies; Part 5 – Individual Study*	
ULEAC A-level Drama	*All four papers*		*Paper 2 – Exploration through Drama*	*Paper 1; Paper 3*
WJEC A-level Theatre Arts	*Objective iv*		*Objectives ii and iii*	
Scottish Certificate (Higher) in Drama	*Investigative Drama*			*Investigative Drama*

Syllabus	Chapter 8	Chapter 9	Chapter 10
GNVQ Advanced, Performing Arts and Entertainment Industries	See pp.xiii–xiv		
AEB A-level Theatre Studies	Paper 1 – Individual Study on Design; Paper 2 – Designing Set Texts; Paper 3 – Commentary and Analysis	Paper 1 – Individual Skill: Masks	
UCLES A-level Performing Arts	4790 Language of Performing Arts; 4796/7 Student Devised Performance	Any of the student-devised modules	4796/7 Student Devised Performance
BTEC National and First Diplomas in Performing Arts	Production Techniques; Setting for Performance I & II; Stagecraft I	Any of the student-devised modules	Arts Administration; Production Techniques
International Baccalaureate (Theatre Arts module)	Part 4 – Theatre Production	Part 1 – Performance Skills	Part 4 – Theatre Production
ULEAC A-level Drama	Paper 3 – Text in Performance	Any of the student-devised modules	
WJEC A-level Theatre Arts	Practical Performance element of both projects	Any of the student-devised modules	
Scottish Certificate (Higher) in Drama	Investigative Drama (folio)	Any of the student-devised modules	

Advanced GNVQ Performing Arts and Entertainment Industries

This chart maps the Advanced GNVQ Mandatory Units against the ten chapters. A tick indicates that there are sections in the relevant chapter which will support the teaching and learning of that element in the particular Mandatory Unit.

UNIT: ELEMENT:	1.1	1.2	1.3	2.1	2.2	2.3	3.1	3.2	3.3	4.1	4.2	4.3	5.1	5.2	6.1	6.2	6.3	7.1	7.2	7.3	7.4	8.1	8.2	8.3
Chapter 1: An introduction to practising theatre	✓									✓			✓	✓			✓	✓		✓	✓			
Chapter 2: Acting				✓		✓	✓	✓					✓	✓										
Chapter 3: Directing			✓			✓	✓	✓					✓	✓										
Chapter 4: Collaboration: devising group work	✓						✓	✓	✓	✓	✓	✓	✓	✓			✓	✓		✓	✓			✓
Chapter 5: Surviving as a practitioner	✓		✓	✓	✓	✓						✓	✓	✓		✓		✓	✓	✓		✓	✓	✓
Chapter 6: The arts in society		✓					✓	✓	✓															
Chapter 7: Theatre and education	✓		✓			✓	✓	✓	✓		✓	✓												
Chapter 8: Design and stage management						✓				✓		✓			✓	✓	✓							
Chapter 9: Masks							✓																	
Chapter 10: Arts administration and management	✓	✓	✓	✓	✓	✓						✓			✓	✓	✓	✓		✓		✓	✓	✓

Core Skills: Application of Number, Communication, Information Technology
Many of the resource activities incorporate the use of Core Skills. Clearly, the use and identification of the Core Skills will be at the discretion of the teacher and students.

This chart maps the Advanced GNVQ Optional Units against the ten chapters. (Each of the three validating bodies offers different optional units.) A tick indicates that there are sections in the relevant chapter which support the teaching and learning of that unit.

	RSA Optional Units						BTEC Optional Units								City & Guilds Optional Units							
	9	10	11	12	13	14	9	10	11	12	13	14	15	16	9	10	11	12	13	14	15	16
Chapter 1: An introduction to practising theatre			✓							✓	✓	✓	✓	✓				✓	✓		✓	
Chapter 2: Acting	✓	✓	✓	✓			✓					✓							✓			
Chapter 3: Directing	✓	✓	✓						✓						✓				✓			
Chapter 4: Collaboration: devising group work		✓		✓			✓	✓		✓	✓	✓	✓	✓	✓	✓	✓	✓	✓	✓	✓	
Chapter 5: Surviving as a practitioner						✓		✓								✓						✓
Chapter 6: The arts in society	✓						✓		✓								✓					
Chapter 7: Theatre and education	✓	✓		✓					✓				✓	✓	✓		✓	✓				
Chapter 8: Design and stage management										✓				✓	✓							
Chapter 9: Masks	✓		✓				✓				✓	✓	✓			✓			✓	✓		
Chapter 10: Arts administration and management								✓				✓										✓

Additional Units

These are different for each of the three GNVQ validating bodies: RSA, BTEC, City & Guilds. Many of these additional units can be supported by chapters in this book. For example, BTEC's Additional U23, 'Performing Arts in Community/Social Context' could be fully studied by addressing Chapter 6, 'The Arts in Society', and Chapter 7, 'Theatre and Education'.

1 An Introduction to Practising Theatre

Sally Mackey

This chapter incorporates a broad range of useful ideas and pieces of information about practical theatre for those beyond the statutory school age. It does not have a particular focus, as do the other chapters, but contains useful material that has not been incorporated elsewhere in the book. It is divided into the following sections:

- Building a broad theatre experience
- Physical and vocal warm-ups
- Practical exercises
- Records and portfolios
- Presentation skills

All these sections are referred to in later chapters, and are intended as a general resource. For example, a number of resource activities in Chapters 2–10 ask for a presentation to be undertaken; guidelines on presentation skills are included in this chapter.

BUILDING A BROAD THEATRE EXPERIENCE

Performing in and watching theatrical productions should be considered an essential form of ongoing research to support an advanced practical study of theatre. If, in addition, you are intending to pursue a career in the field of theatre and the performing arts, it is important to acquire experience early. This experience provides an informed vision of the industry and allows objective and realistic decisions to be made concerning its suitability as an area in which to consider possible future employment.

If you are involved in studying theatre, you are likely to have the opportunity to participate in production work as part of, or as an extension to, these studies. However, there are numerous other ways to gain experience of theatre, either as a performer or as an observer.

Local youth and community companies

These are frequently linked to community centres, regional theatres or other arts centres and venues. Invariably, they provide evening, weekend or holiday workshops and performance opportunities. It is common for these events to have an input from professional practitioners, many of whom are likely to be part of a team with an educational remit for the venue or company. The particular advantage of this type of experience is that it allows direct contact with a range of practitioners in the context of a professional working venue. Some of these youth and community companies also receive financial support, which can provide the means for large-scale productions and even local and national tours.

County or borough youth companies

Providing a high level of experience and training, these are principally aimed at teenagers, and often employ people with professional experience as both practitioners and teachers. Their aim is to provide performance opportunities at a local and national level. Whilst extensive previous experience may not be essential for entry into county or borough companies, there is invariably an audition process, and competition can be stiff, particularly for some companies with a national reputation. (Not all counties and boroughs have a youth company.)

National youth companies

These include the following companies:

- National Youth Theatre (NYT)
- National Youth and Music Theatre (NYMT)
- National Youth Orchestra
- National Youth Jazz Orchestra
- National Youth Dance Company
- National Youth Ballet Company.

These companies are well established, with international reputations, and also have a high level of funding. They undertake large-scale productions and performances, take part in a number of theatre festivals and regularly tour nationally and internationally. Entry to these companies is by audition and interview. Several of the companies hold short residential workshops prior to offering places. These provide a valuable training experience, and also enable the companies to assess the skills of those involved and to offer places to those with the greatest potential. Although the companies are funded, the participants usually have to pay a fee to take part in the workshops, performances and tours. This provides part of the revenue essential for the running of the company. For contact details for some of these companies, see pp.204–206.

Publicly funded local professional companies and venues

These have a significant part to play in the school, youth and community context. If a company or venue is in receipt of national funding from local councils, regional arts boards or the Arts Council, it will generally have an educational policy. This is frequently managed by an education officer. (See pp.242–249 for further details about theatres and educational activities).

The National Youth Arts Network

This promotes young people's participation in the arts through the development of youth arts policy, practice and provision. It publishes a quarterly magazine called *95 percent* and provides an information and network service for subscribers. It is an umbrella organisation and is very useful for contacts. (See page 23 for the contact address.)

Regular national festivals and events

For contact details for all the following, see p.23.

The National Student Drama Festival (NSDF)

One of the oldest of the national festivals, the NSDF is an excellent example of a drama festival which challenges conventional perceptions of theatre. The predominantly post-18 student audience is offered a wide variety of thought-provoking and stimulating student theatre, subsequently reviewed in the special daily festival magazine *Noises Off*. The productions (between 16 and 20 in number) vary each year, and have to go through an adjudication process to be selected for the festival. You may participate in the capacity of performer (if selected) or spectator, but in either case you will have the opportunity of seeing new and exciting interpretations of familiar texts and of being challenged by experimental devised work.

To become fully involved in the drama festivities, you purchase a course ticket, which enables you to participate in a variety of workshops and masterclasses led by professionals in the theatre business. You are also given the opportunity to contribute your positive or negative criticisms of productions in festival debates, held daily. Successful productions at the NSDF may go on to the Edinburgh Fringe Festival, under the banner of the National Student Theatre Company (NSTC). The NSTC attracts good audiences at Edinburgh; it has won the highly prestigious Guardian Student Drama Award there several years in succession.

The NSDF is currently based in Scarborough and lasts for one week in March or April. The festival is reasonably priced, and accommodation is inexpensive as it is out of the holiday season.

THE EDINBURGH FRINGE FESTIVAL

Further examples of original and challenging drama can be found on the Fringe in Edinburgh for three weeks in August every year. As its organisers have pointed out, '. . .the Fringe owes its success to its independence, its freedom, its enterprise . . . Over the years the Fringe has helped to launch the careers of some of the most famous performers, writers and directors the world has ever known. . . the list is endless. They all grasped the unique opportunity that performing at the Fringe can give; the chance to be seen, to explore ideas, to push the boundaries or even simply shock people!' (Edinburgh Festival Fringe Programme, 1995, p.2).

It is well worth getting hold of a festival programme when planning a visit to the Fringe. Anyone can put on a production at the Edinburgh Fringe Festival, which means that there are thousands of performances. This has advantages and disadvantages. For the visitor, there is a wealth of choice and variety, but audience numbers can be painfully low for unknown shows and companies; frequently there is no audience at all for some performances. However, if a production is a success and attracts good reviews, audience numbers will be reasonable. There is a unique atmosphere at the festival, and it is possible to see some of the best theatre in the world there. You are advised to visit the Fringe a couple of times as an observer before taking your own production.

The festival can be expensive: tickets are not cheap for the good shows, and accommodation can be hard to find at reasonable prices. If you are mounting a production, renting a venue and printing publicity can be particularly costly. (See *How to do a Show in the Fringe*: details on p.207.)

The Royal National Theatre
The Education Department at the Royal National Theatre has a commitment to youth theatre nationwide. There have been two youth theatre projects at the RNT over the last few years: the Lloyds Bank Theatre Challenge and BT National Connections. The schemes are different, although both are nationwide and both have involved between 160 and 200 groups producing theatre each year. A selection of these productions have appeared at the Royal National Theatre as the culmination of each project.

The Royal Court Young Writers' Festival
Taking place every two years, this festival is open to writers between the ages of nine and twenty-three. Part of the festival consists of regional workshops. (These operate on a circuit basis. For example, in 1996 the host region for workshops was Scotland.) It culminates in a three-week festival at the Royal Court Theatre in London, where selected plays are given full performances, having been professionally directed and cast. Other selected plays are given readings. The Youth, Community and Education Department at the Royal Court has also introduced an Internet playwriting festival.

National Youth Arts Festival
This annual festival, based in Ilfracombe, Devon, has been running since the end of the 1980s. It is open to all 14–25-year-olds, as individuals or in groups. You do not have to contribute a performance, although these are welcomed; the festival is non-competitive, but there is a high standard of work. A number of workshops take place, such as drumming, mask making and poetry; as it is a festival for all the arts, a wide variety of topics is available. Traditionally it has taken place during the first week of July.

The 'BIG' Festival
Another annual festival, this is run by the National Association of Youth Theatres. Participants are welcome from any youth theatre, nationally and beyond. (There were 36 represented in 1996.) It is residential (including camping in the past) and takes place over a few days in the summer. It comprises performances, workshops, discussions, social events and so on. Participants have the chance to create theatre and work with professionals from around the country. The workshops are extensive and range from creating a night-time, outdoor, site-specific event, to stage fighting and African Caribbean and street dance.

PHYSICAL AND VOCAL WARM-UPS

These physical and vocal warm-ups have been included because students and teachers have frequently expressed a need for brief but thorough guidelines for warm-ups at an advanced practical level.

Many practitioners in this book stress the need for a good warm-up, both at the beginning of practical sessions and before performing. These can take a variety of forms, from short games to extended workouts. Here we outline basic, yet reasonably serious, warm-ups for the body and voice. They are designed to take between 20 and 30 minutes altogether, if you do most of the activities. They appear roughly in sequence, with an element of progression. Clearly, warm-ups can move towards more interactive games or exercises as they progress.

All warm-ups have five basic functions:

● to warm up the body and voice so that muscles are not strained in subsequent activity;
● to help train the voice and body for performance work;
● to focus your attention and engender a sense of community within the group;
● to energise the group;
● to help release nervous tension: 'Activity prevents anxiety'.

(See pp.38–42 for further information about preparing the voice and body.)

Physical warm-up

Part 1

● From a standing position, let your head drop onto your chest. Gently circle it, so that the side of your head drops towards one shoulder, then the head returns to upright (not dropping backwards, as this can hurt your neck), then the other side of the head drops towards your other shoulder, and you bring it round to the front again. Do this about four times (if you can without feeling dizzy). Repeat in the other direction.

● In a standing position, let your head drop onto your chest. Then relax forward from the waist, so that your hands are dangling on, or near, the floor. Keep your legs relaxed, not stiff. Slowly raise yourself up, uncurving the spine vertebra by vertebra; your head must be the last to come up.

● Roll one shoulder back eight times, leaving your arm hanging loose. Repeat with the other shoulder. Then roll each shoulder forward.

● Raise your shoulders up, hold for a couple of seconds, then release. Repeat a few times. Shake the shoulders out.

5

Part 2

● Half-walk on the spot, by lifting only the *heels* of your feet from the ground alternately.

● Continuing this, lift your arms into the air together, keeping them parallel, and push them up in time with your walk. They will be loosely above your head for one beat, then taut for the next beat and so on. Repeat 12 times.

● Continuing the half-walk, rotate an arm backwards for four and forwards for four. Repeat with the other arm.

● Repeat the last two exercises, but this time whilst jogging on the spot (rather than the half-walk).

● Standing still, twist from the waist so that you are looking back over each shoulder in turn. Continue this for several turns.

Part 3

● Go back to half-walking on the spot, with your arms by your side. After a few beats, wriggle your fingers.

● Let this wriggling extend to your wrists, your lower arms, your upper arms and your shoulders, so that your whole arms are being gently flung around in the air.

● Stop the walking and start the same wriggling exercise with one leg and then the other, beginning with the toes. Try to keep your balance: stare at a spot on the floor about six feet in front of you if you have problems.

● When the legs have completed their 'fling', bring the arms back into the movement, so that both your arms and legs are moving at random. Start to walk about the room, continuing the random 'flinging'.

● Standing still, bend the knees and 'ski' on the spot, going up and down as you do so.

Part 4

● Jog around the space. Keep your arms quite loose. After a while, jump occasionally, lifting off from one foot and landing on two.

● Continue this movement, but as you jump push your arms up into the air. Do not strain the arms: keep the movement quite gentle.

● Turn this into a sideways jog, so that your feet are coming together every other step.

● Jog around the room; every few steps change into a 'high-stepping' jog, bringing your knees much higher up towards your chest. Continue the 'high-stepping' jog for several paces and then alternate with ordinary jogging.

● From a standing position, do star jumps, where your hands and legs form the shape of a star on the outward jump and come back together on the inward jump. Repeat this at least 12 times.

Part 5

● From a standing position, gradually stretch your arms right up above you. Stretch the whole body, then relax. Repeat this three or four times.

● Sit on the floor, with your legs outstretched in front of you. Bounce your leg up and down, without taking your foot completely off the floor. Repeat with the other leg.

● From that sitting position, lean forwards, stretching your body over one leg and reaching your arms towards the toe. Stretch and release gently and continuously. Do this six times, then change legs.

● Stand up and shake your arms and legs out.

Vocal warm-up

It is important to recognise that the body should be relaxed and warm for a good vocal warm-up. Your voice needs all the supporting systems in your body to be released from tension. For example, tight stomach muscles will prevent the diaphragm from working effectively and the chest from expanding properly. The back and shoulders are important: too often, tense shoulders inhibit the larynx from operating fully. The tongue, palate and lips are all affected by a face and jaw that is cold or stiff. Clearly, a physical warm-up should lead into a vocal warm-up. The vocal warm-up below includes releasing tension, warming and exercising the face, breath control, resonance, articulation and singing.

Part 1

● Lie on your back on the floor. Bring your knees up to your chest. Focus on the width and length of your back, letting it 'spread' in both directions. This 'spreading' is important for releasing tension.

● Bring your knees down and straighten your legs out. Mentally focus, in turn, on your head, shoulders, torso, arms, hands, legs and feet, relaxing each of these in turn. As you focus on each part of the body, breathe in and tense yourself in that part of the body; as you breathe out, relax that part.

● Roll onto your side and stand up. Centre your body by resting on the balls of the feet rather than the heels.

● Remember to keep your body relaxed, particularly your shoulders. Shake out occasionally during these exercises.

Part 2

● Push your lips out, then stretch them back into a wide smile where your cheekbones are raised and your teeth show. Repeat this several times.

● Massage your face all over with your hands.

● 'Chew toffee'. Move the mouth round as you do so.

● Imagine you have pieces of chocolate caught in various cavities in your mouth. Try to get them out with your tongue.

- 'Blow' kisses in swift succession; your lips are pushed out again.

- Stick your tongue out. Raise it to the nose, drop it to the chin and then move it from side to side.

- Yawn, or appear to, making the sound of the yawn quietly as well.

Part 3

- Breathe in evenly through your nose for a count of five. Feel your chest cavity expanding with your hands. Hold for five. Breathe out through your mouth for five. Feel the cavity contract. Repeat this several times.

- Repeat the exercise but increase the number count for the breathing out section by three or four each time until you reach the number 15. Continue to feel the chest expanding and contracting. This is an excellent exercise for breath control.

- Add in a vocalised count to this exercise on the out breath; keep the voice at a quiet volume.

- Roll the head gently. Raise and drop the shoulders. Gently shake out. Don't let the body become stiff.

Part 4

- Breathe in fully, and as you breathe out let out a series of short 'huh' sounds. This can exacerbate phlegm; you may find yourself coughing. Be careful not to hyperventilate by breathing in too much. Stop the exercise if you feel lightheaded.

- Breathe in, and as you breathe out hum quietly on one note. You should be able to feel the vibration around your lips. Repeat a few times.

- Repeat the exercise, but after you have hummed for four or five seconds, open this out to an 'aah' sound. Repeat this, raising the volume slightly. Try to move the 'aah' sound so that it is coming from your chest and diaphragm rather than from your throat.

- Breathe in, and on the out breath 'sing' on a monotone: 'may, mee, mah, maw, moo'. Repeat this, extending your mouth to facilitate the vowel sounds further. Repeat this with other consonants such as 'b', 's', 'p', 'z' and so on. It may help to work with a partner who can check your back and front. Can he or she feel the resonance around the rib cavities? Male voices are likely to vibrate more than female.

- Find your optimum pitch. Do this by finding your glottal fry – the lowest note in your register, where you can hear a pitter-pattering sound deep in your chest. Then work up the scale about three or four notes. This level is your optimum pitch. Work in that register; you will feel more resonance. Your habitual pitch, your 'everyday' voice, is likely to be different from this.

- Speak the 'may, mee, mah, maw, moo' sounds rather than singing them. Stress the first consonant of each sound. Repeat this with other consonants.

● Hold your nose and speak these sounds, trying not to sound as if you're holding your nose. This makes you very aware of speaking from your diaphragm rather than your throat.

Part 5

Tongue-twisters are helpful for articulation. Do not speak the tongue-twisters at a very fast speed, but concentrate on articulating fully and resonantly, extending parts of your mouth to help articulation.

Tongue-twisters can be divided up according to the different parts of the mouth they exercise:

● Lips, for example Ps, Bs, Ms and Ws:

Peter Piper picked a peck of pickled pepper
A peck of pickled pepper, Peter Piper picked.
If Peter Piper picked a peck of pickled pepper
Where's the peck of pickled pepper Peter Piper picked?

Wendy watched the weasel walking.
My mother will moan, 'Move my map'.
Betty bought a bit of butter.

● Tongue (and teeth), for example Ls, Ds, Ss, Ts:

Leave the lazy lion alone.
Des does a deadly dastardly deed.

Sister Susie's sewing shirts for soldiers
Soft white shirts for soldiers, sister Susie sews
Some soldiers send epistles
Saying they'd rather sleep on thistles
Than the silky soft white shirts for soldiers sister Susie sews

● Palate (top of the roof of the mouth) and back of the tongue, for example hard Cs, Ks, Gs:

Giggling Katie Coe kicked the garden gargoyle
The garden gargoyle kicked giggling Katie Coe

Mixed tongue-twisters are useful too:

Red leather, yellow leather
Peggy Babcock, Peggy Babcock
Round the rugged rock, the ragged rascal ran.

Part 6

● Breathe in. On the out breath, make one long 'aah' sound, starting at a high pitch and ending on a low one. Hold the lowest pitch for a few seconds. Repeat a few times.

● Repeat the exercise, but starting from a low pitch and moving to a high one.

● Choose a reasonably low musical note. Sing up and down three notes of the scale to 'mm' and then to 'aah'. Move up one note and repeat the exercise. Continue to move up the scale.

● Start singing tunes at this point, concentrating on the articulation. For example, sing 'Many men' to the tune of the *William Tell* overture, raising and lowering the volume at various points.

● Singing familiar rounds is a good way of warming up the voice and energises the group. You may know some of these: for example, *London's Burning, Cookaburra, Rose, I Like the Flowers*.

PRACTICAL EXERCISES

There are many books available which contain numerous suggestions for advanced practical work. In the bibliography on pp.24–25, we have listed several that are recommended for further ideas. It is not possible to offer a wide range of activities here, but the ones below have been selected for the following reasons:

● They are *general* practical exercises; the other chapters in this book include their own *specialist* activities.

● They have been tried and tested in further and higher education and work well. (Practical exercises do not come across well on the printed page, but these are all strong in practice.)

● Most of the exercises can be led by a tutor or student; they can act as a resource for student-led sessions.

The last five exercises are particularly useful as stimuli for devising work, one of the core requirements for advanced practical theatre work. (See pp.132–154 for more information.) Alternatively, they can be adapted for projects where an initial outline is in place.

Group count
The aim of this exercise is to help develop a group awareness and sensitivity and to encourage students to use intuition and concentration.

● Stand in a circle.

● As a group, count to the number equivalent to the number of students in the group. (For example, 15 students will count from one to 15.) Each number should be called out by one member of the group.

● Only one person should speak at one time, and each person must sit as he or she calls out a number. Nobody gives more than one number. There is no prior organisation of who will speak each number: it should be done at random.

● If more than one person calls the same number, the process starts again from the beginning.

Fast familiarity
This is an ideal exercise for a group whose members do not know each other and are beginning to work together for the first time.

- Each person needs to be equipped with a sheet of blank paper and a pen.

- Working alone, each person thinks up two questions (or more if the group is under 15 in size) to ask a new acquaintance. Think laterally (and inoffensively): for example, 'What supermarket do you prefer to shop in and why?'; 'If you went to a zoo, what animal would you go and see first?'

- When everyone has thought of two or more questions, the group should move round quickly, asking each other the questions that are on the paper and making a brief note of the answers with the person's name.

- Stop this part of the exercise when most members of the group have talked to each other.

- Ask individuals to stand up and say their name. Ask others in the group to shout out some of the things about this person that they have just learnt and written down.

This is a similar exercise, which achieves some of the same results:

- Each person has a pen and paper.

- Move around the group, writing down the names of six people you meet. Next to the name, put two things that you have in common and one thing that you do not have in common with each new acquaintance. For example, you might share an interest in paragliding and your birthday is in the same month, yet one of you is vegetarian and the other eats meat.

- Try to make one of the common points an unusual one.

- The 'winner' is the one who completes a list of six people first and has the list agreed by the facilitator.

Tag debate

This exercise uses debate to develop group support, negotiation and flexibility. All individuals in the group should aim to contribute to the ebb and flow of the debate, trying always to continue the line of argument in a coherent manner.

- The whole group is given an issue to debate, then splits into two groups, representing the two sides of the argument. For example, your debate may focus on reasons for or against supporting the homeless. An abstract idea can be equally effective: you may wish to argue that circles are better than squares, for instance. It helps if the groups are given time to marshal their arguments.

- A spokesperson from each side of the argument starts the debate. The two spokespeople stand in the centre of the circle and face each other to conduct their debate.

- Any member of either group who wishes to contribute to the central debate must raise his or her hand and be tagged by the facilitator of the exercise (by pointing or tapping). The tagged student then enters the debate, replacing his or her side's spokesperson physically and verbally.

This exercise can become more challenging if the turnover of the spokesperson becomes more rapid; the facilitator could take control of tagging to increase the pace. The facilitator may also choose to change the subject of the debate at intervals.

Positive greetings

This exercise requires generosity, and can help to develop a positive and personal working environment for the group. It can take place only with a group whose members know one another. There is an emphasis here on trust, creativity and physicality.

● Take time to observe the fellow members of your group and consider the positive comments that you could make about different individuals before moving into this exercise.

● As the group moves around, offer a greeting and positive comment to anyone who crosses your path. For example, you may say something like: 'Hello. I'd just like to say I thought you handled that awkward incident yesterday really well. You were quite obviously in control of the situation.' This part of the exercise is done with most of the group talking to each other at the same time.

● Stop the exercise once everyone has said something positive about most members of the group.

This exercise can then be extended:

● Everyone should remember and focus upon one of the complimentary phrases that they used about someone else.

● Stand in a space. Speaking to an open space, a wall, the facilitator or the group in general, say the individual phrase that you have selected when the facilitator gives a signal for everyone to start. Everyone then speaks at once.

● Repeat the line immediately, building upon the level of delivery each time by increasing the volume and/or extending the gesture. Experiment with the degree of expression in your delivery each time as well. It may be easier if the facilitator calls out 'level one', 'level two' and so on, or some other 'trigger' phrase, so that students build their delivery simultaneously.

● When everyone has developed this phrase both physically and vocally to about the equivalent of 'level five', the facilitator should stop the group and ask them to remember the level of volume, gesture and expression that has been reached.

● The facilitator points at individuals in the group, who perform their phrase and then freeze in their position.

● This exercise can be explored and manipulated by the facilitator.

Each student contributes to a three-dimensional image, and individuals may be 're-animated' to perform again. The result is a unified, constructive mass of positive, physicalised expression about the group.

The seated group circle

This apparently simple exercise is an effective test of group unity and support. It requires concentration, sensitivity and trust.

- Stand in a close circle, facing inwards. Turn to your right so that you are facing the back of the person in front of you. There must be no gaps in the group circle, so you will have to bring the circle in, making it tighter.

- Concentrate on synchronising the group's breathing rhythms to create a sense of group unity and awareness.

- When group intuition determines the moment, slowly bend your knees and rest on the knees of the person behind you. The final product should be a perfectly balanced seated group circle.

The group as a jigsaw

This exercise is useful for demonstrating unity and teamwork on group projects. It can be used only once.

- Small groups are each given a jigsaw puzzle which is made up of a *few* pieces (more than ten or twelve pieces would be too time-consuming). If real ones aren't available, cut up photocopied pictures.

- Ask each group to make up the puzzle.

- When this has been done, ask the groups to brainstorm the way in which the jigsaw puzzle has the characteristics of successful group work. For example, 'Every piece of the puzzle is needed to make the complete picture.'

- Share the results with the whole group, reminding yourselves of the important characteristics of positive group work.

Starter questions

This exercise should be repeated throughout a group project. When small groups are working on projects, it can be useful to have a regular way of starting the session, which stimulates thinking and activity.

- At the outset of the project, everybody writes a couple of questions on a piece of paper. Questions might be: 'What has been the most interesting thing that you have done in the last week?' 'What is your favourite film?' 'What is the funniest thing that ever happened to you?'

- The papers are then folded and put in a suitable container, such as a bag. This is kept centrally.

- At the beginning of each session, a question from the bag is asked. Each member of the group has 20 seconds in turn (depending on the size of group) to answer the question.

● This is more effective if each person *enacts* the account, however roughly.

Reduced Project Company

This is based on the idea of the Reduced Shakespeare Company, who 'abridge' great works or periods of history into one short show. The company's first piece incorporated all the plays of Shakespeare in about an hour: hence its name.

The exercise is particularly useful for energising a group which is losing pace in the middle of rehearsing or devising a production or project.

Simply, the group has a few minutes to prepare a 'reduced' or abridged version of the work so far. This should bring out the key features of the narrative and performance. Use instant props such as bags, chairs and so on to take the place of people, scenery or objects. It works best if the group can be smaller than the actual company, so try dividing the company into two.

Status

An old favourite, this exercise has many variations. This version uses playing cards, a method which was popularised by Max Stafford-Clark (see p.70). Status games are useful for developing clear character types.

● From a shuffled deck, two people take a card each. Ace is low and king is high. The two participants know their status from looking at the card. For example, one might be a four and therefore of quite low status. The other might be a ten, which is a reasonably high status.

● The two start walking directly towards each other from either end of the room. They imagine they are walking on a very narrow pavement which allows for only one person to pass; the gutter of the road is full of deep puddles.

● When they are close, a scenario is improvised where each person wants to pass the other on the pavement. This would mean one walker has to step into the puddles. Words can be used, or not. The two participants have to judge the status of the other person from his or her behaviour, words and mannerisms. The person with the higher status ('ten' in this example) is likely to be the one who stays on the pavement, and the one with lower status has to step down into the puddles.

● The rest of the group, who are watching, try to determine the status level of the participants after the issue has been resolved.

This can be repeated many times. As the improvisations develop, participants will develop confidence in their adoption of a 'status'. It is even possible for a lower-status character to 'win' the situation, perhaps by using this lower status: for example, 'I've got a terrible cold today and I daren't get my feet wet, as I've got holes in my shoes.' Where the characterisations are particularly interesting, they could then be developed in other scenarios.

It would be possible to use this exercise in the context of a specific period or place (as suggested on p.17). Look at p.124, where Tim Hibberd discusses the first ideas for *Peasouper*. The context could be Victorian Britain, and the status of the randomly chosen card could be translated into a character type, such as a Victorian gentlewoman.

The basic exercise can also be adapted in other ways. For example, each member of the group can be given a card, and the scenario is a party. As they mingle, the students play their own status and attempt to judge the status of others.

Facial masks

Another character-building exercise, this is also useful for beginning mask work (see pp.336–337).

- Four members of the group sit on four chairs. They are asked to make a face. This can be anything: a grotesque or an innocent, a grumpy or a humorous face, for example.

- Show them their faces in a mirror and allow them to make some changes if they wish. They should begin to think about how the 'mask' can be carried through to the rest of the body.

- Ask them to interact with each other. The setting and situation are entirely open; they should pick up each other's hints on context and respond appropriately.

This exercise can be developed by asking four of the watching group to take on the 'masks' of the first four and add or change one aspect. Repeat the exercise, then change again. After the final grouping, take the four developed characters and build backgrounds for them. Alternatively, build on the storyline that has been developing.

Freeze circle

This is useful for initiating bizarre storylines.

- The group is in a circle. One person begins with a solo activity in the middle of the circle.

- Another person goes in and adds to the 'scene'. This is likely to incorporate speech. A couple more people go in, and they build the scene together.

- At an appropriate moment, the facilitator calls, 'Freeze'. Another person is selected and is asked to 'change' the scene, based on the frozen image.

- When the 'changer' first speaks, those in the 'freeze' immediately become part of the new scene. The changer's first words must be said as *part* of the new scene and should contain enough information for those in the 'freeze' to understand the new situation.

● More people can be added; the scene can be frozen again and another new situation started.

● In order to create unusual and exciting dramatic possibilities, each command of 'Freeze' should be called when the group is in an odd position. The 'freeze' should capture that 'oddness' and lead to lateral thinking in the changer.

● Particularly successful scenes could be extended beyond the bounds of the exercise.

See 'Freeze tag' on p.105 for adaptations of this exercise.

Leading with parts of the body

This is a method of creating larger-than-life characters which can then be developed further.

● The group members are scattered around the room, having warmed up. When instructed, they should move around the space, 'leading' with a part of the body. Try the chin, knees, belly button and so on. Allow this to develop for 30 seconds to a minute.

● Then split the group, so that half are watching, and continue.

● 'Freeze' the performing group and ask the watchers to suggest character types for the frozen individuals, then continue.

● Change groups and carry on, with different body parts leading. Again, take suggestions for types.

● Add in a status level, if appropriate, to develop the characters.

● Play around with this exercise. For example, ask a couple to improvise with each other, spontaneously.

This can lead into further work on archetypes: the villain, the heroine, the pimp and so on. See p.109 for a variation of this exercise, on physicality of character.

Play and the provocateur

There are many ways of 'playing' in drama. Here is one suggestion for play between a character, an object and a *provocateur*. This is a rough approximation of an exercise that John Wright (see pp.79–85) uses to perfection.

● One of the group sits in front of the others. A facilitator takes on the role of *provocateur* and leads the 'performer'.

● Give the performer an object from the room: a bin, a bag, a chair.

● As *provocateur*, ask the performer to do things with the object. For example, 'What happens if you pick that up?' 'Do you like it?' 'Why don't you try wearing it?' 'Try something else with it.' The performer is likely to build a character as he or she plays with the object.

● The *provocateur* can adopt a persona. This could threaten the performer – 'I'm beginning to get angry with you. Why don't you like that bag? It's not done you any harm, has it?' – or be encouraging: 'The audience laughed at that. Do it again. That's very good, well done.'

Extensions can be added: for example, two people could work together; the watching group can talk to the performer as well; you could put an object in the middle of the group, and let the group build an improvisation around it. For further exercises on 'play', see pp.104–106.

Developing the work

The last five exercises above can be adapted to help a group *develop* a scenario, character or idea, rather than being used simply to initiate them. For example:

● The situation in 'Status' can be made appropriate to the period or environment that has already been suggested for a project.

● Again in 'Status', the whole-group 'party' suggestion could be adapted for a large group scene that has already been suggested for the rough scenario.

● In 'Facial masks', the setting can be given, based on the rough scenario (rather than allowed to develop as suggested above). In addition, the first four performers can 'make their face' based on certain characters that have already been outlined, but wildly exaggerating their characteristics.

● In 'Freeze circle', the first freeze image can be altered to a situation that is within the rough scenario.

● For 'Leading with parts of the body', after working on the exercise for a while, prompt the members of the group to develop characters and scenarios from the given narrative: 'What would the anarchist lead with?' 'What would the army general lead with?' Once movement has started, the exercise can be developed by asking further questions, such as 'Where are they?' 'How did they get there?'

● 'Play and the provocateur' can easily be adapted to use characters and appropriate props from the outline of the scenario.

RECORDS AND PORTFOLIOS

Practical theatre is essentially practical. However, it is advisable to maintain a record or portfolio of your practical work. In addition, an evaluation may be appropriate (see pp.150–154), and a comprehensive record will facilitate this.

Guidelines are given below for a personal and a group record, both of which should be ongoing documents, updated regularly. These guidelines apply to practical project work rather than one-off sessions.

Personal record

A personal record should include the following elements.

A list of personal objectives

What do you wish to achieve during the practical project? You should note your objectives in terms of the specific performance, design, technical, research and personal skills you wish to develop. For example:

Within this project, I wish to:
- *gain experience and confidence in spontaneous improvisation work;*
- *improve my performance skills by working in a different style to my usual work and increasing my range of vocal and physical skills;*
- *work on designing and creating props for the piece which are of a near-professional standard;*
- *research my area of the project thoroughly and comprehensively;*
- *work on creating a piece of devised theatre with others in the group, maintaining a positive and constructive working atmosphere.*

Your personal objectives should bear some relation to the assessment criteria or the brief for the project, if these have been given.

Research material

All documentary research material that you have collected should be included. If this is a group project, some of this material may be placed more appropriately in the group record, particularly when it has been of direct use in the process (see below).

Session plans

If you run any sessions, including warm-up exercises, at any point in the project, an outline of these should form part of your record; include brief comments about the success of the session.

Performance notes

Keep and file any personal notes that relate to your own performance. These might include character study notes (see pp.55–57), detailed research into the character, and a brief account of key moments in the process when you made specific decisions about your role.

Notes on other responsibilities

Research and work that you have undertaken for your other responsibilities in the project should be recorded. For example, if you are responsible for publicity, you might have initial designs for a programme cover, copies of letters to newspapers and radio stations advertising your project, examples of publicity material from other productions which you consulted, and an ongoing list of acknowledgements that you will put in the programme.

Key session notes

It is worthwhile to make a record of key devising sessions or rehearsals which were particularly important, interesting, productive or difficult. These brief accounts should include your thoughts about *why* the session was so interesting, and should suggest contributory factors. This does not mean writing a day-by-day diary, unless you are asked to.

Other productions
It is useful to keep details of productions that you have seen which have influenced your thinking during this project.

Group record
If you are working on a group project of any kind, it is worth considering a collective record of this nature. The responsibility for maintaining and collating this document could be a joint one, or the task could be allocated to one individual but with contributions from the whole group. The following elements could be included.

A list of group objectives
These objectives may be adjusted as the project evolves. The following list is an example:

The group's objectives are:
- *to experiment with and create an innovative and exciting piece of theatre, in which content and form are integrated;*
- *to select and tackle a topical issue with sensitivity, yet with force;*
- *to ensure that the piece of theatre is appropriate for the target audience;*
- *to root the piece in research, without allowing factual information to dominate;*
- *to work co-operatively, constructively and sensitively;*
- *to identify each person's individual objectives for this project and to attempt to meet these if possible and appropriate;*
- *to produce a piece of documentary drama using various different styles of performance;*
- *to produce a piece that is of a near-professional performance standard.*

Your objectives should match the assessment criteria or the unit brief for the project if these have been given.

A list of initial ideas and practical work
Keep a list of all of the ideas which are discussed and experimented with in the early stages. It is easy to forget good practical ideas.

Research material
This will include any material collected which is directly relevant for the project. It would be useful to name the person who contributed each piece of material, and it is important to make a note of where it came from, so that you can acknowledge all your sources. Examples might be:

- photocopies of short extracts from books;
- newspaper/magazine articles;
- poems;
- copies or originals of photographs, pictures, diagrams, etc.;
- interview notes;
- programmes;
- other archive or documentary material;
- a collated video tape of extracts or full-length television programmes that have been useful as source material;
- audio tapes from any interviews that company members have undertaken, extracts from radio programmes that have been useful and so on;

● audience research such as questionnaires.

Information about venues
This might comprise measurements, technical facilities, the nature of the likely audience.

Bibliography
It is good practice to include a list of texts that are relevant to the subject matter, explaining how these have been useful to you.

Design plans
Include final drawings of plans or designs for the project. Earlier design work is likely to be in the personal record (see above).

The text
Particularly if the work is devised, a final portfolio might include the completed text. This could be a 'clean' copy or a running document (see p.301).

PRESENTATION SKILLS

A number of the resource activities in Chapters 2–10 include tasks that require students to make presentations. These guidelines are useful for most presentations, taking you through the stages of planning and presenting.

Setting yourself objectives
Examples of objectives might be as follows.

My objectives for this presentation are:
● *to pass this aspect of the project (if it is being assessed);*
● *to enlighten and entertain my audience, which will consist of fellow students, tutors and others, and to ensure that I communicate the required information successfully;*
● *to gain knowledge, understanding and experience of formal presentations for the future.*

Preparation and planning
Your preparation should run along roughly the following lines:

● Allow time for ideas to develop; do not prepare at the last moment.

● Define the topic clearly for yourself to limit the field.

● Remember your audience and prepare your presentation with them in mind.

● Gather and select the relevant material.

● Select a title, if appropriate.

● Structure and write your speech. Keep it simple, enthusiastic and original.

● Prepare your support material (e.g. handouts) thoroughly.

● Always return to your objectives and brief: check that your speech fulfils the requirements of the brief and your personal objectives.

When structuring your speech, remember that it must have a narrative: it must take your audience on a journey. Divide it up into appropriate sections and give it a clear beginning, a middle and an end. Introduce your presentation by briefly summarising for your audience what you are going to say. Give them the information you have selected in a coherent and lucid order. Be sure that you explain all your points thoroughly: most audiences take in less than you expect, so do not be afraid to repeat the key point that you wish them to understand. Finish by summing up what you have told them.

KEY POINTS
Your speech is a conversation.
Be yourself.
Keep it simple.
Avoid: mistaken grammar; clichés; foreign words and phrases; jargon and abbreviations; exaggerations; remarks in bad taste; name-dropping.
Handle with care: new vocabulary; numbers; examples and illustrations; humour.
(Adapted from Bostock, *Speaking in Public*, p.58.)

Presenting
- Rehearse until you are thoroughly comfortable with the material and can precisely fill your allotted time. (Allow a good minute for delays of some kind.)

- Do not read your entire speech. Use notes as memory-joggers.

- Ensure your volume is loud enough. Use your optimum pitch (see p.8).

- Vary your pitch to enhance expression and clarity, and articulate clearly.

- You will almost certainly try to talk too rapidly. Use pauses to allow material to be digested by your audience, and vary the pace to maintain the listeners' interest.

- Dress appropriately: be comfortable, but be aware of the impression you are making.

- Be aware of body language: avoid annoying mannerisms; maintain a good, strong posture that looks as though you are at ease; take care not to move too much; ensure you maintain pleasant eye contact with all your audience. Finally, hand gestures should add to the presentation, not distract from it.

- Be aware of your facial expression: smile, but not excessively.

- Overall, be conversational, natural, energetic and enthusiastic, and use your drama skills.

- Deal with nerves by doing deep breathing or a brief vocal warm-up before the presentation, if appropriate. The best way of avoiding nerves is to be extremely well prepared and rehearsed, so that you look forward to the presentation.

- What are the memorable points of your presentation? There are likely to be other presentations; how will yours be remembered?

Using technical equipment
The following may be available to you:

- television and video recorder;
- slide projector;
- overhead projector (OHP), with prepared and blank acetates;
- white board;
- white screen;
- flipchart;
- appropriate thick and thin felt tips for blank acetates and white board/flipchart.

Check what is available before you plan your presentation. You should rehearse as much as possible, so that you are at ease with all the resources that you intend to use. Do not overuse them! For instance, if you are using a video extract, make sure it does not run for too long: it is not supposed to replace your presentation. Make sure everything is correctly spelt and punctuated, and that tapes are exactly cued in.

KEY POINTS
Use visual aids to illustrate, clarify and add interest.
Choose the visual aid that fits your need.
Ensure that your visual aids support rather than compete with the spoken word.
Keep it simple.
Don't use too many aids.
(Bostock, p.66)

Guaranteeing success
To sum up, before coming to the presentation, you should follow these points to guarantee success:

- Check your presentation against the relevant objectives, criteria and guidelines, including your own objectives, the guidelines we have given you here and any brief that you have been given. Does your presentation comply with most of these?

- Rehearse often.

- Ask friends, family and strangers to watch or listen to your presentation and to give you feedback. Sift the feedback and alter your presentation accordingly.

USEFUL ADDRESSES

The National Student Drama Festival
For further details, contact:
Clive Wolfe
20 Lansdowne Road
Muswell Hill
London
N10 2AU
Tel: 0181 883 4586
Fax: 0181 883 7142

The Edinburgh Fringe Festival
For further details, contact:
The Fringe Office
180 High Street
Edinburgh
EII1 1QS
Tel: 0131 226 5257/5259
Fax: 0131 220 4205
email: admin@edfringe.org.uk

The Royal Court Young Writers' Festival
For further details, contact:
The Royal Court YPT
309 Portobello Road
London
W10 5TD
Tel: 0181 960 4641
Fax: 0181 960 1434

The BIG Festival, The National Association of Youth Theatres
For further details, contact:
NAYT
Unit 1/304
The Custard Factory
Gibb Street
Digbeth
Birmingham
B9 4AA
Tel: 0121 608 2111

Royal National Theatre
For further details, contact:
Producer, Youth Theatre Projects
Royal National Theatre
South Bank
London SE1 9PX
Tel: 0171 928 2033
Fax: 0171 928 2868

National Youth Arts Network
For further details, contact:
National Youth Arts Network
Weston Corner
Station Road,
Fladbury
Worcestershire
WR10 2QW
Tel and fax: 01386 860390

National Youth Arts Festival
For further details, contact:
Penny Jackson
National Youth Arts Festival
The Lantern
Ilfracombe
Devon
EX34 9QB
Tel: 01271 862419
Fax: 01271 863477

ANNOTATED BIBLIOGRAPHY

This bibliography includes volumes relevant to this chapter which are considered suitable for student research. See also the general bibliography on p.380.

Berry, Cicely, *The Actor and his Text*, Virgin Books, 1992 (first published by Harrap Ltd, 1987)
> Particularly useful for voice work.

Boal, A., *Games for Actors and Non-Actors*, Routledge, 1992
> One of the best books around for improvisation work. There are many ideas, and a distinct sense of Boal's voice coming off the page.

Bostock, L., *Speaking in Public*, HarperCollins, 1994
> This small 'pocket' book contains all you would wish to know about presentations. Although it is aimed at the business marketplace, it is useful for any situation.

Fo, D., *The Tricks of the Trade*, Methuen, 1991
> This book reports faithfully on the work of Fo and Rame: it is a combination of an actor's manual and Fo's ruminations on theatre. It is an important book for understanding the work of two of our greatest modern practitioners, but is not improved by a dense layout style.

Frost, A. and Yarrow, R., *Improvisation in Drama*, Methuen, 1992
> This is a slightly heavier read, but it is most useful for a broad understanding of the history of improvisation.

Hickson, A., *Creative Action Methods in Groupwork*, Winslow Press, 1995
> A photocopiable (and therefore expensive) book, this has a huge number of exercises in it. The work is focused towards drama therapy, but nonetheless there are many useful exercises, and good, brief warm-up work as well.

Hodgson, J. and Richards, E., *Improvisation*, Eyre Methuen, 1967
> An old text, typical of the 1960s and 1970s, but still worth having. It is of particular interest to see how improvisation was viewed at the time!

Johnstone, K., *Impro: Improvisation and the Theatre*, Eyre Methuen, 1981
> A classic text. It has many improvisation exercises and is written coherently and with integrity. Highly recommended.

Neelands, J., *Structuring Drama Work,* CUP, 1990

> Neelands' book is a standard text for school drama. Many of the ideas and exercises are perfectly appropriate and useful for post-16 work as well. The divisions in the book are particularly helpful for student-led sessions; identifying appropriate exercises is made easy.

Spolin, V., *Improvisation for the Theatre: Including Two Hundred and Twenty Theatre Games,* Pitman and Sons, 1963

> A dated text in many ways, but Spolin's classic is still useful. It has a wide range of exercises which can be adapted for many different purposes.

2 Acting

Kate Firth

This chapter contains the following sections, aimed at providing background information for those studying or practising acting:

● Acting in theatrical history
● Methods of actor training in the 20th century
● Interviews with two actors
● Guidelines for acting

ACTING IN THEATRICAL HISTORY

An actor should have an awareness of the history of his or her profession.

The role of the actor has evolved over the centuries. Today's actor is a product of that evolution. In order to understand the present-day actor's role in theatre, it is useful to have an appreciation of the cutural and historical background of theatre and the actor's place within it.

Early drama as ritual

Drama evolved from rituals.

The earliest drama evolved out of religious rituals and the human need to make sense of the world. Seasonal changes came to be linked with ideas of birth (spring) and death (winter). People believed that by imitating an object or re-enacting an event, they gained power over it. This was done through dance, chanting or singing, and the wearing of animal skins. Rituals also fulfilled a need for shared experiences of celebration and worship. (See also pp.114–115 and 319–324.)

The first actors would have been priests or shamans, who acted out the ritual on behalf of the community. Ritual and religion were synonymous, and drama in its own right did not exist. As myths developed about the community's beliefs, the shamans or priests took on a new role beyond that of simple imitators. They evolved into storytellers and interpreters.

Actors in the Greek theatre

Greek theatre originally celebrated the festivals of Dionysus.

Early Greek theatre also evolved out of religious ritual, namely the worship of the god Dionysus, who symbolised fertility and rebirth. The festivals of Dionysus were spectacular events, which took place in early spring and combined religious worship of the god with athletic contests, singing and, progressively, the performance of plays. The events were presided over by the priest of Dionysus, and plays were acted out by non-professional male volunteers from the community, who made up the main body of the acting company, known as the chorus. There was therefore a close relationship between the audience and the actors.

The structure of the amphitheatres affected acting styles.

The outdoor amphitheatres were vast, with the capacity to seat an entire town and the rowdy atmosphere of a modern sports stadium. It is important to note that the physical structure of the theatres directly influenced the style of the performances.

Firstly, their size meant that the majority of the audience were some distance from the actors on stage. The area was too big for people to see subtle details, so acting in Greek theatre was not realistic. Actors wore coloured masks to enhance their visibility, and their portrayal of character was stylised into defined categories, conveyed through the use of movement, gesture and voice. Gestures such as those for grief and fear would have been immediately recognised by the audience, and would have been exaggerated so as to be clearly visible to everyone. (See also Chapter 9, pp.324–325.)

Excellent acoustics enabled the actors to be heard at the back of the theatre, compensating for the poor visibility. The masks they wore had large, deep mouthpieces, possibly designed to have a megaphone effect. The primary information about characters came through the spoken word, so the actor's voice was his most important acting tool. Actors needed breath control and vocal flexibility in order to dance, speak, chant and sing challenging and poetic texts. They warmed up their voices before performances, and were put on special diets and told to refrain from sexual relations before a performance. Clearly, they were expected to be physically fit.

Gradually actors moved out of the chorus.

Originally, the role of the chorus was to narrate the story, but gradually individual actors were given a role outside the chorus. This change is attributed to the poet Thespis (from whom the word Thespian is derived), who wrote the first play in which one character stood out from the chorus. Subsequently, the playwright Aeschylus put a second individual character on stage, and later Sophocles introduced a third.

Public speaking skills were highly desirable.

Although we know little about actor training, we do know that public speaking skills, called oratory and rhetoric, were of great importance in ancient Greek culture. Politicians were frequently trained by actors, who themselves often moved into public speaking and politics. By 449BC *hypokrisis* (acting) was seen as an art in its own right. Aristotle explained acting as the way in which the voice was used to express different emotions (see Arnott, *Public and Performance in the Greek Theatre*).

Medieval actors

Medieval drama was still linked to religion.

Close links between religion, ritual and drama were also a characteristic of the early Middle Ages. Christianity had assimilated many pre-Christian rituals and was itself theatrical, featuring chanting, singing and the performance of ritualised actions. Simple biblical stories emphasising the dramatic aspects of struggles between good and evil were often performed inside churches. However, by the end of the 14th century, the non-Christian aspects of performances made them less popular with the clergy, and this brought about a final split between the church and the theatre (see Tydeman, *The Theatre in the Middle Ages*).

The setting influenced the performances.

By the 15th century, theatre had evolved into two main types of performance: mumming and street theatre. Mumming involved travelling in masks to private houses and performing songs or dances upon arrival. More public were the street performances of 'mystery' plays, depicting biblical stories, devised by the local trade guilds. Plays were generally performed outdoors, often on wheeled carts which took the actors to the audiences.

A model of the stage used for mystery plays at Valenciennes in France in 1547

The outdoor setting of these plays would have had a direct influence on the style of acting. While little is known about how the performers trained, we do know that acting styles would have been larger than life, to maximise visibility and audibility. As in Greek theatre, it is likely that stock characters were used, with immediately identifiable gestures. Performers would have needed vocal strength to be heard above an excitable and rowdy audience in an acoustically unfriendly environment.

Performances involved such skills as singing, juggling, slapstick comedy, wrestling, archery and stone-throwing. There was a strong link between theatre and sport, and the visual aspect of theatre was of prime importance. There are accounts of distinctions between actors (*histriones*), buffoons and acrobats, but it is probable that a medieval entertainer would have had to be versatile in his or her performance skills. (There is evidence to suggest that women took part in some performances.)

(See pp.210–213 for a further account of medieval theatre.)

Elizabethan acting

Actors were now professionals.

By the 16th century, all actors were male professionals, who provided entertainment for profit. London had become a theatrical centre, with established venues. Whilst it was not a particularly reputable profession, acting was becoming a clearly defined skill: the tragedian was gaining popularity over the clown and the acrobat.

There were two types of company. Boy companies developed out of school companies, where the training involved the classical oratorical skills, which emphasised gesture and speech. Boys trained by their managers were better educated than the adult players, but not necessarily better actors. Nevertheless, much of our terminology for acting comes from oratory, the art of formal speaking for public or ceremonial events.

In the sixteenth century the term 'acting' was originally used to describe the 'action' of the orator, his art of gesture. What the common stages offered was playing.
(Gurr, *The Shakespearean Stage*, p.99)

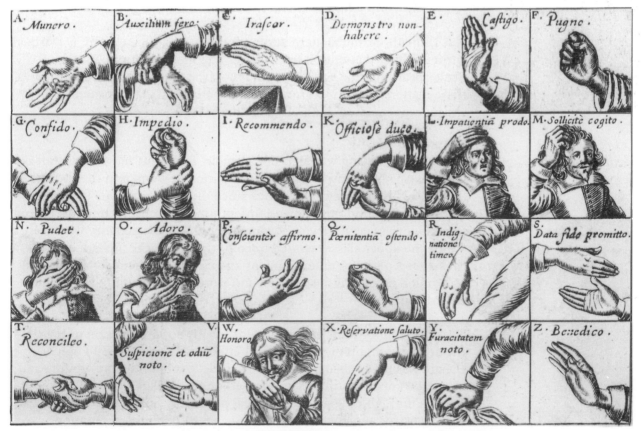

Mime gestures used by actors in the 17th century

The adult companies operated an apprentice system, whereby boys or adults trained with their fellow actors for several years before buying into the company as shareholders.

Actors had a demanding schedule.

Whichever the company type, the players' repertory changed constantly, which meant there was little rehearsal time and most of the actor's responsibilities lay in line learning. The Admiral's Men, for example, worked a six-day week, and in their 1594–5 season performed 38 plays, 21 of which were new. Actors were often required to perform in a different play every day (see Gurr, *The Shakespearean Stage*, p.103).

A schedule of this kind would have influenced acting styles in several ways. Firstly, lack of rehearsal and private preparation time would have prevented any attempt at the type of detailed psychological character study which a modern actor playing a part such as Hamlet would doubtless prepare. It is also very likely that actors knew only their own lines, having been given 'cue sheets' containing their lines and cues but no other part of the script.

A time limit for performances of three hours was laid down in 1594. The three hours had to include songs and jigs at the beginning of the play. Players adhering to this official performance length must have raced through longer playtexts, speaking their lines at a remarkable speed. This swift pacing, together with barely rehearsed staging, would have resulted in a highly energetic and spontaneous delivery.

It is difficult for the modern audience to imagine Shakespeare performed without detailed attention to character and interpretation, but the Shakespearean actor simply would not have had time to pay attention to these matters. For this reason, actors portrayed stock characters and type casting was common, both of which made their jobs easier.

Victorian acting

Acting was not respected as a profession.

By the 1830s, acting was seen not as an art form, but rather as a craft or trade unworthy of respect. The participation of women in the theatre (which had been common practice since the Restoration in 1660) was deplored for being immoral and unfeminine. (Ironically, this was one of the only professions in which women could achieve equality with men.) While the upper classes tended to go to the opera, the 'masses' saw the theatre as a place for entertainment and escape. Audiences grew rapidly as London became industrialised and work opportunities drew people to the capital.

This demand for mass entertainment led to the construction of bigger theatres, which, predictably, had an effect on performances. Popular theatre was dominated by farce, burlesque, pantomime, melodrama and musical comedy. Acting styles focused on the declamatory presentation of roles through exaggerated physical poses and vocal inflexions; it was customary for audiences to applaud scenes of heightened emotion.

Because acting was considered a natural ability, rather than an art that could be cultivated and refined, there was no call for actor training or a theory of acting. Instead, star actors chose pieces that showed off their talent to maximum effect, rewriting plays to their own whim.

Theatre moved towards realism at the end of the century.

By the 1880s, however, the public attitude was changing. The arts were shifting towards realism, the growing middle classes were developing a greater respect for literature, and educated actors were beginning to enter the profession. These factors all contributed to a shift in the audience's demands and a new approach to acting styles. In response to the increasing demands for a systematic and theoretical approach to acting, the first British drama school, the London Academy of Music and Dramatic Art, was established in 1861.

METHODS OF ACTOR TRAINING IN THE 20TH CENTURY

The actor's role continually evolves.

The role of the actor has continued to evolve in the 20th century, alongside the development of theories about the nature of theatre, which in turn have often emerged in reaction to dramatic theories and styles that have gone before. Drama schools in Britain have been influenced by these changing attitudes. Most of them introduce a varied range of acting methods, in an attempt to equip young actors with a physical and theoretical approach to their work which is both informed and flexible, and which will enable them to cope with the wide-ranging demands of the profession. This section provides a summary of just a few of the key practitioners who have influenced actor training in Britain during the 20th century.

Konstantin Stanislavski, 1863–1938

Stanislavski reacted against mechanical acting.

Much has been written about Stanislavski (see Cooper and Mackey, *Theatre Studies*, for example), the deviser of a system which promoted radical changes in actor training and which continues to have an influence today. Reacting against the artificial acting styles of his contemporaries, Stanislavski argued that the aim of theatre was to be a truthful expression of life on the stage. Truthful acting could be encouraged through exercises which developed the actor's entire physical, emotional and spiritual being. In *An Actor Prepares*, he advocated:

- using the imagination to answer the questions 'who, what, where, when, why?' to build a specific physical and emotional profile of the character;
- using the 'magic if' to ask: 'What would I do if these circumstances were real?';
- justifying the character's actions by asking 'What do I want?', where the answer provides the character's objective, motivating his or her action;
- dividing the play into a series of 'units', each with separate objectives to be analysed in detail;
- linking these units by an unbroken through line, leading to an ultimate 'super-objective'. This ensures logical progression between

all units within the play, and the matching of the physical acting style with the style of the play and the director's concept;

● drawing on personal experiences and the emotion memory links which are to be found between actors and their characters. This enables actors to breathe life into the 'inner images' of their characters. At the same time, the actor maintains conscious control of the character played;

● imagining an invisible so-called 'fourth wall' between the stage and the auditorium;

● daily relaxation exercises for the release of vocal and physical tension, in preparation for the physical and psychological demands of the performance.

Stanislavski's approach was ideally suited to the performance of realist plays, such as Chekhov's *The Seagull*, which he directed in 1898. The psychological aspects of Stanislavski 's system were readily received in the United States, becoming the foundation for Lee Strasberg's 'Method'.

Bertolt Brecht, 1898–1956

Brecht reacted against bourgeois realism.

To Brecht, realism and the styles of acting that had developed in response to Stanislavski's System and the Method seemed dull and bourgeois. Influenced by the new expressionist drama, with its cinematic style, which incorporated larger-than-life sets and elaborate and symbolic lighting, he saw theatre as a powerful political force, capable both of entertaining and of changing society for the better. He felt that audiences should learn to be emotionally uninvolved: if the spectator watched objectively, he or she could then think objectively. This new view of the purpose of theatre came to be known as Epic Theatre, and was characterised by an acting style called the *Verfremdungs Effekt* (distancing or making strange). This affected acting in the following ways:

● a return to the idea of the actor as presenter. Emotions are externalised; actors frequently comment on their characters or on the action. The actor may also function as narrator, addressing the spectators directly. This is the crux of the *Verfremdungs Effekt*, drawing on techniques from classical and medieval theatre;

● replacement of the question 'How do I feel?' by 'Have I ever seen it?';

● the elimination of the fourth wall: actors do not try to re-create reality;

● the use of various techniques to maintain freshness and objectivity in characterisation, including swapping roles in rehearsals, rehearsing in dialects or accents, and speaking parts in the third person, using 'he said', or 'she said'.

In addition, Brecht also strove to establish the formation of a close-knit company in which all actors had creative input, and rejected type casting and the star system. (For a more detailed analysis of Brecht's theories, see Cooper and Mackey, *Theatre Studies*.)

Michel Saint-Denis, 1897–1971

Saint-Denis looked for physical truth on stage.

Saint-Denis' concept of actor training was greatly influenced by his work in France with Jacques Copeau and the Compagnie des Quinze. Copeau believed that the essence of theatre was based not just on text, but also on ritual and physicality. Disillusioned with productions in which actors imposed their own psychological truths on non-realist plays, he sought to return to the origins of theatre, in order to find its *physical* truth. The Compagnie des Quinze rejected the proscenium arch and the illusory fourth wall, allowing greater freedom in the use of space. The actors were versatile, and their physical performances combined the text with song, the use of masks, mime and acrobatics.

He founded five drama schools.

In 1931, Compagnie des Quinze was enthusiastically received in London by actors and the press alike. Saint-Denis remained in London, and in 1936 he founded the London Theatre Studio. Passionate about actor training, he also founded five drama schools, including the Old Vic Theatre School and the Julliard School in New York. In 1962, he became a co-director of the Royal Shakespeare Company, together with Peter Brook and Peter Hall.

He rejected specific methods of acting.

Saint-Denis was suspicious of specific methods or systems of acting. Like Brecht, he rejected the idea of the 'fourth wall' and any attempt to create the illusion of reality on stage, but he also saw some virtue in Stanislavski's system, which, used selectively, could be made 'the grammar of all styles' (Saint-Denis, *Training for the Theatre* p.38). He aimed to train actors to be physically and vocally prepared to meet the demands of various different classical and modern texts, as well as the demands of the director and those of the performance space. Training was a means by which actors could discover the physical essence of theatre and find a balance between the role of inventor and the role of interpreter who brings a vital and truthful reality to the text.

Training should last four years.

In *Training for the Theatre*, he outlines a four-year training programme. The first year should focus on the discovery of natural physical, vocal and imaginative abilities. In the second year, the actor would work on the imaginative development of physical and vocal expression; the training would build on an awareness of the need for technique in order to transform. In year three, the actor's new creative and expressive abilities would be applied to the interpretation of texts in varying styles. This would include styles of vocal delivery and movement. Finally, year four would be spent performing plays to be seen by agents and the public.

Training involves five specific disciplines.

This syllabus is broken down into five specific disciplines, as follows:

- **body**: to create awareness of the body in space, incorporating movement exercises from Rudolf Laban; to develop physical agility; to achieve physical alignment, balance and freedom from muscular tension using the Alexander Technique (see pp.40–42);
- **voice/diction**: to awaken an awareness of the expressive quality of the voice; to build vocal power, breath control, resonance and

range, focusing on non-verbal expression in the first year; to free the voice from tension, which inhibits its expressive power;

- **speech/language**: to find the relationship between form and meaning; to explore the effects of style on delivery; to develop interpretative skills and sensitivity to varying forms and styles;
- **imaginative background**: to build cultural and historical resources as reference points to fuel the actor's imagination;
- **improvisation**: to discover the essence of acting through purely physical expression, including the preparation of a silent scenario, mask work and animal studies; to discover the actor's own inner creative resources without texts, in order to encourage the creative interpretation of texts.

Many aspects of Michel Saint-Denis' system are now standard elements of actor training, including mask work, animal studies and experiments with improvisation.

Peter Brook, 1925–

Brook bases his philosophy on the idea that all art forms are changing.

Brook takes as one of his starting points the idea that all art forms are constantly changing and evolving, which would partly account for the contrasting approaches to theatre that we have seen so far. New theories of theatre and acting techniques quickly become obsolete, because theatre, like society, does not stand still. According to Brook, 'the only thing that all forms of theatre have in common is the need for an audience' (Brook, *The Empty Space*, p.142).

Brook initially outlined his view of theatre in *The Empty Space* (1968). Here, he suggested that British audiences have come to expect theatre to be 'deadly', because most performances have fixed and lifeless acting, as though they were aiming for a definitive performance style. 'Immediate theatre' (Brook's name for his ideal theatre) reflects what is happening in the moment: the actors recognise the changing responses and expectations of the audience, and this contributes to a dynamic and spontaneous actor–audience relationship. Immediate theatre would also include 'holy' elements of ceremony and ritual, which would re-establish the theatre as a magical place 'where the invisible can appear' (ibid. p.47). The holy would then combine with the anti-traditional 'rough' aspects of theatre, such as makeshift sets and the possibility of improvisation, allowing for spontaneous and lively performances.

Brook wanted to find the essence of performance.

Brook was interested in finding the point at which performance begins as an inner impulse inside the actor, and in how the actor makes this impulse visible to an audience. He was influenced by the experimental work of Antonin Artaud and Jerzy Grotowski, which examined the fundamental nature of performance and the actor–audience relationship. Like Grotowski and Artaud, Brook hoped to find central images, whether verbal or gestural, which would be lasting in the mind of the audience. However, he did not believe that he could do this work in the commercial theatre.

*He established a
company in Paris.*

In 1970, he left a successful career in England to establish the
International Theatre Research Centre in Paris, bringing together a
company of actors from diverse cultural and linguistic backgrounds.
Since then, the Centre has been a unique place of intercultural exchange
and theatre experimentation. It seeks to find and develop a universal
theatre, in which actors communicate through a common medium of
sound and movement which supersedes language barriers. Such a
theatre could be understood and appreciated by audiences anywhere in
the world. For example, Brook discovered that vocal sounds such as
vowels in their purest form are a sort of emotional language or code,
which can produce lasting images in the mind of the listener. Simple
sounds such as 'ah' could have a more direct effect on the emotions of
the listener than long speeches, and could cross cultural barriers.

Motivated by his search for a universal language of sounds, he worked
with the poet Ted Hughes to develop a new language, 'Orghast'. In 1971,
a play of the same name was performed at the Shiraz Festival. Although
it was widely acclaimed, Brook felt it was too narrow in its approach
and not truly accessible. Other famous projects have included *The
Conference of the Birds*, a 12th-century Sufi play, taken to six African
countries in 1972–3, and a production of the ancient Hindu myth *The
Mahabharata* in 1985.

A scene from Peter Brook's production of The Mahabharata

Brook works with actors from all over the world.

Because he works with actors from all over the world, Brook does not impose a particular method or style upon his cast. He wants his actors to find their own ways of bringing about a cultural exchange. This imposes a number of requirements on them. Firstly, there is a need for vocal freedom. Humans express themselves audibly through their voices; the voice is the actor's primary mode of communication. Actors should therefore explore the vocal language of tones, vowels, cries and chants. For the voice to be free, the emotions must also be free, as must the body: early rehearsals focus on releasing habits, clichés and learned conventions. The absence of a common language enhances the dissolution of habitual vocal and physical mannerisms.

A second important requirement is spontaneity, which actors should seek in their daily life as well as at work. Performances should never be fixed and simply repeated without variation. The actors must respect their audiences and listen to them, encouraging a two-way relationship: they should always ask themselves what it is that they wish to leave with the audience.

Within this philosophy, the director's responsibility is to assist the actor to find his or her character, and to work out how this character develops in relationship to the audience. Brook believes that the theatre does not exist to preach or lecture: it is there to create a shared experience, in which the audience assists with 'eyes and focus and desires and enjoyment and concentration' (ibid. p.156).

Mike Leigh, 1943–

Leigh trained at RADA.

Mike Leigh is known for his improvised plays, developed in collaboration with a cast of actors. When Leigh trained at RADA (the Royal Academy of Dramatic Art) in the early 1960s, the school had not as yet been influenced by the new approaches to training coming from practitioners such as Saint-Denis. The school's approach to actor training was traditional: the actor was still seen as an interpreter, not a creator. It was not until he left drama school and became aware of the work of practitioners such as Saint-Denis, Brook and Peter Hall that Leigh began to see the actor's potential for creating original work.

His work is based around improvisation.

Leigh's first directing experience was working on *The Box Play* (1965) with a group of inexperienced amateur actors, at the Midland Arts Centre for Young People in Birmingham. He was dissatisfied with the results, feeling that the production was superficial. In his next production, *My Parents Have Gone To Carlisle* (1966), he began to establish the principles from which he continues to work. In 1967, he was asked to join the RSC (the Royal Shakespeare Company) as a director. Since then he has continued to base his work around improvisation, working in both theatre and film.

Leigh develops ideas with the actors, and has no preconceptions before

There are characteristic stages of rehearsal for the actor.

he begins work. He also has no set rules about how rehearsals progress, stating that each rehearsal is a new and different experience. Nevertheless, there are characteristic stages of rehearsal through which the actors generally progress. The following is a summary of Leigh's rehearsal process, as explained by Clements in *The Improvised Play* (see bibliography, p.63.)

Actors often base characters on people they know.

Leigh's first rehearsal stage is concerned with finding the inner reality and the external physicality of a character. After casting, actors are asked to bring to rehearsal a list of people they know. The first rehearsal is essentially a private discussion between Leigh and the actor about people on the list. Leigh chooses one of the characters for the actor to develop during a number of private rehearsals. Through a series of improvisations (each based on the previous rehearsals), the reality of the character is played out in a chronological sequence of events. Private rehearsals help to build a trust between the actor and director, and diminish the pressure to 'perform' too quickly.

The character is developed in private rehearsals first.

The actor is encouraged to stay with the improvisation until he or she is asked to come out of it. The director then asks questions about any discoveries made by the actor regarding how the character felt, what he or she was doing and why. The aim of talking about the character in the third person, as 'he' or 'she', is that the actor should maintain a degree of detachment, in order to understand the character better.

Characters are also developed and expanded by active research or investigation into why the character thinks in a certain way, and what his or her belief systems are. Research is also done into the character's physical mannerisms and habits. This might involve going out into the community *in character* to discover how the character would behave in certain situations. (This is only if the actor thinks it would be helpful, however.) Action has to come from inner motivation: the focus should be on *why* as opposed to *what*. This inner motivation provides the impetus for action, whether this means speaking or moving. Because improvisation involves working from the self, there can often be a tendency towards introspection. This eventually needs to shift to a performance level, where the audience can see and hear the character's actions.

Finally, they develop relationships with each other.

Once the actors have established their characters' identities, they are introduced to the other characters. As they interact and their relationships become established, work begins on the structure of the play through the director's written scenarios and exercises that are acted out. The actors never know the motives of the other characters, or the purpose of the exercises. This avoids working towards an imposed goal and maintains spontaneity and an interest in discovery. Equally, the actors are not allowed to invent information about each other that is not already generally known, such as non-existent relatives or unspecified life events.

There are three main stages in structuring the play.

According to Clements, there are three main stages in structuring the play:

- **rough assembling**: scenarios are put together, and a basic through line is established;
- **second draft**: details are considered and revised;
- **final phase**: this involves editing and polishing.

The characters' inner lives motivate their physical actions.

An actor working with Leigh via improvisation in this way will have channelled all his or her creative energy into this work. The initial impetus for the character comes from personal experience. This is then expanded physically and emotionally to discover the character's inner desires, relationships and motivations. This inner life of the character is the source of his or her physical actions. Clements states that 'in essence, the process of arriving at a play is one of refining each pulse of action until what is reached is a text without a script' (ibid. p.55). Eventually, the improvised play becomes a published script, available to be interpreted by other actors and directors.

Voice and movement training

Actors need to train physically and vocally.

The focus in this section so far has been on the influence that practitioners have had on actor training. Every practitioner has stressed the importance of physicality, which involves freeing the body and the voice so that the actor can maximise his or her ability to communicate; it also means building physical and vocal stamina, necessary for the demands of the profession. This section briefly introduces examples of *general* approaches to voice and movement training, which aim to encourage a more free and efficient use of the actor's voice and body in preparation for the demands of performance. These methods are not dependent on any particular style of acting or notion of performance, and are often used in training people outside the acting profession. (More specific exercises are given in Chapter 1, pp.5–10.)

Cicely Berry's approach to voice training

Cicely Berry is currently voice director of the Royal Shakespeare Company. She has been one of the most important practitioners of voice in this century, and has had a huge influence on voice teaching methods in drama schools.

Tension blocks vocal expressivity.

Many people continue to think that voice work is about elocution and 'speaking properly', and that regional accents should be ironed out. Berry has proved that these attitudes are limiting. She feels that, although there is no such thing as a 'right voice', unnecessary tension and constrictions can block the natural creativity of the voice. This is because tension limits the actor's ability to be vocally expressive, as well as his or her vocal power and range. All of these are needed both for audibility in a large auditorium and to maintain the audience's interest. However, a technically perfect voice which is not *emotionally* free can sound imposing, insincere and even dull. Berry aims for a free voice which will give the actor a more creative choice of self-expression in terms of range, pitch and resonance.

Four factors affect the voice.

In her first book, *Voice and the Actor* (1973), Berry outlines her approach to the voice. When we speak, we are unconsciously affected by four factors: our environment, from which we pick up our speech patterns; our ear and how we perceive sounds; physical agility or awareness of our muscles; and personality, which determines how we deal with the above.

The aim is a voice free from tension.

The first element of Berry's form of voice training is relaxation and breathing. The aim is to eliminate constrictive tensions and to discover how a free sound can be made. Actors discover the relationship between relaxation and good breathing habits through a series of exercises performed while lying on their backs on the floor. In this position (known as 'semi-supine'), it is easier to relax and keep the spine straight. Actors can feel sideways lower rib movement and movement in the back against the floor, without lifting the upper chest or the shoulders as they breathe. The aim is to feel the breath as low in the body as possible as the abdomen relaxes, and to become gradually familiar with the sensation of breath that is 'rooted'.

Sound is linked with the impulse to speak, and thus connects with the out breath. It is breath flowing over the vocal cords which powers and supports the sound, not the vocal cords themselves. Voiced sound is introduced gradually, on a 'mah' sound, and any tension that occurs as new pitches and tones are explored is eliminated through relaxation. With the right balance of relaxation and tension, the sound will resonate in the chest, pharynx, face, nose and head. Tension caused by pushing the sound through the vocal cords creates a sore throat and can seriously damage the vocal cords. Yawning helps to release this tension.

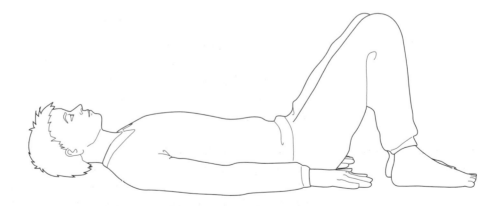

The semi-supine position

Muscularity allows you to reduce volume and still be heard.

The second area on which Berry works is muscularity. The muscles of the lips, tongue and jaw are the articulators, which form consonants and help to power the sound out of the mouth and project it forward. All these muscles need constant exercise. With increased muscularity, speech can sound clearer and will fill a space more efficiently. The bigger the space, the more muscular power is needed in the articulators. Muscularity also allows the actor to reduce his or her volume (as in a stage whisper) and still be heard. Practice is needed to find the right balance of tension. Too much tension in the jaw, for example, will trap the sound inside the mouth. On the other hand, someone who mumbles is probably unsure, and is not allowing the muscles to do enough work. Finding the right balance of tension and energy helps actors to project both the sound and the meaning of the words.

Emotional scenes can cause vocal tension.

However, this newfound vocal freedom and power can easily get lost as the actor becomes physically and emotionally caught up in a character's lines and with the stress of rehearsing and performing. Once the actor is aware that energy is not the same as tension, he or she must monitor any tension that creeps in, but without losing vocal energy. Vocal tension is often discovered only when the actor develops a sore throat.

Berry is particularly interested in the interrelationship of voice and text and the delicate balance between the sound of the voice and the meaning of the word. Speaking poetry, for example, can awaken emotional responses which can result in a new vocal tone or resonance. (In this respect, Berry's approach is very similar to that of Peter Brook, with whom she has worked.)

Sounds have emotional and physical qualities.

Work on the very basic sounds within a text, such as the vowels and consonants, can reveal emotional and physical qualities which give us clues about the underlying emotions and meanings. This can help actors explore characters as they discover energy and rhythms through the imagery and speech patterns. For example, punctuation is directly related to thought patterns and consequently to breath patterns. Long passages with little punctuation feel vastly different from jerky, halting passages with short sentences and many breaks. Scenes of heightened emotion are usually full of open vowel sounds. (See Berry, *The Actor and his Text.*)

Truth comes from connecting sound to intention.

To sound truthful, actors must connect to the language physically and emotionally. This means discovering the emotional intention behind each word, which is then revealed as a thought 'in action'. When the voice is free, the sounds and meanings will be merged, which will bring the text to life.

The Alexander Technique

How you use your body affects how it works.

The Alexander Technique aims to develop an awareness of the body. The technique is named after F.M. Alexander (born in 1869 in Australia). The basic underlying principle of Alexander is that there is an intimate relationship between our *use* of the body and how the body *functions*. This means that if we misuse the body, it will not function efficiently. The term 'use' applies to all our conscious and unconscious physical movements, whether we are standing, sitting or lying, and whether we imagine ourselves in a state of rest or of activity.

Alexander developed his technique after recognising vocal problems.

Alexander came to this conclusion after extensive observation of his own use of his body. Originally an actor, he continually experienced hoarseness and voice loss after or during performances. At that time there were no voice or speech specialists; doctors could not explain the cause of the problem, and just told him to rest his voice. Obviously, this was only a temporary solution, as the voice problems returned when he started work again.

He discovered the link between posture and voice.

Alexander eventually began observing himself in a mirror, watching what he was doing with his throat and neck. He found that he was pulling the back of his head backwards, putting strain on his throat and vocal mechanism, as though the force of gravity was dragging him down. He discovered that if he lengthened the back of his neck and improved his posture and balance, the vocal problems began to decrease. Alexander ultimately turned these discoveries of the link between his 'use' and his physical 'functioning' into a complete system. He came to England in 1904, established a teaching practice in London and trained teachers in his technique. Alexander's methods are used in many drama schools, not simply because of the strong link between voice use and body use, but also because Alexander Technique aims to bring about a new physical awareness.

Benefits include an awareness of the interrelationship of the neck, back, shoulders and pelvis. Freedom and release in these areas are developed through a series of exercises, starting with floor work in the semi-

A slumped posture (left) and upright posture (right)

supine position, with a book under the head to support the neck.
Standing and walking exercises focus on the creation of a free neck.
The knees are flexible, not locked, when standing: as the knees unlock,
the spine lengthens, the tail bone drops down and the back straightens.
Improved posture is thus based on lengthening and widening the spine.
Flexibility as opposed to rigidity is the aim.

A second benefit is kinaesthetic awareness. This helps individuals sense
where their body is in a physical space and where they are in relation to
others, and leads to improved awareness of tension and relaxation in the
muscles. This in turn makes it possible to learn to inhibit unnecessary
tension, for example tensing the left arm when only the right hand is
needed to pick up a pen. This is known as conscious inhibition, and in
this context means simply 'non-doing', as opposed to active prevention.
Non-doing, or allowing the body to function naturally, as a baby does
when it learns to sit, stand and walk, requires less effort than doing,
which involves the interference of unnecessary muscular tension.
Because the muscles are allowed to function efficiently, the breathing
and vocal mechanisms are released, and balance, flexibility and stamina
improve.

The technique helps actors understand their bodies.

Because the Alexander Technique involves releasing longstanding
physical habits, it can be deeply personal work, and like any new
physical and mental discipline it takes time to master. As an exploration
of the potential of the body, it promotes the idea that actors, as physical
performers, should understand the relationship they have with their own
bodies before beginning work on the physical aspects of a character. It
also shows them that as professionals they must take responsibility for
the choices they make about the use of their bodies, and helps them find
a place of neutrality in which to begin and end their work.

INTERVIEWS WITH TWO ACTORS

Geraldine James

Geraldine James entered the profession more than 20 years ago, in 1972.
With a child studying Shakespeare at school and a husband who teaches
acting at RADA, she is as passionate about the need for actor training as
she was when she was a student. Theatre directors she has worked with
include Peter Hall (*Cymbeline*) and Dustin Hoffman (*The Merchant of
Venice*). She has a broad experience of working in television and film.

Acting is transformation.

Q How do you begin working on a character?
I have to have an affinity with it. I've just turned down a play: nothing
echoed in me about the character. Because of the way I work, I like to
find a character who I don't think is me. Acting is transformation.
Training is to prepare the actor in the broadest possible way – vocally,
physically, emotionally, intellectually, psychologically – so the actor
can go, 'If I play Othello, I use this part of myself. If I play a part in a
police series on the box, I use this part of myself.'

Q **Are those parts of yourself conscious choices, or do they just develop?**

They echo. It's unconscious; we don't necessarily know what it is. A lot of amateur actors will say, 'I'll put this sort of voice on...' That to me is the antithesis of acting. That's performing. I don't think performing is acting. I do a lot of work with children; some are able to *demonstrate*, very ably, an old lady with a cockney accent. That is not acting. Occasionally, you'll find a child who can actually respond on another level, but it's usually the child who's very quiet; she's not just bending her back, talking in a funny voice. There's something she's observed about old men, and she's translated it, and I believe her as an old man. That's acting.

Performing is not acting.

Q **Do you think society has got confused between actors who transform and people who perform?**

Yes. There are a lot of young actors, particularly in television, who are doing incredibly well, and they may not have trained at all. They are not real actors, though they often become stars. I doubt they will last long. There are definitely those who really can learn how to act by doing a long-running series, but I think they're still limited in their range. I met someone recently who said, 'You do acting, don't you? I think I'd like to do that.' He said, 'What do you do to start acting?' and I said, 'Well, you go to drama school for three years, you study, you work on your body, you stretch your voice, you explore yourself, you understand what plays are for, and you find out about why we have theatre and culture.' For example, why is the greatest thing about England William Shakespeare?

You need to train to be an actor.

Q **Why is it important for actors to understand the historical development of our culture and the theatre?**

Culture is what separates the human being from anything else. Civilisation has developed for better or worse, but culture is what makes people sane. Culture is what we need in society, and one of the fundamentals of culture is the theatre.

Culture is part of humanity.

Q **Do you build a life for your characters outside the text, or can you get all the information you need from the text itself?**

I think (and this is what the Drama Centre taught me) in the end every answer is in the text, if you've got a good play. Ninety per cent of the time you haven't. Then you create a character. When I was working on *Dummy*, I had to work on the part intellectually and practically. How do you behave if you can't hear? I went into a shop and asked for something as a deaf person, pointing and talking the way deaf people talk. And this girl turned away, giggling behind my back. (I wouldn't have heard if I really was deaf.) I heard the other

You have to try your character out.

43

girl saying, 'Look, she's deaf, did you hear the way she spoke?' It was very frightening, because they could have said, 'Why are you pretending to be deaf?' You take a risk.

Q Do you think directors view actors as interpreters or creators?

Good directors work collaboratively.

People have different ideas. I think the good directors believe it's a collaborative journey, and they need actors to go on it. What we've got involved in recently is pictorial theatre: we have 'directors of idea', who want actors to embody their own idea. I love working with a director who's interested in asking you to help find what they're doing, whether it's their own play or a play that we've all seen 50 times. Why do we keep doing *Hamlet*? Is it endlessly worth re-looking at and re-searching it? I doubt any actress who's played Portia would say she got it right. I talked to an Australian friend about playing Portia. When she did it she was a 26-year-old Australian, I was 30-something and English, and we both had very different experiences playing the same lines in the same order; we were both Portia. These plays are great because there's no one way of playing them.

Q You both created something different beyond interpreting the lines?

Acting is not about interpreting.

It's not about interpreting. It's about those trains that go through coal mines and get loaded with coal; it's about going somewhere dark and dangerous: you trundle along picking up things as you go. And at the end there's light; you come out and you've got something on your back you didn't know you had.

Q Do you find that drama schools turn out very different actors?

You cannot necessarily teach people to act.

Yes, although I do know very good actors who haven't been to drama schools, and actors who've been through very good schools and they've never made it. You need to really find one that suits you. People are very prejudiced about drama schools. You can't *teach* people to act. You can *allow* them to act.

Q Do you think that talent can be cultivated?

Training encourages talent to emerge.

I think that talent is intangible, indefinable, but immensely evident. Good training allows talent to come out. If you've got a trained voice, it's going to be easier to perform a difficult piece eight times a week. If you've got a good body (it doesn't mean a pretty body, it means if it's supple and worked on), then you'll be able to use the body to become the physical life of the character you're playing.

Q In your experience, do many theatre actors work on their bodies and their voices when they're not working?

Acting is hard work physically.

No, not in England. I'm at my fittest when I'm in theatre because it's such hard work. People don't know how physically taxing it is to go on stage and play parts like Hedda Gabler, eight times a week, wearing those costumes and under those lights. You have to be fit. Actors are very rarely ill. It's adrenalin, I suppose. But when I'm not working, I'm very lazy, and I'm impressed with actors who go to the Actors' Centre [for contact details, see p.204] and do classes. It's an American habit, not British.

Q Do you think American actors have a different approach generally?
I think the essential difference is the British are much more based in language, and the Americans are more based in feeling. That's slightly to do with the Method: we're terribly impressed with Americans, because for them it's not about the word, it's about what's behind the word. When you work with an American director, they say, 'just throw it away, throw it away'. But it's not that we're overacting; the English hit consonants, we articulate much more. That was illustrated to me doing Shakespeare with Dustin Hoffman, because he would just throw it away. He would also pretend it wasn't there. He'd go, 'I don't need to say those words, I can say my own words.' And then you'd go, 'Well, no, your words aren't as good as Shakespeare's, why don't you have a go at *his* words?' He would come on and go, 'Hey, what the f**k?' and improvise. He tried desperately to get inside the language, and eventually he succeeded. He'd take me aside, and say, 'Do that speech', and I'd go, 'The quality of mercy is not strained', and he'd go, 'The quality of what? The what? What? What are you talking about?' He'd say there's more to it than just the word.

Q So it was about the intention behind the word.
Yes, but he was saying you can't just *know* you've got to do that, you've got to actually *do* it. One day he came to rehearsal and said, 'I've just realised about Shakespeare, you can't improvise this shit.' Once he realised Shakespeare did it best, then he did it, and did it brilliantly. He had to work his American way, whereas we go, 'I know my lines, what more do you want?'

Q Possibly it's easy to do with Shakespeare, we look at the words and they're so beautifully written...
That's why we shouldn't study it at school. Shakespeare didn't write it to be studied at school, he wrote it to be experienced in the theatre. Most of us have gone through school loathing Shakespeare, but we go and see a good production, and we're mind-blown by it. But it should be scrapped from schools, or anyway treated as theatre, not an intellectual exercise.

Q Why do some professional British actors seem generally to dislike improvisation?
Because it's frightening; they're suddenly being put on the spot. Because, if you ask me to do this part, you've asked for *me*, and *I* will do the part. Improvising can be (and should be) very revealing of us as people, not just characters. You can't hide behind the character. The minute you have any sort of reputation, the more difficult it gets, and you don't want to risk that. I believe any time you do a job, you've got to be prepared to fail.

Q When you are rehearsing, do you ever get to a point when you feel, 'Yes, I'm there', or 'Yes, at least I'm nearly there'?
Rarely, and it might be dangerous. You have to need the audience to complete the event. We all pretend we don't care what critics think, but we do desperately long for their approval, and the approval of the

Improvisation is not popular with many British actors who have gained fame.

audience. If you really believed you'd cracked it, there'd be no point in doing it again tomorrow night. All I ever want to hear is someone to say, 'Yes, this is good.' We can't look at ourselves in the theatre. It's extremely tough.

Drama school shows you if you have made the right choice.

Q How would you advise someone who wants to be an actor?
I would always encourage young people to go to drama school, because it allows them to find out if they've made the right choice. If you can turn up to a course for three years, you know you can turn up to the theatre. You have to find out whether you have a gift for it. It's taken me *25 years* to admit that I do. You have to ask yourself, 'should I take a risk?' and it can be horribly soul-destroying.

Q What keeps you going?
Mortgages? The knowledge that someone might send me a script to read and I might get that thump in the solar plexus. That's what keeps me going.

Colin Firth

Colin Firth left drama school in 1983, and has worked extensively in theatre, film and television. Directors he has worked with include Richard Eyre (*Tumbledown*) and Harold Pinter (*The Caretaker*). He was recently seen as Mr Darcy in *Pride and Prejudice*, and at the time of interviewing he was filming *A Thousand Acres* in the USA.

Q Do you think that actors are artists or craftsmen?
Artist is such a big word. I think a mechanic can be an artist, and a painter can be nothing but a manual labourer.

Q Do directors understand the actor's process?

Directors have different approaches with actors.

Some do. I like nothing more than working with a director with a strong vision, and nothing less than working with a director without strong vision but with very strong opinions. Two of the best directors I've worked with have completely different approaches. One was a dictator with a very strong vision: he started the rehearsal process by expanding on the concept of the play, the universe of the writer, and he blocked everything in absolute detail. He had a very exciting end in mind, and inspired everybody with his concept. That's the key: inspiration rather than direction. The other director was the opposite. He never theorised about it. Some actors feel liberated by a director who puts you through the blocking tightly, because if you're not thinking about where you move you're completely free to fill those moves with substance. Likewise, with a director who's not theorising about anything, you can supply your own approach. The only time I feel stifled is when the director doesn't have an understanding of drama, or story. He doesn't understand an actor's process, but he's pushing you in a direction that goes against any sort of emotional logic. He wants to see a result on the cheap that he's unable to communicate or justify.

Q How do you deal with that?

Actors have to make the material their own.

It depends. Sometimes there's no way to do what's asked of you truthfully, although you try it. You have to debate it. The actor's imagination is really all you're left with in the end. You've got to allow for it. There has to be a kind of aspect of rebellion at some point.

Q Can you explain that?

Well, you have to run with the material, and have the confidence to bluff a bit. A writer who is writing about a historical fact often goes beyond his research and uses his imagination. There's a stage where you have to make it your own, or people aren't going to believe you on stage. It's no longer the writer's material, it's yours. You are interpreting it, but there's got to be a *reason why*.

Q Why do some actors end up doing the same performance for months on end?

If you stop challenging yourself and asking questions, the thing stops being alive. Sometimes the material is limited and there's little more you can find. If you treat it as a repetition, you're going to stagnate.

Q If you're going to start work on a piece of text, do you do any kind of character or text analysis?

Academic analysis on its own is not helpful: you have to find your own relationship with the character.

I think 'analysis' is an extremely academic word. We're talking semantics, but the word 'analysis' doesn't really help me. The text has got to fire your own imagination. Of course, I study it, but the struggle is to make it specific to *you*. You've got to make the stakes very high for yourself, because *you've* got to live it. There's a lot of judgement in academic and critical analysis, but I think it's not appropriate for an actor. You're taking a critical approach when you first read something, to decide whether it's something you should do or not. But once you've taken on a character your exploration has got to be about justifying, not judging.

Q Can you explain justifying your character?

Someone said to me the other day that the character I'm playing is a bastard and how do I feel about playing a bastard? But I couldn't play somebody you could *just* say that about. No matter what someone might say about them, however you feel when you read the book, *I'm* the guy doing what *he* does. I have to find my reasons for doing what he does. *He* has his reasons for doing it, and those have to become *my* reasons. You have to be able to see that they're motivated, that it comes from something. I have to defend him as I would myself. This is what made playing Darcy difficult. I didn't want to strut around just showing how pompous he is; I had to say, well, I understand he's not *only* pompous.

Q In a way, he's struggling against himself.

You have to see the world through the character's eyes.

He's emotionally disabled in some way. He's a product of his class or period. Various insecurities motivate his behaviour; it's important to see the world through his eyes, rather than flaunting his characteristics. Actors sometimes play the result. The result has to be the by-product of the character's needs and characteristics.

Q What kinds of questions do you have to ask about a character?

Ask your character questions.

Just basic questions: who, what, where, when, why? When do I exist? What is my context? Where am I on the map? What are my circumstances? What do I want? When do I want it? Why do I want it? How am I going to get it? Your means, your 'how' is very important. Your character is revealed in the means you use to get what you want.

Q Do you find it frustrating when you work with actors who have a different approach?

All actors work differently.

I can't afford to. Everyone's got a different approach. Some actors are just show-offs. Others are wrapped up in their own internal stuff. I worked with an actor once who went on and on about his 'need' as a character. He wouldn't do anything on stage unless his 'need' required it, even if it meant not coming in with his line for five minutes, because a teacher had told him, 'Don't *do* anything; your *need* summons it.'

Q That sounds like his personality taking over his character.

You have to consider other actors' needs.

You can't get away with that kind of selfishness. An actor cannot take off on their own agenda. I've seen actors do all sorts of things to prepare for a performance. It doesn't matter if it doesn't faze anybody else. But sometimes it does. If an actor needs to start screaming before a take, they'd better be sure that that's OK with everybody, because everyone else is just about to do a take as well. You constantly make compromises. But in the most productive situations you are able to work together.

Q Do you usually need some sort of physical and mental warm-up before going on stage?

I've always had a physical warm-up of some kind, and always prepared myself mentally. After a long run, the need to psychologically prepare diminishes, because you slip in and out of that world more easily. I've worked with brilliant actors who appear to have no preparation, but it's very rare. It depends on a scene. Often actors get into agonies and think they're not working because something's come first time. With theatre you can get a rehearsal right almost by accident; you try it again, and it never happens again, and you've got to work to find it. With film, if you get something right by accident, leave it alone. It's there, you don't know how or why, but you've got the take, it's printed and it's brilliant.

Q **Are you as emotionally involved with your characters when you're filming as you are on stage, even when it's shot out of sequence?**

You use your imagination in the same way in film and theatre.

Absolutely. It's all artificial: theatre may not be in sequence, it depends on the play. Sometimes you're jumping two years, that's a leap of the imagination. I don't find it that difficult to inhabit a different reality, because that's all you're doing anyway as an actor. You have to examine the script to see where you are in the story. If you've done that homework, the 'out of sequence' thing isn't a particular problem.

Q **What are the most exhilarating aspects of your work?**

It's very exhilarating getting something right which is very difficult, and communicating it to people. It is a wonderful feeling if you're inspired and moved by what's happening on stage, and you sense that hundreds of people are having that experience too.

Q **How do you deal with a hostile audience?**

Performing on stage has positive and negative aspects.

You just plough on. It's frustrating and painful, but you just renew the effort. It's not the audience's fault, but it feels like rejection and you have to deal with it. On the other hand, you've got these wonderful moments. There's a story about Olivier, having played a night of *Othello*. He got a standing ovation, and the cast lined the corridor to his dressing-room and applauded as he went by, and he went in and slammed the door. When asked why he was so pissed off, he said, 'Because I don't know how I did it; I'll never be able to do it again.' You've got your basic foundation for your performance, and it seems magical one night, and depressed the other. It's often difficult to know why. Sometimes the audience are just not going to like it. Every single audience has a different identity. You are in a relationship in the theatre.

Q **Are you ever completely satisfied with your performances?**

No!

Q **So how do you get the confidence to go on?**

Your work is never finished.

You go on whether you've got the confidence or not. You just do it. You can't say, 'I'm sorry, can we wait until tomorrow night, I'm not ready.' You never finish it. As Beckett says at the end of the *Unnameable*: 'I must go on, I can't go on, I'll go on.'

GUIDELINES FOR ACTING

Developing a performance from an extract or a full text

There are no set methods.

This section is designed to assist you through the rehearsal process on your way to finding a character. There can be no definitive approach to acting, and it is not the aim of this section to set out prescriptive rules: all actors eventually find their own ways of working. Nevertheless, it is hoped that everyone has the same ultimate aim: to create truthfully acted characters on stage. You must find some way to convey the truth of your character, regardless of the type of reality the character inhabits

The actor's aim is truth on stage.

This section gives you some suggestions to help you find this truth, along with some clues to the purpose of rehearsals.

As we have seen, theatre practitioners have different views about what we mean by 'truth' on stage and how to achieve this. How you approach rehearsals and the performance will ultimately depend on who you are, the play, the director and your fellow actors. Your performance will also be determined in part by the performance space and the audience.

Whilst these guidelines refer to a 'director' figure, they can be used successfully if you are working without a director.

Read the whole play.

How much preparation you do before the first rehearsal is really up to you. It is not enough just to read through your lines, however. You should read the whole play thoroughly: even if you are doing only one scene, you will need information from the whole text to create a full character. Some actors suggest you read the play at least three times before starting rehearsals.

At the first rehearsal, you will sometimes have the opportunity to read through the play with your director and discuss his or her view of it. Directors use this time differently: some will have a more concrete vision of the play than others at this stage. If you have read your text thoroughly, you should have basic information about your character for discussion, but do not be surprised if the director has a different impression of your character. Remember, the rehearsal process is about finding the reality of the character, with guidance and suggestions from the director. The following suggestions are aimed at assisting you with discovering the world of the play, which will enable you to build a truthful character.

Suggestions for finding the world of the play.

Piece together a character history from information given in the text. Find as many specific clues about your character as possible: references to age, place in society, education, behavioural characteristics and so on. Look at what your character says and does. If it is helpful, and applicable to the style of the play you are working on, these questions can be explored further, as advocated by Stanislavski (see pp.31–32) or as described below.

Who am I?

Find out who your character is by examining what he or she says, as well as noting references to him or her by other characters in the text. Explore your character's relationships with other characters on stage. Look at what other characters say about each other. If they do not talk to each other, ask why not. Never disregard anything in the text because you think you have thought of something better.

When do I exist?

The structure of the play as a whole provides clues about the world of your character in terms of time. When does the play take place? Is there a linear plot, with a steady progression of time? Does the action take

50

place over hours, days, weeks or years? Are there flashbacks? Is the character living in a dream world, or metaphorically living in the past? If the action takes place in a period of history, research will tell you more about how people behaved and dressed.

Where am I?

Where does the character live geographically? Does the setting change during the play? Is it a real world? Is it an imaginary world full of fictitious or mythical characters? Ask yourself why the playwright has chosen that world for your character. If it is an abstract world, you will need to give it substance and make it real to your audience. This is something to discuss with the director and other actors, to make sure you end up sharing the same type and level of 'reality'.

What society do I live in?

The social world in which your character lives directly affects how he or she thinks and behaves. What place in society does your character have, in terms of education, class, occupation and wealth? What are the belief systems operating in your character's world? Does your character share these belief systems, or is he or she in conflict with society?

If you do not understand the social background of the period of the play, you will fail to find the reality of the character. Research the background of the play: when was it written, and who wrote it? The answers to these questions are crucial for insights about the meaning of the play, as they will tell you why certain subjects are being dealt with, as well as why characters behave in particular ways. For example, *Death of a Salesman* by Arthur Miller is ostensibly about the character Willy Loman's failure to live up to his dreams of success and popularity. However, viewed in a broader context, Willy can be seen as one of many individuals who fell victim to the myth of 'the American dream', an unquestioning faith in capitalism which preoccupied Americans in the prosperous years following the Second World War. This makes Willy a universal figure, giving the play greater political relevance. (See also pp.55–57.)

Your world has to match the world of the other characters.

Although any imaginative work you do outside rehearsals may be useful for you to get a feel for the character, remember that he or she inhabits a world with other people. If you need to fill information gaps in the text, you must be careful that what you create matches what your fellow actors decide. You must be in the same reality in the play. Ideally, these things should be discussed with the director in rehearsal.

Look at the language.

Clues to the characters and to the style of the play can be gleaned from the language. Does your character use the same style of speech as other characters? Does he or she use a more or less educated vocabulary and sentence structure? Is the language formal or colloquial? Is it modern language, or is it antiquated? Is it full of short lines and rapid exchanges? Are there many pauses? What does this tell you about the energy behind the characters?

Ideas for physical and vocal development

Do not just think; try ideas out.

There is no need to fix on a physical and vocal interpretation too early: try to remain open to development. Let your movement be motivated by something, rather than imposing a physicality or a voice onto the character. Equally, do not be afraid to go with your instinct in rehearsal: this is the creative process at work. As far as possible, work on your character by doing and speaking. If it does not work, at least you will have ruled out some possibilities.

A warm-up is extremely important.

Before you do any physical or vocal work, a thorough warm-up will help focus your energy on your body and voice, preparing you physically and emotionally for work. In addition, it will prevent vocal and physical injuries. Rehearsing and performing is a physical activity: actors, like athletes, need to prepare their muscles for use. Many warm-up exercises used in sport are useful here, but particular attention must be given to the voice, as this often gets neglected, resulting in injury. Without a voice, you can't say your lines! For a detailed physical and vocal warm-up, see pp.5–10.

Developing the character physically

These ideas can be tried in any order.

It is sometimes useful to set yourself a list of questions about your character, which you will then answer quickly and instinctively without looking at the text. Possible questions could be:

- What colour is like me?
- What season is like me?
- What animal is like me?
- What piece of music represents me?

Questions like this can be useful for helping you get a feel for your character using pictures, images and sounds. Imagery accesses a creative part of the brain which sometimes gets left behind when we only analyse. There are many other questions that you could develop practically:

- Consider how your character moves in space. Where is your character's focus of energy? For example, does the impulse to move come from the head, chest or pelvis, or somewhere else?

- Does your character move in straight lines or curves? Does he or she move quickly or slowly? What kind of contact with the floor and the rest of the physical environment does the character have? Is it strong or light?

- Once you've explored some of these aspects of the character, experiment with the text to discover if and when these physical characteristics change, depending on the situation in the scene.

- What is the physical environment like? Do you need to fill in gaps in the text to specify where you are in time and place in order to make it more real to you? How does your character react to the physical environment, or handle objects and furniture? If you are portraying the character in an everyday world, you must convey familiarity with your environment.

- How does your character perceive the world around him or her: through the senses, thoughts, feelings or inhibitions?

- Can you base any qualities of your character on an animal? If so, study the animal carefully: don't just reproduce clichés. Could the sound of the animal help in your vocal characterisation as well?

- Can you base your character on someone you know? If so, don't impose the character on the text. Let your text determine it.

- What costumes will you be wearing? Rehearse in something similar, such as a long skirt, or a particular style of shoes.

Developing the character vocally

Feel the intention behind the word.

All actors develop their characters' voices at different stages of rehearsal. It is important not to impose vocal characteristics on the character too early, because surprising discoveries can be made about your character's voice as you work on his or her intentions. Voice, after all, is a means through which we express ourselves. If you want your character to have a reality on stage, then you must find out what it feels like to *need* to speak those lines. What is it that your character wants to express? Where does the impulse to speak come from? The following include suggestions from Cicely Berry's *The Actor and his Text* for possible ways to develop your character's voice:

- Make sure you understand your lines. If the language is complicated, try rephrasing the lines in your own words. This will help you understand what is being said. If you don't understand every word, why should your audience?

- Working with a partner, speak your lines in character. Ask your partner to say 'What?' every time he or she doesn't 'believe' what you are saying. This focuses your attention on the meanings of individual words, and will also help you to communicate your intentions more effectively.

- What does the language of the play tell you about how your character speaks? Are there lots of complicated grammatical structures? Experiment with the connection between language and thought, by taking a speech from your text and reading it aloud while walking. Every time you come to a punctuation mark, change direction. Does the punctuation indicate a change of thought? What happens to your walking if your character speaks fluidly, with sentences free of commas and colons?

- What sounds does your character make? Does he or she use lots of open vowel sounds, or lots of hard consonants? Try speaking a couple of lines of text using just the vowels, and then try again with just the consonants. Imagine that all your language has been taken away. What kinds of emotions or feelings come out of these sounds? Now read these lines again in full, bearing in mind any new qualities you discovered in the sounds of the words.

- What does the language tell you about the demands that are going to be made on your voice? Are there long monologues, with long sentences? If so, you will need to begin to think about your breath, making sure you have enough power and energy to send the sound out, and making decisions about where to breathe in each line. If you practise, you will achieve a smooth flow of speech, instead of running out of breath when you get caught up in emotional scenes.

● If the sentences are short and naturalistic, do not be fooled into thinking that naturalistic acting means mumbling; you will need vocal energy so that your audience can hear you.

● Consider the performance space. Rehearse in it if possible, or visit it and try out your voice. Ask someone to stand at the back of the space and make sure they can hear every word you say. The acoustics will affect how your voice carries. Remember that a performance space filled with people will absorb your voice, so you will need to work harder to make yourself heard.

● Does your character have an accent that is different from your own? If so, you should listen to a recording of an authentic speaker of this accent. Tape yourself, comparing individual sounds such as vowels and consonants.

Other points to consider

● Do not worry about learning your lines too early. Although some directors prefer this, many actors find that they cannot learn their lines until the intentions of the character are clear and they can fix the lines in their heads as expressions of the character's inner self.

● Consider your audience: if you perform to adults, as opposed to an audience of schoolchildren, for example, will this affect the performance? What are the expectations and needs of the audience? These are points that should be discussed with the director.

Unspoken rules distinguish professionals from amateurs.

Lastly, it is important to point out some aspects of rehearsal etiquette, which are crucial for creating trust and teamwork in rehearsal:

● Some directors are more democratic than others, but even with a dictatorial director you will need to find some way of working together, in spite of disagreements you may have if your interpretations do not coincide.

● Unless this is an entirely devised and collaborative piece (and, even then, sensitivity and constructive comments are preferable), do not criticise your fellow actors.

● Always turn up to rehearsals on time, or you will end up losing the trust and respect of your company. Drama schools expel students for being late. In the profession, bad reputations follow you about: being late means being unemployed.

● If you are preparing a speech for assessment, you are often expected to work on your own. Do not neglect the long, hard preparation work involved: it will show in the performance of the piece.

Creating a character study

*This is just one
approach.*

The following is a sample character study, focusing on the character of
Willy Loman in *Death of a Salesman* by Arthur Miller. However, note
that it is not intended to be exhaustive: there is scope for a lot more
study than these examples show. This is also just one possible way of
approaching a character study.

This approach aims to reveal aspects of Willy's character, together with
the implications these revelations might have for performance. As we
have seen in this chapter, most practioners of actor training have
stressed the need to find the truth behind the physicality and voice of
the character. In keeping with this, the focus here is on using the text
for clues to the the inner life of Willy. These indicate the motivating
impulses for movement, action and vocalisation.

The page numbers quoted are from the Penguin edition, 1989.

Questions to ask about the character	Information from the text	What this reveals about the character	Implications for performance
Who am I?	p.8: Travelling salesman past 60. Miller's description: *his mercurial nature, his temper, his massive dreams and little cruelties.*	Reaching retirement. May be thinking about his future and old age.	A man past his prime. Note his use of arch supports, p.9, and unwillingness to get glasses. Does the trouble with his feet affect his walking? If so, is this constant or occasional? How bad is his eyesight? How is this evidenced?
	Married to Linda.	Has stayed married to one person.	Familiarity and intimacy of a long-term relationship. Perhaps they have private gestures, or glances.
	Father of Biff and Happy, two grown boys.		Two boys now stronger and more virile than him.
	He had an affair (p.30, p.94).	He hasn't been faithful to Linda.	A furtive side of Willy's nature: hiding a guilty secret.
	p.9: *I opened the windshield and just let the warm air bathe over me. And then all of a sudden I'm going off the road! I'm tellin' ya, I absolutely forgot I was driving.*	Is aware he is showing signs of mental instability.	Bewilderment about not being in control? The struggle of a man to maintain his sanity? How is this shown physically? Is Willy constantly tense, for example?
	p.29: *I joke too much, ...I'm fat, I'm very foolish to look at.*	Not physically attractive? Awareness of physical shortcomings, but has a sense of humour.	Overweight, perhaps embarrassed by his appearance, makes up for it with too many jokes? Does Willy laugh at his own jokes? What kind of laugh is it?

Questions to ask about the character	Information from the text	What this reveals about the character	Implications for performance
What do others say about me?	p.15: *Biff: Everything I say there's a twist of mockery on his face. Happy: He just wants you to make good, that's all. I've wanted to talk to you about Dad for a long time, Biff. Something's happening to him. He – talks to himself.*	Reveals a shaky relationship with his son Biff. The boys are aware of his mental problems.	Is the facial expression overt, or subtle? Perhaps only Biff can see it? Maybe Willy looks differently at Biff (for example, with sorrow), when Biff isn't looking. Compare this scene with the flashback scene pp.22–27. This shows that Willy once had a good relationship with Biff. Also, here Willy is physically strong and emotionally in control.
	p.45: *Biff: I know he's a fake and he doesn't like anyone around who knows.*	Biff has discovered Willy's affair. Biff no longer idolises his father, and Willy knows this.	More tension between Biff and Willy. Perhaps Willy avoids Biff's gaze, or perhaps he seeks eye contact. Willy is physically and psycho-logically weaker than his son. Improvisations around status would be useful here.
	p.73: *Willy: ... a salesman I know, I heard him say something about a walrus. And I – I cracked him across the face. I won't take that.*	Willy knows others ridicule him, but will defend himself. His response is over-reaction.	Perhaps Willy remembers the pain of humiliation here; does it hit him in a particular place? Does it make him feel sick or angry to recall? How would this be conveyed?
Where am I?	Author's notes: *the action takes place in Willy's house and yard, and in the various places he visits, the New York and Boston of today* (1940s)	Significance of family life and the home as a place of security and predictability.	Can Willy physically relax at home? Can he relax knowing he's failed himself and his family? How is this reflected in his breathing patterns when he's talking to Linda and his kids? What is his posture like?
When do I exist?	In the recent past: Willy lives in America in the late 1940s. But Willy frequently slips into the past (e.g. p.29, p.86).	Willy is not in control of his life or his daydreaming. He slips into the past easily. It is easier to control the past than the present.	What is the physicality of absent-mindedness? Perhaps improvisations of direction would be useful, trying curves as opposed to straight lines. Are jerky movements more appropriate than smooth movements? Would it be possible to study people with mental problems? Willy must be physically stronger and younger in the flashbacks.

Questions to ask about the character	Information from the text	What this reveals about the character	Implications for performance
What do I want? **Because much of this play is set in the past, it is worth asking yourself: What did I want in the past?**	pp.25–26: *Willy: Be liked and you will never want.* p.23: *Willy: Someday I'll have my own business and I'll never have to leave home any more.*	Willy has ambitions for popularity and success. He wants to impress his children. The present shows that he has never achieved this dream, and still does his travelling sales job.	How can depression be reflected in his posture? If Willy has given in to depression, he might be slumped, with a more monotone voice. If he's trying to cover up his feeling, there could be a forced stiffness in his body and brightness in his voice
What do I want in the future?	p.61: *Willy: I've come to the decision I'd rather not travel any more.*	He needs to change his job because he can't cope with the driving.	Does this decision really make Willy happy? What do his body and voice reveal here?
	p.62: *... I was with the firm when your father used to carry you in his arms.* p.65: *I gotta earn money, Howard.*	Willy's status is much lower than Howard's, even though Willy is older.	Focusing on the need to hold back his feelings while trying to retain his dignity will be more interesting than giving in to temper and desperation immediately. The rise to the outburst of temper can be gradually reflected in Willy's voice and body as he gets increasingly agitated.
What's at stake if I don't get what I want?	p.88: *Willy: Was it my fault? ... It keeps going round in my head, maybe I did something to him. I got nothing to give him.*	Willy's deep regret at losing the respect of his son. Perhaps he's never come to terms with his responsibility for this.	How does Willy look at Biff when Biff isn't watching? Is the twist of mockery really there, or does Biff imagine it?
	p.66: *Willy: I can't throw myself on my sons. I'm not a cripple.*	Willy is afraid of being dependent on Biff and Happy, and is concerned they won't be able to support him. Willy has never lost his pride or dream of being independent. All of this shows Willy's increasing lack of control over his life and his diminishing grasp of reality, and contributes to his suicide.	Desperation can be reflected in physical tension and agitation (think of a caged animal pacing) and a rising voice. Is Willy holding back tears?
Other notes	Willy's entrance is accompanied by the sound of a flute. His father was a travelling salesman who played the flute. His brother Ben says p.38: *Father was a very great and wild hearted man... And we'd stop in the towns and sell the flutes that he'd made.*	Reveals Willy's reverence for his father as a salesman. Why has Miller included the flute? What qualities does a flute have that can tell us about Willy's character? How does the general use of music in the flashbacks contribute to the mood of the scene?	A flute is soft, dreamy and innocent. These could all be parts of Willy's character, so the flute reveals his emotional vulnerability. These images could be useful in developing Willy physically and vocally.

Resource Activities

1. CREATING A CHARACTER STUDY

Aim
To find ways of exploring a character in depth.

Objectives
● To understand a character based on information in the text.
● To establish the importance of studying the whole play when working on a character.
● To address the importance of understanding the social context of the play.
● To find a means of accessing the physicality and energy of a character.

Background
● Read the section on Stanislavski (pp.31–32), and Colin Firth's comments on questions to ask your character (p.48), and on justifying a character (p.47).
● Read pp.49–57 of the 'Guidelines for acting' section.
● For the purposes of this activity, you will need a copy of Henrik Ibsen's *A Doll's House*.

Tasks
● In pairs, write two character studies of Nora (see pp.55–57). Base one on clues from the text in Act I only; the other should be based purely on clues from the text in Act IV.

● Discuss any differences you discover in your studies of Nora's character.

● Answer the following questions orally or in written form:
i) What does this tell you about building a character history?
ii) After reading the whole play, what would you consider to be Nora's super-objective?
iii) Why is it important for the actor playing Nora to be familiar with the background of the play and the society in which the play is set?
iv) Refer back to Colin Firth's comments on justifying, rather than judging, your character (p.47). How can you justify Nora's final actions in the play? Why is it important for an actor not to judge Nora's character?

● Find an animal on which to base Nora's character. Referring back to the exercises on vocal and physical development (pp.52–54), find ways to discover Nora's physicality.

2. EXPLORING THE LANGUAGE OF SHAKESPEARE

Aim
To explore how much you can discover about Shakespeare's characters and the purpose of the scene from the text alone.

Objectives
● To develop ways of accessing the atmosphere of the scene through the sounds and rhythmic patterns of the language.
● To think of characters in terms of speech, voice and body.

Background
● In a group of three, read aloud from *Macbeth*, Act IV Scene 1 lines 1–38 (the three witches).
● Refer to the sections on Peter Brook and Cicely Berry for approaches to the emotional language of sounds (see pp.34–36 and 40.) Review Saint-Denis' methods of training (pp.33–34), and the notes on developing a character physically and vocally (see pp.52–54.)

Tasks
These should all be practical tasks.

● Explore your characters by experimenting with the rhyme schemes and rhythms of their speech. Can you sense any kind of atmosphere through speaking the text?

● Does the text reveal any differences between the characters of the three witches? Look at the sounds of the words, as well as the meanings: do they all use similar vowels and consonant sounds? Are these sounds long and open, or short and cutting?

● Can you improvise with chants and cries using the consonants and vowels from the text, and still get the same intensity of feeling?

● What do you need to think about in terms of body, voice, speech/language, imaginative background and improvisation? Try out the scene with simple masks, to experiment with how this affects your physicality. Does your voice change when you use a mask?

● Are there any gaps in the text you need to fill? If so, why?

3. IMPROVISATION

Aim
To work on characterisation through improvisation.

Objectives
● To explore the possibilities of developing a character beyond the text, using clues within the text.
● To explore the uses of improvisation in fleshing out a character.

Background

Working with a copy of *Death of a Salesman*, refer to the sample character study of Willy Loman and the section on Mike Leigh (pp.55–57, 36–38). The plan of action for developing a performance, pp.49–54, will also be useful here.

Tasks

● Based on the character study and what it reveals about Willy's character, devise improvisations around the following:
i) Willy parking the car and preparing to come home. What happens before his first entrance?
ii) Willy getting ready to go to bed.
iii) Willy getting up and getting ready to go out to work in the morning.

● Experiment with physical details, using the information you already have, such as his age and failing eyesight. Find out how Willy parks the car and opens the door. Does he shower or bath in the morning or evening? Does he talk to himself? If so, how?

● Discuss your discoveries about Willy's physicality in the third person: for example, 'Willy walks like...'.

Clearly, this activity could be undertaken using a character in a different play, providing the character is roundly drawn in the text.

4. PREPARING FOR AN AUDITION

This activity can be adapted for examination speeches. It could usefully follow on from Activity 3.

Aim

To help you find your own way of preparing a soliloquy for performance.

Objectives

● To concentrate on the physical and vocal aspects of performance.
● To prepare you for the pressure of an audition situation.
● To practise two pieces that would be appropriate for a real audition.

Background

You are auditioning for a drama school, and have been asked to prepare two contrasting speeches of no longer than two minutes each. One should be classical, the other modern.

● Refer to Saint-Denis' specific disciplines (pp.33–34) and the notes about body and voice in the sections on Cicely Berry and the Alexander Technique (see pp.38–42). Also look at the notes for developing a character physically and vocally on pp.52–54 and the warm-ups on pp.5–10.

● Read the character study of Willy Loman as an example of a detailed character study that you might prepare (pp.55–57).

Tasks

- Take some time to research before you select the two speeches.

- Using some of the ideas arising from your background reading, find your own ways to work on the characters physically and vocally. Think carefully about exercises that you can set yourself in order to explore the character. Warm up: whilst solo warm-ups may feel strange, they are an ideal way of preparing you for work. Bear in mind where you will be performing the audition, and who your audience is.

- Work through a detailed character study. Try not to let this become a dry exercise; combine it with the physicalisation and vocalisation of the piece. Experimentation is vital.

- Once you are ready for the audition, perform the pieces in front of the class, wearing what you would wear to the audition. If possible, try re-creating an audition (or examination) situation, with interviewers and an interview room.

- Identify in retrospect what happens to your acting when you are nervous and pressurised. What does this tell you about ways in which you should prepare yourself physically and emotionally for performance? Remember: activity prevents anxiety.

5. DEVELOPING AN ARGUMENT FOR ACTOR TRAINING

Aim
To consolidate your understanding of the importance of actor training.

Objective
To prepare you for the possibility that you might need to convince a funding source that you have a valid argument for seeking training.

Background
Your audition (see Activity 4) was successful, and you have been offered a place at an accredited drama school. Now you need to get sponsorship to fund your way through drama school. You have been asked to write a letter to a potential sponsor. Refer to the Geraldine James interview and the sections on Saint-Denis, Brook, Berry and Alexander (pp.42–46, 33–36, 38–42) for arguments in support of actor training.

Task
How are you going to argue your case? State why you think training is necessary for actors entering the profession. Develop these arguments into a formal letter or a presentation. (See pp.20–22 for guidelines on presentation skills.)

6. EXPLORING ACTING STYLES

Aim
To examine the practical results of Brecht's style of acting.

Objective
To experience contrasting methods of working on the same character.

Background
Read the section on Brecht, p.32. It may be useful to do further research. (see Cooper and Mackey, *Theatre Studies*, for example.)

Tasks
● Choose a speech from Brecht's *A Caucasian Chalk Circle*. Work on a performance of this speech using Brecht's guidelines, given on p.32. How does this approach to your work differ from the approaches in the other exercises?

● Now experiment on this piece using the 'who, what, where, when and why?' approach to the character.

● Discuss these questions retrospectively:
i) How does your acting change?
ii) Do you think it is acceptable to use alternative approaches when preparing a character in a Brecht play?

7. RATIONALISING YOUR OWN ARGUMENT

Aim
To understand the evolving role of the actor.

Objectives
● To develop an argument based on relevant information from this chapter.
● To gain an overview of acting history.

Background
Read pp.26–31 and the interview with Geraldine James (pp.42–46). Start thinking about your own reactions to what you are reading.

Tasks
● In your opinion, why is it important for actors to have an understanding of the historical development of the theatre and acting techniques? Discuss this question in class, and make notes on some of the points raised.

● Write an essay referring to at least three of these main points and explaining your views. Use evidence from this chapter to support your arguments.

ANNOTATED BIBLIOGRAPHY

This bibliography includes volumes relevant to this chapter which are considered suitable for student research. See also the general bibliography on p.380.

Arnott, Peter D., *Public and Performance in the Greek Theatre,* Routledge, 1989
> A thorough study, looking primarily at performance, with emphasis on the social context.

Baker, Michael, *The Rise of the Victorian Actor,* Croom Helm Ltd, 1978
> Fascinating reading for those interested in the state of the acting profession in Victorian England.

Barlow, Wilfred, *The Alexander Principle,* Victor Gollancz Ltd, 1973
> A sound explanation of the Alexander Technique; selective reading is advisable, as it does go into some depth.

Bentley, Eric (ed.), *The Theory of the Modern Stage,* Penguin Books Ltd, 1968
> Still useful for summary chapters on Stanislavski, Brecht and others. Limited to pre-1968.

Berry, Cicely, *The Actor and his Text,* Virgin Books, 1992 (first published by Harrap Ltd, 1987)
> Explores ways of accessing the meaning of the text through physical and vocal exercises. If you read only one book on voice and text, read this.

Berry, Cicely, *Voice and the Actor,* Virgin Books, 1993 (first published by Harrap, 1973)
> Clear and accessible, with useful exercises written in detail.

Brook, Peter, *The Empty Space,* Penguin Books Ltd, 1990 (first published by McGibbon & Kee, 1968)
> A detailed account of Brook's views of theatre prior to 1968. Readable and inspiring.

Clements, Paul, *The Improvised Play: The Work of Mike Leigh,* Methuen, 1983
> A readable and thorough account of Mike Leigh's working methods, as well as an account of Leigh's background.

Cooper, Simon and Mackey, Sally, *Theatre Studies: An Approach for Advanced Level,* Stanley Thornes, 1995
> As well as useful guidance on many aspects of theatre study, this book contains detailed and accessible chapters on Stanislavski, Brecht, Antonin Artaud and Edward Gordon Craig.

Frost, Anthony and Yarrow, Ralph, *Improvisation in Drama,* Macmillan, 1990

> This book looks at the development of improvisation and its role in theatre today. Useful for an overview of Mike Leigh's work.

Gurr, Andrew, *The Shakespearean Stage, 1574–1642,* Cambridge University Press, 1992

> A very informative book, recommended for background on the evolution of acting companies, acting styles and the staging of performances.

Roose-Evans, James, *Experimental Theatre from Stanislavski to Peter Brook,* Routledge, 1991

> Useful for contextualising some of the main movements in experimental theatre, providing links between them. Brook is discussed in a chapter on Roy Hart and Alfred Wolfsohn. An academic text.

Saint-Denis, Suria (ed.), *Training for the Theatre: Michel Saint-Denis,* Heinemann, 1982

> Fascinating reading about Saint-Denis' work and acting background. It contains useful examples of exercises.

Stanislavski, Konstantin, *An Actor Prepares,* Routledge, 1936

> Essential reading for anyone interested in Stanislavski's techniques, and reasonably readable. His second book, *Building a Character*, addresses physical technique.

Tydeman, William, *The Theatre in the Middle Ages,* Cambridge University Press, 1978

> Shows the evolution of drama in Europe from pagan ritual to the mystery plays and beyond.

Willet, John (ed.), *Brecht on Theatre,* Methuen, 1957

> Contains a selection of Brecht's own writing on theatre.

Willet, John, *The Theatre of Bertholt Brecht,* Methuen, 1977

> Written by Willet himself, this is a critical study of Brecht's theatre.

Williams, David, *Peter Brook: A Theatrical Casebook,* Methuen, 1988

> A broad compilation of articles and interviews documenting Brook's work since the 1960s.

3 Directing

Janette Smith

The aim of this chapter is to give the student an understanding of the role of the director. It contains the following sections:

- The development of the director
- Interviews with contemporary directors
- Guidelines for directing

THE DEVELOPMENT OF THE DIRECTOR

The word 'director' was first used, in today's context, by Edward Gordon Craig (1872–1966) to describe himself; the term became popular in the 1950s with the influence of cinema. Prior to this, 'producer' had similar connotations, and in the 19th century the closest equivalent to the 1990s director was the 'actor–manager'. Actor–managers such as Charles Kean (1811–68) and Samuel Phelps (1804–78) used lengthy rehearsal periods to perfect the stage design and costumes; however, there was little concern for interpreting the text, as in the work of contemporary practitioners.

Even today, there is no absolute understanding of the position of the director. Charles Marowitz (a contemporary director and playwright associated with the Los Angeles Theatre Centre) thinks the role should be split down the middle: 'Half of directing is . . . taking charge, making decisions, . . . The other half of directing is maintaining the right direction' (*Prospero's Staff*, p.xi). Stephen Daldry (artistic director of the Royal Court, London) says the 'director's art is to facilitate [the release which is] unique to each actor' (Ratcliffe, *Platform Papers*, p.4).

So we can see that directors themselves perceive the role differently: Marowitz sees it as leadership, Daldry as facilitating, but both functions can be called 'directing'. Directors also have different skills and different strengths. For example, Peter Brook is seen as a guru in many directors' eyes for 'the directness and simplicity of his work' (see interview with John Wright, p.80). Katie Mitchell (artistic director of The Other Place, Royal Shakespeare Company) is admired for her use of minute detail and Stephen Daldry for his vision (see interview with Max Stafford-Clark, p.72). Each of these directors has a different working method.

Whilst a precise definition of the term 'director' is difficult, and whilst the modern sense is less than 50 years old, it *is* possible to trace key moments in history which provide a context for the late 20th/early 21st-century director. The following timeline briefly identifies certain key practitioners in the history of Western theatre who could loosely be called 'directors' and who have helped shape our modern understanding of the term.

c.500BC	It is thought likely that **Sophocles** (496–406BC) and some other Greek and Roman playwrights 'directed' their own plays on the stage.
16th–17th century	**Shakespeare** (1564–1616) collaborated with his principal actors and managerial associates to stage his plays.
	Writers such as **Ben Jonson** (1572–1637) collaborated with artists such as Inigo Jones in the staging of plays.
Late 19th century	The first recognisable director was the German **Duke of Saxe-Meiningen** (1826–1914). He ran his own company with his stage manager Ludwig Chronegk, a strict disciplinarian. The Duke believed 'all effects of the production should be subordinated to a single unifying artistic aim, with particular emphasis on the visual aspect' (Bradby and Williams, *Directors' Theatre*, p.4).
Early 20th century	**André Antoine** (1858–1943) was an actor/manager/director who founded the Théâtre Libre in Paris. He was influenced by the Meiningen Players, whose European tour he saw, and by Emile Zola's theories on naturalism.
	Adolph Appia (1862–1928) was a Swiss designer, who advocated that actors should be drilled, and saw them as simply one facet of the performance. His vision was symbolic and anti-naturalistic: atmosphere and location were of primary importance.
	Konstantin Stanislavski (1863–1938) founded the Moscow Arts Theatre with Nemirovich-Danchenko. Fascinated by Meiningen's focused scrutiny of all theatrical elements, he created a detailed 'system' to help actors find psychological realism in performance. (See pp.31–32 for further details on Stanislavski.)
	Vsevolod Meyerhold (1874–1940) was an actor in Stanislavski's company, but did not agree with all of Stanislavski's techniques: he believed an actor needed to play. Consequently, he returned to traditional skills such as clowning and *Commedia dell' Arte*. Meyerhold developed a training system for actors known as 'bio-mechanics'. He placed himself between the author and the actor, because, he believed, 'it was the director's responsibility to develop a style or idiom specific to the theatre within which every element became a significant bearer of meaning' (Bradby and Williams, *Directors' Theatre*, p.15).

Early to mid 20th century	**Edward Gordon Craig** (1872–1966) wanted to be in full command as a director, so that 'supreme achievement can be accomplished'. He used actors as marionettes to express his ideas: the elements of 'line, movement, colour, rhythm and space' were Craig's key creative concepts (ibid. p.13). **Max Reinhardt** (1873–1943) was an Austrian actor/director/manager, whose productions used a large number of techniques in terms of both design and acting. He believed that each play necessitated its own style, and loved huge casts and spectacle. 'Reinhardt's method as a director was essentially one of showing the actors their parts – not by fully acting them out, but by a kind of actor's shorthand, a brilliantly concise indication of the essentials of a given gesture or intonation' (Esslin, M, *Max Reinhardt – High Priest of Theatricality*, 'The Drama Review' Vol. 21 No. 2. p.7, quoted in Braun, *The Director and the Stage*, p.98). **Jacques Copeau** (1879–1949) focused on an acting environment with a variety of levels and a rudimentary set. This opened the way to a style of acting that was concerned with movement, diction and the rhythms of the play. Being faithful to the intentions of the text was important to Copeau. **Antonin Artaud** (1896–1948) was interested in the myth and magic of the theatre, and moved far away from realism. He created the idea of 'total theatre' and the 'theatre of cruelty' and was fascinated by the language of gesture and sound. Although he was not a successful director himself, his book *The Theatre and its Double* (1958) has been a notable influence on the way directors work. **Bertolt Brecht** (1898–1956) was founder of the Berliner Ensemble. He devised a number of techniques to ensure that the spectators were kept at an emotional distance, so that they could think objectively about the production they were watching. He directed mainly his own writing, but was a collaborative director, seeking the opinions of the creative team. (See p.32 for further details on Brecht.) **Joan Littlewood** (1914–), the founder of Theatre Workshop, Stratford East, was dedicated to the ideas of Brecht and the collaborative experience: 'She exemplifies the perfect fusion of ensemble work and spontaneity' (Rea, *Better Direction*, p.17).
Late 20th century	**Jacques Lecoq** (1921–), a teacher of acting, focuses on the importance of play and mime. He is highly respected, yet Dario Fo says of Lecoq's mimes: 'They never manage to rid themselves of the mechanical, gestural stereotypes they have been taught' (*The Tricks of the Trade*, p.148). **Jerzy Grotowski** (1933–) is a Polish practitioner, who runs his theatre laboratory in Wroclaw. He works with minimal props or setting to concentrate on the body and voice. He sees his role as 'that of a catalyst of others' creativity' (Bradby and Williams, *Directors' Theatre*, p.112).

Peter Brook (1925–) is a British director, who left the RSC to set up the Centre International des Recherches Théatricales in Paris. He believes that fusing the actors' creativity is central to his role as a director. He then moulds this work to create a piece of theatre. (See pp.34–36 for further details on Brook.)

This timeline shows how the director's role has altered over time. Innovative work by directors today represents only the next phase of a long history of theatrical creativity, experimentation and ideology.

However, it is not just the influence of past directors that dictates the methods and style used by directors today, but also the type of theatre in which they are working. In Britain, you can divide theatre into the following broad categories: commercial theatre (West End or repertory, where budgets are reasonable and which is often run according to Equity rules), fringe theatre (with low budgets, often performing experimental work) and community theatre (where members of the community are actively involved in the production, but it is not their professional job).

The directors interviewed in the next section work in these different types of theatre. They are all contemporary practitioners of some stature, with strong reputations within their own field for their working methods and creative integrity.

INTERVIEWS WITH CONTEMPORARY DIRECTORS

On the following pages, eight diverse and innovative directors, all working in Britain, give their views on directing. The aim of this section is to give the student some insight into the working techniques of a professional director. To enable you to find information quickly, the following key words have been included in the margin to sum up the paragraphs at a glance:

● ADVICE – general advice given by the director;
● BACKGROUND – background on the director;
● EXERCISES – exercises used by the director;
● TECHNIQUE – techniques or approaches used;
● PROCESS – elements of the process of their practice.

Max Stafford-Clark

Background
● Founded Joint Stock Theatre group (see pp.227–229).
● Spent 14 years as artistic director of the Royal Court Theatre, London.
● Currently artistic director of Out of Joint.
● Author of *Letters to George,* his diaries from the rehearsal periods of *The Recruiting Officer* and *Our Country's Good*, both produced at the Royal Court in 1988.
● Type of work: new and classical.

Q **In your book *Letters to George*, you say your main influences are American companies of the 1960s, such as La Mama Troupe, The Living Theatre, The Open Theatre. What was it that excited you about these groups?**

[BACKGROUND]
He is influenced by directors with different specialities.

Their influence on the work I'm doing at the moment is probably imperceptible, but what was exciting at the time was that they involved a kind of total theatre. They had a physicality that was rather lacking in the text-based avant-garde theatre in this country at the time. I was at university in Dublin, and Hilton Edwards, who ran the Gate [Dublin], gave me the first idea of what a director did. There was a governing aesthetic that controlled his work: the importance of design and overall concept. The second director who influenced me was Tom O' Horgan, who was the director for the La Mama Troupe, and the third would have been Bill Gaskill, who was one of my predecessors at the Royal Court, whose work was focused on text and detail. So that is three very different influences: one is the aesthetics and design, the second is the physicality of theatre and the third is the dominance of the text, so the three add up to quite disparate influences.

Q **What was your starting point for *Our Country's Good*? Why did you stage it and *The Recruiting Officer* together?**

The idea was mine. It was important for the Royal Court to undertake the occasional classic. I had read a book by Tom Keneally which was called *The Playmaker*, which was about convicts putting on *The Recruiting Officer*, so I approached Timberlake [Wertenbaker, author of *Our Country's Good*] with the idea that an adaptation could be a companion piece to *The Recruiting Officer*.

Q **Is that always the way you begin, by reading something then appointing a writer?**

No. Projects are most often initiated by the writer, although occasionally it happens the other way round. For example, *Serious Money* came out of a discussion with Caryl Churchill. The Royal Court had done plenty of plays about disadvantaged people, and we thought it would be a good idea to do a play about advantaged people. What better in the late 1980s than the people working in the financial market? The impetus for doing plays comes from different directions.

The impetus for doing plays comes from different sources.

Q **In your book, you say you cast your actors by who you've seen before, and you take advice from the writer. In addition, you bring in new talent. Is this combination of familiar talent and new faces the best approach for casting?**

Yes it is. A permanent company would be ideal. Often, Eastern European countries have an ensemble. So getting some continuity

[PROCESS]
Use a combination of new and familiar talent when casting.

[TECHNIQUE]
Cards can be used for measuring all sorts of things.

[EXERCISES]

A rehearsal schedule is dependent on the needs of the writer in the early stages, if the play has not yet been written.

[TECHNIQUE]
Discussion with the whole company may solve a problem.

and working with some actors you have worked with before is very important. At the same time, you can renew that by involving new young people.

Q **How would your approach differ if you were *given* a group of actors to work with?**
It wouldn't differ materially at all, and often you do work under those conditions. I did *Our Country's Good* in Los Angeles, and the play was completely cast before I had even got there. If you work for the Royal Shakespeare Company, you have casting meetings with the directors who are directing other plays in the season, and the art of compromise is very much present. You can put forward say three actors who are your first choice, but you also have to accept other directors' first choices.

Q **You are renowned for using playing cards in your rehearsals to quantify levels of emotion. How did you discover this technique?**
I worked with Keith Johnstone, who was an influential director of the Court before my time, and status games, and games generally, were quite a feature of his work. I developed them from that, and I'm inclined to use cards to measure all kinds of things. For example, while working on *Three Sisters*, I would ask, 'Out of ten how good is Andre as a husband?', 'How many out of ten does Natasha think he is?', 'How good a mother out of ten is Natasha?', 'How ill is the child who is just off stage?'. Or you just give the actor a card, and say he is that ill (referring to the number on the card). What you find is that the actress often makes the assumption that the child is not ill and Natasha is manipulating the situation, but if you don't take it as a given and make it a variable then you open up the scene to fresh interpretation.

Q **For *Our Country's Good*, you said you workshopped for a couple of weeks, followed by a nine-week gap for writing and a five- to six-week rehearsal period. Is this a set schedule for all newly written productions that you do?**
No: the next two plays I'm doing have already been fully written. I've worked on a number of plays where there has been little beyond the subject determined before rehearsals start, so there has been a period of research during the workshop. So no, the pattern you have just described is a pattern that is probably productive when the writer knows the area, but has many problems or questions which are open to research.

Q **Have there been any key moments in any production when it changed direction or emphasis? How can you recognise these moments?**
There was a moment during the rehearsals of *Serious Money*, when we were all committed to a certain number of songs and to a structure. One weekend, the third week into rehearsal, we all went off, and on Monday morning everybody said, 'It isn't quite working.' I began that rehearsal with a discussion, and an hour and a half later we had cut two thirds of the songs and restructured the first act so that scene

four actually began the play. That restructuring determined the eventual play. No-one had the answer; we just knew we had a problem, so we addressed it. So that was the crucial moment: we were heading down one road and we turned back.

Q **How did that make you feel as a director, when your actors came back and said, 'This is not working'?**

When you start as a young director, what you are desperate for is control. Any moment when you lose control is frightening, probably one of the most alarming moments there are. When you are more experienced and you assume control with more ease, those moments are often very creative, because you can admit, 'I don't know what to do. I'm no longer the leader in this expedition.' This opens it up to other suggestions. This is just experience.

Q **Is there any advice you would give a young director about progression through a rehearsal period?**

Directors arrive at different technical points at different times. For example, I do tend to run through a play very late in the day, and probably not nearly as much as the actors would like. John Dexter [a British director who has done a wide range of work in the UK and the USA] used to run the whole play at the end of the first week, and that gave him a structure the actors could assimilate. I think directing is a pragmatic art, it is both an art and a craft/trade, and what works is what you do. Personally I prefer to accumulate details, and I think a run-through is simply a statement of what you have got in your account at that moment. The more detail you put into the account, the more you have to draw on when you run through.

[ADVICE]
Young directors are likely to suffer from fear (see Wong, p.79).

[ADVICE]
[TECHNIQUE]
Some directors do run-throughs very late in the rehearsal process.

A scene from Our Country's Good *at the Royal Court Theatre, directed by Max Stafford-Clark*

A director reiterates his or her findings from the rehearsal room through the elements of a technical rehearsal.

Q In your book, you said you have a different function in the technical rehearsal.

Yes, that's true. The first section of rehearsal is in the privacy of the rehearsal room, where you are finding the play with the actors. The final part of rehearsal is much more to do with technique: what will help you to repeat that mood, what will help you in terms of lighting, pace of the scene, costume changes.

Q What qualities and skills should a director possess?

Firstly, with a new play, a forensic kind of skill for opening up the play and exploring the right themes. You then need to know when to finish it off and close it down. Secondly, patience is very important. Thirdly, pacing a rehearsal is important. Fourthly, you are a leader of people, and as a leader it is important to involve people and draw on their skills. I think the best theatre is collaborative, and the balance between the different areas has to be held by the director. Fifthly, a lot of rehearsal is about organisation and research; Katie Mitchell is a director whose detail and research is impeccable. Finally, a visual imagination is important. Someone like Stephen Daldry has the ability to turn a play on its head and make you re-examine it, because he has changed the visual and spatial relationships. All those skills are essential to a director.

[ADVICE]
Directors need many qualities and skills.

Q How do you learn those skills?

Visit art galleries, look at some of the performance artists for spatial awareness, look at groups who are doing site-specific work. You can learn from all that. You've got to keep moving. You have to have a just and ongoing assessment of your own work.

Q Is a reflection time important?

Yes, but it is not always possible immediately after a production, no matter how reflective and objective you are. To assess the value of your own work may take a year before you can tell the worth of your own achievement.

Phyllida Lloyd

Background

- A freelance director.
- Nominated as best director for the Olivier Awards, 1994, for *Hysteria*.
- Received the John Fernald Award, 1989.
- Received the *Manchester Evening News* Award for best production of a play, 1991, for *Death of the King's Horseman*.
- Type of work: innovative, new and classical texts and opera.

[BACKGROUND]

Q Who are your influences?

I was very inspired by international theatre that I saw in the late 1970s

British theatre relies heavily on words.

and early 1980s. It struck me how dependent in this country we are on words as a means of expression: often words and nothing much else. I saw work by Pina Bausch, Tadeusz Kantor, Ariane Mnouchkine. I saw work from India, Africa and South America – countries that had not lost touch with their dances, songs and traditional methods of storytelling. All this excited me.

Q **What is your starting point when you direct a show?**
I'm usually working with a text, so that is not only the starting point but the place to which one keeps on returning throughout the rehearsal and once the play is in performance.

[TECHNIQUE]
Keep returning to the text.

Q **When you begin a play, what is your approach, and is this the same approach for all your work?**
There are certain things I always do when preparing a production. There are many areas of investigation happening simultaneously. At home and usually alone, I will read the text over and over, sometimes aloud. I will break it down into units of action, and make all sorts of lists – all the things the other characters say about a character, all the things a character says about him or herself – perhaps lists of images in the play. At the same time, I'll be spending time with other members of the production team – principally the designer. This is an absolutely crucial relationship. We may go on expeditions together to places that connect with the play, and look at architecture and painting, listen to music, go to the cinema. All of this helps us to understand the play more fully, and to decide how best we will realise it on stage. The problem is that often decisions about set designs have to be made before rehearsals start.

[PROCESS]
Read the text many times.
[EXERCISES]
Lloyd uses the Stanislavskian technique of 'units of action'.

Q **Do you find it difficult if once in rehearsal you go down a different path and you realise that the set will have to be redesigned?**
Yes, I've had one experience of the disastrous consequences of designing the production in advance of the read-through. The rehearsal process was a real voyage into the unknown, a voyage of discovery. By the time we were six weeks into the work, it was developing in a way that had little to do with those early design ideas, but the set was being built: it was too late to stop that process. I had to wrench this beast that had been born in the rehearsal room, sort of cram it into this shape that it wasn't meant for. It was painful.

[PROCESS]
It is not ideal to design the set in advance of the initial stages of rehearsal.

Q **What do you look for when casting your actors?**
Courage, inspiration, humour – people with whom one thinks one will be able to have a dialogue. I like actors who can develop an athletic relationship with a text – who can seize it, hurl it about, close the gap between their imaginations and that of the author so you cannot believe they are not making it up as they go along. I like actors who are dissatisfied with the first safe choice they make, but go on and on searching for another way.

Q **How do you see that quality in an actor?**
Often you've seen actors on stage, film or TV, so you have an idea of

[ADVICE]

Instinct is important when auditioning actors for the first time.

what they might be capable of. If you've never seen their work and are meeting them for the first time in an audition, then you rely on instinct. Perhaps you have some idea of how you think the character might be, and you are testing an actor against that. You want to be surprised. I might give an actor a piece of text or ask them to improvise. Then I might ask them to change or develop what they are doing, just to see how they respond. This is a microcosm of how one will work in the rehearsal room.

Q **If you were *given* a group of actors, would your approach in 'gelling' the group be different than if you chose the actors yourself?**
Absolutely the same. What you are trying to do is create a team and make people feel safe in the room in order that they can be daring, as dangerous as they need to be; getting them to work and play together.

It is important to make actors feel safe in the rehearsal room.

Q **Do you have a set method of process?**
Yes and no, in the sense that one knows that one is going from point A to point Z, and therefore it would be worrying if one got to press night and had not run the play. On the other hand, I find myself responding to different plays, different groups of people, different countries that I've worked in, in different ways. I approach from two angles in rehearsal. Firstly, I look minutely at the text, sitting around the table, analysing it as if we were in a laboratory dissection. On the other hand, I would be working completely freely with improvisation, playing games. That is within one day. I'm thinking particularly of Congreve's *The Way of the World*, where we spent the first ten days in the mornings paraphrasing the text. In the afternoons we played games, improvised, sang, danced. I set them tasks, all to release ideas and energy. Then after a few weeks we would put the scenes on their

[PROCESS]

[TECHNIQUE]
Dissect the text as if it was a laboratory experiment and play games.

A scene from The Way of the World, *directed by Phyllida Lloyd, at the Royal National Theatre*

feet, but even then we might improvise them first, or I would give them an objective: for example, 'in this scene your objective/intention is to seduce each other'. In this instance, I was trying to create a shared experience between them; they must all know each other well – they share a social world.

Q Are there moments of inspiration or failure in rehearsal? How do you recognise this?

Of course! And often there's more failure than success. The director has to be very patient, an excellent listener and, crucially, be prepared to let an idea, a line of enquiry that might seem central to things, go – in order to allow new things, more important things, to come forward. Often there's a shared sense of when something important has happened, a crackle in the air. Sometimes one might drive the cavalcade forward that last inch, when actors are sick to the back teeth of it, because one has a hunch that something exciting lurks there. It's like helming a boat – you rely on your instincts as to when to consolidate by leaving your sails as they are, when to put up more sail, when to reef them in. Looking and listening is often more helpful than talking.

Q Is there any advice you could give directors on the progression of rehearsals?

Have people in to watch it long before it is ready, and ask people what they are getting from it. Then go away and think about that. Remember that rehearsing is a process, a journey. Don't expect it to happen on day one. Be very well prepared, but don't cling on to ideas that the actors have improved upon. Let actors try something if they feel they want to – even if you feel instinctively it won't work, you'll often be wrong. Try to keep things open for as long as you can. It's a balancing act.

For actors to chart the course of a play they need to have run it, to get a sense of the rhythm of the whole, but as soon as you have run the play something happens. You can never get back to that earlier place. I know I often put off running the play for too long, but there's nothing more deadly than just running it and running it for its own sake. Try to give each run an objective: everybody must think about one particular character for the whole run, or the weather, or their clothes. More and more detail will creep into the performance.

Q Is there any advice you can give a young director?

To listen and be open about being prepared to see things afresh every day. You sometimes have to destroy in order to create. You are part of a creative team. Let actors try something if they want to. As a director, you try and do two things at once. One is to mould the piece like a piece of clay. The other is to release something, and sometimes the two are in opposition. I think the greatest directors are those who manage both.

Denise Wong

Background

- Became artistic director of Black Mime Theatre Company (BMT) in 1986.
- A founder member of Black Mime in 1984.
- Her work has taken her to Holland, Germany and South Africa on tour.
- Her work looks at the emotions and is based in physical and mime theatre.

[BACKGROUND]

Q What or who have been your influences?

When I first became interested in movement theatre, I worked with a company called *Moving Picture Mime*. I found that their work was incredibly visual and exciting and gave a quality of cinema on stage, and that is what I try and create with the work BMT does. Also, Steven Berkoff is very visual and alive and works towards a heightened reality. Another director who had a lot of influence was Mladen Materick, a Yugoslavian director. He was the one who suddenly triggered me into working more with emotional content and also actors' personal histories.

Q How did you become a director?

I spent three years doing a community and theatre arts course and then I worked as an actress. I then spent some time at another drama school in New York. In terms of directing, it has just been learning on the job and doing a few training workshops with people like Philippe Gaulier [a French writer and teacher of theatre craft, who runs an international theatre school in London specialising in physical techniques; he is a follower of Lecoq].

Q When you are starting to direct a production, what is your starting point?

[PROCESS]
Black Mime always begins its work with a theme.

Whenever Black Mime starts, we always begin with a theme that is decided prior to casting. There is no script at all. Then it is a case of assembling a group of actors who I feel have something to offer to the subject matter but also I feel will work well together and will be willing to explore these issues on stage. It is a case of building group dynamics very quickly within the group, and establishing a level of confidence. They are willing to expose themselves, because a lot of the time the work not only relates to the subject matter but it also relates to the individual and their personal histories.

[TECHNIQUE]
[PROCESS]

Q How do you go about casting? What is it that you look for in actors?
We spend Saturday and Sunday working with a group of people, and whether or not they are selected they have had a weekend of training with Black Mime. What we are looking for is physical ability; they have got to move very well in the space. We look for inventiveness and creativity, in terms of creating situations on stage and creating the characters and also the ways in which they assemble the material together, because we always set them tasks in terms of working on themes. We don't have a writer. The actors have to have something akin to writing skills, or at least one or two of them should have it. We also have an interview afterwards, so they've got to be interested or fired by the subject matter. By talking to them, I'm looking to see if they could give a lot of input, and if I find it is quite laboured in the interview process then I'm quite wary of taking this individual on board. For me, that is the best way of selecting, through the weekend workshop process and then the interview afterwards. It is such a very difficult thing, because they are going to be on tour for five or six months, so they've got to be people who are very, very committed to the subject material, prepared to go through the extraordinary highs and also the lows that the material takes them through, and willing to work together as a group.

Q How do you work on group dynamics with the actors you have chosen?
We don't stick to a group of set exercises. We tend to spend the first couple of weeks in the rehearsal process playing, and also exploring movement vocabulary, so that we have common ground to refer back to.

Q If you were *given* a group of actors, would your approach change?
I would try and gauge what the group is like. If I feel that it is a group which possibly is leaning towards feeling embarrassed or uncomfortable, then I would start with the play section of exercises. For example, I would go at it via an exercise that Philippe Gaulier teaches. There are four people in a row, and they are looking at a sort of cinema scene, and they are imagining that something on the screen is making them angry, and they 'pass' the anger down the line to each person. Once it reaches the end of the line, that person then sees on the screen something that makes them even more angry, and you just see how far they will go.

What we try and do is get our actors to explore emotion, and usually if I feel the company is quite settled within itself we will go straight into exploration of it, by creating situations where people just spend time, for instance, being angry with one another. In pairs, you get two people being angry, and you usually find someone will take on the responsibility of being angry and the other person will be very passive. What we try and do then is say, 'No, you have to be equal in terms of your commitment to the anger.' There are ground rules: you mustn't hurt anyone, you must stay with your partner, in terms of supporting your partner with the emotion they are going through, even though you are going through it at the same time, and they try and pitch it at 50–50, so that they are both equal and at the same

[PROCESS]
Casting takes the form of weekend workshops and an interview.

[PROCESS]
It is important to find a group of people who can maintain commitment through a long tour.

[PROCESS]

[TECHNIQUE]

[EXERCISES]
Do exercises which physicalise emotions.

[EXERCISES]
Ask actors to commit themselves to an emotion.

Dirty Reality II *by Black Mime, directed by Denise Wong*

level. We also work from another route, where you look to find the expression of anger or sadness or laughter through just purely movement on your own, and it is for the actor to find a way. We find it most successful when everyone in the room agrees that they have seen that particular emotion.

[TECHNIQUE]

Q **Why do you feel it is important to begin with those three emotions?**
We see them as being the primary emotions: the other emotions are the spin-off.

[PROCESS]
Set yourself targets.

Q **Once in rehearsal, do you have a set schedule that you keep to?**
What we try and do is set ourselves targets: to say that by the end of the fourth week we will have 20 minutes' work that we will start to build towards creating a show. What usually happens is that you don't stick to the schedule and the deadline has gone. Then it is a case of moving towards that target but knowing you are behind schedule. It usually comes at the end of rehearsals when we are working long hours trying to make up the lost time.

Q **Are there moments in the rehearsal when you recognise the piece is changing direction?**
In *Dirty Reality II* we were creating it and there was a point when the actors created this character which I absolutely hated with a vengeance. I thought if I said I absolutely hated it, their creativity would be quashed. We did a showing to some people three weeks prior to its opening, and the character was jarring. By that time, the performers could see it was irrelevant to the piece, and it was time to

[BACKGROUND]
[ADVICE]
[TECHNIQUE]
*Black Mime use
techniques similar to those
of Brook and Complicité.*

Do not rush into changes which may upset the company's creative energy.

let it go. Sometimes if you let go of something too quickly you block the creative process. What we were trying to do was keep the process open, even though we knew at some point this character would have to be axed.

Q **You mentioned that you show your work to a select audience before the opening – a technique that Brook uses. Why do you do this?**

[TECHNIQUE]

It started with our Black Women's show *Drowning*. We wanted to see whether or not we were on the right track with the material. We wanted to test it in front of an audience and see the reaction. It is vitally important that we don't get too indulgent, so that we cease to communicate with our audience.

Q **Are there certain qualities the director should possess?**

[ADVICE]
Be sensitive to actors' moods.

Be sensitive to actors' moods. For example, they may be touched by the material they are dealing with; therefore a director must guide them through the situation. It is a bit like counselling. Directors are facilitators more than anything else.

Q **Is there any piece of advice you could give a young director?**

[ADVICE]
It is normal to feel threatened.

A director should encourage creativity.

It is really hard and lonely being a director. With that loneliness come a lot of defence mechanisms, paranoia and feeling threatened by the acting group. The director should abide by the rule that it is the actors who do the performing, and not just pay lip service to this, but encourage their creativity in the space, allowing them the opportunity to speak out. I feel that the role of the creative team – director, designer – is to service the actors. At the end of the day, it is important that the actors have ownership over the material. If they do not feel good about the material, then it is going to show night after night. Also [the director's role is] to guide actors, which is quite draining, because you feel like you are giving out a lot, and you may sometimes feel that you are not getting anything back. The reward is when the show opens and the audience respond to the piece.

John Wright

Background

- Co-founder of Trestle Theatre Company (see pp.337–338) and Told by an Idiot.
- Principal Lecturer in Acting and Theatre Making at Middlesex University.
- Type of work: devised theatre that has evolved from orchestrating the physical play of actors. He often uses masks as part of his working process, although he rarely makes mask pieces now. 'I want something

poetic, and what I mean by that is something visual which brings the word and the movement together to make a surprise, a new meaning.'

[BACKGROUND]

Q **What have been your influences?**

Peter Brook's work has always fascinated me, largely because it's always so fresh. He is so articulate about what he does, and his ideas are so provocative and stimulating. I like the directness and the simplicity of his work. I remember being knocked out by his production of *A Midsummer Night's Dream:* it was so physical and so fast, on a set like a white squash court with Oberon dangling on a trapeze, spinning plates. I came to the conclusion that theatrical magic was not about a literal representation so much as a potent surprise that fixes everyone in the moment. But teachers like Philippe Gaulier, Monika Pagneux [a specialist in movement] and Jacques Lecoq have been a very big and lasting influence on the way I direct and the way I look at theatre. Gaulier and Pagneux taught me the value of play, and Lecoq showed me how movement precedes everything – even thought. I have always found devising and adapting the most satisfying of processes in the theatre, and Lecoq, Pagneux and Gaulier have given me tools and principles that I have been able to develop and re-invent for myself.

He has been influenced by teachers of acting.

Q **Where did your use of masks come from?**

I basically taught myself about masks. Ironically, I did very little mask work with Lecoq, because I haven't done his two-year training, but I first used masks at drama school. We had a choreographer called Molly Kenny, who asked us to improvise some movement in mask, and I became fascinated, not so much by the movement that we were trying to do but by the moment the movement stopped and the actors started to walk off the space in their mask – at that moment I started to get really interested in what the masks were showing.

Wright taught himself about mask work.

[BACKGROUND]

At drama school, a visiting lecturer, Keith Johnstone, arrived with a tatty suitcase and some equally tatty half masks. These were so effective that we could talk about little else for weeks. But I didn't start using masks for myself until I was asked to teach acting – I suppose this would have been in the late 1970s. I was deeply frustrated with the static, text-based approaches to acting, and in a desperate attempt to find another way of approaching the subject I thought masks would be a good starting point, so I got my students to make a mask and then we would dress the masks and then make small visual scenarios.

[TECHNIQUE]

It was never my intention to get involved in mask theatre. Trestle was a sort of by-product really. But we did make some interesting discoveries in using masks. For example, we found that we could double up the characters by simply having identical masks and costumes, and this gave us a tremendous freedom. We could cut instantly from scene to scene just like in a film, we could create montages and move forwards and backwards in time, and we made characters with such a strong visual persona that the audience could

[PROCESS]

Masks are a rehearsal device for imagination and spontaneity.

empathise with them immediately. Today I try to use masks as a means of developing an actor's physical and imaginative range – for me they are a rehearsal device for exploring economy in action and for freeing our imaginations and inspiring us to play spontaneously.

One of the most important lessons in working in masks is the importance of the audience's response, and the moment you look at the audience and break down this imaginary fourth wall you invite the audience to become involved and to share each moment with you on stage. Peter Brook's work is often like this. You frequently get the feeling that the actors are talking directly to you personally.

[TECHNIQUE]
Most of his work comes from the creativity of the actors.

Q **Your work seems to have crossed the water and brought European theatre to Britain. Do you think you have done that?**

I don't know. I always see myself as a European, but I suppose my influences are without exception 'continental'. Certainly I have no interest in making theatre within the very British tradition of the well-made play. Probably 90 per cent of all my productions are devised and have evolved from the physical invention of the actors I'm working with. I rarely work from a literal interpretation of a text. I read a text initially to engage with a narrative or to try to come to terms with the metaphor behind the writing, and from these initial impressions I try to create action and images with the actors. I suppose to that extent my work could be seen as European.

[PROCESS]
Read the play for the narrative and then find actions to encapsulate the images of the play.

Q **So is that your basis for starting a production: reading the text, then finding the action?**

Broadly speaking, yes, but every play's different, and I don't have any hard-and-fast processes or methods. Because I spend so much time

I'm so Big *by* Told by an Idiot, *directed by John Wright*

81

[PROCESS]
When you are familiar with devising, you have no inhibitions about inventing things.

devising, I have no inhibitions about making things up, and for me a text is never a complete piece of theatre in itself. It's a bit like a piano score – reading a text is like reading the melody in the treble clef or simply playing the right-hand part. My job as a director is to try to work out with the actors what happens in the bass clef: what harmonies can we find to bring the melody alive?

Q How do you go about casting? What qualities do you look for in actors?

[PROCESS]
Actors have to have an instinctive sense of play.

I look for actors who have a good awareness of their own physicality and an instinctive sense of play. They have to be able to work from the slenderest of ideas and feel completely happy in that work. They have to be open and rigorously honest with themselves. If I become aware of them 'acting' in a casual conversation, then it's unlikely I would want to work with them; if I'm constantly aware that they're acting all the time as opposed to simply playing in a scene, I'll lose interest very quickly. My nightmare is an actor who wants to be told exactly what they're going to do before they do it. I remember once asking an actor if she could do a particular speech with the quality of being lost. 'What sort of lost?' she said. 'Physically lost, spiritually lost or emotionally lost? I can do any sort of lost you want.' 'Fine,' I remember saying, 'just choose one you like and be lost.' 'But it might not be right,' she said. 'That doesn't matter,' I said. 'It's just an idea. If it doesn't work, we'll think of something else.' This actor had trained in America and she prided herself on her ability to create what she called psychological truth [a Stanislavskian technique]. Because I tend to work from external references and external impulses, in an attempt to open up the action or to find some fresh meaning in the text, this particular actress was constantly at odds with my work and fearful of playing with an idea outside the given circumstances of the scene.

An actor must have the ability to play with an idea.

Q How do you advise a director to draw this instinctive play from an actor?

[TECHNIQUE]
Wright makes up extremely simple 'games' for his actors to play.

I can only say what I do rather than give advice. What might work for me could be a complete disaster for someone else. I get actors to play by making up disarmingly simple games, much more simple than anything you might read in Keith Johnstone's *Impro* [see bibliography, p.112]. I might ask you to find a game of sitting on a chair, for example, or of combing your hair, or of eating a banana. I find that once I've established the idea that the most mundane activity can be turned into a game, most people rediscover their instinct for play. Once you accept the idea that something as simple as sitting on a chair can be a game, you realise that you don't have to be good at it, and that anything you do within the context of a chair is acceptable.

[EXERCISE]
Find the game using the objective of the scene.

It's a very short step from applying simple games like this to playing within a scene. For example, if we had a scene and we decided that your objective in the scene was to come in and intimidate somebody, I would simply say, 'Find a game of intimidating him,' and I would encourage you to play with that idea until we found a particular game of intimidation that we both found amusing and effective. And working like this stops us getting bogged down into 'types' of intimidation, and rather than making decisions, we make discoveries, we find things, and for me this is liberating and exciting.

Q **If you were *given* a group of actors to work with, how would your methods for starting a piece differ?**
Everything depends on the group, and on the atmosphere we all make in the room at the time. I need a very relaxed and very casual atmosphere before I can start work. Nerves and inhibitions are infectious, and don't think that experience makes this process easier – it doesn't. If anything, it just makes you more aware of it.

I've evolved a game called 'The Compliments Game', which I often use to break the ice. I usually start it off by suggesting something really stupid, such as 'They tell me that you know all the movements.' At this point, people who are not familiar with my work look at me with a mixture of incredulity and pity. 'Excellent,' I say, 'do some of the movements you know.' In an attempt to humour me, and with a wry smile on their face, they normally start moving about a little. I respond to this with yet another compliment: 'That's magnificent, some of the best work I've seen all day.' The point of the game is to get people to credibly accept a stupid compliment, and I'm emphasising the word 'credible'. You have to believe in the compliment. I would normally do the game in pairs – one person making the movements and the other person offering the compliment, which has to be accepted. So it would go something like: 'That's very good'; 'Thank you very much,' the other person would say. Then I would ask the person who is giving the compliments to watch their partner and compliment as soon as their partner looks uncomfortable or inhibited. The fact is we all like compliments, and we grow from compliments. We get confident through compliments, and by credibly accepting a stupid compliment we can become quite comfortable, instead of being inane and stupid.

I can take the exercise a stage further by simply asking the question, 'Is there more?' Often this will produce an expression of panic in the person who is working. As soon as I see the panic, I come in with another compliment: 'That's excellent, such a good idea.' The game is liberating because it's inane, and because it never leaves anybody in difficulties for too long. The more credibly the compliments are accepted, the more you appear vulnerable and open, and this vulnerability is the quality I admire enormously in actors.

Q **Do you have a set method or process?**
No, but I can recognise three distinct stages of my production process. The first one is a pre-production period, and this is one of research reading; I like to involve as many members of the company as possible in this, and I don't like it to be too systematic. I like to work from as broad a range of influences as I can.

The second stage is the making stage, and this takes up the bulk of my rehearsal time with the actors. Because of my history of devising,

[EXERCISE]
Actors learn to accept a compliment and oblige the complimenter with action.

[PROCESS]
Stage 1 is pre-production: this involves research.

83

Stage 2 is devising: evolving the design alongside the action.

Stage 3 is rehearsing in a more formal way, delving into the text and developing the characters.

[ADVICE]
Experiment with masks if you have never used them before.

where often we're starting from absolutely nothing, I have developed the habit of trying to evolve the design and the action and the through thread of the production all at the same time. In the making stage, I try to work in very broad strokes, and the first decision I try to make is that of what shape we are playing in. The organisation of the space is the most important question for me to answer, because it influences everything from the design to the style of the action; I really believe that there is an ideal space for every story.

Once the play is on the floor and the second stage has been completed, I start rehearsing the play in a much more formal way. This process involves digging into the 'text', developing the image system of the piece and plotting the emotional journeys of the actors. Some people think that the term 'emotional journey' is a bit pretentious, but I make no apologies for it. The word 'journey' implies distance and a change; it suggests a movement from one point to another, and this is exactly what I want each of the actors to find in the piece. They have to undergo a change, an emotional change, from the beginning of each scene to the end of each scene, and from the beginning of the play to the end of the play. The final rehearsal stage is a process of plotting and developing these journeys.

Q If a director who has little experience of using masks wants to use a mask in their work, how do they begin?

There's an awful lot of nonsense and mystique that surrounds the use of masks, and I would advise anyone who wants to start using masks to simply start. Get a set of masks, or even an object like a paper bag, or any sort of object, and try to observe what you see. Trust your own sensitivity and your own powers of observation, and try to avoid any dogmatic approaches or theories of how masks should be used. In essence, masks do two things: they transform you by making you look completely different, and at the same time they reveal you. That is to say by covering the face a mask makes us read the body, and the way we move the body, with much greater sensitivity.

Whenever you cover your face with a mask or an object, you get an impulse, and this is not a very profound impulse. The impulse could probably be no more than you find it difficult to breathe or difficult to see. In order to breathe easier, you will have to slow down and find moments of stillness. To see and to focus clearly, you will have to be very still and give yourself plenty of time to be able to focus on an object before you pick it up, or to focus on somebody else's face if you're going to start to interact with them. Everything concerning mask work boils down to common sense, and anyone can find this for themselves.

Q Is there any advice you could give directors?

I have a little maxim that I keep at the back of my mind whenever I'm working with actors, and that is to try to say exactly what I see and not what I think, which is actually much more difficult than it sounds. I try to be a mirror that speaks, because, having set the ball in motion with the actors, namely having decided on the theme or a

[ADVICE]
*Tell the actors exactly
what you see and not
what you think.*

particular game in a scene, I try to give the actors as much space as possible, and to do this I find it much easier to focus on the event or the action rather than on the ideas or issues surrounding that action. I find myself using words like, 'You look uncomfortable,' meaning that your work was not completely credible, because all I saw was a very uncomfortable actor who was struggling; or I might say that something is 'fruitful', meaning that it has potential.

Q What qualities should a director possess?

I think you can probably divide these qualities into three rough categories. Firstly, I think you must have a good theatrical imagination. You have to come with some sort of a vision, a hunch about how something should look, about how something should be represented on stage. Secondly, I think you have to be ruthlessly honest about what you see when working with actors. This is getting back to my idea of trying to be a mirror that speaks, because, for me at least, a director is, to a large extent, a facilitator. And the third quality I think a director needs is to be a good time manager. You have to keep a constant eye on where you are in the process, and what this means in terms of the clock. A lot of my time when I'm directing is taken up in trying to organise the different events in a way that uses what is nearly always very limited time and resources to the best effect. But even if you possess all these three qualities in abundance, I feel that unless you can surround yourself with actors with whom you have found a mutual trust, then the work can become very difficult indeed.

*A director must have a
theatrical imagination, be
ruthlessly honest, be a
facilitator and be a good
time manager.*

Jude Kelly

Background

- Artistic director of West Yorkshire Playhouse since 1988.
- Previously artistic director of Battersea Arts Centre.
- Has worked with the National Theatre of Brent and the Royal Shakespeare Company.
- Type of work: making theatre accessible to all.

[BACKGROUND]

*She was inspired and
motivated by the political
stance of other
professionals and the
function of art.*

Q Who were your influences when you began directing and who are they now?

One influence was Charles Parker, who developed the radio biographies on the BBC. They were celebrations of the lives of working people and the approach he took to them was fascinating. [Another was] Peter Cheeseman [director of the New Victoria Theatre, a purpose-built theatre-in-the-round], who came to talk at the university. This coincided with the time when I was thinking about the power of art and how devastating it is that if you create a

civilisation where you subsidise art because you recognise its power and the importance of the imagination, how wrong it would be if people can't have access to that for whatever reason – financial, educational, political. I was also interested in the work of artists who had made it their mission to see how they could extend both the use of art through different roles, whether it be educational use or psychotherapy, and also the framework in which art is received, and also whose stories are told. When I first left university, I knew I wanted to direct, and I wanted to find out what it was like on the receiving end as an actress. I set out to work with Michael Bogdanov, who ran Phoenix Arts, a company who combined education, community workshop shows and main stage work. He was a great influence, because he was so brave about trying things out.

She worked as an actor before becoming a director.

Q **When you begin a play, what is your starting point?**
It varies. For years, it would be the audiences I would want to talk to. I would be thinking, 'What particular dialogue do I want to have with that section of the community?' After I had been working in the theatre for ten years, I wanted to study text – which I hadn't really done since university. Nowadays, my starting point is what I want to speak to the audience about, what are the texts which do that and who are the actors that I trust to share that.

[TECHNIQUE]
[BACKGROUND]
The focus of the work was the audience Kelly was trying to reach (see Wong p.79, Verma p.92).

Q **How do you go about casting? What is it that you look for in actors?**
Genuine application to skill. Acting is a very skilful job, demanding minute decision-making all the time. I value bravery, lack of competitiveness with their fellow artists, self-knowledge (whether actors can understand their body and face and how to use it), and those who don't pretend to have what they haven't got using what they have got – intelligence, sense of humour.

Q **If you were *given* a group of actors to work with, would your approach to a text be different than if you cast it yourself?**
Not necessarily. It would be very important to me that any group of actors felt I was delighted to be working with them. If you find yourself in the situation where you've got to teach actors to act, that does change the nature of your directing. It is a terrible moment when you realise that you are not in love with your leading actors – I don't mean romantically attached, but you've got to really find them interesting to work with, and if you can't find that feeling then you've got to search harder for it.

[TECHNIQUE]
As a director you must be intrigued by your performers (see Lloyd, pp.73–74).

Q **Do you have a set method of process through rehearsal?**
No, although I feel increasingly that there is a huge gain if actors are off the text before rehearsals begin, in terms of a real ability to play the scene in different ways. The only difficulty about that is that actors get stuck in a method of delivery and can't get out of it, which is why some actors like to find out what they are doing before they learn the text. I try to ensure actors learn the text as quickly as possible, so we have more time playing and looking at the real shape of the text.

[PROCESS]
There can be a freedom if actors are off-text before entering the rehearsal room.

A rehearsal of King Lear *at the West Yorkshire Playhouse, directed by Jude Kelly*

Q **Is play an important part of your rehearsal process?**

[TECHNIQUE]

Yes: I enjoy having fun in the rehearsal room, and I like the actors to have fun. I don't like to block too early; I like them to find a lot more of the shape. But to do that they need the freedom of being off-text.

Q **In directing any production, were there any key moments that you felt changed the whole emphasis of the play, for better or worse? How did you acknowledge those moments when they happened?**

[TECHNIQUE]
An appropriate level of
'self' can be shown.

I think you have many frightening moments in rehearsals. As a director, you have to decide how much you're going to show the actors, because I think it is very important that the director doesn't set herself up as a guru. Directors are artists, and they are there to experiment and discover like everyone else, but they are also there to lead the process. There can be an ambivalence about which way you

The rehearsal room is a
place of discovery for the
director, too.

move psychologically. When you look at a scene, and you think, 'I've really missed its central focus', you've got to go back to it. There can also be moments when you might have a revelation about the meaning of the play – and then that is very exciting; it is a creative feeling which you want to pursue. The frightening feeling is when you think you don't know what you are doing with this. You have to acknowledge it.

Q **If a director hits this point, what does he or she do? Should it be acknowledged to the cast?**

[ADVICE]
[TECHNIQUE]

It depends on the relationship. There are two things I would do. One is to go away and rethink it, although before I did I would ask whether anyone else has a view. Secondly, it is important that you don't con actors. But it is also important not to let them feel you may never discover the answers to the problem. This is about management style.

87

[ADVICE]

Q **So you are empowering your actors as well as sharing?**
Yes: often actors come up with brilliant ideas, and they've got to feel they are allowed to.

Q **Is there any advice you would give young directors about the rehearsal process?**
Firstly, it is important to get an ensemble piece going. Although you are with complete strangers, you have to try and make them feel they are a company. Secondly, it is a mistake to have them hanging around the rehearsal room unless they have a reason for being there. Thirdly, you've got to give actors who have got a lot of lines to learn proper study time. Finally, actors must have clear goals.

Gain a company integrity.

Use actors' time wisely.

Q **What qualities do you think a director should possess?**
Firstly, [you must] enjoy working with actors and understand actor processes: actors don't work just because you tell them what to do and what it means. Secondly, it's about creating energy in the room and recognising that most of the time you are investigating what is beneath the words. Thirdly, I think that directors have to have a lot of stamina, mental and physical. You are a manager and an investigator, and you are up against your own frailties. It helps not to be too insecure, because the actors look to you for confidence.

[ADVICE]
Be actor-friendly.

You have to possess a degree of strength and containment

Q **How do you deal with the insecurity a director inevitably feels whilst rehearsing?**
You have to give yourself some talking time. What I've tried to learn, which is hard sometimes, is that the rehearsal room is also the director's rehearsal room. Sometimes you just have to stop and find a creative idea for yourself: for instance, 'We will all act the story of the barber just to get your energy going again.'

[ADVICE]
[TECHNIQUE]

Jatinder Verma

Background
- Founder and artistic director of Tara Arts, a British Asian theatre company.
- Has written, adapted and directed over 50 productions.
- Type of work: sees storytelling as the key to theatre practice.

Q **Who are your influences?**
There hasn't been any kind of direct influence. Certainly, I admire the work of Peter Brook. There are directors I have worked with who are from India who are quite exceptional directors. Also directors here like Anthony Clark at Birmingham Rep., who provided a very useful stimulus early in my career. I see more influence in productions that I like. The productions vary quite considerably:

[BACKGROUND]
He has been influenced by productions rather than individuals.

just to give you an example, Brian Friel's *Translations* at the Hampstead Theatre, the original production of *Woza Albert* at the Riverside Studios, an Indian play that came to London in 1981 called *Gashiram Kotwal*, the original production of *Bent* and Ninagawa's *Macbeth*, which came to the National in 1986. They provide for me a very useful guideline as I come to do my own work.

Q **What was it in these productions that makes them stand out for you?**

Complete commitment by a company makes for exciting theatre.

An absolute commitment by everyone: the actors, the designers. This was not a piece of *theatre* I was watching, but something that people wanted to do, so it transcended questions of excellence, and that is the best and only theatre. It is more than just a job.

Q **How did you become a director?**

[BACKGROUND]

I was a performer, and I fell into directing by default. In 1976, when Tara Arts started, there wasn't any company of this type. Two friends and I formed a company, and I think when you form a company you end up doing everything. It fell upon me to direct, but I also acted and wrote. It was only over the years that I began to shed some of those skills, such as acting, and focus on what I really wanted to do.

Q **Would you advise young directors to do all the jobs first and then focus on directing?**

[ADVICE]

Even if you decide to be an *actor,* it is good to do all those things – much in the same way that I would advise anyone who wants to get into the profession of theatre, don't read drama, don't read English when you go to university. Don't specialise.

Q **Why is that?**

[ADVICE]
Know the world outside the theatre.

I think theatre is a passion. What is useful about having some other background or study is that it provides a context for your work; otherwise, I think there's a danger of becoming too precious. There are many in the profession who don't know the world around them . . . we must always remember that plays exist *in the world*.

Q **When you begin a production, what is your starting point?**

[TECHNIQUE]
He uses different techniques from around the world.

It has tended to be the text or the story, and the first thing I am looking for is the theme. So my approach to text is not to come into it directly, but to come to it in a circular route, so I go somewhere else first. It may be that the theme is explored in the actor's own words, so I try and tease out some understanding before one comes to the text. I think this thinking comes from Indian, Chinese and Japanese theatres, where there are certain sets of principles of movement. For

[EXERCISES]

example, if you want to turn right, you first go left. It sounds a paradox, but it becomes a simple way of utilising space, because if you go left when you mean to go right you are in fact describing a circle. It becomes a neat way of increasing space, and now I can see connections between that, as forms of movement on the stage, and my own approach to the text. It frees both myself and my actors and their imaginations.

[TECHNIQUE]

He explores memory in workshops through use of the senses.

[PROCESS]

[EXERCISES]

[TECHNIQUE]

[PROCESS]
Auditions consist of several stages.

[TECHNIQUE]
You can use similar exercises for different objectives.

Q **Do you find the theme and then explore it with the actors, or do you sit down with your actors and draw the themes out of them?**

I rarely read the text with the actors initially. In *A Midsummer Night's Dream*, the first thing that hit me was that it is very much a journey. I am now spending a long time in workshops trying to explore this idea. I'm not necessarily trying to push that idea up front, but I'm asking, 'What kinds of baggage are you carrying with you?' The biggest baggage is memory, but what does memory consist of? It consists of sounds, smells, gestures, tastes. So in each workshop I have been exploring these, and I've been saying to the actors, 'Come in with a sound that is yours.' I then got them to work with the sound, and use the text with the sound; I have given them the extract. So initially it becomes like a character exercise, but they are exploring their sound in relation to the text. At a later stage, I have asked, 'What is the story behind the sound?' and often I have heard personal stories, and then the question arises: is there a way of connecting that personal story with the text? I know that by the time we get to rehearsals a lot of this exploration will have been done. So how will I begin rehearsals? I might have found something that I am quite intrigued by; like at the moment I am very intrigued by Chinese ribbons, so I might dish them all out to every member and say, 'We are simply going to do a reading of the play and I want you to use this, so keep moving with it.' Part of it is to distract them from the play, so that they don't get too precious with the words, part of it is just to see what is the benefit, what are the images coming out. So for me there is a concern to keep the actors in charge, to be inventive, to be authors and not just be spoon fed.

Q **How do you find your actors?**

Auditions take several stages. Initially, I see them on their own; usually we do exercises, so that the half-hour audition becomes interesting for them as much as it is for me. It is not just me listening to them give speeches, but I actually work with them. Then we meet in groups, to see one actor in combination with others, and for me that is always the best one; it usually takes a day. We are working on something, so that there is an objective in sight. At the same time, I am looking at the dynamics of what works well.

Q **How different would your approach be if you were *given* a group of actors?**

For the first hour, we would do physical exercises that I always do. It would be a way of judging who is good at movement, who is physically open, who has problems, so getting some sort of sense from that. The exercises will be very similar to the ones I've already done with existing actors, though the objective may be different.

Q **What sort of exercises would they be?**

A whole range: I've gone away from any set movement. The actors take a movement as simple as a disco dance movement or a jig, and then I co-ordinate it by something as simple as 'follow my leader',

Tara Arts' production of The Mufti from Istanbul

[EXERCISES]
The actors produce a co-ordinated dance movement.

[EXERCISES]
He does a concentration exercise using sticks.

Storytelling is central to all the work.

[ADVICE]
It is important to make a personal connection with your work (see Magni, p.94).

and before people know it they have developed a dance. This is possible now because I have done so much work with dancers. Another thing that I like very much is concentration exercises. I love using sticks. You stand in a circle with the canes on the floor, holding one end, with the other end touching the floor, and looking at each other across the circle. In complete co-ordination, the sticks must be made to rise as one, without touching one another – they can rise and drop, very difficult. When it is achieved, what people notice is that their breathing is co-ordinated.

Q **Do you have a set method of process, or does it change with each production?**

I think the emphasis and types of exercise change. However, there is one constant in my work, and therefore in my approach, and that is storytelling. How I get to storytelling differs from project to project. It is something that we have completely lost in modern theatre. At the heart of theatre is language, is words: all words have a physical dimension.

Q **What advice would you give to a director who wants to work on a piece of devised narrative theatre, on how to draw these skills out of their actors?**

Exercises are just trial and error. I've realised that the most important thing is knowing why. If you don't have a sense of 'why am I doing it?', forget it: there is no point. It is so obvious, the difference between someone who wants to tell a story and someone who doesn't. This need to tell a story about a journey is important to me, beyond my production of the *Dream*, because, being black or Asian in this country, our stories are hidden. That is almost the definition of being black in Britain today: your stories are hidden. Play is another key thing: to be playful. I've increasingly started thinking in terms of

Doing is better than asking too many questions.

[PROCESS]
Question your material even when it is good: it should always serve the story.

children's games. There must be an element of play which is genuine fun in its own right, and it opens up so many possibilities.

Q Why children's games?
Because as adults we've lost something, and one of the things we lose as adults is the unquestioning naivety of the child. You say to a child, 'You are now a donkey, and you take three steps and then you become a horse.' The child will do it. An adult will ask, 'What is my motivation?' Very much a Western problem is that we ask too many questions: one of the things, for example, that my martial arts tutor does is that he never tells you the *why* of a particular move or pose. He insists you first do the move. And in the course of doing, I begin to focus more on what precisely is the question I want to ask.

Q Have there been any key moments, of either success or failure, in rehearsal, of which you were aware? How do you recognise those moments?
I think you have a sense of what is good, and I'm not sure that sense can be taught. Working with a group of actors you know what is good. However, a second question of 'Yes, that was good – but was there any point to it?' is more difficult to answer. You've got to say, in the cause of the story which you must ultimately serve, 'Is there any point?'

Q Is there any piece of advice you can give a young director?
It is a vague thing, but a director must always remember they exist in the world. Awareness of the world – of your own world – is crucial, because at the end of the day you could create art for just its own sake. The primary objective of the art is to communicate. How can you communicate with your work if you are unaware of the world? Therefore your audience are never wrong: *you* are wrong. You have not connected to their lives.

Marcello Magni

Background
- Born in Italy (the interview reflects his Italian accent at times).
- Trained with Philippe Gaulier and Monika Pagneux and was a pupil of Jacques Lecoq.
- A founder member of Theatre de Complicité.
- Co-directed *Foe* with Annie Castledine. *Foe* was based on the novel by J.M. Coetzee. It tells the story of Susan's experience on the island with Robinson Crusoe and Friday, and how each deals with the world once they leave the island. It is a play concerned with race, language, culture and history. It was

first performed at the West Yorkshire Playhouse, Leeds, in February 1996. The following interviews with Magni and Castledine refer briefly to this production as a clear example of the directors' work.

● Type of work: based on play, physical theatre and ensemble work.

Q I am interested in the elements or ingredients that Complicité has. Would you class them as elements of your training? Is it to do with your process?

[BACKGROUND]

It is both things at once. We have a language of an experience that we share. The experience has gone beyond the school and gone into years of working together. So we understand each other quicker. Lecoq is in the back of our minds. We work in a team, we have learned to play together, I don't know how many companies have learnt how to be an ensemble. We change actors, but there are always four or five that are the same, so this guarantees that somewhere there is unspoken understanding of the spirit of the work.

Q The idea of play and the use of energies is a fundamental part of your training and rehearsal. Why is that?

[TECHNIQUE]

Games are important to group dynamics.

The company has spent an enormous amount of time playing games, games like children, to develop a spirit or a team. You develop an understanding, a physical capacity, physical patterns, or rhythms and energies. We as a group play games to make one another familiar. Then we play games/exercises that are based on concentration and awareness of what is the tension, the dramatic tension, the playing tension like children play. Children always have an eye on each other . . . it is jealousy, it is fun, they interact a lot but they also are very creative. So in order to find that thing you have to go beyond the children's games. It creates a pleasure of interacting with the other person, to the point that you tease the other person or you hit or tickle them. You go beyond the child's level of play, because you are aware of the objectives of the game. So you achieve *complicité* rather than competitiveness.

Q If a director was *given* a group of actors to work with, what process should he or she adopt in getting to know the cast?

[PROCESS]
[TECHNIQUE]
A strong company needs loyalty and stimulating people.

Actors are very much part of the creative process.

A process where the actors go off by themselves and create part of the story from the imagination. To do a lot of experience together, to create loyalty, to create a certain trust and team, then you can achieve. You must find people you can work with: you have to choose the right friend, the collaborator who is both loyal and stimulating. The director has the responsibility to gel the actors together.

The other thing is the method. There is lots of responsibility to the performer to create their own material. So very often we give the task to go into a corner and start to create a piece of theatre, a moment which will fit in with the process that is part of the show. Even when we do a text, like *Foe* or *The Winter's Tale* or *The Visit*, we always have the moment in rehearsal where we went away from the story in order to come back. So very often we had a picture in front of our eyes, or a single event, on which we would improvise and create a five-minute piece and present it to the group, and then we say, 'This moment, we will keep that and that and that,' – so that is how we devise.

Q How do you choose a cast?

I don't like it when people cast types; these are mistakes for me, there is too much stereotyping. I would like to see *Romeo and Juliet* where they are both ugly, and this would speak much more about their love and what they thought about each other. When I cast a couple of shows, I looked for friends, people that would have understood the spirit of the work – not the character necessarily, but the spirit of the work, so that they were familiar and were able to come on a journey together. I thought they had a spirit as performers.

So I go back to the question you asked before: what is the spirit of Complicité? *Complicité* means when people share a delinquent act together, evil act . . . you have to have something very wicked in your eyes and with the audience. I think when performers have that kind of spirit, anarchic, then they always create something more dangerous that the audience will recognise, that element, that spice. You must put a strange, exotic, erotic little thing in, otherwise you can't make theatre. There must be a little 'Oh, that was not clean', or 'That is a little bit dirty' . . . otherwise we always receive too many bland foods.

Q So you are making your audience more active, by making them come with you?

Yes, and I think it is all down to energies and trust – a sense that this person, this action, could surprise me, amaze me!

Q What was your starting point for directing Foe?

Annabel Arden and Annie Castledine asked Mark Wheatley to write a play based on the novel *Foe*, because in the past Complicité have often devised shows. So they wanted to go to a new stage, a new departing point to provoke the work, but using some elements that are Complicité. It is not like a kind of chemical formula that shows that you have success; it is like cooking – you put things together and then you taste it until you are happy. The difficulty, when you improvise, is that your text, the words that you speak, are always slightly banal, because we do not come out with fantastic words. Now, with that premise, Mark was helped by the workshops that Annie and Annabel led, and in these workshops the stories emerged, and little by little Annie and Annabel cast it. I arrived at the very last workshop of all. I did not make many of the initial decisions, but was given the responsibility to carry on with the task. The reason why I decided to do the play is because I believe Kathryn [Hunter] is a wonderful performer [she plays Susan, the lead]. Also I really wanted to work with Annie and learn from her. I believed that the story was very topical and resonant for England today; words enslave people, and that is what we do in society. I sometimes have a similar feeling of dependence and enslavement as an Italian in England.

[TECHNIQUE]
Choose a cast who share the same spirit.

Complicité means people who share and commit themselves.

[BACKGROUND]

[TECHNIQUE]

A personal connection with the play is important (see Verma, p.91).

Q **How did you find the route to enable the character Susan to talk directly to the audience?**

We went through many different options. So physically you say to Kathryn [Susan], 'Only talk to Mr Foe as if he is in the air.' [Mr Foe is the author of *Robinson Crusoe*. Susan is relating her story to him as it is happening on stage.] 'You focus on one point, and then you talk.' Then we put Foe present on the side of the stage, and when she had to talk to him she turned to him. Then we tried that she had a paper and quill, so when she was talking to Foe she would write. Or talk to objects, so suddenly when I'm talking to you I might say, 'So that is how it happened [while doing this Magni picks up a piece of paper on the desk in front of him and looks at it while talking to me]: that's how I felt everything.' Now the object could remind her of another intention; instead of talking to Friday or Crusoe, she could be talking to Mr Foe. It took a long time to make the audience part of her thinking.

Q **Can you explain the 'rhythms' of a play? The different rhythms of the four elements [earth, air, fire, water] were so prominent in *Foe*. How do you make a cast aware of the rhythms of a play?**

Life has rhythms, a wave has rhythms [he demonstrates by building the sound of a wave into a crescendo]. A day has a rhythm: it starts very quiet and reaches a peak, after the peak in some countries there is almost a rest, then it starts up again, and then you go towards the quiet of the evening. Now if you observe life or music you know when there are things that engage you, because they have a big pattern. If you compress these things like if I was compressing a day [he demonstrates], you compress your story, and you will feel what

A scene from Foe, performed at the Young Vic and directed by Marcello Magni

are the rhythms and you will realise if you are reaching the peaks or not. So you have to push them and really go for them. If you live them in the normal pattern of life, you can lose the rhythm. If you push them to a heightened level, then you make them aware.

[ADVICE]
Formulas are traps:
listen to your actors.

Q **What qualities should a director possess?**
Be ready to learn all the time, to receive every single experience as different and possible, and any single experience is a step forwards, not an end: it is never an end. Formulas are traps, and preconceived ideas about shows are mistakes. The play has to happen in the rehearsal space. The actors will tell you where they can go. You must have your reasons for why you did that play, to have a flavour. You have the responsibility to give them the energy. If you give the actors the solution, they will never surprise you or the audience. The audience will receive the idea, see the idea and not the play.

[TECHNIQUE]

Q **How do you block a play?**
We never block; we choreograph. Blocking is not a good system; but at the same time you have to give a pattern, give a game of ping-pong, or give and take, in which people are framed. If it was a free response all of the time, then there would be no form. Blocking is wrong: organising is important.

[ADVICE]
[TECHNIQUE]
It is good practice to ask
an audience in to watch
your show before the first
night (see Wong, p.79).

Q **How do you recognise a moment in rehearsal that has gone well or failed?**
Experience accounts for a lot, but I think the best judges are the collective energies of the group and the audience. The public is the best judge. There are directors like Peter Brook who before opening allow the actors to perform in front of schools; I think that is a very good practice. As we did in *Foe*, we invite friends in early on. The friends can be cruel but they are the best . . .

[ADVICE]
A director must know
what it is like to perform.

Q **What advice can you give a young director?**
Not to think that you know all of it. Let the other people believe they have done the steps; otherwise they will be like good soldiers only. A director must be an actor – not necessarily a performer, but they must have felt somewhere what it was like to perform, so that they can relate to the difficulties that a performer goes through.

Annie Castledine

Background
- A freelance director.
- Artistic director of the Northern Studio Theatre.
- Associate artistic director of Theatre Clwyd (1985–7).
- Artistic director of Derby Playhouse (1987–90).
- Type of work: Extensive work with

96

new plays, and detailed text analysis.

Q **Who have been your influences?**

[BACKGROUND]

I've done an enormous amount of assistant directorial work, so my early influences, I would say, were Trevor Nunn and Ronald Eyre; they were two informative influences on me in their thinking, if not in their methodology. Also, I was always having very close discussions with all my colleague directors. In the 1980s a lot of women directors were getting together to talk about the nature of the work; that was a huge influence. I've always been influenced by European theatre, so Ruth Berghaus, Ariane Mnouchkine, Peter Brook, Peter Stein, Zadek have all been influences on my work because of the way they work. [See Bradby and Williams, *Directors' Theatre* for further information on many of these directors.]

Q **Is the normal practice for you to begin with a novel or text, or have you ever started from an actor or writer?**

There are various starting points.

All those ways of beginning a piece of work happen. I am sometimes actor-centred, because I've wanted to work with a certain performer. Sometimes I'm writer-centred, because a writer writes a play for me to direct, or indeed we want to explore adaptation into a theatre form.

Q **How do you go about casting?**

[PROCESS]

She uses familiar talent (see Stafford-Clark, p.70).

I went about casting *Foe* with Annabel Arden [Theatre de Complicité] by asking people with whom we'd worked before. The casting really solved itself; in other words, we did not cast in a conventional way. People were associated with the production from the beginning, because they were associated with us and because we wanted to work together again.

Q **Do you find it positive, having worked with someone, to work with them again?**

[TECHNIQUE]
[ADVICE]
The concerns of the theatre can override those of the production.

I think it is a very positive way of working, because each production is not an end in itself. It is part of a continuous working process. It is a part of a continuous canvas, so the same concerns are being explored from one production to another. The nature of the production and really the nature of the text doesn't necessarily affect the concerns you want to explore.

Q **If you were *given* a group of actors, which is the situation for most students, would your initial approach be different?**

[TECHNIQUE]
A successful workshop period will create the casting.

No, it would not. I would work with the group without casting the piece in the first instance. Then and only then, after I had got to know the group, would I venture onto the casting procedure, which I believe if the workshopping sessions had been successful would happen organically.

Q **Do you find this the best approach, to workshop into a play?**

[TECHNIQUE]

No, not necessarily, it differs from text to text. It also differs according to the context, where you are. If you are working in regional repertory, that context will be slightly different from

*The context of the
production determines the
approach taken.*

working at the Royal National Studio, where I would choose a group
of actors to experiment with, and the experimentation will be the
nature of the work. It also depends on the length of the rehearsal
process.

[TECHNIQUE]

Q **Do you have any set methods or techniques that you use?**
I do have a methodology, but that methodology doesn't mean that I
use the same exercises or the same methods all the time. But the
theatre concerns will be the same. I am always interested in how to
push forward, with what is the nature of theatre – what is the *making*
of a piece of theatre.

Q **Are there any qualities you can draw out of yourself or colleagues
which you would advise others to work on?**
Directors have to know the kind of questions they are going to ask,
not the solutions to the questions. I think directors have to be
incredibly curious, curious about everything. I think they have to
acknowledge and be curious about their colleagues' work. I think
they have to have an inner vision, a preoccupation, a concern. I think
they have to be driven to explore what it is to make theatre.

[ADVICE]
*A director should know
the questions the play is
asking.*
Be curious.

[ADVICE]
[PROCESS]
Reflect on your work.

Q **Is there a piece of advice you would give to young directors?**
I always feel as if I'm working through vast seas of inadequacy, so of
course I am always concerned and very introspective about the
process as it is happening, and indeed after it has happened.
Hopefully I will learn from one process before I begin and enter into
another process. So I think periods of reflection and of dream time
are absolutely crucial.

GUIDELINES FOR DIRECTING

It is clear from the interviews above that all directors work in their own
way. They focus on different aspects of theatre, and they have a wide
range of experience in directing different companies and styles of
theatre. However, a young director will not have such experience to
support his or her work.

This section offers you a directing checklist, which may help you as you
work on a project. It is not intended to be exhaustive, and it may be
inappropriate for some directors. However, it may be useful as a basic
structure, to which you can return during the project. It focuses upon
directing texts rather than devised pieces, although many of the points
will be relevant for devised work. (For further information on devising
theatre, see Chapter 4.) In addition, it assumes that you are directing for
a performance. If you are limited to a directing exercise, some of the
points will not be relevant.

At the outset of the project, start a personal record of your work, and
continue it as a form of portfolio (see pp.17–19).

Before rehearsals

There are several points to consider when choosing a text to direct.

First, choose your play. This is largely instinctive: you read something and you immediately see its possibilities. However, there are other areas to consider. Before choosing a text, answer the following questions:

● What type of performance space is available to you?

● Is that space available to rehearse in? This has ramifications for the complexity of the design.

● How long will your rehearsal period be? Don't attempt four hours of *Hamlet* if you have only six weeks. Choose a shorter play.

● How many actors do you want to work with? Is this appropriate for the size of the space?

● What is your budget? This will have a crucial bearing on the style of the piece.

● What type of play interests you: modern, historical, political, moral, comedy? Are the language, style and so on appropriate for you, your actors and the audience?

● Who is your target audience? Make the play 'connect with their lives' (Verma, p.92).

Having chosen the play, read it thoroughly and research it with your designer, if you have one (see Lloyd, p.73).

Next, find your technical team. In the professional theatre, this is usually done for you. In student productions, it tends to be left to the director. Make sure you have a stage manager, a sound and lighting person, and someone co-ordinating the publicity, if possible.

With your stage manager, construct a rehearsal schedule. It is best to do this at this stage, so that when the actors audition they can see the commitment you require and the dates of the performance. Begin constructing the schedule from the performance dates and work backwards. (See Chapter 4, pp.148–150, for further details.) Make sure you include all technical meetings. This is very important, as it concerns people management and shows efficient organisation. You must give the technical people the time and respect they deserve. If all meetings and rehearsals are set from the beginning, everyone knows what is expected of them.

Auditioning

Look at the different audition techniques used by Wong, p.77, Verma, pp.90–91, and Wright, p.82. List the objectives you think each of them has and the techniques they use. Use these as a base for your own auditions, if appropriate.

Study the characters in your chosen text. Set yourself objectives, so that you know what you are looking for in your actors. Make a list for each character, describing his or her physical appearance and character traits.

This will help you decide whether or not an actor is suitable for the part.

Create an audition including exercises which will identify the actors' potential to fufil your objectives. Think about whether it is best to audition singly or in groups. Do you want them to work from the text or improvise? Is it more important to you that they look right, that they have the potential to create the right group rapport, or that they have the ability to develop the relevant character?

Once you have chosen your actors, offer them the part, and make sure they accept before you turn anyone else down: your first choice may not want to do it!

Rehearsals

The rehearsals will depend upon the nature of your own project.

Clearly, your rehearsal period is the most important stage of the project. The content and style of the rehearsals will depend entirely upon your text, the company and other particulars. The resource activities section may help you in this. However, there are certain common elements which are worth considering:

● How can you develop group rapport? The resource activity on 'The purpose of play' might help you (see pp.104–106).

● For each rehearsal, set yourself objectives; list games or exercises and techniques you may use within the rehearsal. For example:

Objective	Exercise	Outcome
Warm up (See pp. 5–10 in Chapter 1)	Physical/vocal limber	Physically prepared and focused
Build energy	Volleyball; football; stuck in the mud	Encourage sense of play; develop group dynamics
Find the characters' histories	Hot seating; improvisation of first meetings; improvisation of different childhoods	Development of whole, rounded characters
Spatial awareness	Physically create the characters' living space	Development of the characters' environment

● Set yourself targets for the development of the text. Directors work differently; you may want to work on the text in the early stages (see Lloyd, pp.73–74). Alternatively, you may not approach the text for some days or weeks. Think about whether you want to keep running 'completed' sections, and the advantages or disadvantages of this (see Stafford-Clark, p.71). Beware of leaving the realisation of the text too late (see Wong, p.78).

- Try to keep a reflective diary of the process (refer to *Letters to George* by M. Stafford-Clark). It will make you reflect on the questions and problems raised in rehearsal and spur you on to find ways of exploring them in the next rehearsal.

- Ensure you leave enough time for technical and dress rehearsals. See Chapter 4, pp.148–150, for further details about these rehearsals.

First performances

- Support your team fully, and try not to show your own nerves.

- Play familiar games that you have used throughout the rehearsal period, so that you can support your actors.

- Create a very tightly structured warm-up, to make sure you give your actors enough time to get ready and have a few moments on their own. For example:

Objective	Time
Loosen muscles and relaxation exercises (see pp.5–7)	10–15 minutes
Vocal warm-up (see pp.7–10)	10 minutes
Familiar energiser exercises	10 minutes
Character work	5–10 minutes
Brief supportive chat and focusing	5 minutes

During the run

- Give notes to your cast before subsequent performances. It may be more appropriate to do this before the warm-up.

- Try to enjoy the performance and see it from the audience's perspective. This will help you when taking notes on the performance. It is more important to note things like pace, timing and the intensity of relationships than to worry about whether an actor walked around the table the wrong way. Try and keep notes brief: nobody can take in six pages of notes, but they can work on four points in the following performance.

- If you and your cast realise that one aspect of the show is not working in performance, call a rehearsal. Remember to set your objectives and give the actors plenty of time to adapt to the changes.

Post-production reflection

Both Castledine and Stafford-Clark stress the importance of reflection (see pp.72 and 98). It is worth listening to comments from your audience. You may also wish to run a post-performance discussion, as many theatre companies do. Read and/or listen to criticisms, but try to view them objectively. Did the critic have a point, or did he or she miss your intention completely, and if so what could you have done to improve that? For your own personal use, you may wish to write your own criticism of the production. This will make you look at the show as a whole and really think about how all the different aspects came together.

Reflect on all aspects of the director's role: rehearsals, people management, your role in technical rehearsals, the overall concept, the focus of the production. This reflection will be more focused if you have maintained a personal record from the start of the project (see pp.17–19).

If you are expected to write a detailed evaluation, see pp.150–154 for further advice on this.

Resource Activities

These exercises should be viewed as a starting point to launch you into further exploration of your own. They are rooted in the exercises and advice given by the directors in the interviews. When undertaking these activities, refer to the interviews and guidelines for further ideas.

It is important to recognise that many directors decide what they wish to focus upon in a session and then create their own exercises to encourage that exploration in the rehearsal room. This is a skill you will develop as you gain experience.

1. TEMPO–RHYTHMS

Aim
To gain an understanding of the pattern of a text.

Objectives
● To verbalise and physicalise a text in 'compact' form.
● To construct a chart which shows the peaks and troughs of the text's rhythm.

Background
Tempo: speed at which music is . . . played, as a characteristic rhythm
Rhythm: the pattern produced by various relations of emphasis and duration . . . by long and short or accented and unaccented syllables.
(Hawkins, J.M., (ed.), *Oxford Reference Dictionary*, Oxford University Press, 1989)

In theatrical terms, the tempo–rhythm is the speed and emphasis of the delivery of the text, whether it be verbal or non-verbal. Every text has a tempo–rhythm, which the director must access to find the play's natural flow. In the same way, your life has peaks and troughs, which are dictated by events and mood changes. For example, a slow evening at home changes pace with a phone call from a friend offering you a free ticket to a concert of your choice. The tempo–rhythm changes from slow monotony (trough), through suppressed excitement, to a peak of joy once the receiver has been replaced. (See Marcello Magni's explanation on pp.95–96.) The tempo–rhythm of a text could be recorded on a chart like the one over the page.

Tasks
● Think about the tempo–rhythm of a specific day, such as yesterday, so that you can draw on real events and detail. Physically enact moments of the day, not using sound at first. Then add vocal sounds to your physical actions. Finally, focusing on the sounds only, condense the day's tempo–rhythm into one minute. (Exaggeration helps to highlight the different rhythms, so don't hold back!) For example, you begin asleep, vocalised as soft breathing; the alarm

clock rings and you spend the next hour rushing around, vocalised as an alarm clock sound, shouts and screams; the tempo changes as you sit down for your first lecture, which you find boring, vocalised as a flat drumming sound; you meet friends after the lecture and the tempo and rhythm rise, vocalised as light chuntering.

● Now record your day's tempo–rhythm on a chart like the one below.

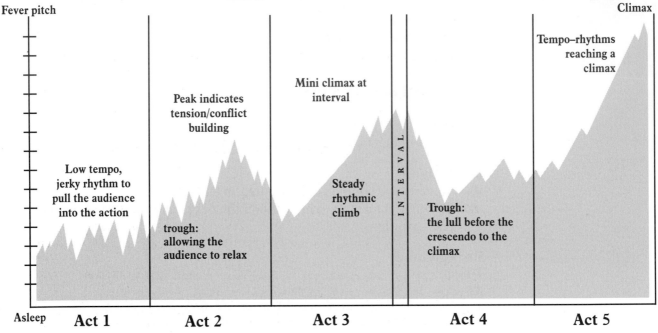

A chart showing the tempo–rhythm of a hypothetical text

● Create your own tempo–rhythm chart for the opening scene of a text you have been studying. Ask your cast to do the same, but from the point of view of one of the characters. Compare the different charts to see how an individual's tempo–rhythm influences the tempo–rhythm of the scene as a whole.

For further research into this topic, look at Stanislavski's *Building a Character*, Methuen Drama, 1991, p.224.

2. THE PURPOSE OF PLAY

Aims
● To gain insight into the different functions of games.
● To understand the place of play in the theatre.

Objectives
● To establish a group's identity and *complicité* through play.
● To find the different uses of a game.
● To develop your own resource of theatre games.

Background
Refer to Magni, p.93, Lloyd, pp.74–75, Wright, pp.82–83, Kelly, pp.86–87 and Verma, pp.91–92. See also pp.119 and 124–126.

Play is important to make actors engage with one another. When one actor engages with another and there is a genuine sense of *complicité* they become interesting to watch: an audience will be drawn into the delight and enjoyment of the actors.

Tasks

- Denise Wong often plays football with her casts. Any team game will help the group work together. For example, divide the group into two teams and give them a small beanbag to throw. Allow the group to make up its own rules. (Can you run with the beanbag or must you stand still? Is there a goal?) This will give them ownership of the game.

- As the group progresses with the game, give it other functions within the rehearsal. For example, play it in character, in different moods or while saying the text (see Lloyd, pp.74–75).

- Tuck a sock into the back of your waistband, so that you have a tail. The aim of this game is to pull off your partner's tail before he or she gets yours. The objective is to find that 'something very wicked in your eyes' (Magni, p.94), that enjoyment of play.

- Write down every children's game you know, and list the uses of each one in a rehearsal room. You may want to list the games under headings: group awareness, *complicité*, team work, energising, concentration, imagination.

- Find or devise a game which would be appropriate for 12–15 people playing the chorus in *Oedipus Rex*. Your objective should be that you want to enhance the group's ability to work as a unit, often speaking and moving in unison.

- Look at John Wright's 'Compliments Game' (p.83). Put your cast in pairs and call them A and B. A is the complimenter and B is the performer. A must ask B to show him or her a movement using a similar phrase to 'I'm told that you know all the moves; could you show me the steps?'. Once B has performed some little movement, then A must compliment him or her. 'The point of the game is to get people to credibly accept a stupid compliment.' Continue, then change over. It is an ice-breaking exercise.

- Freeze tag is a game for a group of actors. One person is frozen in any position in the centre of the circle. A second person enters the circle and, using the shape of the first person's position, begins to make a scene. The first person joins in, feeding off the ideas given. At any point, someone in the circle can call 'freeze' and take over the position of either person in the middle. The new person begins the next scene. There are many variations on this game. (See Chapter 1, pp.15–16, for one variation.) For example, instead of having only two people in the circle at any one time, you can add to the number by never letting anyone leave the circle. So when 'freeze' is called that person adds to the scene, rather than taking someone else's position. The game may also be used as a brainstorming exercise: for instance, it is played as originally stated, but all the scenes have to relate to green issues, or relationships. Write out five different versions of this game with the objective of opening the imagination. Remember that to make the performers more creative you should use constraints (e.g. impose a topic or the use of a prop).

3. EXPLORATION OF TEXT

Aim
To discover different ways to make a text accessible.

Objectives
- To understand the uses of a blind script.
- To discover the 'architecture' of a play.

Activity A: Background
A script is like a set of instructions. If you follow those instructions carefully, you can produce a coherent piece of theatre. As a director, you can then colour in the path you have taken.

There are an infinite number of ways to explore a text. For you to gain the best from your actors, they must be curious about the text: they must want to find out what the meaning is behind the lines, why the playwright has used certain syntax and how this can be executed in performance. It is the director's job to provoke this interest. Blind scripts are a useful way of attuning actors to the language of the text and making them examine every word.

Tasks
- Give your actors the text below; they should learn it. Using only the words provided, create a scene, giving A and B characters, a relationship and a setting. Work with your actors to make sure the lines are given meaning.

  A: You
  B: Yes
  A: I thought you had . . . you know . . .
  B: I changed my mind.

- Create your own blind script of approximately six lines, but give your actors one piece of information ('character A dislikes B', or 'it is set at midnight'). By giving your actors constraints, you are making them work within the criteria set by the hypothetical playwright.

- Follow the instructions below with three actors, whom you should call A, B and C. Without adding any words or changing the instructions in any way, give A, B and C characters, relationships and a setting. The instructions and your concept should interlock perfectly. You will need three chairs, set in a row and numbered 1, 2 and 3.

i) B strolls in and sits on chair 2.
ii) A runs in and sits on chair 3.
iii) A gestures to B.
iv) B reacts to A's gesture (laughs, cries).
v) C enters and sits on chair 1.
vi) A stands up, looks left then right, then sits back down.
vii) B gets up and walks to stand behind C.
viii) B whispers to C and then exits right.
ix) A sits on chair 2.
x) C moves to chair 3.
xi) They stare at each other, and react differently to each other's stare.
xii) A exits left.
xiii) B returns and sits on chair 2.
xiv) A returns and sits on chair 1.
xv) They all sit in identical positions.

Activity B: Background

Annie Castledine has developed an exercise on text analysis which allows the actor and director to discover the 'architecture' of a play. The architecture is the construction or implicit structure of the text. By analysing this, a director will understand the pattern of the text and its significance. For example, *A Doll's House* has a three-act structure, which suggests that the play has three significant developments. We can also note that Nora is the first person we see. If we liken the architecture to a musical score, we then have a male–female duet between Nora and Helmer, followed by a female duet between Nora and Mrs Linde. By following the entrances and exits of the characters and the number of characters on stage in their different combinations, we are able to learn an enormous amount about the play and how the playwright is working. This architecture helps us to reveal the fundamentals of the plot. For instance, at the end of Act I Nora is once more on her own, revealing to the audience her true feelings and her frustrations at being confined to her mother/wife role.

Tasks

● Using a text which you are studying, write down the architecture of the play. First, look at its structure by identifying the acts and/or scenes. Then identify the number of characters on stage, who they are and their gender, in terms of duets, trios and chorus. This pattern should be an indication of how the story is being told, and how it progresses through the play. Look for any *changes* in pattern which will highlight dramatic points in the text.

● Look at Phyllida Lloyd's text exercise using an objective on p.75. This exercise should be conducted when your actors are well rehearsed but you want to push them to discover more. Choose a scene which your actors know well. Ask them to run the scene, concentrating on one particular thing, such as the furniture in the room, the clothes everybody is wearing, or a certain character or incident in the play.

4. WORKING ON CHARACTER

Aims
- To understand the director's role in character exploration.
- To aid actors in their understanding of the role they are playing.

Objectives
- Studying the text to gain as much information about the character as possible.
- Contextualising the character in time, place and period.
- Encouraging the actors to connect the character to their own experience.
- Working beyond the text to encourage the actors to form a rounded character.

Background
It is not the director's role to provide all the answers for an actor who is discovering a character; rather he or she should ask questions and aid the search for the answers. To be able to ask the questions, the director must have a thorough knowledge of the play.

If you have read all the interviews in this chapter, you will be aware that directors' approaches to characterisation differ greatly. Before you embark on characterisation with your cast, make sure you understand the function of the characters in your text. Are they a vehicle to tell the story? Are they rounded characters or are they types – stereotypes or archetypes? Are they a symbolic representation of a concept? The function of the characters will determine how you approach the exploration.

Tasks
- This exercise was created by Stanislavki, but is used widely by directors (see Lloyd, p.73) to enable them to understand fully the characters and their relationships. (Also see Cooper and Mackey, *Theatre Studies*, pp.20–25 and 130–137.) An extended version of this exercise for actors is given on pp.55–57 in Chapter 2. Write down for each character:
  i) everything he or she says about him or herself;
  ii) everything others say about him or her;
  ii) everything he or she says about others.

- This is a similar exercise to one Max Stafford-Clark did when directing *Our Country's Good* (Stafford-Clark, *Letters to George*, p.107). Make a timeline for your cast of the events in history that may have affected their characters' lives. (See pp.66–68 for an example of a timeline.) Begin the timeline at the start of the oldest character's life (or before, if the play requires it). Include all the significant events in history which would have touched the lives of the characters. Also include the events that happened to the characters themselves, so that you can see how they interlock.

- If your actors have not experienced the situations of their characters, help them find a similar situation in their own experience. This is an early Stanislavskian technique – emotion memory. For example, if the character is mourning over the death of a loved one, but your actor has never experienced a death, find an incident in his or her life when he or she lost an object that was of great importance. Ask the actor to explain the feeling he or she had on realising that that object had gone. Find a way of enhancing that feeling so that it is on a par with the loss of a person.

- Hot-seat the characters. Sit the actor on a chair, in role. Referring back to the timeline, question the character on the effect of world events, as well as domestic events, on his or her life.

- Ask your actors to improvise the scene highlighting the subtext. ('The subtext is the information in the text about events and characters that is not directly made clear by the dramatist's written lines. It is the impressions we receive by "reading between the lines".' [Cooper and Mackey, *Theatre Studies*, p.323])

- Improvise the moments before a scene begins. This helps the actors to understand what has led up to the scene, which will affect the subtext of the scene itself.

- Ask the actors to improvise situations that are mentioned in the text but not seen on stage. By doing this, the actors will know how to react when the situation is mentioned, because they have gone through the situation themselves. Again, this supports the subtext.

- While your actors are playing a scene, give them different numbered playing cards which can indicate their status level (king high, ace low). Find other ways of grading the scene. This is an exercise used by Max Stafford-Clark; read p.70 for other ways of grading the scene. It opens up different possibilities for exploring the subtext.

- Refer to John Wright's thoughts on the physicality of character on pp.81–82. Ask your cast to walk round the space in as neutral a way as possible. Call out a part of the body, which is going to be their 'centre of personality'. For example, you may call out 'hands'. The actors need to make their hands the focus of their physicality, so that if that person walked into a room you would immediately look at their hands and think, 'this person is a hands person'. Ask your cast to add a voice to this focus. Note how the voice and the rhythm of the walk change with the different parts of the body. (See p.16 for a variation on this exercise, 'Leading with parts of the body'.)

- Give your cast neutral masks, then divide them into pairs; they should stand about three metres apart. Ask them to stand in a neutral position, then give them instructions: for example, slowly tilt the head to one side and back to neutral, now raise the head slightly upwards and back to neutral, then look downwards. Observe how these slight head movements change how we read the body's different attitudes. Now ask the cast to make bolder movements, but remembering to return to neutral and to move slowly so that the changes are clear. Next, try this exercise without masks: when the actors move out of neutral, it is the *character* who is moving out of neutral.

5. REFLECTING ON THE WORK OF THE PROFESSIONAL

Aim
To assess the techniques and choices of professional directors.

Objectives
- To note the significant working methods of the directors interviewed in this chapter.
- To evaluate a professional production.

Background
Refer to the interviews with directors on pp.68–98.

Tasks
- Skim read some or all of the interviews, using the key words in the margin to make lists of the directors' exercises, techniques, process and advice.

- Choose a text with which you are familiar and which interests you as a piece to direct. Write a clear evaluation of the directors' approaches, explaining which appeal to you and would be useful in the process of directing this piece. Say why you feel these would be appropriate, and give a few examples of how you envisage these approaches being developed in rehearsals.

- Watch a production and write a review of it with emphasis on the director's input. Consider the following questions:

  i) What was the overall concept of the production? The text is just the blueprint; it is how the director interprets the text for performance which should be your focus. This may mean familiarising yourself with the text before you see the production. For example:

  The director developed the idea of Coriolanus as a strong, Mafia-type character, using an ensemble of actors to represent the army/pack. The choreography of the ensemble was regimented and unified, enhancing the idea that they were a strong, well-drilled male unit.
  (Based on Steven Berkoff's *Coriolanus*, Mermaid Theatre, 1996)

ii) How did the stage picture appear? The stage picture is how the production is actually blocked into the space. The staging may be naturalistic, or it may be stylised. For example:

The director chose to stage Flesh and Blood *in space-specific areas of the stage. The stage picture created in the intimacy of the living room, stage left, depicted a family who were used to order and routine, but who lived isolated lives. Each character kept to his or her own chair and never used another's, highlighting the isolated existence of the farming family, however close they were in blood.*
(Based on Mike Alfred's production of *Flesh and Blood* by Philip Osment, 1996)

iii) What struck you about the character interpretation? It is often difficult to know the relative degrees of director and actor input into the interpretation. One question you may ask is: is the acting style of the actors unified? If not, why? Is it to do with the function of a certain character, or is it due to the personality or star status of the actor? For example:

The actor playing Constance in The Three Musketeers *played the role with the naivety of an inexperienced actress. This was a deliberate interpretation by the director, because the fictitious company presenting the show were supposed to be semi-professional; the 'actress' was completely new to the profession.*
(Based on Marina Calderone's production of *The Three Musketeers*, 1996)

iv) What was the tempo–rhythm of the production? (See the section on tempo–rhythms above, pp.103–104, and Magni, pp.95–96.) For example:

The tempo–rhythm of The Changing Room *reflected the subject matter of the play: a rugby match. As the conversation flew from one player to the next, it was like watching the ball being passed from player to player in a match. In the opening of Act III, there is the excitement after the match. The rhythm of the speech is light and full of banter, but it is not as charged as in the pre-match scenes in Act II. The atmosphere of the post-match 'aftermath' slows the tempo.*
(Based on James Macdonald's production of *The Changing Room* by David Storey, 1996)

ANNOTATED BIBLOGRAPHY

This bibliography includes volumes relevant to this chapter which are considered suitable for student research. See also the general bibliography on p.380.

Bradby, D. and Williams, D., *Directors' Theatre*, Macmillan Modern Dramatist, 1988
>   An excellent book for research on particular innovative directors.

Braun, E., *The Director and the Stage*, Methuen 1987
>   A succinct introduction to the work of selected directors. Gives an idea of the changing emphasis of the role.

Johnstone, K., *Impro: Improvisation and the Theatre*, Eyre Methuen, 1981
>   An accessible book, full of useful ideas and exercises for a workshop context.

Marowitz, C., *Prospero's Staff*, Indiana Studies in Theatre and Drama, 1986
>   An interesting introduction and chapter on the definition of the director. A fairly general resource book.

McCafferey, M., *A Phaidon Theatrical Manual: Directing a Play* (series editor David Mayer) Phaidon Press Ltd, 1988
>   See p.378 for details.

Miller, A., *'Salesman' in Beijing*, Methuen, 1991
>   A fascinating account of the directing process from Miller's diaries.

Ratcliffe, M., *Platform Papers: Directors*, The Royal National Theatre, 1993
>   This is good if you are interested in the views and productions of the three directors included, but is quickly dated, as it focuses on particular productions.

Rea, K.A., *Better Direction*, Calouste Gulbenkian Foundation, 1989
>   Good for brief historical background on directors. Looks at the director in relation to the professional business.

Stafford-Clark, M., *Letters to George*, Nick Hern Books, 1990
>   An excellent insight into the trials and tribulations of a professional director.

Stanislavski, K., *An Actor Prepares*, Methuen, 1991
>   Rather long-winded.

Stanislavski, K., *Building a Character*, Methuen, 1991
>   As above.

4 Collaboration: Devising Group Work

Sara Liles and Sally Mackey

Group-devised pieces of theatre are standard for most advanced practical theatre courses. Sometimes, these are based around texts or theatre periods. More often, a group is expected to devise its own theatrical or combined arts piece, demonstrating an ability to work collaboratively and with theatrical awareness.

This chapter seeks to offer information for students involved in group practical projects. It comprises the following topics:

- An introduction to collaborative devised theatre
- Collaborative devised theatre in history
- Interviews with contemporary professional companies
- A practical guide to collaborative devised work

AN INTRODUCTION TO COLLABORATIVE DEVISED THEATRE

Collaborative devised theatre is created by the company.

The term 'collaborative' refers to a negotiated group process where three or more people work as a collective or co-operative company in an amateur or professional capacity. Collaborative *devised* theatre implies that the work is original and created by the company. It may contain extracts of previously published work such as music, playtexts, novels, short stories, poems or journal articles.

It is organic.

This form of theatre demands an organic process; it is evolutionary by nature. If a script is produced, one person may write it, or several people may write sections. However, it will be a result of extensive group experimentation. This creative process is unique and differs from the more prescribed roles usual in non-devised theatrical forms. Occasionally, a scriptwriter is employed to work with the company.

It evolves over time.

The continual evolution intrinsic to such a process allows the piece to be 'living' theatre. By this, we mean that it can constantly change, even during its performance run. A sense of freedom in the work encourages flexibility, with a resulting immediacy and sense of growth.

Improvisation is key.

Improvisation is always an important aspect of collaborative devised theatre. This is usually undertaken as part of the devising, creating process. Occasionally, however, improvisation is used within the performance, as well.

There are common characteristics of collaborative devised theatre.

There are certain characteristics of this form of theatre which are common to many pieces. Frequently, such work:

● addresses topical social, cultural and/or political issues;
● experiments with form and style and is inventive and innovative;
● uses other art forms, such as music;
● challenges the audience's perceptions;
● is associated with fringe theatre spaces and is performed in diverse venues (the Edinburgh Fringe Festival in August sees thousands of performances in an eclectic range of venues, from the Assembly Rooms to a tiny bubble tent erected in a cobbled courtyard: see pp.3–4 for further information);
● 'is transient and ephemeral, which makes the documentation of the form difficult' (Oddey, *Devising Theatre*, p.21);
● is minimalist in its production values, especially technically, as many companies tour their work. However, the design realisation is often fully integrated into the conception of the piece as the devising process facilitates this;
● is multi-roled. Actors double up parts, because companies are small and because of the style of the work. In addition, small companies need multi-skilled members who can, for example, construct a set, play an instrument and drive a van, as well as perform a role;
● is poorly funded. The unknown element of the work and the lack of documentation do not assist funding applications;
● is site-specific and/or audience-specific;
● lacks star status.

COLLABORATIVE DEVISED THEATRE IN HISTORY

First rituals were a form of early collaborative devised theatre.

From the first rituals onwards, there are many examples of this form of theatre. The need for a collective dramatic experience and for performance has existed since the time of the earliest civilisations. Paintings of early humankind give us accounts of such activity. For example, in southwest France, markings on the walls of the Trois Frères caves suggest that people took on the garb of animals, impersonating them in a form of ritualistic dance. Possibly this was to recreate a hunt for, and with, fellow members of the community.

As there are few records of such rituals, it is difficult to confirm the exact nature of these early forms of collaborative devised theatre. However, they clearly had a specific purpose.

Ritual, which is common to all ancient religions, derives from the belief that the imitation of an action can have a bearing on the action itself. The imitation of rain, or sound of rain, was thought likely to make it rain, for example . . . Agricultural communities believed that the wooing of the Spring Queen by the Corn King was necessary to ensure the success of the spring sowing.
(Allen, *A History of Theatre in Europe*, p.7)

Of particular relevance is the fact that rituals were both participatory and topical; here, 'collaboration' often extended to the whole community, and the rituals addressed issues that preoccupied that community. (See pp.26 and 321 for further references to ritual.)

The earliest theatre was improvised by the performers.

Devised and collaborative drama has its roots in ritual. It can also be traced to the ancient Greeks. As Aristotle noted in *The Poetics*, in Dorian Greece (sixth century BC), small companies of masked actors improvised rude comedy scenes based on the experiences and concerns of the townspeople; this was *before* the great Greek tragedies were written. These devised scenes are likely to have been burlesque in quality and would have contained elements of variety acts, such as acrobatics.

Guild plays of the Middle Ages are further examples.

Aspects of collaborative devised theatre can be seen in many periods of theatre history. From the early part of the 14th century, the trade guilds devised their own versions of Bible stories for performance in the town square as part of the great mystery cycles. As with all devising theatre companies, they would create stories that were central to their own preoccupations and interests: the shipwrights would perform the Noah's Ark story, for example. (See pp.27–28 and 210–213.) Centuries later,

Shakespeare gives us accounts of devising in the 16th/17th century.

Shakespeare's *Hamlet* has the Players redrafting an old play, *The Marriage of Gonzago*, and in *A Midsummer Night's Dream* Bottom and company devise a play around the story of Pyramus and Thisbe. These references suggest the presence of such professional and amateur devising companies in the late 16th and early 17th centuries. Both these 'plays within plays' are produced in response to topical events immediately concerning the performers.

Bouffants were less famous devisers.

There are less famous examples, as well. In Europe in the Middle Ages, *Bouffants*, or 'buffoons', were physically disfigured people who were sent away from their own towns for displeasing society by their appearance and their inability to contribute to the everyday work of the community. They would form bands of 'entertainers', living in the surrounding rural areas, who were allowed to come and perform to the townsfolk on special occasions, amusing them with rough skills and simple devised scenarios. Some *Bouffants* became well known; the Prado Museum in Madrid has three tiny portraits of southern European *Bouffants*, who must have gained sufficient reputation to be painted.

Commedia dell' Arte is a famous example of theatre that is collaborative and devised.

Europe of the 15th, 16th and 17th centuries was home to a more famous form of collaborative devised theatre: *Commedia dell' Arte*. Roughly translated as 'comedy of the professional artists or actors', the genre was Italian by birth and in nature. *Commedia dell' Arte* comprised improvised storylines with stock characters, many of whom were masked. Traditional *Commedia* characters are: Arlecchino, who became Harlequin in Britain; *Il Dottore*, the doctor, an elderly cuckold; Pantalone, the miserly old man; the lovers (various names); *Il Capitano*, swaggering, boastful and probably cowardly; *zanni*, servants. Actors tended to specialise in one mask, developing and honing that particular character.

115

The Rejects tour to a number of small-scale venues.

Q What types of venue does the company perform in?

Anybody who will have us, really! Arts centres, theatres, small scale, under-200 seaters really, although we are starting to play to bigger venues at the moment. Village halls are a very important circuit at the moment. A third of our work is village halls.

Q Can you talk a little bit more about that?

Cheshire, Lancashire, Scotland, Nottinghamshire, for example, are starting to bring together village communities who aren't getting any theatre. They send us, and other companies as well, who are small-scale, professional companies. We go into village halls, take our own lights, take our own sound, and actually set up in these places where the community are used to going. People are being given theatre and they don't have to go to professional theatres.

Q In this book, we look at 1960s/70s fringe theatre, and that had very much the same ethos. You took theatre to the community; the more unusual the space the better, in a way.

Yes. I am a bit hesitant, because I would never want to get away from the joy you can get if you go to a theatre as well, because there is something different. Going to your community hall to see a piece of theatre is fine, and I wholeheartedly agree that, yes, people are given theatre and it's great and it should be somewhere they accept and somewhere where they don't have to feel out of place, but there's a great joy in feeling out of place sometimes, to give you that added boost. It doesn't mean you have to pay big-price tickets. It doesn't mean it should be the West End of London.

Q Is there a particular design style that's used, or does that evolve out of the nature of the work?

The design has to be based on the fact that we can fit it into a van along with four people! Anything more than that is no good. We design something that is simple but can be used in a number of different ways.

Design impetus can be crucial for the devising process.

With *Crumble*, we had ladders. We played on stepladders and a plank. That was half the fun of devising. You get ladders in the devising thing, and you swing them about and you stand on them, you stand under them, you pick them up, you make a boat, you make a plane, and you see what you can do. Almost the entire show of *Crumble* is based on the fact that we picked up ladders and played about with them.

With *Peasouper*, we said, 'Let's have screens on either side, and then let's have a cloth at the back.' We developed by saying, 'We have a cloth, but we'd like to stand on it. So let's make it a box. If it's a box, let's see if we can crawl through it, so let's make it a hollow box,' and that was that. We could then spend three weeks seeing if we could stand on this, crawl under it, appear between it, push the boxes apart.

Q The company consists of three performers. What do their roles entail?

For the first five years of the company, the roles of the company were

As with Kneehigh, members of the company have to be flexible.

completely interchangeable, in that we all ran the company. We ran it from Anne's front room for four years. We answered the letters. We wrote out funding forms. We went to visit people. We devised all together. We paid ourselves exactly the same as each other, as we do now. It developed that I enjoyed writing and could write, and so I ended up doing the writing; David plays music, so he does the music, and so on. Since January [1996], we've employed a full-time company manager, so things are changing. She has taken over most of the administrative work.

Q **Does the company have a specific education policy?**
Education is about a third of what we do. It really is a fairly important part of our remit. We're performers, not teachers, but we like taking workshops and are becoming quite good at it; now we are trying to focus these workshops at the age range with which we work best.

Q **Do you have any ideas at the moment about the future of the company?**
We are hoping that the company expands. Anne, David and myself live, eat, sleep Rejects, and have done so for the past five or six years. At the moment, we are taking a two-month break, which is the first period longer than two weeks that we have spent apart from each other in six years, and it's worked very well. We get on with each other, we enjoy each other's company, we have outside friends and we have managed to put a lot of work into the company, and so we have come on very well. What we need to do is start looking at the other skills and the outside skills we have. I want to be writing for radio. David wants to do a bit more music. Anne wants to act with other companies. We all want to involve other people, but we hope to do that within the guise of the Rejects.

The future revolves around further productions and expansion.

We are going to do at least one other show, devising show, when we will work with Bim Mason again, which we will take up to the Edinburgh Fringe and which we will tour. I think after that we will start using other actors and possibly use other formats and start combining with other companies to see what we can come up with – just playing about, having more fun. Devising is fun, and it is fun to be in there with nothing but your imagination and a couple of planks – that's great. Sometimes maybe it's good to step out of that and do Shakespeare and then go back to doing the two-plank stuff. So it's open.

Gavin Robins, a member of Legs on the Wall

Background
Legs on the Wall is an Australian company, which first performed in the UK at the 1996 Edinburgh Fringe Festival. Its production was entitled *All of Me*. This company is unique in its conception of using acrobatics and circus skills as a theatrical medium for communicating with an audience. The linking of form and content in *All of Me* is a superb example of collaborative devised theatre.

127

All of Me is about having children, losing children, behaving like children. Narratively it follows a nuclear 1940s family – a mother and father, their little boy and his baby sister who dies – and their changing from closeknit joy to desperate clinging need.
(*The Times*, August 1996)

Just extraordinary . . . Legs on the Wall more than lives up to its name with a gravity-defying spectacle that combines physical theatre skills with a rare emotional eloquence.
(the *Guardian*, August 1996)

. . . it is inspired . . . What is phenomenal about this company is that their acrobatic feats, throwing themselves from great heights into each other's arms, are searingly charged with emotion and dramatic meaning.
(*The Times*, August 1996)

The four performing members of the Legs on the Wall company

Legs on the Wall started with circus skills, acrobatics and magic.

The company is publicly and privately funded.

Q **Why was the company formed?**

The original members were actually buskers; they were doing a lot of clowning workshops and different styles of street performance back then. They were using circus skills and juggling and some acrobatics; they ended up winning the 1985 Australian Busking Award, or something like it! That took them into more interesting work. Circus Oz is often quoted as a direct influence on Legs on the Wall, because they were one of the groups that were using circus skills and techniques in more of a theatrical convention. And Legs on the Wall were interested in taking that use of circus skills – particularly physical theatre – the use of acrobatics and balance acrobatics – to explore a theatrical narrative. Trying to work on new techniques and breaking new boundaries physically – this is what we want to do.

Q **How are you funded?**

By the Australian Council, mainly, and also the New South Wales Ministry of the Arts, but we also do corporate work, which enables us to kind of make more money. For example, BMW or Telecom might ask for an aerial show. A lot of our work we do is outdoor aerial work. We use harnesses and rescue equipment and do choreography off the side of buildings and things like that.

  The company has made the decision this year to put everyone on wages: a full-time administrator and four performers. As much as that's a risk, we see it as an investment, because it's the only way that we can keep ourselves supported financially to train each day, which we need to do, to work in the office and to perform. Whereas it gets difficult when you're doing obviously project-to-project funding, which is how the company has worked in the past.

Q You've said there are five members of the company – the administrator and four performers. Is that always the composition?
Yes. Entering the international market, I think it's more important, maybe, to make our next show at least five performers on the stage, just to create a bigger scale of performance. I think it opens up choreographic possibilities with more members than just four.

Q In terms of the organisation of the company, do you have many roles? Are you just performers, or do you take on other functions as well?
No, to administrate this company is definitely more than a one-person job, so we often do training in the morning and in the afternoon we're in the office, if we're not rehearsing. On one hand, it is difficult to balance the physical training with the administration, but there is the other side that we as performers are artistic controllers, and we employ directors, we employ designers, we employ production teams, so we have that artistic control. Unfortunately, often the financial decisions and administrative decisions of the company are in opposition to the artistic needs, and so therefore you do get that struggle.

Again, company members have to be flexible.

Q Can you give me an example?
I remember one time when we needed to cut our budget a bit, because we were going over budget. And we said, 'Right, we'll cut the design slightly.' So we'd tell the designer, and then suddenly you're in this terrible confrontation with the designer. As a performer, you don't want to have to deal with it. You think, 'I don't want to jeopardise our relationship here: we're in the precarious process of creating a work, and now we're arguing about money.' The administrative side of the company is saying, 'We've got to cut, and this is an area that we can

Artistic and administrative responsibility can clash at times.

cut, and the designer will just have to make do.' And as a performer I was saying, 'The design is really crucial, especially for this show; we want to work with design *more*', or 'We can't jeopardise the relationship with this designer. And this is an important project. If this project doesn't come off we mightn't get funding for the next round.' There is that real dilemma where you're caught in the middle. Often the administrative needs are in opposition to the creative needs, and so it is difficult. At the same time, I think it is important to keep in perspective what both needs are.

A move from Legs on the Wall's All of Me

129

The company members are all highly skilled physical performers.

Serious physical training is part of the company's routine.

Q **What are the skills of the company?**

Most of the members have had a very substantial physical history in terms of being either excellent sportspeople or good gymnasts or dancers or acrobats in the past. There was one member of the company who didn't really have so much of a background, and you can't teach that when you need to be performing next month. It takes a lifetime to develop.

For training, we do a lot of flexibility work, a lot of stretching, and then we work on fundamentals of handstands and getting the strength up. Then we have just a general repertoire of balances and balance acrobatics that we use and we've seen. We always try to deconstruct the balances and make them more interesting. This gets on to the notion of devising work, because I feel that the training and the practical approach to training is very much linked to devising; the language *informs* what you say theatrically. One of us might be in the middle of a balance and we'll say, 'That looks like someone really taking control of you, but you're trying not to let them.' So you can see almost a little bit of a story evolving through the balance. I have noticed that we've been much more interested in the ways into and the ways out of balances and that whole area of 'contact improvisation' explored by similar companies like La, La, La, Human Steps [a Canadian company].

Q **What sort of work had you done before *All of Me*?**

The company worked more in a revue style or cabaret style, where there was a lot of comedy involved. We would have juggling, fire eating, balance acrobatics and trapeze work, magic – there was quite a bit of illusion work. [One of the company is a magician.] We try to use these techniques in an analogy way, so that there's a story, with definite characters that are developing their relationships with other people: characters that juggle together, then balance on top of each other according to a situation of danger, for example.

Q **How was *All of Me* devised?**

Devising work has led the company away from a revue format to more serious storytelling.

The company have been moving away from comedy into how we can use the drama, or use the techniques in more of a dramatic sense. It mightn't always deal with frivolous situations or comedy situations, but it could also reveal certain things about human life and the experiences that we go through every day: they're not always joyful. The proposal for *All of Me* was to explore the theme of the extremes of human bonding. Nigel [Jamieson, the director] was working with the company and finding ways of pushing each other to their limits – to their physical and emotional limits – exploring to what extent we rely on each other as people in life, what are our thresholds of trust, and all of those kind of themes. Using a family unit made perfect sense, with Bernadette [Regan, a member of the company] being so small and like a tenacious child. There was the caring big brother and the passionate mother and father, wanting to push each other to those limits. It seemed like the perfect scenario for that theme to be communicated. Everyone relates to at least one of the characters in the piece, because of their experience in life. So the piece explores the joys of family life and the joys of human trust and bonding, as well as the disintegration of values and trust and human bonding within the family unit.

Q **Having started with that, how did the storyline develop?**
There was a writer on the process, Mary Morris. The company have a few problems with the role of a writer in a physical theatre company, when often you're saying one thing physically and it's very clear. To reiterate it vocally doesn't seem necessary, or if we want to say something different are we creating more ambiguities than it's worth? At the same time, I think the writing helped frame the scenes, indicating that this is a scene in its entirety, this is another scene in its entirety. [The few lengthy speeches in the show came at the end of 'scenes'.] The writing helped set up that idea of the flash-forward convention that's used in the play, as well. Some people find the non-linear structure confusing, and other people really enjoyed the ambiguity of it. I think it's always an interesting thing to keep the audience working to some extent; that's partly the reason for that episodic structure.

Working with a writer as well has been a new development which has led to different methods of working.

Q **The episodic structure allowed for the extremely powerful motif of the dead child to return throughout the piece.**
Yes. On the one hand, we have a scene like 'Second Steps' [the child develops her ability to walk: Regan 'walked' on the bodies and hands of the 'family'], which is full of life, with the child running over people, and then from that vitality she falls into a lump of dead bones. I think that's something in physical theatre that can work so powerfully. There is the sheer life force in movement and the physical risks taken. As an audience, we watch them, we revel in it – and then to see death in someone's body, which was just so active, does seem to work a lot better, I feel, than poetry can in some ways.

A single motif can bind a piece and add theatrical resonance.

Q **Where do you think the company will go on to next?**
Creating a new theatre work, a vibrant piece of theatre. We do want to pursue our outdoor stuff, but I think our passion lies definitely in theatre work, creating a new theatre show, and also some work for video, some physical theatre specifically designed for video or film makers, working with us to create that effect. But it's something that you can't just jump into. You have to work with somebody who's very experienced in that way to be able to recreate, or heighten even, what you are doing on stage. It's really hard, producing such a successful show, to then totally put that aside and go on and create one that's equally successful. It just doesn't happen like that, and I think that's why we've given ourselves three or four months' creative development for this next show, to really explore a lot of things.

A PRACTICAL GUIDE TO COLLABORATIVE DEVISED WORK

The aim of this section is to give guidelines for the various phases of group projects. It is based on research done with many students who have already undertaken such projects; their advice and comments have been included in the margins.

Phase 1: Basic considerations

These considerations are divided up as follows:
- Considering external factors
- Initial preparation for group work
- Starting points
- Allocation of job responsibilities

Considering external factors

There are a number of external factors which will influence the nature of your collaborative devised piece *before* you start working. It is worth considering these before developing a piece of theatre.

1. Assessment criteria

Assessment criteria will channel and focus your work. Assessment usually focuses on three main areas: process, product and evaluation. The following are typical requirements.

You are likely to be assessed on your process.

In terms of **process,** students are assessed upon their ability to:
- demonstrate an understanding of the collaborative nature of the theatrical process;
- contribute to the process of development;
- do research, for example on issues and themes, theatrical style and the target audience;
- 'recognise dramatic potential in a range and variety of sources, select, use and develop these for the performance' (ULEAC A-level Drama, p.10).

You will be assessed on the product.

In terms of **product,** students are assessed on their ability to:
- use appropriate styles and coherence of form to communicate with the target audience;
- achieve original work of performance standard.

It is possible that you might also be assessed on your ability to demonstrate an awareness of the interactive nature of the performing arts by combining the disciplines (where appropriate).

You will also be assessed on your evaluation.

Students are also assessed on their ability to:
- evaluate the devising, collaborative process and use this evaluation in the ongoing work;
- evaluate and reflect critically upon the effectiveness of the performance and its communication with the audience;

- contextualise their own work and its significance in relationship to similar contemporary and/or historical forms, if appropriate.

2. Time available
Ascertain:
- the time available for rehearsals;
- the performance dates;
- the required length of the piece.

3. Rehearsal space
Appropriate rehearsal space must be available and set up in accordance with the group's needs.

4. Funding
Be aware of any budget available. Consider applying for sponsorship to boost your budget.

Initial preparation for group work
Before you enter fully into the collaborative devising process, there is a certain amount of initial preparation to be undertaken.

1. Research into past and current practice
Look at past examples of collaborative theatre, identifying the key characteristics of both historical and contemporary ensemble groups (see pp.113–131). In addition, carry out some research into recent amateur or professional group projects that have taken place at or near your college or school, in order to avoid close repetition of theme or concept in your own work.

2. Advice from visiting practitioners
Whilst such support may have to depend on funding and budgets, external workshops can be invaluable for raising the group's awareness of such areas as script writing, methods of delivering a storyline, narrative, physicality in performance, mask work and so on.

3. Initial group activities
In collaborative group work, certain social skills are essential to assist the smooth running of the process; these include trust, humour, negotiation, generosity, flexibility, creativity, lateral thinking, sensitivity and awareness. Whilst it may be difficult to switch on these skills automatically, it is certainly possible to work on developing them as part of the preparation for the project.

In the initial stages of working closely with a group, whether familiar or unfamiliar, any number of improvisation exercises can be used to develop rapport and a suitably constructive working atmosphere. All students are likely to have worked in this manner before, but you may wish to refer to some of the exercises in Chapter 1, which focus on teamwork and group unity. (See 'Group count', 'Tag debate', 'Positive greetings', 'The seated group circle' and 'The group as jigsaw', pp.10–13.)

Student advice:
You are about to be working intensely for quite a period of time; people are bound to get annoyed and tempers will probably fray. Develop a thick skin quickly, and if you feel a grievance deal with it calmly.

Student comment:
Initially, the group's energy levels were very low; we weren't much of a 'group' or a 'team'.

133

Starting points

Re-read the interviews with Kneehigh, Rejects Revenge and Legs on the Wall. It is clear from these that there is no set or 'correct' starting point for collaborative devised theatre. Here we identify some potential starting points you might consider.

Starting points vary greatly.

1. Audience research

Consider your audience first, if you know what it will be.

Consider the audience's expectations and the likely reception. The audience might be a particular group: women prisoners or primary-school children, for example. This will affect your choice of ideas.

For example, a group of students recently worked on a TYP (Theatre for Young People) project for primary schools. The primary-school teachers had suggested the Victorians as the general topic, as it was part of the National Curriculum. The students wished to devise their own piece, so they took 'Victorian tales of the imagination' as the genre in which they would work, responding to the needs of the audience. *Alice in Wonderland* is an example of this genre. (For further information on working in TYP, see Chapter 7.)

If the audience is likely to be amorphous, the starting point is less clear and it would be better to look for other routes into the project.

Undertake audience research.

If appropriate, conduct more precise audience research. Interview and/or question the target audience. For example, the following questions were included in a questionnaire given to an audience of female prisoners prior to a devised performance by students:

● What is your experience and knowledge of the theatre?
● Do you watch any particular style of television programme?
● What issues are most important to you at present?
● If you had a choice, would you prefer to see a piece of straight drama, or a performance which includes other art forms, such as dance or music?

Clearly, this is quite a general questionnaire, but it was geared towards a potentially unconventional audience, and the students wished to keep the questions inoffensive.

Undertake research by identifying common features of the kind of theatre your audience would normally see.

Another form of audience research would be to go and see examples of the style of theatre your likely audience would choose to watch. For example, students working on a children's theatre project recently watched a number of such shows, and collated this list of common features, which they used in their devising process and when making decisions about form and content:

● Costumes and make-up were attention-grabbing and attractive.
● Audience participation was important.
● Images were very clear and repetitive.
● The productions were energetic, not static.
● There were not many long speeches.

- There were not many sub-plots.
- The action was easy to follow, with recognisable entities: people, concepts (e.g. good and evil) and so on.
- There were firm character types and contrasting characters.
- Imaginative leaps could be made, with instant acceptance.
- Sick humour was popular!

If the venue is known, this affects early decisions.

Consider the venue or performance space from the audience's point of view. This will affect the choice of topic, as well as form and content. An intimate studio space would be inappropriate for a piece of melodrama, for example.

Match the piece to the audience.

When you have selected an idea, you should return to considering the audience. Is the idea suitable? Will it offend? Is it likely to enlighten and entertain? What do you hope the audience will take away from the piece? Discuss early ideas with potential members of the audience; ideas can be changed easily at this stage.

Ensure there is an audience.

If you do not have a captive audience, start working on publicising your piece more fully once you know the content. If it is an in-house piece for an examination, ensure that you have an audience. It is worth spending some time inviting a good audience at an early stage (see p.139).

2. The nature of the group
At this stage, it is worth undertaking an analysis of the group members' knowledge and experience of appropriate skills, and discovering which skills they wish to develop. Below is an example of a grid sheet that might be used.

Know the group's strengths and interests.

Name	Music skills S = sing; I = instrument; MD = musical director	Craft skills	Technical SM = stage management; LX = lights; FX = sound	Wish to perform	Additional skills	Dance; movement C = choreography; W = warm-up	Wish to develop
Lisa	S; I (guitar)			Y		D; C	props; dance
Paul	S			Y	stilts + juggling	D (African)	physical theatre
Shenghi	S; I (piano + violin)	stagecraft		don't mind			LX; design; SM
Costas	S	props	SM, LX, FX	Y	writing	rave	music
Janie	S	costume; props	LX; SM	Y	physical theatre	D	singing
Sarah				Y		D; W	performing; like to write
Sita	S			Y			singing
Muhammed	S	props	SM	Y		D	movement and voice
David	S; I (piano); MD			Y	sung for big bands	D	craft skills
Shaun	S	art		N		D; W	set; props; costume

Balance skills and desires in the group.

Balance the individuals' wishes to experiment and extend their own skills against the need to utilise their strengths as fully as possible in order to create a skilled and effective piece of drama.

3. Developing ideas

You may have a general idea already, or, at least, certain parameters.

Your topic area may have been decided for you, as with the TYP piece on Victorian tales of the imagination above. You may have a clear idea of the likely audience reception, and you may have undertaken extensive audience research. You may know that your venue is a marquee without electricity, as part of a summer festival at your school. All these will give you parameters for selecting an idea.

You will have certain information to help you at the outset of a project.

If you are starting without any such frameworks, choosing an idea can be the most awkward stage of the process. However, you *will* know the 'external factors': the assessment criteria, the time available, the rehearsal space and the funding. You will have undertaken initial preparation, including working on initial group activities and researching into recent projects. It is possible that you will have received assistance and support from visiting professionals. Also, you should have thought about your potential audience, in however limited a manner. You will have identified the strengths and interests of your group. All these factors will influence your ideas, although they may slip to the back of your mind temporarily. Perhaps it is right that this happens, as the creative energies of the group may be stifled otherwise. Below is a series of suggestions for initiating group project ideas.

It is clear from the interviews with professional companies that *the most effective way of initiating ideas is to 'play'*. Refer to Shepherd, p.119, Hibberd, pp.124–125 and Robins, pp.130–131; in addition, refer to Magni, pp.93–94, Wright, pp.81–83 and Verma, pp.91–92. However, 'play' can be daunting for many, so begin by doing the exercises in Chapter 1 on pp.10–17 and Activity 2 in Chapter 3, pp.104–106. These will help you initiate your work.

When it comes to selecting the specific topic, there are various methods you may wish to use. For instance, each member of the group might select his or her own area of interest, or the group may have had a topic in mind for a while. A third option is that a list of topics is provided for you. These might run along the following lines:

You may be given certain sample ideas.

- Exiles and refugees
- Equal opportunities for women
- The Industrial Revolution
- War
- The Seven Deadly Sins
- Invention
- Time
- The unexplained
- Modern times
- Animal rights

- Too many cooks
- The King's Cross fire

Alternatively, you may be given more general suggestions:

- adaptation of a novel;
- characters from a piece of literature taken out of context;
- a biography of a real or fictional person;
- interpretation or adaptation of a poem;
- building a topical event from newspaper articles;
- interpretation of works such as paintings or cartoons into a drama;
- interpretation of pieces of music into a drama;
- objects that create a story.

A fourth option is that you might be given a list of starting points by an examination board, as in the following examples:

- Not waving, but drowning
- The poems of Roger McGough
- Wilderness
- The myth of Icarus
- *Guernica* by Picasso
- $e = mc^2$
- A modern fairytale
- 'Woe to the land that's governed by a child!'
- Ritual of life
- Uneasy lies the head that wears a crown

(UCLES AS and A-level Performing Arts, 1995, p.27)

Develop ideas individually.

Each person could do research around a topic that appeals to him or her, bringing in relevant 'documentation' (see pp.142–144). For example, if the topic area was 'Equal opportunities for women', the research might include newspaper cuttings covering a trial on sexual harassment, an extract from a video on women in the workplace, and names and addresses of organisations that would be useful for further research. This research could be accompanied by a broad scenario for the piece, or suggested scenarios for fragments of the piece, devised by the student who has investigated the topic.

Student comment: We spent too long discussing at the beginning of the project.

Student comment: We should have written down more, as often ideas were forgotten and we all became very disheartened with what we had.

If you have worked individually so far, you should now make a group decision, narrowing down the choice to one or two of the proposed ideas. Start practical experimentation immediately. One successful method of approaching this is for each student or pair to devise a short drama exercise or session that involves the group working practically on a topic. Once all these have been done, the group decides which ideas offer the most practical potential, given the members' experience.

All thoughts and ideas should be logged in writing at these early stages. It is worth keeping both individual and group files which can act as resources later (see pp.17–20). Trying ideas out practically, as soon as

137

possible, is highly recommended. Do not talk for too long, but do keep a record of your activities.

Allocation of job responsibilities

Another important early step is to allocate tasks to different members of the group, where appropriate. These tasks may include audience liaison and booking the venue, organising funding, publicity, set design, props, lighting, sound, costume, make-up, direction, script writing and researching. While many of these tasks may involve the whole group, it is advisable to have one person who co-ordinates the various elements involved in each area. These are listed below. (See pp.170–180 and 349–353 for further information about roles and responsibilities in theatre.)

Audience liaison and venue booking

● Co-ordinate audience research, as discussed above (see pp.134–135).

● Book specific dates for performances, whether touring or in-house. The management may require a deposit or payment in advance.

● Consider the following points. Is (are) the venue(s) physically appropriate for the piece? It is worth visiting the venue(s) at this stage. Take photographs for the benefit of the rest of the group and take measurements of the space. Check the technical equipment. If you are doing a minimalist touring piece, a venue might have basic equipment that you can use, such as a tape recorder. Is this worth utilising? Are there sockets in appropriate places? Are there facilities for lighting? If you are taking lights, is there enough power to supply them? If you are thinking of simple scenery, will it fit through the doors? If the venue is outdoors, consider the implications of weather. Is it possible to do the show in bad weather? Can you waterproof everything satisfactorily? If it is windy, will the design be appropriate? (See the excellent book about Welfare State International, Coult and Kershaw (eds), *Engineers of the Imagination*, for further ideas about outdoor and community theatre.)

● Liaise with the potential venue and audience: this is crucial to the success of the project, and should begin at an early stage. It is important even if this is an in-house piece. For example, will there be silence around the performance area at the time(s) of the showing(s)?

● Liaise with other people or bodies, such as tutors, about dates and venues, as appropriate.

● Continue to communicate with the venue about specific details, including the length and nature of the performance, the amount and shape of space you need to have at your disposal, the size of the cast, the nature of the set and so on.

● Consider the availability of rehearsal space, and whether you can rehearse in your performance venue(s).

Organising funding

- Estimate a budget for the work.

- Allocate one person to hold the budget.

- Investigate sponsorship from local companies, or further afield.

- Acknowledgement of any external help (financial or other) should be given in the performance programme.

Publicity

- Is there a local radio station that would be prepared to interview you to help advertise your production?

- Can you team up with a photographer to produce a press release for the local paper?

- What possibilities are there for performing extracts of your piece publicly? For example, look out for any imminent local street festivals or charity events that might welcome an extract from your performance.

- Circulate posters as early as possible to increase public awareness of your work. Consider designing t-shirts with the necessary information for effective advertisement.

- Organise tickets and programmes. Allow time for updating and proof-reading the programme.

Direction

The group may decide to direct the drama collectively, within the devising and polishing process. Alternatively, certain individuals may be allocated specific scenes to work on, especially if they possess expertise in those particular areas. Remember to utilise the skills and knowledge of individuals in the group to their full potential. For example, if you have an experienced dancer in the group, you may want to suggest that he or she concentrates on the movement element of the performance.

It is worth remembering that the piece being devised must remain 'collaborative'. It may not be appropriate for one individual to direct the work throughout the process; however, consider the needs of the particular project. Re-read the interview with Tim Hibberd, particularly pp.124–125, where he talks about the need for an outside eye, and the interview with John Wright, pp.84–85, where he describes the stages of the process and how the director acts as a mirror.

Set design, props and stage management

- Develop your ideas for the visual aspects of the performance as the devising progresses. The set will need to be designed at the same time as the piece is created to ensure coherence between style and content. (See Lloyd, p.73, on the problems created if this does not happen.) You are advised to keep the set simple.

- Do you need to research a particular period in depth to give authenticity to your set?

- How flexible does your set need to be? Will it have to withstand being constantly dismantled and reconstructed if you are planning to take your production on tour? Is the size of your set appropriate and effective for your chosen venue(s)?

- Are you going to need to set aside valuable time for the group to work on the set collectively?

- What props are needed? Consider visiting junk and charity shops, circulating an 'items wanted' list and placing classified advertisements.

See Chapter 8 for details about the stage management role and further information on set design.

Sound
- Your group may have specific needs concerning the use of sound in the performance. Any decisions should be a part of the initial devising process, intrinsic to the development of the piece.

- If you need live music, who is going to write it, and are any lyrics needed? Are you able to bring in help from outside the group to help direct this element of the performance, or can you draw upon the group's skills?

- Does somebody need to research and arrange the use of pre-recorded material?

- Will your performance require any kind of microphones, and will these need to be hired?

- How closely do you need to co-ordinate sound and lighting design? What is the relationship between lighting and sound in your performance?

- Arrange all technical requirements early on.

Lighting
- Consider the lighting as part of the overall visual realisation of the piece.

- Is it appropriate to use the expertise of a fellow student from another department?
- The technical element of your performance will depend upon the venues, and on the budget. Look at the equipment available to you and decide whether extra lights, or even special effects, need to be hired.

- Read pp.290–297 for further help in this area.

- Arrange all technical requirements early on.

Costume and make-up

- Develop your ideas as the devising progresses. Experiment at an early stage.

- Do your costumes need to be hired, or borrowed? If this is the case, you will need to consider booking in advance.

- If the garments are going to be specially made, who is doing this?

- If your performance requires the use of masks or puppets, begin to work with them in the early stages of the process. Also, give yourselves plenty of time to make the masks and/or puppets so that they are robust enough to last for the duration of the project.

- Remember the effect of lighting on character make-up, and begin to experiment at an early stage to achieve the desired visual effect.

Script writing

You may want to write up your performance in the form of a script. If this is the case, one person may be made responsible for the collating of dialogue and stage directions. Alternatively, individuals may be responsible for writing short sections as the piece is devised. This script may be submitted as part of your final assessment.

Researching

As mentioned above, research into the audience, the venue, the issues, the historical context and the dramatic style will need to be undertaken in the initial stages by individuals in the group. This collective and individual activity will certainly be a part of the ongoing process, as outlined in the following phase (see below, pp.142–144).

Creating the draft proposal

Once many of the above processes are under way, the group may need to bring together the information acquired and the decisions made. A draft proposal may need to be written, utilising the group's ideas so far. The draft proposal would need to cover such points as:

- the group's overall aim for this project: for example, 'We wish to produce a piece of theatre for senior citizens, which will provide entertainment and enlightenment';
- the estimated budget;
- details about venues;
- other relevant details, according to the project and the group (see Activity 3, p.157).

Producing supporting material

The group may decide to support the theatre piece with additional material and information, such as a teachers' pack, an extended programme offering some of your research material that is relevant to the piece, or an exhibition. Whilst all the members of the group will contribute to this, one person needs to co-ordinate it. This may be part of the responsibility of the publicity co-ordinator.

Phase 2: The process

Having started the project and taken into account the various preliminary points, you will move into the next phase of the work. There are three main areas to consider, some parts of which will run concurrently:

● Research
● Setting targets
● Developing the piece

Researching information directly related to the topic or issue

This is a time-consuming task, so divide it amongst the group members; a comprehensive portfolio can then be gathered. All companies undertake some form of research when they are working on devised theatre. (See Hibberd, p.124, and Wright, p.83, for example.)

Historical research
Key resources for historical research are:

Student advice: Research the period thoroughly and ensure that the performance is historically correct.

● history textbooks;
● diaries and biographies of people living at the time;
● photographs;
● fiction – novels, poetry and films;
● documentary television reports;
● newspaper articles;
● journals;
● paintings.

What local research centres are available to you?

Museums, art galleries, county record offices and libraries may be able to give you access to the above sources of research material.

Be clear about your objectives when compiling information. Ask specific questions. For example, if you were exploring the role of women in the 19th century, you might ask:

Set yourself research objectives.

● Who were the famous women of the 19th century, and what were they famous for?
● How were women in this period of history represented in pieces of art, theatre, novels, news reports and so on?
● What were the expectations of women in both the social and the domestic context?
● How did the 19th-century woman feel about the role that she was expected to fill?

Think laterally for your sources of information.

Thematic research
Your research may be focused on a specific theme, such as the environment. This will require you to contact relevant agencies and organisations to gather the most up-to-date information. For example:

● Interview relevant groups to gather information, such as a representative from the Green Party.

- Locate maps, charts or pamphlets that will give you a broad picture of the situation. For example, you may want to contact the National Trust.

- Target a specific area of your theme, and research one particular organisation in depth, for example the Forestry Commission.

- Use the Yellow Pages for further suggestions on where to look. For example, under 'Environmental Consultants' there is a variety of contacts which may prove useful.

- Television or film documentaries are very thorough in their research, and often refer you to useful information sources.

- Keep your eye on current affairs, on the television and in newspapers.

Literary research

You may be working with a particular literary genre. Identifying the fundamental features of the genre will help you make choices during the devising process.

For example, students working in the genre of Victorian and Edwardian tales of the imagination found these common elements in the stories:

- A magical or fantasy world exists, as in Wonderland, Narnia, Neverland.
- Creatures or animals often possess human qualities. (See the photograph below, where three Victorian children meet a walking, talking coral reef.)
- An object is sometimes used to aid movement to a magical world: there is often a specific way of 'getting in'.
- Grown-ups do not make this journey, unless they are abnormal.

A scene from Land of the Forgotten Tide, *a devised Victorian tale of the imagination. This was performed by students of the Education Department of the Central School of Speech and Drama at the Minack Theatre, Cornwall.*

- Opposing forces of good and evil are often represented by powerful figureheads; the fight between good and evil is all-encompassing.
- Challenges and conflict are integral to the story of some form of quest or journey.
- A clear distinction is made between reality and the other, magical world.
- Mythological creatures often appear.
- Repeated chants or poems assist in magic spells.
- Time does not always pass normally in the magical world; it is often 'suspended'.
- Order and disorder are a recurrent theme, with order always being restored at the end of the tale.
- There is a moral and a happy ending, which shows that something has been gained.
- The characters have appropriate, fitting names.
- Relationships grow between characters from the two worlds; there is sadness at parting.

This research led the students to devise a piece where three Victorian children were transported to a magical world full of mythological creatures. Their task was to find a king and queen and to stop the evil forces in the land.

Theatrical style research

It may be appropriate to undertake research into theatrical styles.

You may wish to research theatrical styles that may suit your devised piece, such as physical theatre, naturalism, pantomime, total theatre, absurdism, mime, expressionism and so on. Again, it is useful to set yourself specific research objectives. Think about compiling a list of the common features that are associated with specific theatrical styles. For example, the list below aims to highlight the common features of performances in the style of physical theatre:

- an extensive use of images throughout the piece;
- the occurrence and recurrence of images and symbols;
- a few actors portraying a number of characters and objects;
- extended gestures and use of voice;
- heightened movement accompanying taut and pointed dialogue;
- originality and experimentation with devised texts or highly visual interpretations of old texts;
- physically demanding, choreographed movement.

In addition, be aware of ongoing developments by building your own theatre experience (see Chapter 1, pp.1–4).

Student comment: We didn't set ourselves targets; we attempted to, and talked about it a lot, but we didn't get down to it.

Setting targets

Setting group targets can seem daunting at the outset of a project. However, it is by far the most effective way of keeping the group on schedule. Although there will be times when you get ahead or fall behind these deadlines, they will form natural short-term 'hurdles' which will help you keep the final stages in sight.

Clearly, the targets will be set according to the needs of the project. We can give only rough guidelines and an example here. In addition, your targets will shift during the process, particularly if you decide to abandon your topic and ideas three weeks into a seven-week project! It is well worth revising your targets periodically.

Identify the first performance and then set a date for your dress, technical and pre-technical rehearsals, and your run-throughs.

Always work backwards. First, you should establish the date of the first performance. After this, you need to set the dates for your dress rehearsal(s), which should preferably be the day before the first performance. (For further details about technical and dress rehearsals, see pp.148–150.)The technical rehearsal should be a day or two prior to the dress rehearsal, and you should leave plenty of time for this. One or two days before the technical rehearsal, you must set time aside to hold a pre-technical rehearsal. Before the pre-technical, allow time to run the piece, non-stop, at least three times.

Break down the remaining time into workable sections.

Divide the remaining rehearsal time according to the length of your piece. For example, you might be preparing a half-hour piece, and have seven weeks' remaining rehearsal time. In this case, you could allow approximately one week for devising and rehearsing each five minutes of the show. Alternatively, if you aim to have a rough draft completed and to have done a rough run-through by the end of week four, three weeks are left for further rehearsals and polishing.

Student comment:
We could have been more organised in terms of planning our time. I think that if we had made better use of our rehearsal times that would have been a great help.

Set targets weekly. For example:

Week 4
Mon am: Run through second quarter (devised in week 3)
Mon pm + Tues am: Devise third quarter
Tues pm: Rough run of third quarter
Wed: Write up script
Thurs am: Third quarter run-through
Thurs pm: First, second and third quarter run-through
Fri: Design realisation day

Student advice:
You've got a short space of time to do a lot of things, so get organised and stick to your plans.

Developing the piece
There is no set format for devised theatre. Every company and every group of people will work differently. We can see this in some of the comments made by Kneehigh, Rejects Revenge and Legs on the Wall, above. As Alison Oddey says:

*The devising process challenges every group member to confront the work, engage with it individually at different levels, as well as developing a sense of group co-operation, affiliation and unity at the same time. **All groups are different** as personalities change the group dynamics and impetus of the work.*
[Our emphasis]
(Oddey, *Devising Theatre*, p.24)

The impetus of the devising process will vary because of the differing composition of each group.

Thus there are few 'givens' in devising theatre; there is no finite set of rules that has to be complied with. In this section, therefore, we offer a few pointers for the early, middle and later stages of devising.

Early devising

- Try ideas out practically as soon as possible. It should be rare for a group to be sitting down and discussing for more than a few minutes at a time.

- Do physical and vocal warm-ups at the beginning of each practical session (and before rehearsals and performances). (See pp.5–10.)

- Elect a chairperson or leader for each session. Decide whether this person is also responsible for planning the practical work.

- If there are some people in the group who have a particular flair and vision for theatrical structure, ideas and so on, allow these people to take the lead at the devising stage. (Everyone has different strengths.)

- When one idea works particularly well in practice, record it closely in writing (as notes or script), or on video or audio tape.

- Consider the design concept as you create the piece. Is the design focus clear? Does it overwhelm the piece or intrude? Is it in harmony with the intentions of the piece? Is there flexibility in the design if you are taking the piece on tour? (For further advice on design, see Chapter 8.) Consider one session where everyone brings in visual material very broadly connected with the topic, to serve as inspiration for design ideas.

- If singing or live music is involved, try this out early on. Learn music as early as possible and practise frequently.

The middle stages of devising

- Concentrate on building the piece. Are you *excited* by it?

- If a session does not seem to be working, finish it by making a clear plan for the next session, which will involve a complete change of direction; leave in a positive frame of mind.

- Each person in the group should have been allotted specific tasks (see above, pp.138–141). Discuss their ideas at regular intervals, with reference to the development of the devised piece.

- Check that you are fulfilling the strengths, expectations and/or desires of the individuals in the group.

- Use your research. Return to it frequently.

- Have you considered specialist help for particular aspects of the piece?

- Go along with quirky ideas, but be strong enough to speak against them if you feel they become inappropriate. Try to identify work of quality. If you feel that one section is not good enough, find a tactful way of changing it.

Student comment:
There are lots of things we would do differently. For example, we wouldn't spend so long on discussing and rejecting ideas without working on them.

Student advice:
Warm-ups are vital: get into a routine as soon as possible.

- Keep to your targets as closely as possible. If you scrap an idea and start again, reset realistic targets.

- As technical requirements become clear, book the equipment. Have you considered Health and Safety issues in your venue(s)? Do you need a performance licence? (See Chapter 10 for further information.)

- Have you considered support material for your piece? For example, you could produce an extended programme, an exhibition or a teachers' support pack.

- Keep your written records up to date. These will be important for post-project evaluation. (See pp.17–20 for details on keeping records.)

The later stages of devising

- Do you have a clear structure? Thinking in terms of beginning, middle and end is simplistic, but still valid. In addition, you should consider the lucidity of the 'narrative'; moments of tension; the setting up of conflict and its resolution – if there is one; pace; and an appropriate balance of ingredients such as humour and pathos, music and dance (where these apply). The through-line may not be a simple narrative; the piece could be epic, documentary or imagistic, for example.

- Be prepared to scrap an idea, even at a comparatively late stage.

- Is the style of the piece appropriate for the content? Is there a coherent and conceptual link between form and content? Does the style of theatre work? Experiment with different styles, even if these contrast with your original choices. Does this encourage you to alter the thrust of the piece?

- If characterisation is important, have you developed the off-stage life of the characters? (See pp.49–54 and pp.108–110.)

- Keep the time limit in view. You will want to experiment with many ideas, but be selective, particularly when there is a tight time limit.

- Maintain an overall vision of the piece. Do not allow the beginning of the piece to have more weight because it has been devised first and rehearsed more.

- Is the piece still appropriate for the audience? Does it communicate clearly to the audience? You may know the piece so well that it is difficult to determine its clarity. For example, if it is important for the audience to know the names of certain characters, are these names established early on?

- Think of videoing your piece towards the end and viewing it objectively. Some syllabuses ask for the final product to be videoed and sent on to the examiner or moderator for reference. It is worth doing a trial run of this.

- Return to your original aims and objectives and ensure you are in line with these. If they should now be altered, does that matter? Are you meeting the brief and/or the assessment criteria? (See pp.132–133 or your own syllabus.)

Phase 3: The final stages

This final phase addresses:

- Final rehearsals (pre-technical, technical and dress)
- Evaluation

Final rehearsals

Pre-technical rehearsal

Prepare for your technical rehearsal.

The director, stage manager, designers and technical operators should meet prior to the technical rehearsal. (In collaborative devised work, these roles may not be clearly delineated.) By this time there should be an accurate script and a rough running document to work with (see p.299), so that time may be used most efficiently.

The following trials should take place during the pre-tech rehearsal:

- Demonstrate suggested lighting states for the approval of the director and designer (or the group).

- Demonstrate suggested sound effects for the approval of the director and designer (or the group).

- Demonstrate other suggested technical effects, such as smoke or pyrotechnics, for the approval of the director and designer (or the group).

- Plot the agreed levels and timing into the script as provisional cues for trial at the technical rehearsal.

In addition, the costumes and make-up should be viewed before the technical rehearsal.

Technical rehearsal

Allow four times the length of the piece for the technical rehearsal – longer if it is a complicated show technically. Run through the following checklist:

- Try out the make-up of a few characters for lighting purposes.

- Make sure all technical equipment – sound, lights, special effects and so on – is in place.

Consider those factors that will affect the technical run.

- Check that your props table is in order (see p.304).

- Position the props and set for the start of the performance.

- If there are any special or awkward costumes, these should be used in the technical to rehearse entrances, exits and key moves. In addition, rehearse any quick changes; these will affect the technical cues.

You may have to remember to adjust props during the performance.

- During your technical rehearsal, you will need to take into account the movement and use of props. Look carefully at maintaining continuity in the appearance and function of these props. For example, you might have to change clock times on the set between scenes, or you may have to empty a wine bottle to suggest that time has moved on. Allow time to make these alterations.

- Attempt to run the rehearsal 'cue to cue'. In other words, leave out sections of the production that do not have any cues or technical considerations. (It may not be possible to leave out any of the text.)

In running each cue, you should take into consideration a number of influencing factors:

- backstage changes;
- the timing and use of lights (referred to as LX or LFX cues);
- the timing, levels and use of sound and music (referred to as FX or SFX cues);
- the position and function of the set and props;
- costume changes and functional changes.

Generally, it is a good idea to set up the cue, run the cue and then repeat it to confirm the arrangement. Depending upon the nature of the performance, it is sometimes worth doing a subsequent 'top-and-tail' technical run of just the LFX and SFX cues.

Dress rehearsal
Your aim should be to simulate the real performance as closely as possible: *every* aspect of the production needs to covered as if it were the actual performance.

Try to reconstruct every aspect of the performance.

Consider the timing of the rehearsal. Aim to hold it at the same time of day as your performance(s), to avoid unforeseen hazards.

The organisation of a dress rehearsal should include the organisation or confirmation of arrangements *off* the stage, as well as on it. Consider the following as a necessary part of the performance:

- front of house: the selling of programmes and other duties;
- foyer displays;
- if appropriate, characters in role showing the audience to their seats or mingling with them in some capacity;
- a person responsible for house lights, and for closing appropriate doors, windows and/or curtains.

It is worth also taking into account the following points:

- Consider inviting an audience to the dress rehearsal, particularly if the production is promenade or if audience participation is part of the show.

- Allow plenty of preparation time for the cast to warm up, dress, make up and be given notes.

- Include a full-length interval.

- Never stop the performance in a dress rehearsal; if possible one member of the group should be responsible for taking notes on the performance during the dress rehearsal and passing them on afterwards or the next day.

For further information about the final stages of rehearsal, see pp.298–305.

Evaluation

What are you being asked to do? Be wary of terminology and work to the highest level of evaluation.

For group projects, some form of record or evaluation is usually required. Often there is ambiguity in the terminology that is used. The word 'evaluation' might be employed, yet when this is explained more fully what seems to be required is a detailed *account* of the work; few guidelines are given about how students should take that a stage forward and *evaluate*. Evaluating your own work is a complex process; many students fall down on this aspect of practical work, yet it is important as a method of learning and improving for the future.

After you finish the practical project, it is likely that you will have to complete a record, essay, portfolio and/or evaluation of some kind. (See below, pp.151–154, for further details of this.) To facilitate this, as well as for ongoing use whilst devising, you should keep thorough records throughout the project. The most effective method of doing this is by keeping both a personal and a group record. (See pp.17–20 in Chapter 1 for further discussion of these.) Add further details to your records where appropriate. These records can then be used to help you write a summative evaluation. (Alternatively, they may be all that is required.)

Written analysis and evaluation

The terms 'analysis' and 'evaluation' are notoriously vague; the following definitions are taken from the *Shorter Oxford English Dictionary*:

Analysis: *The resolution of anything complex into its simple elements; the opposite of 'synthesis'; the exact determination of its components; the critical examination of any production, so as to exhibit its elements in simple form; the tracing of things to their sources.*

Evaluate: *To work out the value of; to reckon up.*

Description alone is inadequate.

For the purposes of a summative piece of written work on your project, these two terms can be brought together. For example, you may be describing a moment in the final performance which was particularly exciting. You would *analyse* why it was so effective by explaining the contributory factors:

The audience knew many of the cast, so that there was a particularly responsive atmosphere in this performance; it was the second show, and the company felt secure in the piece, as the first performance had gone well; the warm-up had been well focused and all the company felt controlled but energised by it; the tension of the last couple of weeks had dissolved as we had seen the piece come to fruition; that particular moment in the show is moving, and Jas and Darren pushed it further than in the previous performance by . . .

When you *evaluate* your work, you should evaluate it against the personal and group objectives for the project (see pp.18–20), which, in turn, are aligned to the assessment criteria for the project. So you might continue talking about the same moment as discussed in the previous paragraph as follows:

This point in the performance was particularly effective in terms of meeting our objectives. One of these objectives was to present a piece which commented on isolation and the inability of many people to form lasting relationships. The group felt that this key message in the piece was communicated to the audience emphatically at this moment of the play. The breakdown in the relationship between the two central characters was clarified; the emotions were understated yet powerful, which left the audience feeling moved and helpless. When Darren said, 'There's nothing else to say, is there?', he spoke in a quiet, disillusioned voice that left you with a sense of bleakness and despondency. The move into naturalism for this particular scene after the overt physicality of the previous scenes helped the poignancy of the narrative, and the effect justified one of our other objectives, which was to incorporate a mixture of styles . . .

Evaluation must explain the value in relation to your original objectives.

There is little point in saying that something was 'good' or 'effective' unless you can relate this to the criteria that you have set yourselves. So the moment was 'good' and 'effective' because it met some of the objectives for the piece to a high level. Clearly, it would be difficult to evaluate your work without analysing it as well, as the above examples demonstrate.

We have included two frameworks for summative written work below. If you are expected to write such a piece, we recommend you look carefully at both of them: they are quite different. The first one is taken from the ULEAC A-level Drama Teachers' Guide.

THE STRUCTURED RECORD

The Structured Record is designed to promote analysis, and should be structured in loose-leaf format to allow flexibility.

By keeping a Structured Record, each candidate will be supported in analysing the following:
- Choice of source material or theme
- Choice of style and form
- Rehearsal progress, including: development of the role
   group interaction
   development of the theme or source material
- Design concepts – set, lighting, sound, performance space
- The relationship of the piece to the practical workshops and individual research
- The relationship of the piece to its audience
- Audience reaction

Candidates should work on their Structured Record during the process of devising drama – it is an integrated evaluation and should prove useful in the development of ideas.

The Structured Record will consist of a total of ten sheets, each sheet covering one of the questions/statements in the Structured Record list below.

- **How the role emerges and how it is communicated:**
  Who is the person being played?
  What is being done physically to communicate the role?
  How does the character feel at specific moments in the drama?

- **How the theme or source material is developed through the drama process:**
  How is the material used in the rehearsal process?

- **How the elements of light, sound and space complement the dramatic intentions:**
  Description of how space is used and how it works for the character being played.
  Considerations made regarding the use of light and sound.
  How does light affect the performance?

- **How group-work skills contribute to the development of the drama:**
  How do members of the group interact at different stages of the rehearsal process?
  What constitutes a good rehearsal? Use specific examples.

- **How the style of acting and the use of dramatic form are consciously employed to create the intended effect:**
  What have you seen which has influenced your work in this performance?
  The choices made about the form of drama/the style of acting at different stages of the preparation.

- **How rehearsals and the production process contribute to the final performance:**
  The ways in which style and form are investigated during rehearsals.

- **How the group envisages responses from the audience:**
  The expected audience response at specific moments of the drama.

Below is a more complex example of a framework for a summative evaluation. It concentrates on *evaluation* and analysis, rather than on descriptive account and analysis. It revolves around evaluating the work against personal and group objectives.

Guidelines for a summative written piece of analysis and evaluation for a collaborative devised theatre project

This written piece can be divided into three sections.

1. Evaluation and analysis of self during process
This refers to your role during the process of the project.
Suggested format:

i) Write out your personal objectives for the project that apply to the process. See p.18, where examples of personal objectives are given.

ii) Divide up your self-evaluation and analysis section according to these objectives. Look through your personal record (see pp.18–19) and make a note of all the points that you think would be relevant for each of the personal objectives. Select the most appropriate examples from the personal record to use as evidence that you have met these objectives.

iii) As you write, give two or three specific examples (pieces of evidence) from your personal record and your own memory for each objective. Ensure that you analyse and evaluate each of these. (See pp.150–151 for an explanation of analysis and evaluation.)

2. Evaluation and analysis of the group during process
Whilst this section is about the group, it is written from an individual perspective.

Follow the same format as for the self-evaluation, above. (For examples of group objectives, see p.19.)

3. End product analysis and evaluation
This will include comments about both yourself and the group, and will refer to the end product.

i) Start by writing out any of your personal objectives that apply to the product. Do the same for the group objectives. For example (as suggested on pp.18 and 19):
- to improve my performance skills, working in a different style to my usual work and increasing my range of skills;
- to work on designing and creating props for the piece which are of a near-professional standard;
- to experiment with and create an innovative and exciting piece of theatre, in which content and form are integrated;
- to select and tackle a topical issue with sensitivity, yet with force;
- to ensure that the piece is appropriate for the target audience;
- to produce a piece of documentary drama using different styles of performance;
- to produce an end product that is of a near-professional performance standard.

ii) Divide up your end product evaluation and analysis section according to these objectives. Look through your personal and group records and make a note of all the points that you think would be relevant for each of

153

these objectives. In addition, if you have a record of the performances in any form, such as audio tape, video tape or photographs, use these as a resource for judging your own work.

iii) Consider the audience's response. Is there a possibility of interviewing audience members about the piece and your own performance? Can you ask them to complete questionnaires?

iv) As you write, give two or three specific examples (pieces of evidence) from your personal and group record, your own memory, any record of the performance and any audience feedback, for each objective. Ensure that you analyse and evaluate each of these. (There are examples of such evaluation on p.151.) Do not try to be exhaustive. You need to select specific moments to analyse and evaluate. You may also wish to analyse and evaluate design elements, such as lighting, sound and so on.

v) Ensure you address the assessment criteria for the project in your piece. Your objectives are likely to reflect the assessment criteria, of course, so it is more than likely that you will have evaluated the work with these criteria in mind.

Summative orals/vive voces
Sometimes, students are asked to discuss their work orally after completion of a project. During such a discussion, you would be expected to analyse and evaluate the conception, process and product. This should be prepared beforehand, just as you would prepare written work. The two sets of guidelines given above for written work could be adapted and used for oral discussion quite simply. One of the resource activities suggests this (see p.160).

Resource Activities

Each of the following activities can be used as part of a major project, although they are written, on the whole, as simulation exercises, for students to gain experience of aspects of collaborative devised work before embarking on a whole project.

1. UNDERSTANDING HISTORICAL AND/OR CONTEMPORARY PRACTICE

Aim

To support your own practice with an understanding of the historical and contemporary practice of collaborative devising theatre companies.

Objectives

- To gather information about a recent or contemporary collaborative theatre company.
- To collate this information into project form.
- To make connections between companies, finding connections between the work of the researched company and the work of similar groups in the past.

Background

- You will need to identify a professional company from the past or present which devises theatre collaboratively. Either turn to Chapter 6 and select one of the companies that is discussed there, or alternatively you may choose one mentioned in Alison Oddey's book *Devising Theatre*. Possibly the best option is to select a company which works locally, or with whose work you are familiar.
- Read the interviews with Kneehigh Theatre, Rejects Revenge Theatre and Legs on the Wall on pp.117–131, together with the material on pp.113–117.

Tasks

- Create a case study of a company. Many of the questions and statements below were used for the interviews in this chapter, and should provide a useful guide for carrying out research into the company you have chosen, although it may not be possible to accumulate such detailed information. Find appropriate materials on the company, such as books, theatre reviews or articles. You may need to send out questionnaires and try to interview people or have telephone conversations. Asking for publicity material on contemporary companies is a useful method of obtaining information. This kind of research can be quite complicated; your local library may be able to help you track down relevant information in books, magazines and so on.

  i) When was the company formed?
  ii) Why did it form?
  iii) How is the company funded?

iv) Does the company have a specific target audience?

v) Is there an ideological basis for the company's work? Does the company have a philosophical rationale for its work?

vi) Find examples of its work from across its lifespan. Does this work represent different periods of its development? If so, how?

vii) Does the company work in a particular style?

viii) What are the devising processes that the group uses? Can you get a description of particular methods?

ix) What type of venue does the company perform in?

x) Is there a particular design style that is used? Can you obtain a description of the different designs used?

xi) Try to find examples of reviews of the company's work.

xii) What is the average size of the company?

xiii) What responsibilities do the different members of the company have? What do their roles entail? Do they look for specific skills in members?

xiv) Does the company have a particular marketing policy? Can you find examples of how it markets its work and to whom?

xv) Does the company have a specific education policy?

There may be a number of further questions that you can add to this list. Write up the information you collect, including relevant documentation such as leaflets, brochures and so on.

● Find features that your case study company and other companies from the past and/or present have in common. Write this up as an essay. For example:

The theatre company I researched, Three Threads, states in its company objectives that its mission is to 'focus on the politics of the everyday, the events in life which affect the people on the street'. This was the case even in the early days of devised theatre. Commedia dell' Arte *troupes would improvise around events happening in the town or city in which they were performing. Companies of the 1970s fringe movement were similarly preoccupied with contemporary issues and produced theatre that focused specifically on these. Monstrous Regiment, for example, addressed the feminist issues of the time.*

2. PREPARING OBJECTIVES

Aim
To understand the importance of setting objectives for a project.

Objectives
● To experience the compilation of personal and group objectives.
● To develop group discussion and collaboration skills.
● To gain experience in starting off a piece of collaborative devised theatre.

Background
You are working in a small group, which has been asked to create a piece of

TYP (Theatre for Young People) for Key Stage 1 and 2 (five- to eleven-year-old) children. The teachers have chosen the topic Victorian Tales of the Imagination. You will be inviting local primary schools to see the piece at an in-house venue. Read the sections on audience research and literary research on pp.134–135 and 143–144. You may also find it useful to read pp.18–19 in Chapter 1 for examples of personal and group objectives.

Tasks
- What would be your personal objectives for such a project? Write these up in detail.

- Suggest a list of group objectives, as well.

3. CREATING DRAFT PROPOSALS

Aim
To gain an overview of the first formal stages of the devising process.

Objectives
- To establish clear headings for a draft proposal.
- To write a mock draft proposal.

Background
A draft proposal for your project establishes a sound base for the subsequent devising process. For the purposes of this activity, assume that the draft proposal will be given to potential sponsors. Read the sections on starting the project, pp.134–138, and creating the draft proposal, p.141.

Tasks
- Devise a list of headings for any draft proposal. What would it be useful for the sponsors to know? For example, one heading is obviously going to be 'Budget', as any sponsors would need to know what the outlay of finance would be.

- Look at the list of suggested topics on pp.136–137 and select one of them. Using your list of headings for a draft proposal, discuss a hypothetical project based on the topic you have selected. You have a completely free hand. The piece can be aimed at any audience group, can be of any length and so on.

- Write up a full draft proposal of the project for sponsors. You may want to add or alter headings if appropriate. What aspects of the project do you want to emphasise? What are its strengths? Ensure that you bear these in mind when you are preparing the draft proposal. This should be approximately two to three close-typed (or equivalent) A4 sheets in length.

4. TOPIC RESEARCH

Aim
To appreciate the complexities of research and the rigour needed in this aspect of collaborative devised work.

Objectives
- To consider the research needs of a project, identifying specific areas to research.
- To locate sources for such research.
- To select relevant information from the research.

Background
You are in the initial stages of a project, and each member of the group has to contribute to the research. (Note that this activity does not ask you to undertake a full research project; it will give you an insight into a full research project and allow you to do a small amount of research yourself.) Read pp.142–144.

Tasks
- You have been given a choice of two topics to research: local drug abuse, or the everyday life of people living in Britain during World War II. Select one of them.

- Compile the following:
  i) a list of what you believe you need to find out about this topic. What information would the group need to know?
  ii) a list of institutions, places and sources of information that you could utilise to find this information;
  iii) examples of any resources you can locate that might be of use, such as a local police force document on how to recognise dangerous drugs or photocopies of pages from *Chronicle of the Twentieth Century* on the years 1939–45;
  iv) suggestions for the particular aspect on which you might focus in the collaborative piece, having undertaken this limited amount of research.

5. THE EARLY STAGES OF DEVISING

Aims
- To understand how practical work can enhance the early devising stages.
- To engage the group in mutually supportive activity.

Objectives
- To develop and run a successful practical drama session.
- To focus this on the early stages of exploring a particular topic, which could be extended into a full project.
- To write up this work in detail.

Background

- From pp.136–137, select a topic that you may be interested in pursuing further for a devised piece. Imagine that you are going to be working in a group of six to eight students on this topic.
- Read through the warm-up and practical exercises in Chapter 1, pp.5–17.

Tasks

- Devise an hour-long introductory session for your peers on this topic, taking into account the following points:

  i) Select a variety of ideas to try, including warm-up activities for the group. Ensure you time them carefully.

  ii) One of the activities must utilise an external stimulus that you have brought in, such as a piece of music, a newspaper article, a picture.

  iii) Make the exercises or improvisations relevant to the topic. For example, if you selected the topic '*Guernica* by Picasso', you might choose an exercise which asks the group to make a still image entitled 'Fear of war'.

  iv) Ensure that you explain each exercise thoroughly. It is useful to write out the introductory explanation of each part of the session fully; it may relieve some of the apprehension you feel before taking the session.

- Write this up as a full session plan and keep it in your personal record. Include the following:

  i) your objectives for each activity. What do you want the group to achieve from each exercise?

  ii) a detailed explanation of each activity;

  iii) the amount of time allocated to each activity;

  iv) some suggested follow-up activities that could be undertaken if the topic were to be used for a full project.

6. USING ADVICE

This activity is for a group which has embarked on a major project.

Aim

To learn to stand back and reflect on a project.

Objectives

- To note areas of the ongoing project that have not yet been addressed.
- To make a plan of action which will redress any balance that is needed.

Background

The group has started to devise the project. Read pp.146–147 on the early and middle stages of devising as a group.

Tasks

- Run through all the statements, questions and pieces of advice on pages 146–147 with the rest of the group. How many of these points does the group need to address at this stage?

- Make a plan of action to address these, and outline the strategies you wish to put in place to achieve this plan. For example, *when* will certain things be achieved?

- There are a number of quotes from students in the margin. Now that you have embarked on your project, is there any further advice you would give to students for the first stages of the project?

7. VOCAL AND PHYSICAL PREPARATION FOR DRESS REHEARSALS AND PERFORMANCES

Aims
- To take reponsibility for your own performances.
- To increase an awareness of the need for good basic skills work.

Objective
To devise vocal and physical warm-ups for individuals and the group.

Background
Look at pp.5–10, which give examples of voice and movement exercises. Try to find other books that give suggestions for warm-up activities.

Tasks
- Prepare a 15–25-minute physical warm-up which is appropriate for the needs of the piece.

- Prepare a 15–25-minute vocal warm-up which is appropriate for the needs of the piece.

- Write up these activities and keep them as a personal resource for the future.

8. WRITTEN/ORAL RECORD/EVALUATION

This activity can be undertaken only after a complete group project has been finished.

Aim
To understand the complexity of evaluation.

Objectives
- To be aware of different forms of 'evaluation'.
- To write a thorough evaluation.
- To consider responses in an oral evaluation.

Background
Look at pp.150–154.

Tasks

- Choose one of the frameworks from pp.151–154. You may need to consult your tutor about this. Using it as a guideline, write a summative evaluation of a collaborative devised piece of theatre.

- After your performance, you may have a group oral with a moderator or examiner. As a preparation for this, consider your responses to the following questions. The questions may be put to you as an individual or to the whole group.

i) Where did the idea for the piece come from?

ii) How did the group pursue it initially?

iii) Did you have a specific job responsibility? Did you prepare for and research this responsibility?

iv) Describe a key moment in the rehearsal process. How did this affect the project or the group?

v) How have you utilised the strengths of individual members of the group? To what extent do you think that this was a successful method of working?

vi) Identify problem areas in the process. What strategies did you put in place to deal with these? How valuable were these strategies?

vii) What sort of research did you undertake individually on theme, period, topic and so on? Where did you go to do this research? What resources did you find? Was it directly used in the piece?

viii) Evaluate the use of research in the piece.

ix) What targets and deadlines did the group set itself? How useful was this?

x) Individually, comment on the strength of your own performance. What were your objectives for your role(s)? How well did you achieve these in performance?

xi) Were there any moments where you felt the performances of others were particularly effective? What were these, and why do you think this was so?

xii) How well did your piece communicate with the audience? Can you give evidence to support this?

xiii) Did you consider the audience during the devising process? How did it influence your decisions? In retrospect, was this influence appropriate?

xiv) Can you comment on the relationship of form and content in your piece? Can you give specific examples which highlight that relationship? In retrospect, how successful was the development of that relationship?

xv) Discuss the design concept and its evolution. Would you alter any aspect of the design now that the whole production has come together in performance?

ANNOTATED BIBLIOGRAPHY

This bibliography includes volumes relevant to this chapter which are considered suitable for student reference. See also the general bibliography on p.380.

See the bibliography at the end of Chapter 1 (p.24) for the following texts, which are useful for improvisation and devising:

Boal, A., *Games for Actors and Non-Actors*, Routledge, 1992
Frost, A. and Yarrow, R., *Improvisation in Drama*, Methuen, 1992
Hickson, A., *Creative Action Methods in Groupwork*, Winslow Press, 1995
Johnstone, K., *Impro*, Methuen, 1981
Neelands, J., *Structuring Drama Work*, CUP, 1990
Spolin, V., *Improvisation for the Theatre: Including Two Hundred and Twenty Theatre Games*, Pitman and Sons, 1963.

The following are also useful:

Coult, T. and Kershaw, B. (eds), *Engineers of the Imagination: The Welfare State Handbook*, Methuen, 1983
> An excellent text for community theatre: a must.

MacLennan, E., *The Moon Belongs to Everyone: Making Theatre with 7:84*, Methuen, 1990
> This is a useful book for understanding the methods of one of Britain's foremost fringe theatre companies.

Mason, B., *Street Theatre and Other Outdoor Performance*, Routledge, 1992
> A useful book; there are very few that explore work like this. Quite academic.

McCafferey, M., *A Phaidon Theatre Manual: Directing a Play*, Phaidon Press Ltd., 1988
> See p.378 for details.

Oddey, A., *Devising Theatre: A Practical and Theoretical Handbook*, Routledge, 1994
> A key text for research into devised theatre. Quite academic in parts.

Rees, R., *Fringe First: Pioneers of Fringe Theatre on Record*, Oberon Books, 1992
> An accessible text about fringe theatre. It consists of various interviews with key fringe practitioners.

Oreglia, G., *The Commedia dell' Arte*, Methuen, 1968

Rudlin, J., *Commedia dell' Arte: An Actor's Handbook*, Routledge, 1994
> Both these books are classic texts for information on *Commedia dell' Arte*. Rudlin's is more accessible for practical work.

5 Surviving as a Practitioner

Peter Nelson

At any one time, it is estimated that 80 per cent of practitioners in theatre are out of work. To stand any chance of working successfully in theatre one needs to possess the following attributes:

- a realistic understanding of what is involved;
- a thorough appreciation of the area of employment;
- good fortune;
- considerable talent.

This chapter sets out to provide a framework of information that addresses the first two of these points. The chapter is divided into the following sections:

- Establishing an 'objective' approach to work
- Employment in theatre
- Education and training
- After training: starting a career

The aim of these sections is to examine the theory behind why work is necessary and to consider the concept of theatre as an industry; to explore the range and scope of employment available in theatre and consider the nature of each job; to look at the progression routes through which vocational and academic qualifications and expertise can be acquired; and to provide information on how to begin establishing a career, and also an insight into some of the survival skills necessary to develop and succeed.

ESTABLISHING AN 'OBJECTIVE' APPROACH TO WORK

The following approach is appropriate for any student who is considering working in theatre. It helps to explore a number of fundamental issues, in a way that should inform and influence the decision-making processes about potential work options. Survival as a practitioner depends on making clear and balanced decisions from the beginning.

Why work?

Three basic questions are worth considering:

- What is a job and what does it provide?
- What is a career and what does it provide?
- What is job security and what does it provide?

To put these questions in context, you should consider your needs. A psychologist named Maslow proposed a theoretical model which he called 'a hierarchy of needs'. This model illustrates what he considered to be the things we need in life. His ideas are represented in the diagram below (which should be read from the bottom upwards). The diagram is constructed like a tall building: the foundations are laid first, and each floor can be added only when the one below it is complete and secure.

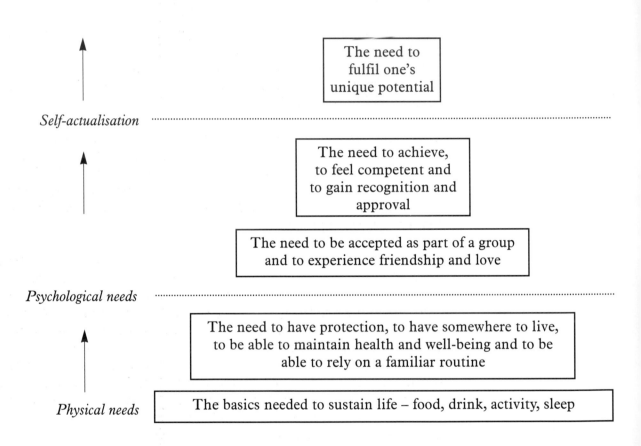

An adaptation of Maslow's hierarchy of needs in Gross, Psychology: The Science of Mind and Behaviour, *p.652*

This theory can be used to help address the three initial questions. For example, *if you have no job*, it is barely possible to establish the basic needs of life. In the UK, the Welfare State provides most out-of-work adults with some sort of entitlement to money from the government, such as the Jobseeker's Allowance (JSA). Therefore, if you have no work, it *is* possible to maintain the basic needs, but the foundations, as represented in Maslow's hierarchy of needs, are shaky. It is difficult to establish a level of personal development, or to progress to a situation where you do have a job. In many other countries, there is no Welfare State, so if people have no job they have few methods of providing even the basics for themselves.

If you have a job, it is possible to provide the basics. If you also have job security – that is, some guarantee of the job continuing for any length of time – it is possible to begin to progress up Maslow's hierarchy of needs: according to his thesis, you can then establish friends and possibly a family, and gain some level of satisfaction in life through being able to afford hobbies, holidays and further 'treats'. The job security can be as important in maintaining this position as the job itself. However, opting for job security may mean sacrificing your aspirations.

If you have a career, this tends to imply specialised training, experience, job security, the ability to progress and develop, higher aspirations, greater earning power and the ability to reach the top of Maslow's hierarchy of needs – to achieve your own unique potential by using your acquired skills and individual talents.

These ideas can be related to the concept of Maslow's hierarchy of needs as a building. The more successful you are, the higher up the building you will be able to live, and, as a result, the better the outlook will be. This position can be maintained only as long as the career structure and work prospects remain secure. If job security falters, your position is likely to be put in jeopardy.

Try discussing your answers to the three initial questions at the bottom of p.163, relating them to other people's views and comparing the similarities and differences of opinion. This will help you to begin to gain an insight into what *you* consider to be the relative importance of work, jobs, careers and job security. In turn, this will give you a more focused approach in considering the way forward and exploring opportunities in education, training and employment. It is also worth bearing in mind that as one gets older one's priorities tend to shift, calling for a change of emphasis or direction. When you are planning your career path it is possible and advisable to allow for changes of circumstance, and if necessary a change of focus.

The next stage is to consider the particular field in which you might wish to seek employment, bearing in mind the above thought processes.

What is the theatre industry?
A description of the processes within any industry might be as follows:

● An inventor comes up with an idea for a new product range.

● Research is done to see whether there would be a potential market for such a product.

● Research suggests that a market exists, so a product team develops the initial idea and creates what it hopes will be a marketable commodity.

● This process involves experimentation, trial and error, and continued consultation and testing to ensure the viability of the product.

- Once the design has been perfected, the product can then start to be manufactured: this process calls upon a wide range of skills.

- A design team comes up with an idea for attractive packaging of the product, and a marketing team prepares for the product launch.

- There is a publicity campaign, followed by an advertising campaign to continue product promotion.

- Another team contacts businesses who might want to carry the product as part of their line, and distribution systems are set up.

- The product is therefore manufactured, marketed and distributed.

The theatre industry, like any other, has a product (or a range of products), a business and organisational structure, scope for employment, a diversity of jobs and careers, and the potential for a multi-skilled workforce. Therefore, 'the ability to fulfil one's unique potential' by selecting a career in the theatre industry can become a reality.

Considering theatre as an industry, as outlined above, also highlights one other fact, which has a major influence on job security: the theatre industry exists to create a *product*. The product is viable only if there is a demand for it, or if a demand can be created. There is no business sense in creating a product that no-one wants to buy. If a product (or performance) is created which is not viable (which no-one wants to see), the result, as in any industry, is that the infrastructure can fall apart, jobs are put in jeopardy, job security is lost, careers are affected, and Maslow's building comes tumbling down. Although the theatre industry has its own particular identity, it forms part of a bigger industry – the performing arts industry. Other parts of the performing arts industry include the film industry, the television industry, the recording industry and the entertainment industry. There is a significant overlap of skills between these parts of the performing arts industry, so that training in one field may allow you to consider developing a career in other fields of the industry.

To sum up, if you are considering training opportunities and career options within the theatre industry, it is worth bearing in mind the following points:

- You must be realistic, and balance your ideals concerning 'the need to achieve one's unique potential' with rational decisions about levels of income and job security.

- If you explore the full range of careers available in the theatre (and performing arts) industry, you are much more likely to find an area which provides the balance of challenge, job satisfaction and job security that is right for you.

- If you understand the precise functions of a number of different careers within the industry, you are much better placed to choose a progression route (education and training) that will enable you to keep your options open.

- If you decide that the industry simply fails to provide the level of income or job security you would wish for, you can use your transferable skills to move into a completely different area of work, without having wasted your training and jeopardised your entire career.

- If you understand how your intended career fits into the greater picture, you are much better equipped to protect your position, deal with problems and maintain your job security.

EMPLOYMENT IN THEATRE

This section examines the nature of jobs and careers to be found within the theatre industry. It considers different modes of employment, provides an overview of the employment structure, comparing small- and large-scale companies, and describes a number of jobs within the industry, including the type of experience and qualifications required.

Modes of employment

As in any other industry, there are two basic modes of working in theatre. Perhaps the most common is for an individual to be an employee of a company and receive a regular salary for his or her work. Alternatively, a person can be self-employed (or 'freelance'). This means that he or she tends to work for short periods of time on one-off projects or assignments with different organisations; for each project a pre-arranged fee is paid, and once the work is complete the freelancer/ self-employed person moves on. Both employment and freelance work are common in theatre, but there are areas where freelancing is more common. The reasons for this are explored later in this chapter.

It is also possible for an employee to be either full-time or part-time. For part-time jobs, the amount of time worked is usually represented as a decimal fraction, so 0.5 would be half-time. When part-time jobs are advertised, the salary is frequently expressed on a full-time scale followed by the words *'pro rata'*, with an indication of the time worked. If an advert were to describe a 0.5 post, with a salary of £16,000 per annum, *pro rata*, the employee would actually receive £8,000 a year.

A structural overview

It takes only a careful browse through a theatre programme to discover how many people are needed to facilitate a particular performance. The audience sees the box-office and front-of-house staff and the performers, but there are many others involved.

The first of the two diagrams below shows the overall structure of the Royal Shakespeare Company. This is a multi-venue company, which operates both as a receiving house, receiving performances created by other production companies, and as a production house, responsible for instigating its own productions. The second diagram shows the overall structure of Green Candle Dance Company. This is a small-scale touring

COURT OF GOVERNORS
THE COUNCIL
EXECUTIVE COMMITTEE
ARTISTIC DIRECTOR

PRINCIPAL ASSOCIATE DIRECTOR
EXECUTIVE PRODUCER
ASSOCIATES
GENERAL MANAGER
FINANCE DIRECTOR
FINANCE MANAGER
ACCOUNTS MANAGER

Principal Associate Director
- PRODUCER(S)
- LITERARY MANAGER
- COMPANY MANAGER LONDON
  - Stage management
  - Company

Executive Producer
- PLANNING ADMINISTRATOR
  - Programme planning
  - Contracts: writers, directors, designers, freelance
- CASTING DIRECTOR
  - Artist contracts
- COMPANY MANAGER STRATFORD
  - Stage management
  - Company

Associates
- HEAD OF REGIONAL DEVELOPMENT
- HEAD OF EDUCATION
- RSC COLLECTION DIRECTOR
  - Audience development
  - special projects
- DIRECTOR OF MARKETING PRESS & PUBLICITY
- HEAD OF MARKETING
- HEAD OF PRESS & PUBLIC RELATIONS
  - Marketing
  - Graphics
  - Mailing list
  - Publications
  - Exhibition & display
  - Press
  - Box offices
- DEVELOPMENT DIRECTOR
- HEAD OF DEVELOPMENT (CAMPAIGN)
- HEAD OF DEVELOPMENT (MANAGEMENT)
- HEAD OF SPONSORSHIP DEVELOPMENT
- HEAD OF SPONSORSHIP RELATIONS
- HEAD OF RESEARCH
- ADMINISTRATOR TOP
- INFORMATION TECHNOLOGY SYSTEMS MANAGER
- RETAIL SALES MANAGER
  - RSC shops
- LONDON ADMINISTRATOR
  - House management
  - Pit
  - Landlord
  - Visiting companies
- MANAGER STRATFORD
  - House management
  - Catering
  - Properties & gardens
  - Visiting companies

General Manager
- HEAD OF OPERATIONS
  - London operations
  - Residency operations
  - Stratford
- HEAD OF RESOURCES
- MANAGEMENT SERVICES CO-ORDINATOR
- HEALTH & SAFETY MANAGER
- HEAD OF TECHNICAL SERVICES
- TECHNICAL SYSTEMS MANAGER STRATFORD
  - Maintenance electricians
- TECHNICAL SYSTEMS MANAGER LONDON
- MECHANICAL ENGINEER
  - Maintenance electricians
- HEAD OF TOURING & SPECIAL PROJECTS
- DEPUTY HEAD TOURING
  - Tours managers; UK and foreign
- PRODUCTION CONTROLLER
  - Sound Staff
  - Design
  - Scenic workshop
  - Property workshop
  - Paintshop
  - Production wardrobe
  - Wig department
  - Maintenance wardrobe/wigs
  - Hire wardrobe
- PRODUCTION MANAGERS LONDON
- PRODUCTION MANAGERS STRATFORD
- TECHNICAL MANAGER
  - Stage staff
  - Property staff
  - Electrical staff
  - Sound staff
  - Stage staff
  - Property staff
  - Electrical staff

Staff structure, Royal Shakespeare Company

dance company, which performs principally in schools and community venues.

Although there are many significant differences between the two companies, the underlying objective is the same for both: to create a piece of theatre and perform it repeatedly to an audience.

If you compare the two structures, you will see that that the Royal Shakespeare Company appears to have narrowly focused job titles, whereas in Green Candle Dance Company the job titles involve broader responsibilities. For a large-scale organisation, although the areas of responsibility for each job appear narrow, the level of experience and

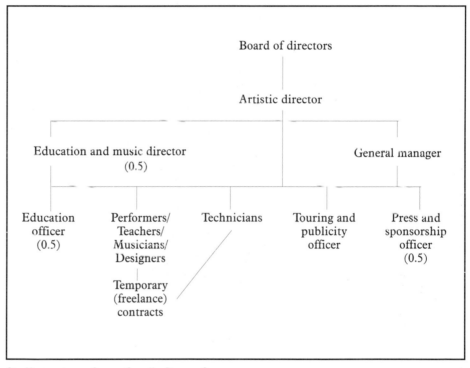

Staff structure, Green Candle Dance Company

understanding needed in any field is likely to be high. Conversely, in a small company, the emphasis is on having a wide cross-section of skills.

Another fact that is highlighted by these two examples is the significance of the freelancer's role in the theatre industry. A company such as the Royal Shakespeare Company has a rolling programme of productions. As a result, at any one time there is always likely to be a range of projects at various stages of production. This means that the company is in a position to offer full-time, permanent employment to people involved in each stage of production, such as construction, marketing, administration, house management and education. In contrast, a small-scale company such as Green Candle works project by project, with each tour lasting for about four months from entering production to final performance. The company may then enter a non-performing phase, to enable planning before the next project goes into production. The core roles of artistic director, general manager and touring and publicity officer are full-time permanent posts. But the company does not have the capacity to maintain ongoing full-time employment for other administrative staff, or performers and production staff. The administrative posts are part-time permanent contracts, while all other posts are offered as short-term contracts and are likely to be carried out mainly by practitioners working on a self-employed basis.

Jobs

This section briefly examines the function of a variety of jobs within the theatre industry. The following information is provided for each job (or group of jobs):

- areas of responsibility for that post;
- the general nature of the work;
- essential qualities needed to carry out the work successfully;
- the training and progression route that might lead to this post;
- work experience worth acquiring at an early stage;
- likely membership of appropriate professional organisations;
- the comparative salary range associated with the work;
- an indication of the possible job security associated with the work;
- the transferable skills which form an integral part of the work.

The jobs are divided into categories, to enable comparisons to be made between jobs that require similar types of skills or training. This is not intended to be a comprehensive guide to every aspect of working in the theatre, but it can be used as a starting point for further research and investigation.

Senior management

Producer/executive director

- **Area of responsibility:** overall financial and managerial responsibility for a production or venue.
- **Nature of work:** to raise (or provide) the financial backing, appoint the creative production team (writer, director, designer, composer, choreographer) and play a significant role in the choice of performers.
- **Essential qualities:** shrewd entrepreneurial skills, a keen feel for the market, a significant level of management expertise for both people and finances, a high level of communication skills and a great deal of experience in all aspects of theatre work.
- **Training and progression:** there is no formal recognised route to becoming a producer. The level and range of skills needed are likely to be acquired over a significant period of time. There is also the need for innate flair. Very occasionally, traineeships are made

available. (In 1996, the Arts Council of England offered one associate producer traineeship, and had over 100 applications.)

- **Salary range:** owing to the level of responsibility of the producer, the salary is likely to be substantial. It would not be uncommon for income to be linked to the success of the production. If a production flops, the producer may make nothing, or even lose money.
- **Job security:** although the producer may have the most to make on a production, he or she may also have the most to lose. Consequently, job security becomes directly related to the skill of the producer; occasionally, luck is also involved.
- **Transferable skills:** the diversity of skills and natural flair required to be a successful producer would be transferable to managerial or entrepreneurial appointments in any number of areas of work outside theatre. (However, as long as a producer can handle the pressure, the financial incentives and job satisfaction are likely to be sufficient to maintain his or her interest in producing.)

Administration

Venue/company manager

- **Areas of responsibility:** overall responsibility for the day-to-day smooth running of the venue or company.
- **Nature of work:** the emphasis is on keeping life as uneventful and as organised as possible, to prevent unwanted distractions and pressure for everyone else. An ability to spot potential problem situations and resolve them with the minimum of fuss is the key. (See also Chapter 10.)
- **Essential qualities:** good organisational and management skills, authority, diplomacy, confidence, tact, and an appreciation of the pressures being experienced by everyone else.
- **Training and progression:** there is no recognised progression route. Most venue/company managers have come from acting, stage management, front of house or occasionally a management role outside theatre.
- **Useful work experience:** any opportunity to gain an insight into the running of a venue or company; any similar organisational experience.
- **Salary range:** most venues and companies of any size have a manager. The salary is reasonable and probably proportional to the size of the company and the level of responsibility.
- **Job security:** assuming the continued success of a venue, the venue manager has a reasonably secure position. A company manager's security tends to be related to the size of the company. Touring companies are more likely to employ company managers on a freelance basis for each tour.
- **Transferable skills:** the knowledge of the theatre industry and the general management and organisational skills needed for such a position would tend to be useful for a significant range of other jobs both within and outside the industry.

Promotion: marketing, press, publicity, public relations

As the diagram of Green Candle on p.169 suggests, in small-scale companies most promotion work is carried out by a small team of administrative staff, or even one administrator. The larger the company, the more likely these jobs are to be carried out by specialists. Therefore, large venues may have a separate department for each of these areas, with several employees in each department, whereas in a small company the administrator may carry out all these functions. (See also Chapter 10.)

- **Areas of responsibility:** informing the public and raising the profile of the production, company and/or venue.
- **Nature of work:** gathering information and compiling promotional material in the form of posters, programmes and press releases; liaising with the media.
- **Essential qualities:** good communication skills, both written and spoken, initiative, a positive image, diplomacy, an understanding of the press world and journalism.
- **Training and progression:** a number of post-16 performing arts courses contain elements of arts administration, and many performing arts degree courses have administrative options. It is possible to study media, journalism or marketing at either undergraduate or postgraduate level. A number of short courses also exist in all aspects of administration, marketing and promotion.
- **Useful work experience:** involvement in promoting any type of event; working in local radio or television.
- **Salary range:** For people with the appropriate levels of expertise, salaries generally start on a par with the national average wage. A higher income might be available for working freelance, but this is reliant on a reputation which has probably been built up over a significant period of time.
- **Job security:** reasonable, depending upon the company or venue.
- **Transferable skills:** all the skills used in this area are likely to be highly sought-after in other fields of work.

Primary creators

This term refers to the team with primary responsibility for the artistic content of a performance. Members of the team work together to integrate the different elements – dialogue, movement, dance, sound, music and design – in order to create a piece of theatre with its own unique identity. As well as defining and upholding the artistic and theatrical integrity of the piece, the team will also be aiming to create a piece of theatre appropriate for the target audience, and which will meet with critical approval.

Director/artistic director

- **Areas of responsibility:** overall artistic responsibility for a production or venue.
- **Nature of work:** the director will lead the creative team, liaise with the production team, choose the cast (possibly in conjunction with

a casting director), lead the performers through the rehearsal period and co-ordinate the technical pre-production period in conjunction with the production manager. (For more detailed information on the director's role, see Chapter 3.)

- **Essential qualities:** absolute determination, leadership, the ability to command respect, artistic, literary and theatrical vision, an appreciation of all the elements of a production and an understanding of performers.
- **Training and progression:** directing options exist in some post-16 and higher education theatre-related courses. In addition, there are an increasing number of specialist directing courses in higher education and drama schools. A number of these courses tend to be aimed at postgraduates who have already managed to acquire considerable theatrical experience. There are also a few trainee schemes, which are offered when funds can be made available. (In 1996, the Arts Council of England offered four associate director traineeships, for which it had about 200 applications, and six assistant director traineeships, for which it had about 350 applications.) Many successful directors take none of these options, but acquire their skills via such routes as acting, mime or dance.
- **Useful work experience:** the skills that go to make a good director come from a deep understanding of many areas, including theatre, literature, art, politics and history. For anyone interested in directing, it is worth being exposed to as much theatre as possible, both as a participant and as a member of an audience. At school or college, it tends to be far easier to create performance opportunities with little or no cost: instigating such opportunities and gaining experience from them is essential.
- **Professional organisations:** Equity, the Directors' Guild of Great Britain.
- **Salary range:** directors are poorly paid until they are very well established. Most young directors are not able to support themselves by directing alone. The few exceptions are mainly freelance directors with an international reputation, who are employed by the largest companies. Such directors become a selling point for the production, at which point salaries or fees can be substantial.
- **Job security:** low.
- **Transferable skills:** directors are frequently able to work in other areas of the performing arts industry, or in education and youth and community theatre. A number may also act, or work in other jobs, such as company management.

Writer
- **Nature of work:** to create scripts, either independently or in conjunction with a company, as a result of a commission.
- **Essential qualities:** substantial skill as a wordsmith, having an opinion, artistic vision.
- **Training and progression:** writing options exist in most post-16 and higher education theatre-related courses. There are some

specialist writing courses available in higher education and drama schools. A number of these courses are aimed at postgraduates who have already managed to acquire considerable writing experience and theatrical appreciation. There are also a small number of trainee schemes, which are offered when funds can be made available.

- **Useful work experience:** the difficulty is not in gaining writing experience, but in obtaining critical feedback and finding performance opportunities for work. There are several venues that operate young writers' festivals and competitions, and some venues run writers' workshops. It may also be beneficial to work in conjunction with youth and community theatre, where there may be opportunities to have work performed.
- **Professional organisations:** Society of Authors, Writers' Guild of Great Britain, Theatre Writers' Union.
- **Salary range:** an aspiring writer would be unlikely to earn a living wage purely from writing. The income of a successful writer with a string of West End successes would be substantial, however.
- **Job security:** directly related to status and reputation.
- **Transferable skills:** any person who is an accomplished writer is likely to have significant scope for work outside theatre, in such areas as journalism, the media and other areas of the performing arts industry.

Composer

- **Nature of work:** to compose music, either independently or as a result of a commission from a company.
- **Essential qualities:** substantial musical skill and creativity.
- **Training and progression:** composition options exist in most post-16 and higher education music courses. It is also possible to study composition as the main part of a degree, or at postgraduate level. There are a number of composers' festivals and competitions which provide an opportunity to get work heard.
- **Useful work experience:** as with writing, the difficulty lies not in composing but in getting work performed. Working with youth and community companies, or taking part in profit shares, may be a way of getting work seen and heard.
- **Professional organisations:** Association of Professional Composers, Performing Rights Society (PRS), Mechanical Copyright Protection Society (MCPS), Musicians' Union (MU), Equity.
- **Salary range:** an aspiring composer would be unlikely to earn a living wage purely from composing. The income of a successful composer with a string of West End successes would be substantial, however.
- **Job security:** directly related to status and reputation.
- **Transferable skills:** there is scope for composing outside the performing arts, in commercial environments such as advertising. A composer might also work as musical director, conductor or musician in musical theatre. There is also the possibility of work in education.

Choreographer

- **Areas of responsibility:** in the context of a dance performance, the choreographer is likely also to be the director (for example, in the Cholmondleys Dance Company, based in London, Lea Anderson is the choreographer of the work and also the artistic director of the company). In other theatre contexts, the choreographer would be likely to work alongside the director on the dance and movement sections of a production.
- **Nature of work:** devising the dance and movement aspects of a production.
- **Training and progression:** choreography is an integral part of dance studies at post-16 level and in higher education. There are also a number of postgraduate or specialist courses for highly experienced dancers.
- **Useful work experience:** any opportunity to perform or choreograph is of benefit, as is regularly seeing the work of leading choreographers.
- **Professional organisations:** Equity, Choreographers' Register, British Association of Choreographers.
- **Salary range:** virtually all choreographers are freelance. Most small-scale, independent choreographers do not make a living purely from choreographing. Work in opera and non-subsidised theatre is better paid, but commercial work for exhibitions and trade shows tends to be the most lucrative field of work.
- **Job security:** low.
- **Transferable skills:** most choreographers may also work as dancers, or as movement advisers in other areas of the performing arts industry.

Performers and entertainers

The most common types of performers are actors, dancers, musicians and singers. There are also a host of others, including magicians, comics, escapologists, jugglers, clowns, aerialists, stunt men and women and hypnotists. (For further details on acting, see Chapter 2.)

- **Nature of work:** to work with the rest of the performance company on the structuring and shaping of a production, under the guide of the director, choreographer and/or musical director. Depending on the nature of the company, the performers may have a significant part to play in devising and constructing the performance. This will depend on the philosophy of the company and the approach of the creative team. (See Chapter 4, pp.117–131, for further details on company-devised work.)
- **Essential qualities:** performers in any area of theatre will succeed only if they possess talent, training and good networking skills.
- **Training and progression:** most post-16 and higher education theatre training courses include elements of technique and units which can begin to provide the basic skills needed to work as a performer. There are then several possible training routes which are examined below (see pp.181–187). It is to any practitioner's

advantage to have a range of performance skills to offer. For example, an actor should have some singing and movement skills as well. The greater the range of skills a performer possesses, the more employable he or she is likely to be.

- **Professional organisations:** Equity, Musicians' Union.
- **Salary range:** varies.
- **Job security:** low, dependent on reputation and versatility to some extent.
- **Transferable skills:** theatre performance skills are useful in other areas of the performing arts industry, such as television and radio. Many performers also work in education and youth and community theatre.

Support

Even in large professional companies, developing the level of skill of the performers is important. This task may be carried out by appointed members of the company, or by specialist coaches. These are people who have acquired skill in their particular field, and have then moved on to work in an education and training capacity with professionals. All the jobs tend to be highly specialised, and there are comparatively few practitioners working in each area. They are likely to be either freelance or employed by a well-established, large-scale company or training establishment. The following are some examples of this type of job.

Staff/rehearsal director
- **Nature of work:** works with a cast during a run, maintaining and developing the quality of the performance. The rehearsal director may also rehearse the understudies.

Voice coach
- **Nature of work:** to maintain and develop the vocal skills of the performers, and to coach any specific style of speech, accent or dialect.

Movement coach
- **Nature of work:** similar to the role of a choreographer, but generally dealing with any movement in a production which falls outside the parameters of dance.

Fight coach
- **Nature of work:** usually a specialist in fencing and hand-to-hand combat, the fight coach will choreograph and direct any fight sequences, with particular attention to safety.

Repetiteur
- **Nature of work:** a musician (usually a pianist) who acts as accompanist during rehearsals, in place of the orchestra or band. (It would be prohibitively expensive to have the band in for every rehearsal.)

Notator

● **Nature of work:** usually works in dance, alongside a choreographer, annotating the movement and choreography. There are several different types of notation, each of which is highly specialised; it serves the same function as musical notation, and allows reconstruction of the movement at a later stage.

Casting

The people responsible for this fall into two groups. First, there are a considerable number of agents and personal management companies who represent practitioners. They tend to specialise in different areas, such as acting, music, dance, voice-overs, composition or script writing. Casting directors, on the other hand, work on behalf of venues or production companies to find practitioners with suitable skills or physical features for a specific role. Both jobs require a high level of communication skills, and the ability to maintain and develop a substantial network of contacts.

Agent/personal manager

● **Nature of work:** to manage the professional affairs of practitioners, using a network of contacts to promote them and acquire work for them. The agent will negotiate fees and contracts on behalf of the practitioner, and will represent his or her client in any disputes with employers. The agent takes a percentage of the practitioner's fee in payment. (See pp.189–190 for further details.)

Casting director

● **Nature of work:** to work on behalf of a venue or company to locate appropriate practitioners for specific roles. The casting director will usually have substantial knowledge of a number of different performers, and will also have strong links with agents and management companies.

Design team

Depending on the scale and nature of a project, there may be one designer who has responsibility for all aspects of design, or the various different roles may be divided up among a number of people. The three main areas are set design, costume design and lighting design. Some designers have the skills to work in all areas, whereas others choose to specialise in only one. However, there will always be close liaison between members of the team. (For further information on design, see Chapter 8.)

Set designer

● **Nature of work:** in conjunction with the director or choreographer and production manager, the designer works to create the design concept for the set. This will usually involve drawing up the technical plans and constructing a scale model of the set for use in rehearsal and when planning and constructing the full set. Liaison with other designers on the project and the construction team is

essential. In small companies, the set designer is often responsible for construction.

Costume designer
- **Nature of work:** working alongside the set designer to develop the ideas for the costumes.
- **Essential qualities:** a substantial knowledge of historical and geographical trends in clothes design and fashion; an appreciation of the needs of the performers when in costume, such as the need of a dancer to be able to move freely.

Lighting designer
- **Nature of work:** to work in conjunction with the design and technical team to create lighting which complements the intended atmosphere and mood of the production.
- **Essential qualities:** a thorough understanding of the wide range and function of technical lighting facilities available, and of the physics of light and colour; practical knowledge of electricity and of loading lighting bars and trusses.

Production and technical team

It is possible to specialise in any one of a number of different areas of production and technical theatre. However, as with performing, the greater your range of skills and knowledge, the more likely you are to find employment. The areas of responsibility and the nature of the work vary between jobs, but in other ways they are quite similar.

- **Essential qualities:** complete reliability and professionalism, with a keen awareness and appreciation of Health and Safety issues relating to theatre; stamina and the ability to work long hours.
- **Training and progression:** most post-16 vocational courses include technical theatre options. There is also a range of professional training courses and traineeships available for acquiring the level of experience to work professionally.
- **Useful work experience:** as with performing, it is well worth finding any opportunity at school or college, or in youth and community theatre, to gain as much experience as possible. An applicant for vocational training will be expected to have a high level of experience and understanding of the field of work at an amateur level.
- **Professional organisations:** Equity; Broadcasting, Entertainment Cinematic Theatre Union (BECTU).
- **Salary range:** technical salaries tend to be low to reasonable. A practitioner who is self-employed, or working in more commercial areas such as trade shows, or who is highly experienced and working as a freelance production manager, may earn quite large sums of money
- **Job security:** if a technician has a broad range of skills, it is usually possible to find work. Contracts tend to be short, with permanent contracts being found only in a few larger venues or companies.

- **Transferable skills:** technical theatre skills are also of use in other areas of the performing arts industry, such as film, television and the recording industry, as well as in areas such as trade shows and exhibitions.

Production manager
- **Nature of work:** liaising between the directorial and design team on the one hand, and the production team and construction workshops on the other. He or she is responsible for the production budget, and for ensuring that this is adhered to. The production manager may also advise the design team on technical aspects of construction and on the costing of materials and resources. Once the show is in rehearsal and production, he or she will oversee the technical and stage management team.

Stage managers
- **Nature of work:** the stage managers are responsible for the management of all aspects of the stage area, and for the general running of the show. Once the stage manager has received clearance from the front-of-house manager, the stage management team has full responsibility for the running of the show, including providing cues to the various technical teams and the performers working on the show. (For further information on stage management, see Chapter 8.)

Technicians: stage, lighting, sound
- **Nature of work:** the technicians are part of the production team, under the supervision of the production manager. They are responsible for setting up, maintaining and operating their specific area of a production.

Theatre workshops
There are a range of creative and craft practitioners associated with theatre who operate within their own production workshops, including carpentry, the paint workshop, the metal workshop, armoury, properties, costume, wigs and make-up. Venues such as the Royal National Theatre and some large production companies may have permanent teams employed to fill these posts, but much of the work in these areas is likely to be freelance.

- **Nature of work:** to use specific craft skills for manufacturing and maintaining elements of the production.
- **Essential qualities:** a high level of skill, training and creativity, with an eye for precision and detail.
- **Training and progression:** a few schools and colleges have the expertise to begin to teach some of these skills on post-16 performing arts courses. Some professional training courses exist at a higher level, and with the development of NVQs limited numbers of apprenticeships are likely to become available via the Training and Enterprise Councils (TECs).

- **Useful work experience:** any experience which can be acquired at school or college or in youth theatre is likely to be useful. It is also possible, and may be easier, to acquire certain craft skills, such as metalwork and costumier skills, outside the world of theatre.
- **Salary range:** the salary for this type of work is not likely to be high, especially during an apprenticeship. As skill levels increase, it may be possible to demand higher salaries, particularly if working freelance. It is likely that the majority of these craft skills could command more substantial salaries outside the theatre industry.
- **Job security:** some larger theatre and production companies may have workers on permanent contracts in craft areas, but it is likely that a good proportion of the available work will be freelance. This tends to be a fairly specialised field, and once a practitioner has developed a high skill level and a network of contacts, it should be possible to maintain a steady stream of work.
- **Transferable skills:** most theatrical craft skills can also be applied outside theatre, where in fact they might originally have been acquired. Depending on the particular craft, work exists in many fields, such as the clothing or construction industries and the fine arts market.

House management
The house management team is responsible for the front-of-house areas, which might include the foyer, bars, restaurants, box office, shops and auditorium. A range of staff will be employed to work in these areas. Although many of these jobs may not require specific theatre skills, they may provide an insight into the day-to-day running of the venue, as well as an opportunity to see a range of companies and performances free.

Education
A number of companies focus specifically on working in an educational capacity. Many other companies and venues have a remit to provide educational support for the work of the company. In these situations, an educational officer is frequently employed to provide this support.

Education officer
- **Nature of work:** to liaise with schools and colleges and to provide educational support for the work of the company or venue. (For further information about the role of an education officer, see pp.246–249.)

Other contexts
There are many opportunities for the use of theatrical skills outside the theatre industry. You might progress from work in theatre to such areas as drama therapy, music therapy or movement therapy, or into education. Such moves may be made for a variety of reasons, but most commonly it is because there is significant scope for further development, a different sense of fulfilment and greater job security.

EDUCATION AND TRAINING

During the 1980s and 1990s, opportunities in training and education in general have changed considerably. A proportion of this change has been brought about through action by the government, including:

- introducing the National Curriculum;
- commissioning and acting on a number of major surveys of current education and training provision (including the Dearing reports);
- altering the levels and methods of funding for schools, colleges and universities;
- establishing National Targets for Education and Training (NTETs);
- reducing student grants and introducing student loans;
- increasing the availability and status of GNVQs and NVQs.

The changes that have resulted from these and other initiatives have led to a wider range of options, but also to far greater financial pressure both on the schools and colleges delivering education and also on the student. This in turn has affected the competition for places.

Historically, only two main progression paths were available. The first involved staying at school and taking A-levels, then progressing on to university or college to obtain a degree, or equivalent. This was the *educational* route. The other option was to enter a trade and become an apprentice in that field: skills were acquired whilst working under the watchful eye of an expert. This was the *training* route.

Each system had its advantages and disadvantages. The educational route tended to carry greater recognition in the form of qualifications, but because of the non-vocational nature of many degree courses it did not necessarily include preparation for employment. By contrast, the training route, as a result of its vocational nature, provided a skill, but rarely resulted in nationally recognised qualifications.

One of the advantages of recent developments is that the new structure acknowledges the importance of both vocational (training) and non-vocational (educational) elements in any one qualification. Some qualifications, such as General National Vocational Qualifications (GNVQs), which are school- or college-based courses, incorporate both vocational and non-vocational elements. Other forms of assessment, called National Vocational Qualifications (NVQs), have also been devised. They allow people in the workplace to be assessed on their skills in a similar way to the old-style apprentice and to gain a nationally recognised qualification with equal status to the school/college-based routes.

There are effectively three progression routes open to a student studying theatre. The routes differ in terms of funding and the means by which a qualification is accredited. However, this does not prevent you from swapping between progression routes. These three different progression routes are outlined below, and on pp.184–186 we consider the funding implications for each route.

Progression route 1 (generally non-fee-paying)

The following courses form the basic framework of the government-supported educational programme available in the UK. The descriptions below indicate the bare facts about the general nature of each qualification. However, individual courses at different colleges are unique in terms of their content (within the confines of any established curriculum), their underlying philosophy, their prestige, the ratio of theory to practical, the standard and the entry criteria. If you are attempting to work out a progression route for yourself, it is essential to carry out extensive background research to find a few options that best suit your own individual needs and interests.

A-levels

These tend to be the most theoretical post-16 options, with some practical work. However, they do not always explore the more vocational elements of theatre. Dance, music and theatre-based A-levels are available separately, or you can study Performing Arts as one A-level.

BTEC Diplomas in Performing Arts

These have a more vocational bias than GCSEs and A-levels. Subject options are available in most areas of theatre. The courses have no final examinations and are continuously assessed through practical assignments. BTEC diplomas are available at two levels: the First Diploma is a one-year course, roughly equivalent in standard to GCSEs, while the National Diploma is a two-year course, equivalent to A-levels.

GNVQs in Performing Arts and Entertainment Industries

These are an extension of the BTEC Diploma. They have a vocational focus, with subject options available in most areas of theatre. The courses are continuously assessed, and selected units also have theoretical tests. The Foundation GNVQ provides a grounding in the basics of the industry; the Intermediate GNVQ is roughly equivalent in standard to GCSEs or a BTEC First Diploma; the Advanced GNVQ is equivalent to A-levels or a BTEC National Diploma. Generally, the foundation and intermediate courses would each be covered over one year, and the advanced course would be covered over two years.

HNDs

Higher National Diplomas are a step on from A-levels, the BTEC National Diploma or the GNVQ Advanced. They are taught at various colleges and universities across the country. Each course is different, with its own particular emphasis and specialism. Virtually all areas of theatre are catered for somewhere in the UK. Like the BTEC National Diploma, the course is vocationally based and is continuously assessed. The courses are generally taught over two years, and although they do not carry the same status as a university degree, certain HNDs are very highly regarded. This is because the practical skills and attitude to work acquired on the course are thought to prepare people well for employment. After completing an HND it is sometimes possible to feed into the second or third year of a degree course.

Degrees

These are available at a number of universities and colleges, and a few drama schools, throughout the country. Courses cover most areas of performing arts, although the particular focus and underlying philosophy vary from course to course. There may be scope for studying more than one subject within the degree course. Like HNDs, degrees are a step up from A-levels, BTEC National Diploma or GNVQ Advanced.

Higher-level courses

Courses available at various colleges, universities and drama schools include:

- Postgraduate Certificate of Education (PGCE): a one-year course taken after a degree, which provides a teaching qualification;
- Master of Arts (MA): a higher-level course, usually with an academic bias; each course has a different emphasis;
- postgraduate diplomas: usually one-year courses, often with a practical emphasis, on subjects such as script writing, directing, acting, community theatre, composition or choreography.

Progression route 2 (generally fee-paying)

The following courses form the basic framework of what is in effect the private-sector educational programme. As with the courses in progression route 1, all that is provided here is an outline. Each course is unique, and if you are attempting to map a progression route for yourself, it is essential to carry out extensive background research to find the options that best suit your own individual requirements.

Stage schools

These are private, fee-paying schools, which provide a general education as well as teaching specialist theatre skills. Generally aimed at the primary and secondary age-group, they usually offer GCSEs and sometimes A-levels.

Drama schools

These are usually fee-paying schools, which provide training to prepare people for employment in the performing arts industry. Students usually have to be at least 18 when they start, and entry is by audition and interview. Courses last for two or three years, and the qualification awarded is roughly equivalent to an HND or degree. Some courses are accredited by universities and carry formal degree status; these may require formal entry qualifications, such as A-levels, BTEC National Diploma or GNVQ Advanced. Some of the university-accredited courses do not charge fees.

Most drama schools carry courses in a range of subjects, including acting, stage management, musical theatre, directing and writing. There are also equivalent dance and music schools and colleges, functioning along the same lines as drama schools. Most of these schools are members of organisations such as the Conference of Drama Schools or the National Council for Drama Training, which provide accreditation and maintain the schools' status, quality and prestige.

Higher-level courses

These are available at many drama, dance and music schools and colleges. Higher-level diploma courses tend to be aimed at students who have already graduated from university, college or drama school, and are usually highly specialised. Students who have done less practically based degrees, or professionals who wish to learn new skills, can opt for a one-year course in a variety of subjects, including acting, directing, script writing and speech. As with the other drama school courses, fees will be charged for many of these diplomas.

Progression route 3: work-based training

These schemes are usually the result of collaboration between industry, which provides the training, and schools or colleges, which provide the assessment. They are a rapidly expanding area, and follow the principles of the old apprenticeship model, with the advantages that the trainee may receive payment, acquires on-the-job experience and gains nationally recognised accreditation.

If you undertake what is known as a 'Modern Apprenticeship' (MAPP or MA – not to be confused with postgraduate Master of Arts MAs), you are likely to spend some time at college and some in the workplace. You will gain qualifications through the National Vocational Qualifications (NVQ) scheme. These are work-based assessment strategies available at five levels. Although highly developed in certain industries, NVQs are in their infancy in the performing arts industry. They are being developed by several organisations, in particular the Arts and Entertainment Training Council (AETC). NVQs are or will be available in a variety of areas, including arts management, venue administration, technical theatre and certain areas of performance, such as circus, music and dance. It is likely that the range of NVQs that are available in the industry will expand considerably over the next few years.

Funding for training and education

There are two areas to consider when researching funding for education: the fees for a course, to be paid to the educational institution, and your own living expenses (maintenance). Seven main categories of student funding are available:

● Local Education Authority (LEA) mandatory awards (for fees and maintenance) are paid automatically if the course falls into a specific recognised category, which includes most undergraduate degree and HND courses. The maintenance part of the award is means-tested. Some further and higher education institutions have been forced to start charging 'top-up' fees, as government spending on education has been cut in the last few years.

- LEA discretionary awards (for fees and maintenance) may be paid if the course falls outside the recognised category. Usually, LEAs have a limited budget for discretionary awards, and applicants are assessed on merit. Each LEA has a different number of discretionary awards to offer, and its own policies on who receives them. These awards are often managed like scholarships, with potential students having to audition and/or interview. Some authorities do not give discretionary awards.

- Student loans (for maintenance) are generally available for all post-18 courses that attract LEA mandatory awards. There may also be the possibility of receiving loans for courses that attract LEA discretionary awards.

- Career Development Loans (CDLs) (for fees and maintenance) are available from the Department for Education and Employment (DfEE), and are available for up to two years' vocational study, for certain courses only.

- Access funds (for maintenance) are held by some colleges, and are made available to students who can demonstrate serious financial difficulties, at the discretion of the college.

- Scholarships (for fees and maintenance) may be available from some schools, colleges or benevolent organisations with an interest in the area of study.

- Other sources (for fees and maintenance) might be found by means of a certain amount of research and perseverance. As with scholarships, there are a number of organisations, many of which are charitable trusts, which have discretionary awards to give to specific categories of people. Information on these organisations and the categories they tend to fund is given in *The Directory of Grant Making Trusts* (full details in the bibliography, p.207). Occasionally, students are successful in gaining funds from a variety of alternative sources. It usually takes substantial commitment, ruthless determination and a hard-sell approach to be successful in gaining such funding.

The following information relates these considerations to the three progression routes illustrated earlier.

Funding for progression route 1
Most GCSE, A-level, BTEC Diploma and GNVQ courses at schools and colleges are free to students under the age of 19. If you are 19 or over, you are likely to have to pay a proportion of the fees, in which case it is possible to apply to your LEA for a discretionary award. If you progress on to an HND or degree you will not normally have to pay fees, and will be eligible for an LEA mandatory award and a student loan to help cover living expenses.

Funding for postgraduate study varies; some courses, such as PGCEs, attract mandatory funding, but many courses may attract only discretionary funding. A number of these courses may have part-time options, which enable students to continue working in order to finance themselves while they study.

Funding for progression route 2
This is the area where funding so often becomes a problem, preventing a student from taking his or her chosen course of study. Many courses at stage schools, and at drama, dance and music schools, do not attract mandatory funding, and students are therefore dependent on the attitude of their LEA to performing arts training. Other alternatives include: Career Development Loans; paying your own way through training, either by trying to hold down a job whilst studying or by saving for several years whilst working and then studying; or researching other funding channels. It is also worth contacting the Educational Grants Advisory Service for further information. (See list of useful addresses, p.204.)

Funding for progression route 3
Some larger organisations run their own training and apprenticeship schemes, but Modern Apprenticeships are government-funded, via the Training and Enterprise Councils (TECs). Trainees will normally receive a training allowance, and they may also be entitled to a CDL or student loan.

The training and progression routes in practice
If you are considering training and education in the area of performing arts, it is worth asking yourself the following questions:

● Are you being completely realistic about your skills, your academic ability and your aspirations? You should gain objective opinions from the people who are best placed to advise you, not necessarily from those closest to you.

● What area(s) of work will allow you to achieve your fullest potential and therefore best suits your needs? (Refer to Maslow's hierarchy of needs, p.164.)

● What level of job security do you want?

● Do you *really* know what your chosen career path entails?

● If you are still undecided about the specific direction you wish your career to take, what courses will allow you to keep your options open?

● Will your needs and aspirations be best served by a general, conventional qualification, such as a university degree, with an educational bias and greater general recognition, or by a vocational training course, which may provide more specific theatre skills but be less well recognised outside the world of theatre?

When looking at course options and course content, try to maximise your scope for acquiring transferable skills: a wider skill base will increase your employability later.

You will need to acquire a real feeling for the institutions and courses under investigation. Read all the literature they produce, attend open days, visit the institution, see its productions, talk to students who are studying the course, and try to find out whether graduates are successful in gaining places on higher courses or in employment.

Do not let possible funding difficulties prevent you from researching all options. If you favour courses in progression route 2, research funding sources (be imaginative – some people manage to fund the course, so why can't you?); if you cannot find potential funding channels, refer back to progression route 1 or 3.

AFTER TRAINING: STARTING A CAREER

In most areas of work within the theatre industry, there is an oversupply of skilled practitioners. This tends to benefit the industry, because it allows a choice from a pool of applicants for any post or role. However, it does not necessarily favour the practitioner, who may find it difficult to establish a foundation of professional experience on which to build a career. Another problem is that the concept of a job for life is outdated, and consequently security is harder to find. The Arts Council of England estimates that approximately 70 per cent of all work carried out in theatre is conducted on a freelance basis (a contract lasting less than 12 months), and this figure is growing.

These factors emphasise the need for:

- a creative and flexible approach to career opportunities;
- an appreciation of the role played by transferable skills;
- a continuous programme of personal development and skill acquisition (lifelong learning);
- the ability to promote yourself;
- the expertise essential for working on a self-employed basis;
- regular assessment of your own development.

This type of flexibility of approach tends to lead to a non-linear career pattern, and the person who is best equipped to deal with such a pattern is most likely to be successful. The term that is commonly used for this type of approach is 'portfolioing'. To be a 'portfolio worker' one needs to appreciate that work can serve one of four functions. These are:

- to provide an income;
- to provide enjoyment;
- to increase experience;
- to refresh and inspire one's thinking and outlook.

These ideas relate back directly to the earlier model demonstrated by Maslow's hierarchy of needs. Each function is important to establish a balance, and each job may provide one or more of them.

The aim of this section is to provide an insight into some of the knowledge necessary to work effectively in theatre, particularly as a portfolio worker.

Self-marketing

A Curriculum Vitae (CV)

This is one of the first documents you will need to draw up. Its function is to act as a clear, chronological record of your education, experience and achievements. It should be a short, concise document, containing the following information:

- name;
- address and telephone number;
- date of birth (and playing age for an acting CV);
- height and appearance (for an acting CV);
- union membership;
- education and training;
- relevant work experience;
- other work experience;
- additional skills;
- interests and hobbies;
- referees.

There are various opinions about how a CV should be laid out. However, it should always be concise (ideally one side of A4), word-processed, clear and, if appropriate, subtly unique.

A portfolio of evidence

It is common at schools and colleges to build up a personal portfolio known as a record of achievement. Producing a portfolio of evidence is a continuation of the same process. The first document you include should be your CV, in order to provide an overview. The rest of the portfolio should contain supporting information, which goes into greater detail. This may include examples of work, portrait photographs, press reviews, evidence of qualifications, citations and any other relevant documentation. It should be presented in a way that enables the reader to build up a picture of you very quickly by simply browsing through the information, without having to read large tracts of text. More detail should be available to the reader if required. The principle is very similar to that of a newspaper: one can browse through it, acquiring information from headlines and pictures but reading only the articles that are of particular interest and relevance.

A portfolio should be put together in such a way that information can be regularly altered or updated. Every job tends to have a subtly different emphasis, so it is in your interest to try and bring out salient points for each application. It is also important to remove information as it loses its relevance. The portfolio is an opportunity to present information clearly, but also in a way that shows your creativity and originality. The information contained in the portfolio provides general information about the individual; the style of presentation can reveal something of the individual's personality. (However, it is worth obtaining a cross-section of opinions about the level of originality and creativity that might be considered acceptable.)

Spotlight

Spotlight is an organisation which produces a national directory of actors and actresses; this runs to a total of eight volumes, each about twice the size of a telephone directory (or one CD-ROM). The entries include photos, brief information and a contact number. Directors, casting agencies and regional theatres regularly use this directory to aid the casting process, so it is essential for actors to have themselves listed. The fee for inclusion is about £100 per year. (For contact details, see p.206.)

Networking

Once you have established a reputation as a practioner, you may be fortunate enough to find that your skills are in demand. Until you reach that stage, it is important to establish and maintain contacts, to be seen, and to make your name and face familiar to people with influence; these contacts can then be used to help find employment. This process is known as networking.

Any ploy that can help increase the number of contacts in your address book will increase your networking opportunities, as long as you stop short of blatant intrusion. Such ploys may include:

● sending a CV or examples of your work, and following up with a telephone call;
● cold calling (ringing with no prior contact having been made);
● regularly attending auditions;
● making the most of chance meetings;
● staging chance meetings.

Whenever you are making contacts, it is important to find out the name and role of the person with whom you are dealing, and to establish a dialogue. Even if it is only a chance meeting, it is worthwhile using the conversation as an opportunity to discuss a few memorable concepts, which can then be used in future conversation as a point of reference to re-establish the link. The importance of networking should not be underestimated, but the skills that are needed to develop and maintain the network can be acquired only through experience.

Agents and management companies

The role of the agent or management company (an umbrella organisation with a number of agents) is to manage the professional affairs of a practitioner through promotion and representation. Agents are most commonly associated with actors, but some specialise in working with other practitioners, such as writers, composers and variety performers. Agents have their own large network of contacts, which they will use to promote the practitioner. They use their experience to negotiate fees and the terms and conditions of contracts, and they will represent the client in any disputes with employers. An agent may also advise a client on the type of job to accept and reject. Agents usually take up to ten per cent of any income from work they generate for their clients; it is therefore in the best interests of the agent to find work for the practitioner and also to optimise the development of his or her career.

There are several possible ways to be signed up by an agent. Frequently, during vocational training courses, a number of agents will be invited to showcases. This enables them to see the practitioners' work, after which they might be prepared to negotiate taking certain individuals onto their books. Alternatively, as part of the networking process, you may be able to persuade an agent to come and see your work, and this may be followed by similar negotiations. The reputation and status of different agents and management companies vary, and it is in your best interests to be represented by a reputable agent, who will treat your career as a priority.

Co-operative agencies

Some agencies work on a co-operative basis; these can be useful for people who are having difficulties signing with an agent they like, or who wish to maintain greater control of their own affairs. A co-operative agency is a group of perhaps a dozen practitioners, who join together to represent themselves. They will usually take it in turns to staff the office, promote the clients and respond to enquiries. The advantage of co-operatives is that a practitioner maintains greater autonomy, but the disadvantage is that the members may not possess the same wealth of contacts or of experience on such issues as fee negotiation, contracts and employment rights as an agent would have.

Joining a union

There are three main unions in the British theatre industry: the British Actors' Equity Association (Equity), the Musicians' Union (MU) and the Broadcasting, Entertainment Cinematic Theatre Union (BECTU). BECTU is predominantly a theatre technicians' union. The unions act to protect the interests of their members by ensuring acceptable working hours and conditions, maintaining favourable standard minimum rates of pay, collecting and distributing back payments such as repeat fees, and providing insurance, advice on social security benefits and contracts, and a variety of other information.

Joining the MU is done by simply completing the paperwork, signing a declaration and then awaiting approval.

Joining Equity is rather more difficult. There are a number of different routes through which to gain membership and acquire an Equity card: each one requires the applicant to produce evidence that he or she is working on Equity-approved contracts over a specified period of time. Full details and a guide to entry are available from Equity.

Joining BECTU involves filling in the relevant paperwork, providing evidence that one is working in the relevant field and awaiting approval.

Auditions and interviews

There is a wealth of advice, training and books available about auditions and interviews (see bibliography, p.207), and opinion is mixed about the best approach to take when preparing for them. Most auditions will require you to perform a pre-prepared piece to demonstrate your skills. You may also have to take part in a workshop, class or improvisation session, and invariably there will be an interview.

Audition and interview skills are acquired with experience, and ultimately you will no doubt develop your own strategies. However, until you have gained experience, the best preparation is research. Important points to investigate might include:

- the details and background of the job or role for which the interview/audition is being held;
- the nature of the company, organisation or production;
- specific facts about the artistic policies of the company;
- any peculiarities or idiosyncrasies which might give the applicant an advantage at interview.

The objective of the potential employer is to find the person most suitable for a specific job or role. Failure, therefore, does not necessarily imply that the person who got the job was better than you, but that he or she was more suitable in this particular instance. It is often possible to request feedback from the interview/audition panel if you are not successful, and this can help further your personal development. (See also p.60.)

Survival information

National Insurance (NI)

Everyone who is employed or self-employed is liable to pay National Insurance between the ages of 16 and 65. This is a form of insurance or long-term investment managed by the state, which may entitle an individual to Jobseeker's Allowance when unemployed, and to state benefits such as a basic pension on retirement. There are four categories of National Insurance:

- Class 1 NI is payable by anyone working with employee status (this means in employment, as opposed to being contracted as a freelancer). Contributions (from employer and employee) are calculated as a percentage of earnings and are deducted at source,

191

before you receive payment. Paying Class 1 NI entitles an employee to Jobseeker's Allowance when unemployed and to a state pension on reaching retirement age. If you are unemployed and signing on, Class 1 NI is automatically credited to your record without you having to make payments. This protects your entitlement to Jobseeker's Allowance and your pension rights.

- Class 2 NI is payable by people who are self-employed, at a fixed rate per week. These payments entitle you to a state pension on retirement, but do not automatically entitle you to Jobseeker's Allowance when unemployed.

- Class 3 NI is voluntary, and can be paid to make up any period of time when Class 1 or 2 contributions were not paid. For example, such a period might occur if you worked or travelled abroad for a period of time, and did not make contributions in the UK.

- Class 4 NI is payable by people who are self-employed, in addition to Class 2. It has to be paid if the total income for a financial year is above a certain amount (in 1996, the figure was approximately £7,000), and is calculated as a percentage of income.

Jobseeker's Allowance

If you are registered unemployed, and signing on, you may be entitled to receive the Jobseeker's Allowance. Rules on eligibility and entitlement to the allowance are complicated. The aim of the scheme is to encourage people to find work, and to accept any job that might be offered to them. The system is not designed to finance students through education and training, or practitioners who are 'resting', waiting for the right job to come along. Anyone receiving this benefit will be pressurised to find *any* work: if they are seen to be exploiting the situation, they will lose their entitlement to benefit. Specialist advice and support should be sought on this issue, and is available from a number of sources, including the various unions, such as Equity, and the Citizens' Advice Bureau.

Pensions

When you are in the process of trying to launch a career, it may seem irrelevant and premature to be considering provision for your retirement, which might be more than 40 years away. However, a basic understanding of pensions and how they work reveals the importance of considering such issues early. With any pension scheme, money is invested over the period of time between making a payment and retirement. The length of time for which the money remains invested is a major factor which will influence how high the pension will be on retirement. The following examples illustrate this.

- You invest £10 per month over a ten-year period between the ages of 20 and 30, but then pay no more money into the scheme. A total investment of £1,200 has been made. The investment keeps on growing, because of the interest earned, even though no more money is paid in.

- You invest £10 per month for a 35-year period between the ages of 30 and 65. A total investment of £4,200 has been made.

When you reach the age of 65, assuming both schemes have been earning the same interest over their investment period, you will get a larger pension from the first scheme, because of the longer investment period, *despite* having invested more than three times as much money into the second scheme. This highlights the importance of considering pension schemes early: smaller investments paid into a scheme early in your career are likely to be at least as valuable as more substantial amounts paid into a scheme later in your career.

There are many different types of pension scheme, but it is possible to classify them into three distinct categories:

- **State Pension Scheme:** as a result of paying National Insurance, you are entitled to a state pension. These pay out a very small weekly sum on retirement. In the next 20 years it is possible that they may be phased out altogether.

- **Company pension scheme:** if you are in fixed, long-term employment, it is likely that 'superannuation' will be deducted from your salary at source. This money is paid into a company pension scheme. Details of the scheme will be available from the personnel section of the company. It is possible to opt out of this scheme, but it is worth taking professional advice before taking such action.

- **Private pension scheme:** there are any number of different private pension schemes. These are run by specialist companies, and can be used either instead of paying superannuation, or in addition to a company pension scheme.

Pensions might not appeal as an important or worthwhile item on which to spend your money, but if you are planning to live reasonably comfortably in retirement they are essential. They can also have certain tax advantages, which tend to make them more attractive as a way of saving money over a long period of time.

Tax

Taxation is the method employed by the government to collect revenue, which it then spends on such things as the National Health Service, education, the armed forces and also the arts. Taxation is calculated as a percentage of income. Different bands of income are taxed at different rates. As an *approximate* guide, roughly the first £4,000 of earnings is tax free; the next £4,000 is taxed at 20 per cent; the next £22,000 is taxed at 23 per cent, and any income above that is taxed at 40 per cent.

Like the schemes for paying NI, there are two 'schedules' on which tax is most commonly paid:

- Schedule E is paid when you are working as an employee, as opposed to being self-employed. The scheme is known as 'pay as you earn', or PAYE. This is because all tax, National Insurance and superannuation are deducted from the salary and paid on behalf of the employee by the company.

- Schedule D is the tax schedule for self-employed people. In this situation, all income is usually received in full, and it is the self-employed person's responsibility to keep a record of income and expenditure, and to liaise with the tax office each year to calculate the amount of tax to be paid.

The potential advantage of working on Schedule D is that you are effectively perceived as a business which has running costs, and all such costs are tax-deductible. Therefore, if a freelancer has a *gross* income in one year of £12,000, but during the year spends £5,000 on allowable expenses, for tax purposes the *net* income is £7,000 (£12,000 minus £5,000), so only £7,000 will be liable for tax.

Allowable expenses depend on the particular area of work, but are likely to include such things as the following:

- agent's or manager's fees;
- accountant's fees;
- secretarial support;
- advertising;
- stationery;
- some postage;
- some telephone/fax;
- tuition and professional development;
- books, journals and trade papers;
- travel expenses (which might include all or part of the cost of running a car);
- some theatre, cinema and concert tickets;
- union subscriptions;
- some subsistence costs (hotel and restaurant bills);
- insurance.

It is crucial for anyone working freelance to acquire some basic book-keeping skills at a very early stage; this will help you to keep clear income/expenditure accounts and to maintain an ordered financial record. Incomplete records may lead to a higher than necessary tax bill. In addition, it can be very expensive to employ an accountant to sort out poorly kept records.

It is not uncommon to carry out some work on Schedule D (self-employed), and other work on Schedule E (PAYE). If this is the case, it is usually worth calling on the expertise of an accountant. With their knowledge and advice, they are likely to be able to save you more money than the amount they charge for their services.

Insurance

Insurance can be a complicated field, but it is in your interests to know a little about why it might be of importance.

Your belongings or equipment can be insured by taking out an insurance policy with an insurance broker. Cover usually includes loss, damage or theft of belongings, but in certain situations, such as being on tour, it might be that your belongings are not protected. It is worth checking with the insurance company to see exactly what the policy covers.

Any company is legally obliged to have employer's liability insurance. This covers it if an employee is injured and sues the company for damages. When working freelance, it is not uncommon to sub-contract work out to other people, in which case the freelancer is effectively becoming an employer; in such a situation, it may be necessary to have employer's liability insurance.

It may also be in the interest of some performers to have personal liability insurance. For example, a fire juggler might risk damaging property, or causing injury to a member of the audience; a trapeze performer might fall, and, quite apart from any damage done to his or herself, might injure a spectator. In such a situation, the spectator (the third party) might sue for damages, and if the claim was successful the performer would be liable; if he or she was insured, the insurance company should pay the damages.

As a freelancer, you are dependent upon your ability to work in order to earn money. In the event of injury or illness, you might not be able to work for a sustained period of time, and might therefore lose your earning capacity. It is possible to obtain insurance cover for such situations, which would pay out if you were unable to work.

Resting

In theatre, the term 'resting' refers to the period between contracts, when a practitioner is effectively out of work. Equity estimates that 80 per cent of its members are resting at any one time. This proportion is high partly because the supply of practitioners exceeds the demand, and partly because it can prove difficult to attend auditions and interviews for new jobs whilst involved in time-consuming performances or a tour. As a result, practitioners often need to complete a run before they can make themselves available to audition for a new job.

Resting can be a stressful time; you are unlikely to be earning much money, and may not know when you are likely to secure the next contract. It is a time for trying to remain positive, maintaining morale and utilising the time constructively. Below are a number of tasks and actions that might be worthwhile when resting.

Signing on

If you were previously employed on PAYE, it is likely that you will be able to sign on as unemployed and available for work. This is important, because even if you are not entitled to state benefits (see above), signing on will credit you with National Insurance contributions, which protects pension rights (see above).

Networking

It is worthwhile for you to re-establish contact with networks of friends and former colleagues while resting. By so doing, you may well hear of work that is coming up, and will also inform others of your availability. Agents are also likely to be working hard for their clients at this time.

Researching for auditions

Before attending any auditions it is well worth investing time into researching and preparing for them (see p.191).

Maximising income

Once the process of finding new work has been put into action, it may be necessary to do some other form of work for a period of time, in order to earn some money. It is usually necessary to take a job where it is possible to attend auditions at very short notice. However, this is likely to mean that the income for the work is not particularly high. It is not uncommon to end up in a job such as telephone sales, where the majority of the money tends to be earned on a commission-only basis.

Unpaid work

There may be a great deal of benefit to be gained from undertaking work for which little or no payment is received. This may fulfil as many as three of the objectives that define portfolio working: providing enjoyment, increasing experience and refreshing and inspiring your thinking and outlook.

Some highly prestigious venues and companies are involved in experimental or innovative theatre, where practitioners rarely receive a living wage for projects. The work done and the public acclaim can, however, contribute significantly to your reputation, thus increasing your prospects. This tends also to be the context in which new practitioners learn their trade. It is not uncommon to work on a project with people who, a few years later, are highly acclaimed practitioners, in a position to offer you substantial work and income.

Unpaid work can be a very successful means of staying involved, being seen and increasing your network of contacts. A few practitioners opt to spend a significant proportion of their time working on such projects, whilst the majority of their income is generated through short-term commercial work that is highly lucrative but not especially challenging or rewarding. This is a classic example of portfolio working.

Taking the initiative

Another option available to a practitioner is to take the initiative by creating and promoting his or her own performances. This is an extremely valuable way of acquiring new skills and broadening your understanding of other areas of work.

It is possible to team up with like-minded practitioners in a similar position and work on what is usually called a 'profit share' (although there is seldom any profit in such a venture). There are a number of fringe venues and festivals around the country where such initiatives are common. The costs incurred can be kept manageable, and the modest nature and facilities of the fringe venues used for such projects do not have to detract from the experience, or from the potential recognition that such productions can generate.

Perhaps the biggest festival in the UK is the Edinburgh Fringe Festival, which takes place each August and includes contributions from every form of theatre (see p.3). This festival attracts many well-known names, but the majority of companies are working on a profit-share basis. The festival personnel are particularly experienced in supporting and assisting inexperienced companies, and hold regular meetings to provide help and information. They also produce a series of extremely useful booklets on putting on a show, marketing and promotion, and Health and Safety issues. The value of such an event is not only in performing, but also in seeing the work of other companies and sharing in the experience of such a prestigious, internationally renowned festival (see bibliography, p.207).

Personal development

Resting is also a good time to undertake training and development. This will enable you to maintain your current skills, brush up old skills that may not have been used recently and acquire new skills. By increasing the range and level of your skills, you will prevent yourself from stagnating, and will increase your marketability. Places such as the Actors' Centre (see p.204) in London, where training and information are available, are useful for this.

Teaching

It is estimated by the Council for Dance Education and Training that within the field of dance 80 per cent of practitioners earn the majority of their income from educational work. It is common for most theatre practitioners to work in education at some stage of their careers, and some choose to train and become specialists in the educational field.

The first experience of teaching can be a shock to anyone, especially if you believe it to be a straightforward area of work. It is therefore well worth acquiring some form of teacher training as part of your professional development (see p.183). Students benefit from working with active practitioners, because their experience and enthusiasm help to provide a direct insight into the essence of the theatre industry.

There is significant scope for education work in theatre, on a part-time, temporary or guest basis, including:

- primary and secondary school teaching (for which a PGCE is required: see p.183);
- further education;
- higher education;
- drama, dance and music schools;
- educational departments of companies and venues;
- TIE companies (see Chapter 7);
- youth and community theatre companies;
- private tuition.

Resource Activities

1. THE STRUCTURE AND FUNCTION OF A VENUE OR PERFORMING COMPANY

This activity has some similarities to Activity 1 in Chapter 4, p.155. It might be appropriate to combine the two, although they have a slightly different focus according to the nature of the chapter.

Aims
- To gain an insight into the infrastructure of a variety of performance companies and venues.
- To develop presentation skills.

Objectives
- To research and identify the objectives of an organisation.
- To analyse the various functions that are carried out by members of the organisation.
- To produce diagrammatic trees to demonstrate the organisational structure of the company.
- To research the funding and financing of the organisation.
- To compare and contrast the differences in structure and funding of different organisations, with reference to their function.

Background
- Read pp.167–180 prior to carrying out this task.
- When making contact with a venue or company, it is important to be diplomatic and understanding. It may be that the organisation cannot find the time to provide the information you are requesting.
- There is value in working as a group and co-ordinating which organisations you intend to contact. This will result in a more thorough understanding and overview of a range of companies.

Tasks
- Pick a company or venue for study. If several people are carrying out the task as a group, make sure a cross-section of organisations is being researched (a venue, a performance company, small-scale, large-scale, and so on). Contact the organisation and locate a suitable individual who can provide the information you require and answer any questions that might arise. Explain your project and arrange a meeting; here you need to acquire information which will enable you to fulfil the task objectives. This may include information about:
  i) the organisation's objectives;
  ii) its mission statement;
  iii) a brief history of the company;
  iv) any particular individuals who might have been involved with the organisation's development;
  v) any other facts that are particularly relevant to the organisation.

If possible, spend some time talking to a cross-section of people who work for the organisation, see it in action and gain the opinions of the organisation's users/customers.

● Using the information you have researched, prepare a short, concise presentation about the organisation, using any available audiovisual aids to help you illustrate your information clearly. (See pp.20–22 in Chapter 1 for guidelines on presentation skills.) Your presentation should enable the audience to gain a thorough insight into the organisation, and should meet all the research objectives. You should provide evidence of the organisation's function and product, diagrammatic trees to illustrate the administrative and organisational structure, and examples of promotional and marketing material and policy.

● Put together a 'summarised' portfolio to complement the information in your presentation

● With the other members of the group, compare and contrast the various different organisations in relation to the task objectives. You may wish to consider similarities and differences in:
i) objectives;
ii) function;
iii) structure;
iv) roles and responsibilities;
v) funding.

2. CONTEXTS FOR EMPLOYMENT

Aim
To gain an insight into two different contexts for employment within one specialism.

Objectives
● To explore contractual arrangements and variations in a chosen vocational area of theatre.
● To investigate working conditions.
● To understand the statutory requirements for different types of employment.
● To gain an insight into regional and national employment trends.

Background
● Read pp.167–180 on employment in the theatre and pp.191–195 on National Insurance, pensions, tax and insurance prior to carrying out this task.
● It is important to be diplomatic and understanding when making the initial contact. It may be that the person cannot find the time to provide the information you are requesting.

Tasks
● Working in pairs with someone within the same specialism as

yourself (drama, dance, music, stagecraft or any other), select two specific, contrasting jobs in which you might both consider working.

- Each of you should establish contact with a person who is currently carrying out one of these jobs and can provide the information you require. Explain your project and arrange a meeting; the aim of this is to acquire information on the specific job being researched and its context within the industry. It is essential to be diplomatic and polite when carrying out this type of research. Make it clear that you are carrying out the research because you are interested in pursuing the same area of work, and be aware that the practitioner may not wish to provide all the information you are seeking. You could try to find out about:

  i) the precise nature and function of the job (it may be possible to obtain a job description and job specification for the post);
  ii) contractual arrangements (full-time, part-time, employed, freelance, temporary or permanent);
  iii) working conditions (pay, benefits, hours, location, working conditions, job security);
  iv) regional and national employment trends for that type of job (levels of employment, male–female ratios, competition, variations in contractual arrangements and working conditions);
  v) statutory requirements (taxation, National Insurance, pensions, benefits, Health and Safety);
  vi) background information on the individual (early work experience, education, training and progression route, professional career path, membership of professional organisations, other work carried out, reasons for achieving success). The person may be prepared to give you a CV or biography.

- Once you have acquired the information, liaise with your partner to explore similarities and differences in the information you have managed to acquire. Use the conclusions you draw to help you plan your own personal development and progression route, if appropriate.

3. SETTING UP A COMPANY

Aim
To gain a comprehensive understanding of company structure.

Objectives
- To define the functions and objectives of a performing arts organisation.
- To plan the job structure and working relationships of the members of the organisation.
- To allocate working roles and responsibilities in terms of functions.
- To define the specific areas of responsibility for each role.
- To explore and assess the benefits and difficulties of team membership in carrying out working roles.

Background

- Read pp.167–170, 'A structural overview'.
- See also pp.138–141 in Chapter 4 on roles and responsibilities.

Tasks

- For this project, you will create your own 'company'. First of all, identify its purpose (such as to produce a successful performance or to set up a venue to receive a touring show).

- Identify all the jobs that need to be carried out within the company, and plan a company structure.

- Allocate roles and responsibilities to different members of the group, making sure all the jobs that need to be carried out are covered.

- Draw up job descriptions and job specifications for each company 'employee'.

- Ideally, this company should then work practically on a production, with each member fulfilling his or her allocated roles and responsibilities. Try to maintain a professional attitude and approach to the work, in particular to the company structure that was originally agreed.

- On completion of the project, assess its success in relation to the function, structure and job descriptions that were originally drawn up. Which aspects were most successful? What would you do differently next time, and why?

4. OPPORTUNITIES FOR EMPLOYMENT AND TRAINING

Aim

To consider and research possible careers and training routes in the theatre (and performing arts) industry.

Objectives

- To identify sources of information on employment and employment routes.
- To collect material on employment.
- To identify employment growth areas using employment trends.
- To evaluate routes leading to identified employment.
- To assess the individual's training needs to achieve progression to employment.

Background

Read pp.163–187. It is advisable to carry out Activity 3 prior to undertaking these activities.

Tasks

- Following careful consideration of the information contained in this chapter, and with the help of other research sources, decide what area(s) of work might interest you in relation to the theatre industry.

- Carry out an audit of your current strengths, including:
  i) skills;
  ii) interests;
  iii) experience;
  iv) qualifications.

- Research training and progression routes through which you might be able to achieve your potential area of work. This should include careful consideration of funding.

- With a teacher, lecturer or careers adviser, discuss whether such a progression route would be realistic for you.

- From your discussions, identify areas where you might need to add to your skills, interests, experience and qualifications.

- Draw up an action plan of how that might be accomplished.

- Draw up a flow diagram illustrating the various possible progression routes you wish to consider.

USEFUL ADDRESSES

The Actors' Centre
1a Tower Street
Covent Garden
London
WC2H 9NP
Tel: 0171 240 3940

Arts and Entertainment Training Council (AETC)
Glyde House
Glydegate
Bradford
BD5 0BQ
Tel: 01274 738800

Arts Council of England
14 Great Peter Street
London
SW1P 3NQ
Tel: 0171 333 0100

Association of British Theatre Technicians (ABTT)
47 Bermondsey Street
London
SE1 3XT

Association of Lighting Designers
3 Apollo Studios
Charlton Kings Street
London
NW5 2SW
Tel: 0171 482 4224

British Actors' Equity Association (Equity)
Guild House
Upper St. Martin's Lane
London
WC2H 9EG
Tel: 0171 379 6000

British Association of Choreographers
204 Westbourne Park Road
London
W11 1EP
Tel: 0171 221 6058

Broadcasting, Entertainment, Cinematic Theatre Union (BECTU)
111 Wardour Street
London
W1E 6JZ
Tel: 0171 437 8506

The Circus Space
Coronet Street
Hackney
London
N1 6HD
Tel: 0171 613 4141

Conference of Drama Schools
c/o The Central School of Speech and Drama
Embassy Theatre
Eton Avenue
London
NW3 3HY
Tel: 0171 722 8183

Contemporary Dance Trust
The Place
17 Dukes Road
London
WC1H 9AB
Tel: 0171 387 0161

Council for Dance Education and Training
Room 101
5 Tavistock Place
London
WC1H 9SS
Tel: 0171 388 5770

For information on Career Development Loans, contact:

Department for Education and Employment (DfEE)
Publications Dispatch Centre
Honeypot Lane
Canons Park
Stanmore
Middlesex
HA7 1AZ

Educational Grants Advisory Service
Family Welfare Association
501–505 Kingsland Road
London
E8 4AU
Tel: 0171 254 6251

The Festival Fringe Society
180 High Street
Edinburgh
EH1 1QS
Tel: 0131 226 5257

Independent Theatre Council (ITC)
12 The Leathermarket
Weston Street
London
SE1 3ER
Tel: 0171 403 1727

Mechanical Copyright Protection Society (MCPS)
Elgar House
41 Streatham High Road
London
SW16 1ER

Musicians' Union
National Office
60/62 Clapham Road
London
SW9 0JJ
Tel: 0171 582 5566

National Association of Youth Theatres
Midlands Arts Centre
Cannon Hill Park
Birmingham
B12 9QH
Tel: 0121 440 2930

National Youth Dance Company
35 Gloucester Road
Kew
Richmond
Surrey
TW9 3BS
Tel: 0181 948 7659

National Youth Theatre
443–445 Holloway Road
London
N7 6LW

National Youth and Music Theatre
2 Bow Street
London
WC2E 7BA

The New Playwrights Trust
Whitechapel Library
77 Whitechapel High Street
London
E1 7QT

Performing Rights Society (PRS)
29–33 Berners Street
London
W1P 4AA
Tel: 0171 580 5544

Production and Casting Report (PCR)
PO Box 100
Ramsgate
Kent
CT10 1UJ

Royal Court Young People's Theatre
309 Portobello Road
London
W10 5TD

Samuel French Ltd
52 Fitzroy Street
London
W1P 6JR
Tel: 0171 387 9373

Spotlight and *Contacts*
7, Leicester Place
London
WC2 7BP
Tel: 0171 437 7631

The Casting Sheet (TCS)
PO Box 145
Horley
Surrey
RH6 7YZ

Universities and Colleges Admissions Service (UCAS)
Fulton House
Jessop Avenue
Cheltenham
Gloucestershire
GL50 3SH
Tel: 01242 227788

ANNOTATED BIBLIOGRAPHY

This bibliography includes volumes relevant to this chapter which are considered suitable for student reference. See also the general bibliography on p.380.

Annett, M. and Simmonds, N., *Actors Guide to Auditions and Interviews,* A & C Black, 1995
> One of a number of books available with advice on the process of auditions and interviews.

Barry, C., Dean, A., Norrish, K., Poynton, K., Wheeler, M. (eds), *Contacts No. 85,* Spotlight, 1995/96
> This is an essential book for locating theatre 'contacts'.

Cassady, M., *The Book of Cuttings for Acting and Directing,* National Textbook Company, 1991
> May contain pieces useful for auditions, or for teaching workshops.

Cohen, N., *Theatre Works: A Guide to Working in the Theatre,* Royal National Theatre Publications Dept. and Theatre Museum Education Dept., 1992
> Informative publication with first-hand comments from practitioners about their jobs

Department for Education and Employment, *Career Development Loans Application Pack,* Crown Copyright, 1995

Duncan, S., *The Guide to Careers and Training in the Performing Arts,* The Cheverell Press, 1993
> Contains useful information for assessing possible career options.

Festival Fringe Society, *How to Do a Show on the Fringe,* Festival Fringe Society, 1996
> One of several highly informative publications produced by the Festival Fringe Society, obtained if taking a show to the Edinburgh Fringe Festival, or on request from the Fringe Office.

Richardson, J., *Careers in the Theatre,* Kogan Page Ltd, 1995
> More useful information for anyone considering work in performing arts.

Villemur, A. (ed.), *The Directory of Grant Making Trusts, 13th Edition, 1993–94,* Charities Aid Foundation, 1993
> An essential publication for reference when trying to find money for training and education. See also publications produced by individual Local Education Authorities.

6 The Arts in Society

Elaine Turner (with assistance from Tamsin Dodgson)

An understanding of the unalterable and interdependent relationship between the arts and society is important for any advanced study and practice of theatre.

This chapter seeks to introduce key aspects of this interrelationship, identifying clear links between society and drama in a historical period and providing a case study on which students can do further work. It contains the following sections:

● An introduction to the relationship between the arts and society
● Medieval theatre
● The alternative theatre movement of the 1960s and 1970s

AN INTRODUCTION TO THE RELATIONSHIP BETWEEN THE ARTS AND SOCIETY

Culture and society are inextricably joined; the arts are an outward demonstration of society's culture.

Even though we are all individual and unique in our own way, we are also the products and the producers of our society and our culture. The society and culture we grow up in is a part of us: what we do and the attitudes we take will either confirm the way society is or make changes in it. The arts are a visible demonstration and outward realisation of our culture. The arts interpret cultural beliefs; often, the two words are used synonymously.

Because this book is primarily about theatre, we are using theatre as a specific example of 'the arts' in this chapter, although many of the points made in this introduction apply to other art forms as well. It could be claimed, however, that theatre and society have the closest links: theatre is the most social of the arts. For example, social relationships are in action not only on stage and in the audience, but also in the relationship between what's happening on stage and the audience.

Theatre is intrinsically 'social'.

Theatre is social in its content, its organisation and its form.

A number of points are worth considering when we address the relationship between the arts (specifically theatre) and society. Firstly, theatre is social. Its content – human interaction – is about society. Its organisation is social; its presentation is social. How a performance is put together, where it takes place, who its audience is and how it relates

208

to that audience all depend on social organisation. In other words, wherever you look in theatre you will find an expression of social relationships.

The form of the play itself is an expression of social and/or political attitudes. For example, a text that comprises a number of short, sharp, aggressive or angry scenes, which confront the audience with the action, suggests the work of a company which is confrontational about and with society.

The content of plays will always be connected to society and society's politics.

The content of a play can be overtly linked to the politics of a society. (See pp.213–233 for clear examples of this.) Even if the content *seems* mild and apolitical, certain social and/or political messages are still being expressed. For example, a protagonist in a West End detective play may express no specific political opinions. However, the character might be given a number of likeable, positive characteristics by the playwright, such as a witty sense of humour, a sharp intelligence and a lively manner. The audience warms to this person and is engaged by the character. The automatic result is that people listen to the character and are inclined to feel sympathy for him or her. Thus, the audience is receptive to the values of the protagonist. So, for example, if the character expresses a condemnation of war, audience members will be receptive to this because they 'like' the character. They may be accepting this mild political message.

Theatre can imply a hierarchy of human worth.

In addition, the other characters might be presented as antagonistic to the protagonist, or they may be written merely as appendages, with few characteristics of their own. Oblique messages are being conveyed here. The play could be suggesting that there is a hierarchy of value in human life: this likeable protagonist is the most *important* character on stage, no matter how 'flawed' he or she is. The playwright is suggesting that in life, as on stage, there are 'important' people and 'less important' people.

There are, of course, other ways to tell a story on stage. A story does not have to centre on only one important character. The play could be written so that a group of people share equal importance, or single characters may have the chance to tell their own stories. These approaches suggest other social values and structures.

Artists are inevitably affected by the society in which they live.

It is romantic to think that artists are special and detached from the world they live in, that a lightbulb goes off in the playwright's head and he or she dashes off a masterpiece consisting totally of his or her 'own' thoughts and utterly unconnected to any outside influence! Clearly, that is not the case. Novelists, painters, playwrights, actors and directors are, like everyone else, both the products and producers of their social context, and that social context is very much a part of their work. Moreover, one might say that it is this very connection to the everyday world that can make their work important. It is this social connection that allows the arts to comment on, reveal and even effect change in society.

How do we examine the relationship between a work and its social context? It is usual to gather historical information and then to look at the work in the light of that information. However, it is also possible to work in the other direction; that is, to draw social implications out of the work.

MEDIEVAL THEATRE

As we have said, the 'social context' of a work is not just to do with the subject matter of a play or performance, nor is it solely a question of events occuring in the society at the time. It is also a matter of how that performance is created and performed. All of these factors reveal not only the intent of the creators but the preoccupations of their particular society.

Medieval theatre can offer us a good example of the close connection between theatre and society.

For an example, we can go as far back as the first recognised British theatre: the drama that developed in the 13th and 14th centuries. We shall now consider, briefly, the relationship between art and society in this period of history.

Medieval society was dominated by the Church.

Although kings and queens ruled over medieval Europe, the most pervasive power belonged to the Church. From Ireland to Turkey, almost everyone shared the same beliefs, symbols, faith and even language: if you knew Latin, you could find people to speak to throughout Europe. Our perspective on the Middle Ages is often coloured by our own cultural assumptions. In the 'modern' West, we tend to assume that 'faith' is rather primitive and that it is 'modern' and 'progressive' to be a sceptical non-believer. Also, culturally, we tend to be cynical and suspicious of religious authority. Thus, for years, when people looked at medieval theatre, they assumed it was a form of Church dogma, that the plays were simply an example of the Church oppressing the people through the constant communication of Bible stories. However, by addressing the development of the plays, it is possible to examine further social implications.

Plays developed as part of church services.

In the 12th century, the Church began to add short episodes from the life of Christ to services on special days such as Easter and Christmas. These liturgical 'plays' were sung in Latin and presented with very simple, stylised movements, often no more than a single gesture. They were written and acted by priests, thus confirming the close relationship between the Church and the 'mysteries of the faith'. However, since the plays were in Latin (which was not understood by most of the congregation), and were accompanied by simple movements barely suggestive of the action, it is hard to imagine what they could teach.

They confirmed the centrality of the Church's position in society.

Rather, the form of the plays suggests they were aimed at an audience which already knew the stories. The emphasis on sound and image suggests that the purpose of the plays was actually the creation of an emotional (if not a spiritual) experience. If this 'worked', the audience would experience an emotional relationship with Christ and, by association, the Church and their own sense of belonging within it. To put it another way, the plays were devised to create an emotional confirmation of community and of the centrality of the Church in that community.

When theatre moved out into the streets, the guilds took over.

However, in 1313 Pope Gregory decreed that all Christian countries would celebrate the Host on Corpus Christi Day, and theatre burst out from the church onto the streets. The creation of Corpus Christi Day happily coincided with the expansion of the merchant class, and the merchant guilds found an outward expression of their professional and civic pride in the production of 'mystery plays'. As the plays moved out into the community, outside the Church's physical centre, a civic power (the merchant guilds) took them over.

The merchant guilds were established in the 12th and 13th centuries by craftsmen who sought to protect their trade by ensuring the quality of the goods produced. One example you will recognise is the assessment of gold and silver in 'carats' and 'sterling', which guarantees the quality you are buying. In order to practise a craft, a worker needed to belong to a guild. The training began with an apprenticeship, which usually lasted seven years; at the end of this the craftsman became a journeyman and could practise the craft. However, to become a 'master craftsman' he (or sometimes she) had to produce a 'masterpiece', which was judged by the master craftsmen of the guild. The skills of the craft were called 'maesteries'; the plays were called 'mystery' plays because they were produced by the guilds.

The word 'mystery' comes from 'maesterie'.

The cycles comprised the whole Bible, from Creation to Resurrection.

The Mystery Cycles were collections of individual plays based on stories from the Old and New Testament, usually covering the Creation to the Resurrection. Each city (Chester, York and Wakefield, for example) produced its own cycle. Each play was the property of a specific guild. The plays were performed over a period of several days, either on 'wagons', which moved from place to place, performing to different audiences en route, or at 'stations', which remained on the same spot while the audience moved from stage to stage. They were performed in the open. Although all European countries produced Corpus Christi plays, only the English produced cycles.

Plays were performed in the open.

The plays contributed to the gradual move from Church authority to civic authority.

We can see that several social influences brought about this break from the Church and the development of public theatre. For example, the increasing power and wealth of the guilds and the merchant class led to a growing civic consciousness and pride. The guilds desired both to show off their professional skills and to gain power and recognition in the community. One could argue that the cycles themselves were instrumental in shifting the central focus from the Church towards the civic community.

*There are several
identifiable links between
the theatre and its society.*

Various aspects of the relationship between theatre and society can be identified here:

- how the plays were produced;
- where they were produced;
- the relationship with the audience;
- the form and content of the plays.

Theatre was financed by a collaboration between the guilds and the Church. The Church now shared its centrality with the guilds, which represented civil, secular power. Plays were created co-operatively by all sections of the population, from nobles to plebians. Clearly, they were both an expression and an experience of community: since the people were working together towards a common end, the strength of the community was confirmed, which, ironically, is as much a spiritual as a social experience.

The emphasis on excellence, which went as far as fining actors who were not good enough, was another expression of pride in the community. Perhaps more importantly, it also emphasised a recognition of the importance of each individual, personal contribution in the creation of this community theatre.

The fact that the performances took place in the open, often in front of the church, on common ground, was another confirmation of community values. The audience surrounded the performance, and often were not only addressed directly, but included in the play. Thus the interactive values of community were experienced even in the process of the play. It is highly likely that audience response would have affected the performance itself.

Since all the plays were Bible stories, the narratives were, by necessity, in keeping with Christian tradition and expressed Christian values. However, the characters tend to be very down-to-earth and involved with the concerns of everyday life. What is more, these plays were in local English, rather than Latin. The content tends to express an interactive relationship between spirit and matter, past and present, and even Heaven and Earth, especially since God is personified and actually speaks in many of them. This suggests that the medieval 'community' extended beyond the city boundaries to include Heaven, Hell, history, myth and legend.

Although every European country developed 'mystery' plays during this period, only the English cycles are marked by a mixture of the serious and the comic. Even the crucifixion play has distinct comic interludes. This distinctive mixture might be seen as another expression of the 'democratic' mixture of high and low in producing the plays. The plays also have a sense of irony, which is still particularly English.

The structure of the cycle is particularly important. It presents a single narrative, made up of a series of individual plays. In other words, each single play is complete in itself, but it gains further significance from its place in the whole. At the same time, the experience of the whole is created through the accumulation of its parts. In fact, each of the major cycles has its own specific concerns, with unifying issues and metaphors that develop through the individual plays. This unusual structure, clearly, has social and political implications. Quite literally, it expresses a statement that the whole is made up of its parts, but that each part has its own unique qualities and its own inimitable part to play in creating that whole. As it happens, this is, perhaps, the most definitive concept in medieval thought.

The development of the plays demonstrates the importance of the community in medieval life.

In this brief look at the development of the plays, we have found a constant confirmation of the importance of community in the Middle Ages. In addition, there is a clear confirmation of the importance of the individual in the community, and even a recognition of the importance of each individual contribution. The Biblical content of the plays strengthens this image by showing humans in communication with Heaven. As we have seen, the singular power of the Church began to be displaced, in favour of a sharing with secular elements, a growing emphasis on civic forces and an acknowledgement of individual skills working towards the common good.

It is not surprising that secular, monetary power began to displace the Church and become the centre of civic pride. When we take into consideration the commitment and attention to quality given to the cycles, it is also not very surprising that many of the participants began to form professional acting companies.

It is often easier to look at the distant past than our own world. The object of this example was simply to illustrate how one might identify the relationship between art and its society. In the following section, we will give a more detailed account of the development of the 'alternative theatre movement' of the late 1960s and 1970s as an example of this process in the context of a society that is closer to our current concerns. Indeed, it was this movement that laid the foundations for the range of theatre available today.

THE ALTERNATIVE THEATRE MOVEMENT OF THE 1960s AND 1970s

When we talk about an 'alternative theatre movement', we mean an alternative to West End theatre. Sometimes this is also referred to as the 'new theatre movement'.

West End theatre managed to establish itself as the 'official' theatre between the two world wars; it promoted and sustained a particular style and approach to theatre, and a particular audience. There are several major elements which define West End theatre, to which the new companies strove to provide alternatives.

Post-war West End theatre has certain characteristics.

Firstly, the main purpose of commercial theatre is to make a profit. This in itself has social repercussions; not everyone can afford to pay the prices that allow a theatre to make a profit. Consequently, a social hierarchy is confirmed, whereby people with wealth are labelled as superior; unsurprisingly, the content of the plays also reinforces these social distinctions. The plays tend to address the personal or social problems of the middle classes and are set in appropriate environments, such as middle-class houses.

In the West End, you will go to a building that is specifically built for theatrical performances and used only for that purpose. It has also been built for a particular kind of theatre. There is usually a proscenium arch, which has the effect of framing the action and gives the impression that the audience is watching the stage action through a 'fourth wall'. The proscenium arch and the architecture of the theatre both separate the audience members from the action and turn them into passive viewers.

Because of the commercial requirements of the West End theatres, they tend to rely on long runs; that is, a play runs for as long as it is making money. If you have ever seen a popular musical years after it has opened, you may have felt that what you saw was only a shadow of what made it so popular in the first place. Casting a star in a major role is often used as a way of drawing in the public. In theatrical terms, the result tends to be that the other roles are overlooked and the other actors are treated as appendages, enabling the star to shine.

Finally, West End theatre production is organised according to a strict hierarchy. Theatre owners and producers make the production possible and make many of the 'artistic' decisions, but for commercial rather than artistic reasons. The hierarchy descends through the director to the actors and technicians, who have little say in what is done or how.

Alternative theatre in the 1960s and 1970s challenged West End theatre.

In the late 1960s and 1970s, a great many experimental theatre companies came into being, whose principal intention was to offer an alternative approach to theatre. Although each had its own character and intentions, they all tended to share certain perspectives, which offered a viable alternative to the mainstream. Crucially, they were non-commercial. Their primary purpose was not to make a profit but to make theatre. The practitioners were supported by the dole, by the Arts Council and sometimes by outside work.

Another central feature was that the focus was on the actor and the performing company, rather than on a producer. The actor was acknowledged as the essential source of the theatrical experience.

Many of these companies placed great emphasis on the audience, and on the audience's relationship to the stage. They were intent on breaking down the barriers between the audience and the performance. This was attempted through:

- the style of performance;
- a search for new audiences;
- the use of alternative venues, places not originally intended for theatrical performance, including warehouses, synagogues, barns, pubs, and so on.

Both their search for new audiences and their use of non-theatrical venues express clearly their denial of the class/wealth hierarchy implicit in mainstream theatre, and demonstrate their 'alternative' socio-political intentions. By seeking new audiences, who may never have had the chance to go to the theatre before, and playing in venues which suited this new audience – and which, moreover, were often places central to community life (pubs, churches, warehouses) – these groups posed a living alternative to the rigid, hierarchical, profit-based establishment of mainstream theatre. They were engaging in the act of creating social equality, social interaction and social change.

The organisation of these groups was essentially democratic: actors made decisions, managed and became technicians. This, at least, was the ideal, and for the most part it was carried out. However, most of these groups were the expression of one or two individuals' creative insight, and thus, in most cases, these people would be the key force; often, when they left, the group either disintegrated or changed its character.

Priority was placed on writing and experimental work. Many of the companies made extensive use of the techniques of Brecht and of popular theatre forms such as music hall, spectacle and melodrama.

In general, their politics were socialist, but some companies had a specific focus: for example, the Women's Theatre Group and Monstrous Regiment dealt with feminist issues, and Gay Sweatshop confronted gay issues. Many groups, however, were also *explicitly* political; that is, the issue of social and political structure was overtly confronted.

The social and theatrical background
It would be a mistake to think that 'alternatives' to the West End suddenly sprang up overnight. There had been a trickle of attempts to create an alternative – to produce new plays and to experiment with new forms – since the 19th century. The struggle, however, was often weak and patchy.

The alternative movement had its base in the theatre work of the 1950s.

In the late 1950s, however, British theatre began to change noticeably. A new crop of playwrights appeared, each of whom offered a different approach to theatre and theatre writing. On the whole, they emerged from George Devine's Royal Court Theatre in Sloane Square, London, and from Joan Littlewood's Theatre Workshop at the Theatre Royal, Stratford East. Many of these writers are now very well known: they include John Arden, Tom Stoppard, Brendan Behan, John Osborne, Arnold Wesker and Harold Pinter, among others.

Social events in the late 1960s

Exciting new plays and approaches to theatre had been evolving since the late 1950s, but in the late 1960s an unusual number of small companies suddenly formed, each with its own ethos, its own style, its own concerns, its own unique approach to theatre, and in many cases, its own playwrights. This creative renaissance produced one of the most exciting periods of drama in Britain since the 17th century.

The movement was in direct response to socio-political events.

Although this occurrence may seem to have been abrupt and spontaneous, the unprecedented emergence of these companies, as well as their work and concerns, can be seen as a response not only to the established theatre of the time, but also to social and political events.

There was a new feeling in the air, a sense of responsibility and faith in the possibilities of change.

We felt ourselves to be like Gods and capable of anything. This was it. The past would disappear forever. Everyone was 'doing their own thing'. There was a mood of positivity in the air which, in our experience, was unprecedented. People were creating things, outrageously extravagant things. Bright colours and optimism were definitely in. Even God was back among us. Inspiring stuff.
(John McGrath in *Theatre Papers*, Volume III, no. 8, 1979, p.37)

One year in particular stands out as a key moment: 1968.

The events of 1968 were a particular catalyst.

It is impossible to deny . . . a link between the most publicized political events of 1968 and the creation in practical terms of the new 'alternative' circuit of Arts Lab, cellar theatres and environmental venues . . . Unquestionably 1968 was the watershed.
(Ansorge, *Disrupting the Spectacle*, p.56)

The year was marked by violent anti-Vietnam war demonstrations, students' and workers' riots in Paris, student sit-ins across Britain and Europe, Russian troops occupying Prague, riots in Londonderry, the assassinations of Martin Luther King and Robert Kennedy, and protests surrounding the Olympic Games in Mexico.

There was a growing sense of global consciousness.

Revolutionary demands were made by students and workers, but they were met by a negative and even violent response from the authorities. A genuine global consciousness was growing – especially amongst the young – which became sharply focused upon similarities in the quest for freedom from oppression and differences of opportunity. Although Britain's economy in 1968 was in a healthy state, the majority of the world's inhabitants were living well below the poverty line, and radicals demanded the equal distribution of the world's wealth. An increase in material freedom brought home to British youth these global inequalities, and at the same time it gave rise to demands for cultural and creative freedom at home.

This new awareness increased the growing disillusionment with the Labour government elected in 1964. Followers of the Left, for whom

Political disillusionment motivated some left-wing theatre groups.

the election had promised a more egalitarian, socially conscious society, realised that Labour was not in fact going to alter anything. This realisation motivated some of the more overtly political theatre groups.

Events in Paris in May 1968 were also significant. Students and workers fought together for political change, and students occupied theatres and art galleries. This united action created a belief that society could be changed through the solidarity of the middle and working classes. The hopes and ideals of the Paris rebellion inspired young Britons and were incorporated into the aims of the new political theatre.

The American war in Vietnam caused particular outcries; one effect of this was a strong American presence in British theatre.

The most important factor, however, was probably the war in Vietnam. 'Global consciousness' had activated British anger against both the implicit colonialism of the war and the plight of the Vietnamese, and protests against the war were growing. The Grosvenor Square riot was a battle between police and anti-Vietnam protestors, resulting in the worst scenes of violence in London for years. A by-product of the Vietnam war was the large number of Americans who came to Britain because they objected to the war, many of whom worked in and influenced the theatre as actors, directors and writers. David Aukin, co-founder of the Foco Novo company and a key figure in 1960s and 1970s theatre, suggests that the entire fringe was run by Americans. American Jim Haynes created the Arts Lab, for example, by converting a former warehouse in Drury Lane into a performance space, gallery and cinema in 1967. For a few years the Arts Lab was London's first, if not only, truly experimental and underground arts centre.

The growing youth sub-culture affected many theatre practitioners.

'Youth culture', too, was coming into its own. There was a desire amongst the young for change, and a will to do something new. Many companies, such as Belt and Braces, Foco Novo and Joint Stock, evolved with strong connections to a surrounding sub-culture that articulated its ideas through political demonstrations, drugs, rock and roll, the underground press and an attitude towards the world which was wholly in opposition to that of the older generation.

Many of the rising theatre practitioners had been born during the war and brought up during the hopeful days of the post-war Labour government, had matured along with the disappointment in Labour's failed promises, and were now inspired by the new global awareness and political unrest. They were sure of the need and possibility for change and aimed to create drama which would stand at the front of political and social upheaval.

You were on the edge of the transformation of the political, personal, social and economic relations and you wanted theatre to be part of that transformation. (Playwright Jon Chadwick, cited in Rees, *Fringe First*, p.10)

A number of new venues opened.

New performing spaces started to open: the Combination in Brighton, the ICA, the Theatre Upstairs at the Royal Court, the Open Space in Tottenham Court Road, and many others. There was no division

217

between performer and audience, and the rigid social behaviour of conventional theatre-going was abandoned for casual informality and a feeling of interaction between performers and audience.

Brecht's practice influenced British theatre in the late 1950s and 1960s.

Given the political consciousness of most of the new theatre groups evolving at the end of the 1960s, it is hardly surprising that Brecht was a major influence on performers and writers alike. (See p.32 for further information on Brecht.) Brecht's theories were given form and inspiration by the visits to Britain of his company, the Berliner Ensemble, in 1956 and 1965. William Gaskill, co-founder of the theatre company Joint Stock with Max Stafford-Clark (see pp.68–72), explains:

I was politicised by the Berliner Ensemble when I first saw them in 1956 . . . I'd never seen such good theatre before . . . there was something about the whole process of work which was serious and thoughtful in a way that we had never seen before, it was a great revelation. We thought, 'that's what theatre should be like' . . . serious theatre, a large-scale company, subsidised theatre and a group of people working as a permanent ensemble – that image of what theatre could and should be like dominated many of our lives for a long time.
(Gaskill, cited in Itzin, *Stages in the Revolution*, p.222)

Playwright Jon Chadwick argues that the plays written and produced in the early 1970s could not have been created without Brecht. Certainly, Brecht's prime intent of using theatre to 'politicise' the audience (that is, to make its members conscious of the political implications and consequences of their own choices and decisions) was shared by a great many of the companies that grew up in the 1960s and 1970s. After the Berliner Ensemble visited England, many playwrights began to make use of Brechtian aesthetics in the structure of their plays (for example, the use of songs), even if they did not share his intentions.

Time Out *helped communicate events to the public.*

Another important contribution to the development of this new theatre movement was the launch of the listings magazine *Time Out* in 1969. *Time Out* listed all the venues and performances taking place in London, no matter how obscure they may have seemed. In this way, it connected the people involved in fringe theatre, maintained the flow of information and helped develop an audience for the performances. David Aukin, a playwright and key figure in the theatre movement of the 1960s and 1970s, says:

The magazine had a definite policy. It was not a critical magazine. That was not its function. Its function was to network what was happening where, and describe what the work was about. Never with value judgements. We are talking of 30 people turning up for a performance, and that was a full house! The buzz was terrific.
(Aukin, cited in Rees, *Fringe First*, p.51)

The Theatre Act of 1968 removed censorship, allowing greater freedom of content.

In addition, in 1968, the Theatre Act was passed, and the Lord Chamberlain ceased to function as the censor of theatre. Until then, all plays had had to be submitted to the Censor, who could ask for any changes he wanted or could actually stop a play from being performed. Writers and performers were now free to express themselves without restriction, which undoubtedly created new and greater possibilities for experimentation.

Where for centuries playwrights had their work hacked about by the 'royal smut hound', alternative theatre from the moment it breathed life was under no restrictions.
(Craig, *Dreams and Reconstructions*, pp.16–17)

The growing Arts Council of Great Britain (ACGB) supported many of the new companies.

The Arts Council, which was set up after the war to encourage and subsidise the arts, had initially concerned itself mainly with major companies, especially 'high' art, such as opera. (For further details about the Arts Council of Great Britain, see pp.240–242.) However, at the beginning of the 1970s, the Arts Council set up a sub-committee, the Fringe and Experimental Drama Committee, to investigate alternative theatre. This resulted in some of the new theatre companies receiving Arts Council grants to produce their work. In 1971, half a million pounds was set aside to distribute to 'fringe groups', and a precedent was set. The possibility of Arts Council support opened the door for theatre companies which could not be self-sufficient.

Civic pride grew and, with it, more arts venues.

During this period, also, a wave of civic pride, probably arising out of the rebuilding after the war, resulted in a great number of local theatres and arts centres being built across the country.

The new theatre toured extensively.

These events influenced and inspired a new wave in British theatre, in which work that was new, revolutionary and experimental could develop, in contrast to the traditional fare of the West End. This theatre played to new audiences, many of whom had never set foot in a West End theatre. Moreover, most of these companies did not sit in an established space waiting for their audiences to come to them, but took themselves around the country to find new audiences for their new theatres: 'New Theatre was not building-based but primarily in origin a touring phenomenon' (Rees, *Fringe First*, p.9).

The new or 'alternative' companies

It is important to identify certain key companies which contributed to the 'alternative theatre' movement of the 1960s and 1970s in order to understand more fully the nature of the work undertaken, and its great variety.

The People Show

The People Show began in 1966. It deserves mention not only as the earliest of the experimental companies and the longest surviving (still lively and active today!), but also as possibly the most eccentric.

Founded by performers from a variety of arts disciplines, the company has always worked communally and has never had a director or artistic director. Its performances are devised around the theatrical skills and artistic concerns of the particular people involved. People Shows tend to be 'structured around a collage of atmospheres rather than narrative or character', (Craig, *Dreams and Reconstructions*, p.24) presented in their unique style which highlights the aural and visual elements of theatre. The work tends to elaborate, comment on and deconstruct elements of popular culture. Its faithful following and lively continuance is proof that there are still audiences who crave exercise for their imaginations.

Since 1966, the company has created 102 'numbered' productions and approximately 30 other shows, including street theatre and one-off events. Recently, The People Show have been awarded £368,000 from the National Lottery, and work to refurbish and equip their base, St James the Great Institute in East London, will begin in spring 1997.

While some insist that companies like The People Show are apolitical, others place their anarchic perspective and their lively disruption of conventional expectation nearer to the agit-prop company CAST.

People Show 100

CAST

CAST (Cartoon Archetypical Slogan Theatre) was established in 1965 by Roland and Claire Muldoon, who had formerly worked with Unity Theatre, and was the first avowedly socialist company in the 'new theatre'. It was born out of the clash between the 'old' and 'new' Left exposed by the Labour government of 1964, and developed out of the Muldoons' break with Unity Theatre.

We weren't in the C.P. [Communist Party], but we were coming round to Marxism. We were young and we were part of an enormous resistance to established politics – CND, Ban-the-Bomb, anti-apartheid, that sort of thing. We wanted to bring this into Unity. We were expelled for our efforts.
(Kershaw, *The Politics of Performance*, pp.75–6)

CAST was basically an agit-prop company. (Agit-prop stands for 'agitation-propaganda', and is a form designed to communicate a political and usually radical message directly to the public. One of the earliest forms was the 'Living Newspaper', where actors performed pieces of daily news in the street to expose the power struggles behind the headlines.) CAST's purpose was to politicise its audiences while entertaining them. Its style was based on music hall – fast-moving, humorous, with broad stereotypical characters (hence 'Cartoon Archetypical') – and drawn from popular forms such as film and TV. The central character in most of the shows was Harold Muggins, played by Roland Muldoon: 'the English archetype of the bloke who does everything and gets no reward' (Muldoon in Itzin, *Stages in the Revolution*, p.14).

CAST toured the pubs and workingmen's clubs of North London. However, . . . whilst CAST approached its material from a Marxist perspective, the shows did not directly present a Marxist analysis in the didactic way agit prop had. Rather, they projected a harsh satirical vision of British society from the point of view of an underdog who was satirised along with the rest.
(Kershaw, p. 78)

Roland and Claire Muldoon later acquired and renovated and now run the Hackney Empire.

Jim Haynes

Jim Haynes was one of the Americans who came to Britain in the 1960s, as mentioned above. He was one of the most influential participants in the 'new theatre movement', establishing the Arts Lab, which provided both a home for experimentation and a centre for audiences hungry for new ideas. When the Arts Lab closed, Haynes went to Edinburgh, where he founded the Traverse Theatre, one of the longest-surviving and most influential small theatres in Britain, which fosters both new playwrights and new companies. For example, Max Stafford-Clark, who was at one point director of the Traverse, began the Traverse Workshops, which eventually metamorphosed into Joint Stock Theatre Company, one of the most successful and influential of the 'alternative' theatre companies (see below). (For more information on Max Stafford-Clark, see pp.68–72.)

Ed Berman – Interaction

Another American, playwright and producer Ed Berman, founded Interaction in 1968. This was described as '. . . the most vital current attempt to relate the art to the needs of a community' (the *Guardian*, 1969).

Based in Kentish Town, London, Interaction was actually an umbrella organisation covering a wide range of community and self-help projects, such as city farms, as well as several different professional theatre companies. One of these was a children's theatre company called The Dogg's Troupe, which toured the local housing estates: 'An innovative street theatre gang who unleashed a thoroughly demystifying theatrical experience on the unsuspecting streets of Kentish Town' (Craig, *Dreams and Reconstructions*, p.92).

Berman was also one of the creators of the Ambience Lunch Hour Theatre Club and the Almost Free Theatre, where, for many years, people paid what they could afford. Both of these ventures extended the concept of 'alternative' to its practical limits. Theatre at lunchtime totally cuts across the conventions of mainstream theatre-going: by offering theatre during the working day, it demolishes the barriers between work and 'play' and opens up the possibility of theatre becoming an inherent part of everyday life. In addition, of course, it encouraged new audiences. Within a few years, lunchtime theatres grew up all over London, especially in pubs.

Berman and his assistant . . . Naftali Yavin . . . sought to illuminate and analyse the social conventions which so rigidly structure everyday life in the Western world and which straight-jacketed personality into a series of stereotypical roles . . . Early Ambience productions were typified by a painstaking concern for language and the absence within the plays of a social reality . . . an obvious reaction against the dominant naturalism of the day. (Craig, pp.148–9)

Asking people to pay what they can afford also cuts across some of the basic premises of mainstream theatre, encouraging new audiences and denying the economic exclusivity of the West End. This arrangement also gave the theatre itself a degree of independence. The Almost Free hosted what were probably the first seasons of women's plays and gay plays. Interaction was probably the first company to create theatre in the community, and was a fundamental inspiration for the community theatre movement that followed.

Red Ladder

Red Ladder began [in October 1968] by answering needs. The first shows were for tenants' associations in Tower Hamlets during the struggle against the GLC [Greater London Council] rent rises through 1968–9. We were asked to open meetings with sketches lasting five to ten minutes about the rent issue. The tenants wanted us to warm the meeting up, help build an atmosphere of solidarity and attract more people to the meeting.
(Chris Rawlence in Craig, *Dreams and Reconstructions*, p.33)

Red Ladder aimed to relate to its audience's concerns. Working from the desire for social change and from socialist ideals, it played to people in factory canteens, union meetings, women's conferences and school halls, focusing its material on the lives of working people.

A Red Ladder production, A Woman's Work is Never Done *(or* Strike While the Iron's Hot*)*

To achieve authenticity in its work, the company carried out a great deal of basic research and often spent months in discussion with workers and their families. As a condition of performance, Red Ladder insisted on holding discussions after each show. This allowed room for immediate feedback to let the company know if it was reflecting its audience's lives accurately and to extend the perspectives of the performance:

The purpose of our work is not to provide ready-made answers, but to present controversial social issues in such a way that the people in the audience feel compelled to ask themselves questions about their prejudices, their beliefs, their world view. So we have a discussion after the play in which the audience moves towards the possible answers to the questions it has asked itself.
(cited in the *Guardian*, 1977)

In pursuit of its aims, Red Ladder developed its own distinct style, incorporating narrative content, the visual and filmic nature of advertising on television, techniques of the British folk song tradition, the participatory and collective atmosphere of music hall, the clarity and charisma of good rhetoric, and the excitement of circus. It used masked figures and brightly coloured props, emphasising the visual elements of performance and using images to extend and give power to the words. A good example is the regular use of the step ladder (from which the company's name originated), which served as the perfect symbol for every kind of hierarchical relationship.

By the mid 1970s, Red Ladder, like many other of the groups which had begun in the 1960s, felt the need of a more permanent home and made its base in Leeds, from which it toured North Yorkshire.

7:84

The name of this company derives from the fact that seven per cent of the population owned 84 per cent of the country's wealth. When he founded 7:84 'to set up a theatre company "in opposition to bourgeoise theatre – a truly revolutionary theatre"' (Itzin and McGrath in Itzin, *Stages in the Revolution*, p.120), John McGrath was already a successful television and theatre playwright. Based in Scotland, and unashamedly socialist and revolutionary, the company encouraged and produced new writing, especially works relevant to the Scottish experience. *The Cheviot, the Stag and the Black, Black Oil* (1973) is one of the best examples of community 'alternative theatre' where popular entertainment is used to express political content.

The Cheviot, the Stag and the Black, Black Oil, *a 7:84 production*

Over time, 7:84 became one of the most influential and admired of all the new theatre companies. It is still in existence, and performed at the 1996 Edinburgh Festival, using members of the community rather than trained actors as the performers.

Belt and Braces Roadshow

Belt and Braces was founded in 1973 by Gavin Richards, who had been a member of 7:84.

Richards wanted to use traditional acting techniques combined with elements of variety and pantomime, to use music as a vital ingredient in performance rather than as decoration. So the Belt and Braces Band came to be an autonomous, but integral part of Belt and Braces Roadshow.
(Itzin, *Stages in the Revolution*, p.199)

The company sought to present entertainment which was articulate and socialist, in order to educate its audiences. It was the first company to produce Dario Fo's *Accidental Death of an Anarchist* in 1977; ironically, this was a huge West End success. The programme for the play contains an article on the history of politics in Milan, a report on contemporary fascism in Britain and a section on the murder of Blair Peach by the police. Thus the programme not only sets the context for the play but also connects its action to events in contemporary Britain.

Belt and Braces intended to make entertainment which would provoke discussion about the processes that affect our lives. Like most of the companies which evolved in this period, it set itself up in conscious opposition to mainstream theatre and the social structure and attitudes it represented and encouraged: 'Abstention is the easiest way to voting for the wrong side. Most theatre in this country is dull piss because it hasn't got the guts to choose sides' (*Accidental Death of an Anarchist* programme, 1977).

Welfare State

Even a minimal list of new theatre companies such as this would be incomplete without a look at Welfare State International (WSI), whose approach towards social change is entirely different from that of its associates. WSI was founded in 1968 by John Fox and Sue Gill (and others), who were then based at Bradford College of Art with Albert Hunt. (Albert Hunt and his students were already breaking new ground in political community theatre.) An early manifesto of WSI states that the company 'believes that imagination, original art and spontaneous creative energy are being systematically destroyed by the current educational processes, materialism, and bureaucratic decision-making of western large-scale industrial society' (cited in Itzin, p.69).

WSI's 12th Annual Ulverston Lantern Procession – How Does Your Garden Grow, *(September 1994)*

Its anti-establishment, anti-capitalist, anti-hierarchical stance and its dedication to the need for change are clear, and coincide with the political commitments of most of the new theatre companies. However, its approach to the instigation of change is entirely different. Where most of the other companies acknowledge their debt to Brecht, Welfare State's approach owes more to Antonin Artaud.

Welfare State International's position is this: the current social system perpetuates itself and its values by dulling the imagination and the creative urge, thus weakening the ability of the populace to create, grow or imagine possible alternatives, or even to change itself. WSI dedicates itself to stimulating these creative energies, releasing the imagination, creativity and spontaneity of its audiences.

To this end, WSI can create enormous, powerful, energetic spectacles: 'Their performances are not plays, but epic poems, visual and aural, though virtually without words. They deal in ritual, myth and magic' (Itzin, p.69).

Particularly central to its creations is the use of universal myths and archetypal stories. It seeks new audiences and works towards creating a sense of community through the experience of its performances, most of which take place outdoors. Unrestricted by architectural considerations, the performances can take on enormous proportions, and the outdoor setting, of course, also attracts audience members who would never set foot in a theatre.

We live in a society that has very little spiritual belief in anything . . . it is a question of how far we as 'theatre people' can relate to or discover alternative spiritual values . . . you cannot forever suppress human energy.
(Fox cited in Itzin, p.72)

In 1972, eight people based in Leeds became the solid core of WSI; the company is still flourishing. Having performed on four continents and spent seven years collaborating with Trident submarine workers in Barrow-in-Furness, it has made its home in the small Lake District market town of Ulverston. It has initiated annual lantern festivals, and produced carnival street bands, cycles of plays, shadow puppet theatre and elaborate sculptural installations. In 1996, the company wrote a book called *The Dead Good Funeral Book* and designed new coffins and urns as a practical way into new rites of passage. A National Arts Lottery Grant of £1.6 million will enable it to build a training centre for the celebratory arts in Ulverston, where its innovative clowning may continue to awaken and celebrate the radical creative spirit of specific communities.

Footsbarn
Little has been written on the Footsbarn theatre, but it is unusual enough to deserve a mention. From 1971, the Footsbarn company lived as a commune in Cornwall and produced a particularly English and

extraordinarily creative form of theatre, often based on English myth and legend and using forms derived from early popular drama such as mumming. It has also tackled Shakespeare in the same eclectic style.

We are as alternative as you can get – no wages, live in a community, grow vegetables, chickens, etc . . . The word 'alternative' alienates the people we play to . . . working people. These working people are not all trade unionists or furry freaks. A lot of them are conservatives, but what the hell.
(Itzin, *Alternative Theatre Handbook*, TQ Publications, 1976, p.25, cited in Kershaw, *The Politics of Performance*, p.138)

Footsbarn toured all over Britain, playing, for the most part, in small theatres and studio spaces. In the late 1980s, it received a grant from the European Commission. The terms of the grant stipulate that the majority of the company's performances must be outside its native country. Consequently, Footsbarn is now based in France, and its appearances in Britain are regrettably rare. (The formation of Kneehigh Theatre in Cornwall occurred partly because of the void left by Footsbarn's departure. See pp.117–121 for more on Kneehigh.)

The new working methods

The new theatre produced work that was new and inspiring. Its organisation was democratic and co-operative, and its rehearsal methods, too, were innovative, inventive and in sharp contrast to mainstream theatre, in which there were designated roles and the only expectations of an actor were that he or she learn the given lines and produce them according to the director's wishes. Although each company had its own methods of working, we can gain some insight into these processes by taking a look at the work of one company, Joint Stock.

Joint Stock

Joint Stock was founded in 1974 by William Gaskill, David Hare, David Aukin and Max Stafford-Clark. In Stafford-Clark's workshops at the Traverse Theatre, all the participants worked on material with the writer, who finally produced a script from the ideas suggested by the whole company. Joint Stock worked primarily with this method.

In 1975, it produced David Hare's *Fan Shen*. 'Fan shen' means literally 'turn over', and is the Chinese term for 'revolution'. The play charts the gradual education of the peasants of the Chinese village of Long Bow as they struggle to *fan shen* from the oppressive regime of the landlords to the responsibilities of communist society. It is based on a book by William Hinton which chronicles this upheaval.

Fan Shen is structured as a series of dialectical arguments: that is, one point of view is countered and expanded by a contrasting viewpoint. Joint Stock explored both sides of the arguments. The company claimed that exploring these arguments made them more critically aware.

Joint Stock's production of Fan Shen, *by David Hare*

Gaskill explains:

We made a decision before we started rehearsal that because of the nature of the material we would work by methods we hadn't used before. Like making group decisions on everything. Everything went through discussions, analysis, everyone spoke. The image of the meetings in Fan Shen *were mirrored all the time by meetings of the group.*
(Gaskill, cited in Itzin, *Stages in the Revolution,* p.221)

Gaskill's argument is that the working method of the company 'politicised' its members.

The two directors (Gaskill and Stafford-Clark) and the writer (Hare) worked closely with the actors in workshops. After a period of relevant research and exploration, David Hare then wrote the play; he stresses that the workshop process was crucial. When you look at the text, you can see signs of the group effort. The way in which each character is allowed to create his or her own story and give full expression to his or her views is a strong mark of the group dynamic, as well as of its political perspective.

Research and improvisation were the mainstays of the company's work methods. For its play *Yesterday's News* (1976), about mercenaries in Angola, the actors interviewed mercenaries. For Caryl Churchill's *Light Shining in Buckinghamshire* (1976), they researched the historical period of the time. This method not only requires thought from the writer and director, but requires the actor to think as well. The actor is a responsible, intelligent member of the company, instead of the director or producer's puppet. 'We have had the Actor's Theatre, the Writer's Theatre, the Director's Theatre. This is the era of the Company Theatre' (Stafford-Clark, cited in the *Daily Mail,* 1977).

228

The key aspects of Joint Stock's work were the material to work on and the actors. Eighty per cent of its money went on actors. Up to a month was spent with the actors in workshops, improvisation and research. Then up to eight weeks might be spent creating the performance.

Improvisational work required thought and responsibility and frequently incorporated the writer, too. Stephen Lowe, a playwright working with Joint Stock, wrote about an improvisation in the workshops for *The Ragged-Trousered Philanthropists* which grew out of the use of costume: 'They were then put through a series of improvisations in which they were not allowed to speak – they all had to do an audition, to wait for their social security benefit, and so on. They had to maintain the characters the clothes had given them for some time . . . ' (*Theatre Papers*, Volume III, no. 2, p.22).

The inclusion of writers in the group creative process was both innovative and productive. Many of the playwrights who worked with Joint Stock are now well known, including David Hare, Howard Brenton, Howard Barker, Caryl Churchill, Stephen Lowe and Barrie Keefe. Some people still argue that these writers' best work was the work they did with Joint Stock.

The chief innovation of Joint Stock was to see the script as an end product rather than a starting point. Also, like most of the new theatre companies but unlike the mainstream theatre, it put creative necessity before supply and demand.

. . . *[Joint Stock's work] has run counter to the whole British theatre tradition in which shows are often mounted simply to keep the existing plant, machinery and company ticking over.*
(Michael Billington, the *Guardian*, 1977)

The theatre of sexual politics
In the late 1960s and early 1970s, sexual politics, too, came out into the open. Women's theatre groups began to develop, partly to redress the conventional balance of power between the sexes, and specifically to begin to foreground sexual politics. Many of the plays were didactic: that is, they used the platform of the drama to illustrate a single, significant point.

The Women's Theatre Group
The founding of the Women's Theatre Group in 1974 coincided with and was a significant part of the growth of the Women's Liberation Movement in Britain. There was a strong desire to make links between life inside and outside the home, between the world of politics 'out there' and power structures in relationships and families. The Women's Theatre Group intended to use its work to explore the dictum 'the personal is political': that is, that the choices we make in our everyday life have political implications and can be changed. Its work was aimed at examining the way in which our personal life reflects the values and power struggles of our society.

The company was an all-women collective, which worked democratically. There was no 'boss'. It was a touring company, performing, for the most part, at women's events and to community and trade-union audiences. Its plays, such as *My Mother Said I Never Should* (1974) and *Work to Rule* (1975), questioned women's subordinate role in society and promoted the possibilities of change. 'To challenge the accepted role of women is, inevitably, a political action, since it raises questions about the structure of our society as a whole, including capitalism' (Women's Theatre Group flyer, 1979).

The company used music in all its performances, but otherwise the style adapted to suit the material, ranging from biting satire to emotionally charged realism.

Monstrous Regiment

Founded in 1975 by a group of actresses including Gillian Hanna, Sue Beardon, Linda Broughton and Chris Bowler, the company's fundamental aim was to fight back against the treatment of women in theatre and society.

The Regiment was established on the basis of feminist principles. It was crucial that it was run by women, that its commitment was to women – good stage parts for women (where women could take centre stage and not be relegated to the sidelines), jobs for women technicians, writers and directors; child-care provision written into the budgets . . .
(Gillian Hanna, interview with Lizbeth Goodman, *New Theatre Quarterly*, Volume VI, no. 21, Feb. 1990)

[Actresses faced more] unemployment, [or] small parts as wives or girlfriends, always serving, never acting on our own behalf. But women always have acted on their own behalf and we want to celebrate that action.
(*Vinegar Tom* programme, 1977)

Monstrous Regiment's production of Teendreams *by David Edgar and Susan Todd*

Thus the organisation itself mirrored the company's feminist political principles. It commissioned plays from women writers, and the plays it produced, on the whole, both exposed the unequal treatment of women in society and highlighted the strength of women, often using history as a focus. *Vinegar Tom,* by Caryl Churchill, for example, is about witch burning in the 17th century. *Scum* is a musical in which the Paris Commune of 1871 and the French Revolution are seen through the eyes of a group of earthy washerwomen scrubbing away in a slum laundry.

These women pooled their performing and theatrical skills in the fight for women's rights. In common with the other new theatre companies, they hoped to challenge, provoke and disturb their audiences through the form of entertainment, in order to encourage social change.

Gay Sweatshop

Gay Sweatshop was set up in 1974 to tackle gay issues through theatre, as it was widely believed that the British Left and socialist theatre were ignoring gay politics. It was then the only gay company in existence; it still exists today.

Gay Sweatshop had both a women's and a men's group, which toured nationally, playing not only to the gay community but to the wider public. It encouraged and commisioned plays which dealt with gay issues. (There is now a volume of Gay Sweatshop plays.) Its continuous presence has opened a previously closed door between the gay community and the public that would have been inconceivable before 1968.

A recent Gay Sweatshop production

231

Of all the companies which created the 'new theatre', perhaps Gay Sweatshop is the one that can see most practically the positive results of its work. It is not all that unusual now for plays about gay issues to be seen in the West End.

Other alternative theatre

The 'new theatre movement' gave birth to many more groups than we have mentioned here. Of special interest is the creation of ethnically based theatre groups such as Temba Theatre Company, Talawa, the Black Theatre Co-operative and Tara Arts (see pp.88–92), which not only express concerns specific to their communities but also encourage black actors and writers. Temba Theatre Company, the first black theatre group, is no longer functioning, but the others are still flourishing energetically. Graeae Theatre Company is a company of disabled actors who produce both their own plays and classics such as Ben Jonson's *Volpone*. In addition, the birth of many theatre-in-education (TIE) companies was a response to the evolution of theatrical practice. (See Chapter 7 for further details about TIE.)

Alternative theatre and society

The new theatre of the 1960s and 1970s has had its effects.

The intrinsic commitment to social change and the pursuit of new audiences characteristic of alternative theatre have had profound effects on theatre audiences, community consciousness and education.

Mainstream theatre has accepted many of the alternative companies and styles.

At the time, political consciousness was raised.

In retrospect, we can admit that the new theatre of the later 1960s and 1970s did not cause a revolution and change the world, but the effects of this movement are manifold. A great many 'alternative companies', such as Theatre de Complicité, Belt and Braces and Cheek by Jowl have performed successfully to West End audiences, suggesting, perhaps, that theatrical taste has been affected, and even that new audiences have been attracted to the theatre. Certainly, theatre-going is a much less formal affair than it was in the 1960s. In addition, although no revolution has taken place, we could argue that these companies have altered the attitudes of the audiences they have reached, encouraging political consciousness and suggesting the possibility of change.

Particular groups have grown in stature as a result of the alternative theatre movement.

Many new, talented and exciting playwrights have been, and continue to be, fostered by the new theatre movement. Most notably, there has been a wave of women playwrights since the 1980s, including Caryl Churchill, Louise Page, Sarah Daniels, Claire Luckham, Clare McIntyre, Winsome Pinnock and Timberlake Wertenbaker, many of whom started out in the women's theatre movement. Black and Asian people, too, have begun to use the stage as a platform to examine issues important to their communities, and this serves as an encouragement to a new group of black writers. (See the interviews with Denise Wong and Jatinder Verma, pp.76–79 and 88–92.)

Theatre is accepted outside traditional theatre spaces.

It is no longer assumed that in order to present a performance you need to hire a theatre building. Theatrical performances are now seen in a variety of venues. (See the interviews with Kneehigh, Legs on the Wall and Rejects Revenge, pp.117–131.) The touring programmes of the new theatre companies, together with the developing interest in community theatre, have, in many places, led to a new consciousness of 'community' and a desire to explore and celebrate community history and experience. (Again, see Kneehigh, pp.117–121.) TIE has been an increasing influence in education, although shifts in funding have reduced the number of TIE companies in the 1990s and moved the weight to theatre education. (For further details, see pp.239–255.)

In all these ways, then, real change did take place. However, when funding problems began, the optimism that gave rise to the new theatre dampened. Looking back, playwright Pam Gems captures how important a time this was in British theatre:

> . . . that lovely time when youth was celebrated with all its dangers and silliness, but with all the good things, was precious. People talk of the French Revolution as if it was only about blood running in the streets. But it changed the world . . . These brief periods make such an impact.
> (Gems, cited in Rees, Fringe First, p.200)

Funding
In 1969–70, the Arts Council subsidy to alternative theatre was £15,000. In 1978–9, the budget of the Drama Panel of the Arts Council alone was over £1.5 million. This agreeable increase over ten years allowed the development of 60 full-time, small-scale theatre companies. The Arts Council, funded by the Ministry of the Arts, exercised its own discretion about how the Treasury's money was to be distributed.

The funding situation changed in the 1980s.

The Conservative government came to power in 1979. By the mid to late 1980s, the Arts Council was to assist in the downfall of many of those touring theatre companies. It decided that companies must find half their income from sources other than subsidy. This had an adverse effect on companies such as Foco Novo, since commercial sponsors tend to favour less politically overt pieces of work. Roland Rees argues that Foco Novo 'went under' because it would not conform to the new priorities. Moreover, its political motivation had been severed by the 'prevailing Thatcherite economic principles' – to put it bluntly, that everything should be done for profit.

The machinations of the Arts Council are complex. Suffice it to say, 20 years on from the time when experimental theatre ignited one of the most exciting periods in theatre history, the Arts Council, on the justification that it had decided to 'inject new blood' into small-scale theatre, cut funds to longstanding companies such as Joint Stock and Foco Novo, which, subsequently, ceased to exist.

Resource Activities

1. POLITICAL TEXT AND HISTORICAL CONTEXT

Aims
To understand the correlation between content, cultural context and theatre.

Objectives
- To gain an understanding of the relationship between theatre and the society of its time.
- To identify the correlation between the content and the structure of *Oh What A Lovely War*.
- To understand how performance can bring out political content.
- To experience the relationship between text and performance.

Background
Theatre Workshop was established at the Theatre Royal, Stratford East, London, (after starting as a touring company) by Joan Littlewood, who had been working in 'agit-prop' theatre in the North of England since the 1930s. The company had a strong left-wing bias. It worked primarily through improvisation, and sought to create a 'popular' theatre that would entertain as well as expose political issues. The acting style was broad and energetic, and the company used elements taken from music hall, such as talking directly to the audience and breaking into song.

Oh What a Lovely War was devised by the company in the early 1960s. Its main point is to strip the concept of war of its romantic, heroic associations, to expose the economic motives and power struggles that

A scene from Oh What a Lovely War *(1963)*

give rise to wars, and to emphasise its consequences for ordinary people. In this way, the intention is to expose 'making war' as an unacceptable choice, especially for the ordinary person.

The actors are dressed as 'pierrots', white clowns, in an ironic contrast to the uniform of soldiers. The clowns take on different parts to illustrate a series of issues in World War I. Because the action is twice removed in this way, the audience is 'distanced' from the individuals taking part, and its attention is focused on the issue the scene is examining. The company also presented information by using projections.

When the play first opened, many people were horrified. They were offended by the main point of the play, 'The War Game', with its suggestion that war was nothing more than a game in which ordinary people were treated as disposable pawns.

Read pp.213–219 on the background to the period, and *Oh What a Lovely War*, or sections of it.

Tasks

- Take one short extract from *Oh What a Lovely War* that particularly interests you. 'Stage' it, in such a way as to highlight its major issue(s) and political perspective. The facilities at your disposal and the time given for this exercise will determine the detail attached to this staging. You may work with only the actors' bodies, or you might develop this into a broader staging exercise. (For example, you could combine this with Activity 7 on pp.313–316. *Return to the Forbidden Planet* is used in that activity. You could use *Oh What A Lovely War*, adding in the overt political dimension of the task.)

- In a piece of written work, answer the following questions:

  i) What was the political mood of the 1960s that provided the context for *Oh What a Lovely War*? Can you find examples of events that could be seen as relevant?
  ii) How would you describe the structure of the play?
  iii) How does the structure affect the content? Use examples from the text.
  iv) In what type of venue would you perform this play? Take two specific scenes from the text and explain how each one would work in the space.

2. THE ARTS IN SOCIETY TODAY

Aim
To address the question of the arts in society today.

Objective
To undertake a project on local arts.

Activity A: Background

- You will need to get a programme of events or productions and, if possible, a policy document from a local theatre or arts centre.
- Read pp.20–22 in Chapter 1 on presentation skills.

Tasks

- Read some of the plays that are being presented at this venue.

- Go to see some of the productions, and read reviews in local (or national) papers.

- Read general news stories in local papers: this will help you to find out about the community's concerns.

- Interview some members of the audience.

- Read the theatre's policy document: how does it relate to the needs of the community?

- Give a formal presentation about this local theatre or centre. As well as giving general information, take these two questions as the key focus of your presentation:

  i) How is this theatre responding to the needs of the audience?
  ii) How does this compare to *your* view on the current position of theatre in our society?

Activity B: Background

- You will need to get programmes from as many different local arts centres and theatres as you can. If a group of you have undertaken the above activities, you may well have a number of such programmes between you. This activity is more interesting if you can work as a group.
- Read the section entitled 'The new or alternative companies' on p.219–232 above.
- Read the three interviews in Chapter 4 with Kneehigh, Rejects Revenge and Legs on the Wall (pp.117–131).
- If you can, find out information about the companies mentioned in this chapter which are still going, for example 7:84. You may find it useful to look at a copy of the *Directory of Alternative Theatre*, which is published annually.

Tasks

- What do you think the objectives of a small-scale theatre company should be today? Draw up a group list.

- Write a proposal for a theatre festival in your area. This proposal should include:

  i) a statement from the organisers (yourselves) explaining what you believe the purpose of theatre should be in today's society;
  ii) a list of events that will be happening. These may be real companies and events that you know of, or you could invent names and types of groups/shows and so on. Include a wide range of companies, such as disability theatre groups;

iii) an explanation of the nature of all these events, such that the public will want to see them;

iv) a description of the venues in which they will be taking place;

v) ideas for funding the festival, if possible;

vi) any other details that you feel are pertinent to such a festival.

This proposal should be drawn up as professionally as possible; drawings or photographs may be included.

● Turn the proposal into a formal presentation.

3. SOCIAL ISSUES

Aim
To develop an understanding of social and political theatre.

Objectives
● To investigate how a play reflects a way of working.
● To understand how information can be 'dramatised'.
● To consider how connections can be made between another culture and our own.

Background
Read *Fan Shen*, which was written by David Hare with and for Joint Stock. It was possibly their most successful play. At first, it is a bit difficult to read, partly because of all the Chinese names, but also because there are so many characters. The play is about how the inhabitants of a small village in China struggled to change their lives after the Chinese Revolution. Even though their lives were improving, it was difficult to turn the ideals of the Revolution into practical, personal behaviour.

Tasks
● Read pp.227–229 on the working methods of Joint Stock. Write a short report explaining in what ways the working methods of the company are revealed in the playtext.

● Choose one scene and stage it so that it expresses an issue you think is relevant to a British audience today. State the nature of your audience in a support document. For example, is it your local, average theatre audience? Is it a student audience at the NSDF (see p.3)? Is it an Edinburgh Fringe Festival audience (see pp.3–4)? Is it a village hall audience (see Tim Hibbert's interview, p.126)?

● Take an incident happening in another country from a current newspaper and write a short scene that will make it alive and relevant to British people today.

For further activities which come under the broad area of the arts in society, consider the resource activities at the end of Chapter 7.

BIBLIOGRAPHY

Some recommended playtexts for further study:

Arden, John and D'Arcy, Margaret, *Our Little Grey Home in the West*
Churchill, Caryl, *Vinegar Tom, Light Shining in Buckinghamshire, Cloud Nine, Fen*
Hare, David, *Fan Shen, Knuckle*
Barker, Howard, *Victory, The Castle*
Brenton, Howard, *The Churchill Play*
Red Ladder, *Taking Our Time*
McGrath, John, *The Cheviot, the Stag and the Black, Black Oil*
Lowe, Stephen, *The Ragged-Trousered Philanthropists*
Theatre Workshop, *O What A Lovely War, Sparrers Can't Sing*
The Wakefield, York or Chester Mystery Cycles
Anonymous, *Everyman*

The following texts all address the theatre of the alternative movement. They are all interesting analytical accounts; all are fairly academic. The most accessible are Rees, Bull, Richie and McGrath. See also the general bibliography on p.380.

Ansorge, P., *Disrupting the Spectacle*, Pitman, 1975

Bull, J., *New British Political Dramatists*, Macmillan, 1984

Coult, T. and Kershaw, B. (eds), *Engineers of the Imagination: The Welfare State Handbook*, Methuen, 1983

Craig, S., *Dreams and Reconstructions*, Amberlane Press, 1980

Davies, A., *Other Theatres*, Barnes and Noble, 1987

Elsom, J., *Post-War British Theatre*, Routledge and Kegan Paul, 1979

Goorney, H., *The Theatre Workshop Story*, Eyre Methuen, 1981

Itzin, C., *Stages in the Revolution*, Eyre Methuen, 1980

Kershaw, B., *The Politics of Performance: Radical Theatre as Cultural Intervention*, Routledge, 1992

McGrath, J., *A Good Night Out*, Methuen, 1981

MacLennan, E., *The Moon Belongs to Everyone: Making Theatre with 7:84*, Methuen, 1990

Owusu, K., *The Struggle for Black Arts in Britain*, Comedia, 1986

Rees, R., *Fringe First: Pioneers of Fringe Theatre on Record*, Oberon, 1992

Richie, R. (ed.), *The Joint Stock Book*, Methuen, 1987

7 Theatre and Education

Chris Elwell

As has been mentioned in Chapter 4, a popular practical project for students often involves performing or creating work for audiences within an educational context. Traditionally, this may be for a local primary school or youth group. However, this is only one element of a much larger field of activity, which for the purposes of this chapter is called 'theatre education'.

This chapter comprises the following sections:

- A brief history of theatre education
- Different forms of theatre education
- A sample theatre education project
- A case study: Pop-Up and *Iron Dreams*

A BRIEF HISTORY OF THEATRE EDUCATION

Theatre education practices are rooted in theatre history.

Theatre history itself has been broadly tracked elsewhere in this book (see Chapters 2 and 4). Theatre education is rooted in this long and varied history. From the rituals and early dramas of ancient civilisations to the present day, theatre has been an important force in stimulating questions and debate; simultaneously, it has entertained and engaged its audience. Clearly, then, it is possible to say that *all* theatre is education.

Contemporary theatre education started at the beginning of the 20th century.

For the purposes of this chapter, however, our definition of theatre education is work produced for and with young people. Within this context, theatre education has a relatively short history. In the late Victorian era, the popularity of pantomime showed a desire among the public to bring their children to the theatre. This continues today; many of the large commercial theatres in the UK will programme daytime productions. Most cities will offer a stage version of a popular TV children's cartoon, such as *Postman Pat*, *Playdays* or *The Mister Men*, at least once a year.

At the turn of the century, the equivalent of *Fireman Sam* gave theatre a new focus. The 1904 production of J.M. Barrie's *Peter Pan* is frequently referred to as the first work especially designed for young people; it was followed by *Toad of Toad Hall* in 1929 (an adaptation of Kenneth Grahame's *The Wind in the Willows*). Two years earlier, in 1927, the Scottish Children's Theatre had become the first full-time professional theatre company for children. However, it was not until 1937 that a

Local Education Authority began to find resources to pay for schoolchildren to attend free theatre performances (other than Shakespeare) during school hours as part of the curriculum. Children's theatre had been established.

The educationalists Slade and Way heavily influenced the development of theatre education in the mid 20th century.

In the 1940s, two important developments occurred which started to shape the theatre education industry as we know it today. The first was the work carried out and documented by the educationalists Peter Slade and Brain Way. Way, in particular, sought to formalise the role of children's theatre within education. He saw the value to children of experiencing theatre not just as a useful social activity, but as a powerful tool in education.

Public funding for the arts stimulated a growth in theatre education.

It was also in the late 1940s that the Labour government established the Council for the Encouragement of Music and the Arts. This organisation was later renamed the Arts Council of Great Britain (ACGB) and became the most important influence on the development of the arts in the UK. Many of the arts organisations or companies which regularly produce theatre education work now receive their major funding from public, state or local authority grants. The major provider historically has generally been the ACGB.

Public funding of the arts grew from demand; a broad cross-section of people had experienced the arts during the war years.

Prior to the 1940s, the British State had not given public money to the arts, unlike most European countries. The ACGB was a development from philanthropic or subsidised arts provided for the troops and the people back home during World War II. For example, the Pilgrim Trust had aimed to promote the arts among the young for their educational and cultural development, while the wartime troop entertainment organisation, ENSA, had become very popular. Subsequently, with peace, there was a new demand for the arts. It seemed right that, just as it was providing a new free health service, the State should also fund arts through a public body. The scene was set for the establishment of the famous companies that we know today. The Memorial Theatre Company, originally privately funded by the Stratford-based Flowers' Brewery, became the Royal Shakespeare Company through public funds.

A Policy for the Arts (1967) ushered in a period of new theatre-building programmes, new opportunities and financial security for the sector.

In the early 1960s – a time of expansion and innovation in the arts (see Chapter 6) – theatre education took a new and firm grip upon the UK's culture. The newly created ACGB published an influential paper written by the first Minister for the Arts: *A Policy for the Arts*. This 1967 report recognised for the first time the importance of theatre specifically aimed at young audiences. It recommended an immediate injection of financial support – £90,000 in the first year – and the establishment of a Young People's Theatre Panel at the ACGB. The 1960s also saw a scale of theatre building not experienced in the country for almost half a century. Four theatres in particular were constructed that had especial significance for the development of theatre education: the Belgrade, Coventry, the Nottingham Playhouse, the Sheffield Crucible and Greenwich Theatre, London.

The Belgrade in Coventry was particularly influential in TIE.

These theatres were concerned with reaching out to new audiences and serving the communities whose taxes had paid for them. One of them, the Belgrade, established a new method of working called theatre-in-education (TIE). This programme went beyond the child-centred and progressive educational theories of Way and his colleagues, and placed a new emphasis upon theatre as *process* rather than as an *end product*. TIE teams were subsequently established at many mainstream repertory theatres.

Youth theatre and children's theatre achieved some prominence in the 1960s and 1970s.

The development of community arts initiatives, including work with schools through TIE programmes, was one aspect of many theatres' work. With the official recognition of the National Youth Theatre by the Ministry of Education, youth theatres blossomed, as did extensive community projects, including community plays. During the next decade, the oldest specialist children's theatre company, Theatre Centre, co-founded by Brian Way, received direct funding from the ACGB, and specialist children's theatres, the Unicorn Theatre, London, and the Polka Theatre, Wimbledon, were established.

Theatre Centre productions of three plays by Brian Way: The Mirrorman, The Decision *and* The Hat

The formation of SCYPT was a sign of the strength of TIE.

TIE began to find regular funding from Local Education Authorities. Greenwich Young People's Theatre in London became independent of its parent theatre and with support from the Inner London Education Authority (ILEA) took a lead in establishing a TIE network within inner London. Such was the strength and importance of the movement across the country that the TIE companies formed SCYPT – the Standing Conference of Young People's Theatre – which became a powerful advocate for theatre education in the 1970s and 1980s. As it saw resources being reduced through government policies, it took an increasingly political stance, which proved unpopular and embarrassing to some local and national funding bodies.

This remarkable growth peaked in the late 1970s. By the early 1980s, the amount of money available from public sources began to be reduced,

The theatre education industry re-assessed itself in the 1980s in the light of major political changes and public legislation.

in response to changes in government policies. This situation was compounded by alterations in the structure of the state education system, most specifically the establishment of the National Curriculum as a result of the 1988 Education Reform Act. The abolition of the ILEA represented a major loss in financial support to London-based TIE in particular. From that time on, it became progressively more difficult for funding bodies such as the ACGB to match the resources once given by local authorities.

In 1994, the arts funding system in the UK experienced a series of major changes. Since this date, the Arts Councils of Scotland, Wales and Northern Ireland have become independent bodies, and the English regions are covered by 12 Regional Arts Boards. The ACGB was renamed the Arts Council of England (ACE). These changes were the culmination of a major shift since 1979 in government policy towards the arts, and were to have an enormous impact upon the provision, role and style of theatre education in the UK. With substantially less funding, TIE companies have been forced to replace their labour-intensive methodologies with cheaper practices; many have chosen to close voluntarily rather than compromise. Schools find it hard to justify spending finite resources on TIE. (See the interview with Mike Shepherd, p.120, for comments on the present situation.)

Education-in-theatre has attempted to fill some of the gap left by the dwindling TIE companies.

During the early to mid 1980s, a new type of theatre education product started to develop, which is known as education-in-theatre. (See below for an explanation of the different forms of theatre education.) Nowadays, most publicly funded companies and venues undertake some form of arts education activity, and many have a special education programme, department and officer; links with the community are central to their work. Education-in-theatre is a direct attempt by the theatre world to fill the vacuum left by the disappearance of almost the entire TIE portfolio. Education-in-theatre in its many forms is the most prolific form of theatre education activity presently offered in the UK.

DIFFERENT FORMS OF THEATRE EDUCATION

The theatre education industry has undergone rapid changes since its early developments in the 1960s. The term TIE is still used to cover wide-ranging practices. However, theatre education today occurs in many settings, not just schools: these might include senior citizens' day centres, prisons, museums and art galleries, or substance abuse drop-in centres. It also benefits many different sectors of the community, including the homeless, single parents and adults with special needs. However, all theatre education activity has one thing in common: an informing or instructional role. In summary, it can be described as using theatre for an educational purpose.

Over the past 40 years, however, theatre education has become most closely associated with schools and young people. This chapter focuses

Theatre education work taking place with youngsters has been grouped under the umbrella term TYP.

on this aspect of theatre education work. In recent years, it has been grouped under the umbrella title of Theatre for Young People (TYP). The term TYP is used for any theatre-based activities presented to young people, and reflects a range of practice taking place in schools, colleges and youth centres.

For simplicity, it is useful to make distinctions between the different types of TYP. This will help focus your thoughts about styles or approaches that may be usefully employed when choosing a playtext or devising a piece to be performed for young people. There are four categories: theatre-in-education, education-in-theatre, children's theatre and youth theatre.

Theatre-in-education (TIE)

Theatre-in-education is an interactive theatre experience.

In describing theatre education work for young people, the term TIE is most commonly used. Theatre-in-education (TIE) is not a generic term, however; it is now recognised to be a specific process. This process is primarily an interactive one: TIE includes interaction between the audience and actors. For example, a TIE programme could be a continuous interactive piece of theatre where the audience participates in some way. Participation is the key aspect of TIE. Another important point is that TIE is not about drama education: it is about education on other topics and issues through the medium of theatre.

Boal is a practitioner closely linked with our contemporary understanding of TIE.

Whilst the process cannot be said to have been introduced by any one practitioner, the work of Augusto Boal has many links with the philosophy of TIE. Boal was preoccupied with the political oppression in many South American countries. He sought to use theatre as a medium for confronting this oppression. One of the key areas with which Boal concerns himself is the role of the audience in the theatre experience. He believes that the purpose of 'theatre of the oppressed' is 'to change the people – "spectators" – passive beings . . . into subjects, actors, transformers of the dramatic action' (Boal, *Theatre of the Oppressed*, p.122).

The role of the audience is central to traditional British TIE methods. Boal's term 'spect-actors' is often used. Clearly, this word combines the role of spectator and actor. Boal's method gives a 'voice' to the audience participating in the theatre event, stimulating the participants to take charge of their actions and make changes in their lives.

Below, Chris Vine outlines an early use of Boal's practices in British TIE in 1982 at Greenwich Young People's Theatre (GYPT) in a programme called *A Land Fit For Heroes*, which took as its starting point the 1926 British General Strike:

The pupils watched this scenario unfold knowing in advance that it contained a series of problems similar to those they had already experienced. When it was over they were asked what they thought she [the protagonist] could do. They discussed the possible options open to her and speculated on their ramifications

Participation is encouraged by the Joker (facilitator) in the Forum (the name Boal uses for this participatory theatre).

. . . They were then asked what they thought they would do if they were in that situation . . . After the different opinions had been clarified, the next stage began . . . A key figure in the Forum process is the 'Joker'. The Joker is the facilitator, the direct link between the audience and the dramatic action; she or he has the responsibility for orchestrating the whole event. The Joker must encourage and enable the spectators (or 'spectactors' as Boal calls them) to intervene.
(Vine, C., 'TIE and the Theatre of the Oppressed' in Jackson, *Learning Through Theatre*, pp. 114–117)

The actor playing the Joker is one of several theatre practitioners guiding the young people through the experience. Most theatre practitioners working in TIE would call themselves 'actor–teachers', acknowledging their dual function as an educationalist – teacher – and as an artist – actor.

A scene from A Land Fit for Heroes *by Greenwich Young People's Theatre*

TIE draws influences from many practitioners, including Brecht, Littlewood and Brook.

Boal acknowledges the influence of other theatre practitioners, especially Brecht, on the development of his work, and particularly on his understanding of the role of the audience. Brecht wanted his audience to question and change their society for the better. (See p.32 for further information on Brecht.)

Closer to home, in the UK, the work of Joan Littlewood and the Theatre Workshop in London's East End in the 1950s and 1960s has also been influential on TIE development. Littlewood's work provided members of the audience with a channel through which they were able to learn, experience and express themselves. By presenting theatre that directly represented the hopes, aspirations and fears of the people who attended her plays, she was able to create 'a continuous loop with the community'. Through this experience, she hoped, the audience would be able to bring about change. (For further work on Joan Littlewood, see pp.234–235 in Chapter 6.)

It would be wrong to give the impression that TIE is inherently political or serious. TIE can also be enjoyable and entertaining, like all forms of theatre. However, TIE is always underpinned by some sort of educational purpose.

Clearly, TIE must have an educational purpose.

The educational purpose of TIE can be complex. For example, imagine that a TIE company is preparing to create a piece of theatre for an audience of 12-year-olds which will explore solvent abuse. The company might recognise the importance of the issues or content, but may choose not to address the topic head-on: 'What would be the point if the theatre piece only said, "say no to solvents", but did not also look at people's lives and how choices are made?' This second level is the educational purpose. On a practical level, the characters represented within the piece provide a human dimension. The individual 12-year-old participating in the theatre piece will empathise with the protagonist, and will simultaneously make a connection with concerns in his or her own personal life. This is *applied* learning.

In 1996, PGCE Drama students at the Central School of Speech and Drama who are training to be teachers of students in the 11–18 age group summarised TIE work as follows. It articulates a philosophy for British TIE.

The policy focuses the practice.

All TIE programmes are conceived as an integral part of the process of education, not as a one-off theatrical event. Audiences do not just sit and watch, but are asked to participate, sometimes playing a role, sometimes as themselves, alongside the actor–teachers. They are encouraged to intervene, to question, to solve problems and to make decisions in a thoughtful and constructive manner, thereby reinforcing the efficacy of the learning method across the curriculum, particularly in respect of oral skills, self-assertion, decision-making, self-assessment and critical analysis.

It is difficult to assess the learning that takes place as a result of a TIE programme. The following comments are made by students two years after seeing *A Land Fit For Heroes*, the GYPT programme cited by Chris Vine earlier in this section:

Serjit: *You were made aware of things you probably wouldn't have thought about if you was watching telly or something.*

Sarah: It was sort of depressing going back into the classroom afterwards, wasn't it? Going back to old boring stuff.

Serjit: Things like that can use so many ideas at the same time and get it over efficiently to kids, whereas if you sat down you'd have to deal with each thing individually and it wouldn't get through as well. Like they could see each side of the point of view and if they did it at school they'd only take their own stand.

Sarah: I think as well as that, all the people who wouldn't usually sort of participate, did, didn't they?

Claudia: Usually if you see that sort of thing on television you just turn it over, but there you had to take part in it and that was it and it was educational, 'cos you did learn.

(Suffolk, L., 'Theatre, Memory and Learning: The Long-Term Impact of Theatre-in-Education' in Tickle, *The Arts in Education*, p.186)

Education-in-theatre

Education-in-theatre practices employed by theatre educators are diverse.

One of the more publicly profiled styles of theatre education practice taking place in the UK in recent years is that carried out by education officers or education departments attached to theatre companies, theatres and arts centres. This is known as education-in-theatre.

Education-in-theatre:

- is not easily categorised, since its nature, role and status vary enormously;
- often focuses on establishing and extending links with the local community (most often schools or youth groups), in order to give an informed awareness of what theatre is and how it works;
- creates an audience for the future, as part of a marketing strategy or community development plan.

Activities generally include lectures, courses, backstage tours, playdays, workshop programmes and so on.

An example of a policy statement could be:

The policy focuses the practice.

Our Education Department aims to bridge the gap between the Company's work on our stages and students, teachers and lecturers throughout the education system and within the wider community context. We work in partnership with participants so that projects undertaken can be integrated into the wider educational process of young people. Our approach is creative and practical. It draws on contributions from the full spectrum of the Company – production staff, voice, actors, movement specialists, directors.

Four main types of theatre organisation have some form of education-in-theatre in position:

- regional producing theatres (for example: Birmingham Repertory Theatre, Watford Palace, Nottingham Playhouse, West Yorkshire Playhouse);
- producing theatres operating a repertory system (for example:

Royal Shakespeare Company, Royal National Theatre);

- arts venues supporting visiting theatre companies (for example: Bury St Edmunds Theatre Royal, Warwick Arts Centre, Battersea Arts Centre, Bath Theatre Royal);
- touring theatre companies with their own defined 'education, community and outreach programme' (for example: Oxford Stage Company, Method and Madness, Trestle, Theatre de Complicité, English Touring Theatre).

The workshop is a popular method of practice used in education-in-theatre work.

The most common form of work practice or methodology used by theatres such as the West Yorkshire Playhouse is the workshop. A good workshop is a carefully crafted activity which responds to a play in performance. A good workshop – like a piece of theatre – will take account of various points:

- what is to be taught: the content;
- how this is realised: the form;
- the intended audience: the reception.

Workshops usually focus upon a performance taking place in the theatre building or arts centre. They tend to comprise two areas of activity. The first aims to teach skills, or to illustrate theatrecraft and/or technologies. For example, this could involve students working in detail on the text with the production's director, or taking a class with the movement director or lighting designer. These workshops will attempt to enhance the participants' theatre skills base, for example by developing improvisation skills. They will directly develop acting or technical training or the more practical elements of examination syllabus requirements.

Secondly, workshops may also explore the concepts or themes of the play. For example, a typical workshop may look at the portrayal of women in Shakespeare's plays, using *King Lear* as the focus. The workshop could involve the actors who are playing the three sisters, Cordelia, Goneril and Regan. They may be asked to hot-seat, improvise or work off-text directly with the participants. In general, the participants are not being taught how to perform, but instead are learning about the play's themes or its contemporary resonance for an audience.

The education officer is the major player in theatre education practices.

Workshops are led by actors or directors, or possibly by the designated education officer at the theatre. Education departments within theatre companies or venues vary enormously in size, ethos and function. They may consist of one individual, a small team or an eclectic group of individuals; these people may be working on short contracts, on a daily basis, or part-time on a specific project. Such individuals have many titles: education officer, education liaison officer, community director, associate director (education and community), education manager, head of education or schools' officer.

An education officer will want to develop good relations with local

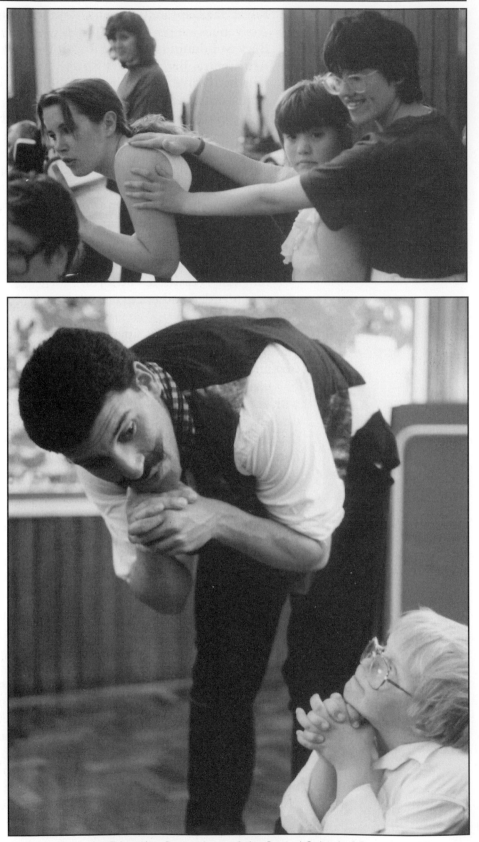

Students from the Education Department of the Central School of Speech and Drama running workshops while in residence at Curnow School, Cornwall, in 1996

Education-in-theatre aims to promote art activities with and for a theatre's communities, using the theatre as its resource.

schools and community groups, as well as being part of the artistic and administrative team at the theatre. His or her main role will be to bridge the gap between the two worlds, providing access for all those who want to take advantage of the theatre's resources.

Public policy influences contemporary practice in theatre education.

The ACE (Arts Council of England) has firmly indicated that theatre education provision should be placed at the heart of all theatre companies' and arts venues' work. This shift in policy is a natural response to the changes that have occurred in the UK over the past ten years, socially, politically and economically. There has been a noticeable re-allocation of resources from educational theatre companies (TIE companies most obviously) to theatre companies and venues producing educational work within existing or newly created education departments. This has demanded a re-assessment of 'theatre education':

Recent changes in the education system (e.g. the loss of the national drama advisory services and education authority funded theatre in schools) have had a critical impact upon arts education and the ability of young people to attend theatre performances. The introduction of the National Curriculum has made it more difficult for drama teachers to maintain the previous levels of involvement in curricular and extra-curricular drama activities, or their own specialist, professional development. The theatre industry has had to adapt and develop its activities to achieve its objectives of access and participation. Specialist theatre companies, particularly, have had to meet the challenges resulting from these changes.

Theatre for Young People and Theatre in Education are areas of work which have, over many years, cultivated relationships with a large and important audience. This work tends to have a low profile – and it can have a low status within the theatre profession. It is, however, critical to the development of theatre since it can offer young people an experience of great educational and artistic value, which helps create the audiences of the future.
(The Policy for Drama of the English Arts Funding System, 1996, p.19)

Education officers in the 1990s have a significant role to play in the delivery of arts education practice in the UK.

Children's theatre

Theatre created with a young people's audience in mind is called children's theatre.

Education-in-theatre practices use the workshop to carry out much of their activity. However, some people believe that a workshop 'added on' after a theatre performance is not appropriate. Some theatre companies do not do workshops, but rather devise or write productions *specifically* for young people in their own right. The producers have this audience in mind, and believe that such theatre can stand alone as an educational experience. Companies which create theatre of this type are usually described as producers of children's theatre. This type of theatre has the following characteristics:

● It is a performance designed either for non-traditional venues (schools, for example) or for local arts centres or theatre studios (for example: the Old Bull Arts Centre, Barnet, the Derby Playhouse Studio, the Young Vic Studio).

- It is primarily, but not exclusively, created with a children's or family audience in mind.

- It is funded by the Regional Arts Boards or the four Arts Councils of England, Scotland, Northern Ireland or Wales to produce theatre specifically for young people. Some children's theatre companies are building-based (for example: the Unicorn Theatre, the Polka Theatre, the Little Angel Marionette Theatre). Others are touring companies without their own theatre base or studio space for rehearsal (for example: Theatre Centre, Quicksilver Theatre for Children, Pop-Up, Oily Cart Theatre Company).

A typical children's theatre company's policy might read:

The policy focuses the practice.

Our aim is to present productions of the highest possible artistic standards to as wide an audience as possible, ensuring accessibility and relevance to young people and adults; to respect the maturity and diversity of young people's emotions and perceptions; to encourage and facilitate performers, directors, writers etc. to develop and enrich their professional expertise when working with and for young people.

As with any type of theatre, the style and content of productions staged by children's companies vary enormously. For example, they include:

- adaptations of traditional children's stories or books (for example, *The Jungle Book, Beauty and the Beast, Grimm Tales* – all produced by the Young Vic, London);
- stories drawn from fables from many cultures (for example Half Moon Young People's Theatre and Kazzum Theatre, both based in London);
- curriculum-based or focused work (especially the Young National Trust Theatre and Floating Point Science Theatre);
- issue-based or child-centred new writing (Theatre Centre and Quicksilver Theatre, both based in London);
- focused age-specific shows (for example, *Houseworks: An Installation for Under-5s*, produced by London International Theatre Festival/Theatre Rites in June 1996).

Understanding children creates theatre of quality and relevance.

Two of the leading UK practitioners in this field are Vicki Ireland (artistic director of Polka Theatre, Wimbledon) and Michael Dalton (artistic director of Pop-Up, Islington). They are both concerned with the quality and nature of children's theatre, and suspect that too often the quality of a theatre piece is judged by the excitement generated within an audience as it leaves the theatre, a view they consider patronising. Michael Dalton explains:

> We want to make shows that are not just non-patronising to the child, but are also relevant to the children. I think we forget that young people's level of comprehension is at an adult level, although their level of expression is not. So, too often, work is directed towards the children at the level of their expression, not their comprehension,

so it becomes patronising. When I work with actors, the first thing I will do is ensure that they have an understanding of a child's sophistication . . .

I think that ultimately adults will get the same from a performance as the young audience. A good example was our 1992 show written with Penelope Leach, the child psychologist, called *Snap Happy*. Our philosophy behind the show was 'speaking out against conflict', and young people identified with this. For the adults watching, they were moved – remembering their childhood and particular difficulties they may have experienced at that time. Through this experience, they may then realise that the child they are with is going through the same difficulties as those being explored by the play. The play is not, therefore, working above the child – with 'in-jokes' and innuendo at worst – it is being experienced from different perspectives.

If this is coupled with production values of the highest possible standard, the audience will respect the play. If it is of visual quality, it is saying to the audience that it is worth seeing. I love to see an audience of young people leave a show not terribly excited, but walking out as you or I as adults would, talking – saying, 'this is good', 'I like that' – and being stimulated or moved by it. Often people will look and think that the children didn't enjoy the play very much because the children are not running and jumping, or screaming. This in itself is quite a patronising view.

A scene from Pop-Up's production of Snap Happy

Integrity in practice will create quality theatre.

Practitioners like Michael Dalton would warn against 'singalong' productions with lots of pastel colours and adult actors pretending to be children. Occasionally, an actor will portray a child with a squeaky voice and a shuffling, pigeon-toed gait, which is not how a young person perceives him or herself. This is an example of children being treated at their level of expression, not their level of comprehension.

This does not mean that children's theatre should be a sombre affair. Vicki Ireland uses three words to sum up what she expects of her work at Polka Theatre. Polka produces theatre for young people, but Ireland would use these words for all theatre. It should, she says, *entertain*, *educate* and *enthral*. She would argue that there should be no difference in the quality of theatre presented whether the age of the audience is 3, 13, 30 or 80.

Many of the issues raised in this section are addressed in the following article, 'The Kids Are All Right. Oh No They're Not', by Tim Supple, who is the artistic director of the Young Vic. This article was originally published in the *Independent* in December 1994.

Children get a bad deal in the theatre at the best of times and Christmas is the worst of times; 'tis a season to be vacuously jolly with cannibalised plots, lazy direction and celebrity casts.

Children should be offered the best we can give. Few people would disagree with this and good theatre is produced for children all over Britain throughout the year. However, and especially at this time of year, a remarkable amount of bad theatre is forced on children. Moreover, the adult theatre is rarely as bad as children's fare can be; and children's theatre is rarely as good as the best offered to adults. Children should be offered serious theatre: a full repertoire of work of all kinds – contemporary and classical, devised and scripted, of easy pleasure and intense meaning – created with the highest artistic intentions. This is what we give ourselves; so why do we settle for less for our children?

Perhaps because children are a guaranteed and lucrative audience who go to the theatre in their thousands on the advice of other people (a bit like tourists, although tourists have some choice in what they see).

Many theatres and producers make a lot of money from Christmas shows and where profit is certain, laziness will want to follow. In England (this is less true of Scotland) the pantomime is too often a dustbin for low standards of performance, writing, design, music and direction. Short rehearsal periods, small vision, big ego, long run: big money. Bits and pieces borrowed from the true pantomime form, variety, pop and television are thrown in to ruin wonderful folk and fairy stories. In the worst cases English panto simply exploits and insults its audience. In what other circumstances can we imagine sports stars taking the place of actors?

'But they love it' I will be told of the audience. Maybe so, but that doesn't make it good theatre. I could imagine Ian McKellen playing cricket at the Oval for a one-off charity match; but for a whole season with Surrey? The sporting world has too much respect for itself and its supporters.

'But they love it.' It's a cry which lies at the root of so much poor quality in children's theatre. However bad a piece of theatre looks to me, when asked 'Did you like it?' I have never heard a child say 'No'. The experience itself is electric for children: waiting in the foyer, sitting down, the empty stage or closed curtain, the dimming light, backstage – and if they get to laugh and shout, even better.

Perhaps later a longer discussion will reveal true feelings, but we in the theatre only hear 'They love it!'. Every time we hear it we are flattered and relieved and forget that this is what we always hear. We must look for the difference between superficial pleasure and real, lasting effect. The point here is not that I would wish children to be denied pleasure, however superficial I may feel it is, but that they must be offered a different experience of theatre as well. The experience of theatre that corresponds to their deeper, more difficult and dangerous thoughts and feelings. If all a child finds in the theatre is life-never-quite-taken-seriously, then no wonder most people are uninterested by the time they are teenagers.

So how do we tell the difference between what is deep and lasting and what is superficial? With difficulty, obviously. One of the hopes behind the Young Vic's *Grimm Tales* is that if we allow ourselves to be guided strictly by the stories themselves, we may learn some answers to that question. When children read *Ahsputtel (Cinderella)*, all they need is for it to be told well. Their pleasure does not rely on funny voices or faces, contemporary characterisations, sentimentality or censorship of violent or frightening passages. So why should such approaches be necessary in the theatre? The stories are extraordinary and, if dramatised faithfully, precisely, seriously and well, they will correspond to feelings children struggle with all the time. Children have a fear of abandonment and of the terror they would face as a result. Sometimes their mother is an object of fear. But the fear is also pleasure, a source of fantasy and adventure. *Hansel and Gretel* brings the imaginative world to life brilliantly, and on stage, as on the page, children can take it undiluted. Only adults think children need gags, colour and razmatazz. And only adults think children need contemporary reference, issues and characterisation. They may like these qualities and should be given them, but they must also be offered worlds that are secret, mysterious and unlike life as it is. In the Grimms' stories we find life as it feels, which is every bit as important and real to the child.

I know children as young as three who are enthralled by *The Lion King*. It gives them characters and situations to act out and sparks fantasies and emotions. Yet it seems to me that the impact of *The Lion King* is superficial while that of the story of *Hansel and Gretel*, told well, is lasting. It is the experience of *The Lion King* that impresses, of the film, the colour, the fights and emotions stirred, but it is the story of *Hansel and Gretel* that sticks in the mind. The story of *Hansel and Gretel* is weak, a patchwork that includes *Hamlet* and *Macbeth*. Furthermore, however many millions see *The Lion King*, many more will have heard a version of *Hansel and Gretel* told with its inherent, fierce economy intact.

The surest indication of the difference is merchandise: if the stories are told in their true force there is no desire for it. Simba, Scar, the Seven Dwarfs, Beauty and her Beast, are animated in a way that makes the child greedy for objects to tickle the memory. But the witch in *Hansel and Gretel* is too fearsome, too seminal, too likely to pop up in the form of one's own parents. She is not suitable for merchandise and is best kept to the limitless terrors and pleasures of the mind and the playground. It is in the very nature of characters like Hansel and Gretel that they are unsentimental, basic, archetypal. They are unfit for plastic dolls; like Jack and Jill they live only, but brilliantly, on the page and perhaps, for a moment, on the stage.

Children are not imbeciles: theatre should not treat them as if they were.

Youth theatre

Theatre presented by young people themselves, facilitated by a professional theatre worker, venue or company, is called youth theatre.

Youth theatre takes place outside the statutory education sector, most often through the youth services (funded by local authorities or their equivalent) or, increasingly, on a semi-voluntary basis. Youth centres have traditionally provided a focus for this activity, although there are many other locations where youth arts work takes place. Youth work involving the arts tends to focus on the 14–25 age range, and is most successful when integrated into a larger picture of social activity and participation. Youth work is often an opportunity for participants to work with other young people in their own community, on their own terms. Youth arts activity provides a positive arts experience, re-affirming clear cultural identities and articulating common interests.

Mary McCluskey is Artistic Director of the Scottish Youth Theatre, based at the Old Athenaeum Theatre in Glasgow; she suggests that youth theatre is about 'participation, the creative artistic experience, and learning from an encounter with the arts'. The Scottish Youth Theatre and others like it across the country are ideally suited to meet the needs expressed by young people. As SYT says in its publicity brochure: 'All you need to decide is which skills you would like to learn and we will provide an appropriately qualified tutor.'

The policy focuses the practice.

A brief example of a policy for a youth theatre might read:

The youth theatre, as a provider of drama activity for young people, organises workshops, courses and large-scale theatre events. The work includes special provision for physically disabled/able-bodied integration; reflects cultural diversity; provides drama in areas of multiple deprivation; and organises a young playwrights' project and an annual festival of youth theatre. It provides opportunities for young performers and technicians to work intensively with the technologies of theatre-making and presenting.

A workshop at the Scottish Youth Theatre

All youth theatres do not have the same ethos. Youth theatres can exist to promote the 'star' or gifted practitioner. Conversely, they may provide an opportunity for all young people, regardless of ability, to learn through an encounter with all aspects of theatre-making. Activities taking place in youth settings might be:

- youth arts leaders co-ordinating a production;
- artists or youth arts practitioners working with an organisation to develop the range and quality of existing youth arts activities, through the introduction of new skills or approaches (choreography, composition, devising, etc.);
- artists or youth arts practitioners offering technical support or workshops for a youth arts event (for example: lighting design for a theatre production; sound engineering skills for a recording or video session; marketing and design skills for an exhibition, etc.);
- youth arts leaders working on the development of new writing skills with young people, culminating in a festival of new plays.

Youth theatre is an important sector of the theatre education industry. Youth theatres are often the training grounds for young people eager to pursue a career within the theatre industry itself as actors, directors, designers or technicians. Anyone working in this area of theatre education needs to have a strong skills base themselves, as well as the ability to devise activities that teach skills and those that provide opportunities to try these skills out in a professional and non-competitive environment. (See p.23 for useful national contact details.)

A SAMPLE THEATRE EDUCATION PROJECT

The purpose of this section is to provide a model theatre education project that could be used as a guide for similar work.

Appropriate and thorough research is essential if theatre education practices are to be of quality and relevant to their intended audiences.

A successful theatre education project takes into account three important starting points, or criteria:

- the audience;
- the form: the style or nature of the performance;
- the content: what the piece may be about.

In this section, we are assuming that the theatre education project will take place in a school setting. In addition to the three principal criteria above, a further three points should be taken into account when creating a theatre education product for such a setting:

- the expectations of the young people and their teacher, and the age range and ability of the targeted group;
- the formal requirements of the particular drama curriculum and the syllabus for examinations;
- the place drama holds within the published whole-school policy, and the place of drama across the whole curriculum.

255

Understanding the needs and expectations of a potential audience is essential for all good-quality theatre education.

Initiating a theatre education project

A theatre education project always needs to identify and justify its role and value. Within a school or college context, it is important to remember that all state-funded schools in the United Kingdom are required to follow the National Curriculum. Drama and theatre practice are one part of this published curriculum and appear mainly within English.

Any project needs to take account of the National Curriculum Programmes of Study, Key Stages and Statements of Attainment in related subject areas. Collectively, these set out to describe what students should be taught, what opportunities they should be given and what they should be encouraged to do. At the end of each Key Stage, at the ages of 7, 11, 14 and 16, the students are expected to have achieved a minimum attainment, reflecting appropriate stages of development and learning for their age.

Identifying areas of the curriculum that may usefully be addressed through a theatre education piece often begins with a discussion with a teacher or group of students. If this is not possible, a questionnaire is useful. The discussion will touch upon:

- **Previous experiences:** What is the level of appreciation and understanding of theatre education work among all the potential participants? What theatre education activities have already been hosted at the school? Why did they choose to receive any specific piece? What was it about? What style or form did the activity take? What follow-up work did it generate? Was it useful? Was it successful? How and why did the participants make these judgements? Did they feel comfortable?

- **Present needs:** Are the teachers looking for activities directly related to the curriculum or a specific syllabus? Would this be from a cross-curricular basis, making links with other subject areas? How does the project fit into a term's plan of work?

- **Enthusiasm and interests:** What is a particularly burning issue at the present time among young people? What theatre skills would be exciting to explore in depth? What plays would be exciting to study if they were explored actively in a workshop or by experiencing a short performance?

- **Resources:** What time, space and equipment are available? Where and when can the theatre education piece happen? How many young people will be present? Do the teachers need specific training themselves before they feel happy with hosting the product?

- **Progression and continuity:** Do the students follow a year-by-year programme in the arts? How does the school or teacher actively link work together? Is the experience part of a developing programme of activity? Would a resource pack left behind once the project has finished be useful?

- **Assessment and evaluation:** How is the students' progress to be evaluated? What methods of assessment are being used in the school? What methods of evaluation could usefully be incorporated into the theatre programme offered? Could there be a questionnaire, or an opportunity to talk with the young people again in the future or to make a follow-up visit?

- **Special Educational Needs:** Does the product take account of all the abilities within the group? Is there too much reliance on reading? If there is a wheelchair user or partially sighted student, for example, would he or she be able to complete or join in all the tasks set? Is the programme taking advice from specialist practitioners?

Planning a theatre education project: a working example

As a result of this initial research, a specific request could be made. For example, the class teacher wants the theatre education project to consider ways of working with 13-year-olds in preparation for the Shakespeare examination paper which her students take as part of National Curriculum English at Key Stage 3. The theatre education piece is to be a simple workshop aimed at students who have a limited experience of working practically using drama techniques.

Objectives are set.

The first stage for the group undertaking the theatre education project is to set its objectives, which could be as follows:

- to introduce specific active methods and suggest future strategies that can be used in the classroom;
- to address the meaning of the text (theme, plot, character, dramatic structure);
- to employ teaching methods which encourage the pupils' participation (for example, speaking the original text out loud);
- to encourage pupils across the ability range to be engaged and excited by the study of Shakespeare;
- to place such active methods within the framework of classroom learning (talking, listening, reading, writing) specifically reflecting National Curriculum requirements.

Plan using the options available.

The project then moves on to the planning stage. When devising the workshop, the group considers a whole range of activities, which together can form a complete workshop experience:

- a cartoon strip;
- writing in role;
- tableaux or freeze frames of character relationships or significant moments;
- the workshop leader being in role;
- devising short versions (e.g. five-minute plays or mini-scenes);
- creating missing scenes (e.g. the murder of Duncan in *Macbeth*, or an encounter between Romeo and Rosaline);
- creating pre-text (e.g. what is the ancient grudge in *Romeo and Juliet*?);
- starting in the middle (e.g. Perdita is found on the shore in *The Winter's Tale*);

257

- changing the story (e.g. Duncan survives the assassination attempt);
- forecasting (predicting what might happen in the next scene);
- having the whole class in role;
- improvising from theme/plot/character;
- poem work;
- editing the dialogue;
- chorus work on speeches or passages of dialogue;
- physicalising the speech (with gesture and movement – simple directing);
- creating tableaux or still images of key lines or textual images;
- improvising from the text;
- translating into modern language or ethnic language;
- paraphrasing.

Decide on a product.

The group decides that it is not always desirable or practical to read a play in full, particularly when the student group does not have to study the whole text in detail. A knowledge of the story is important, but not a line-by-line dissection.

Two workshop ideas are detailed below.

Two alternative workshop ideas are proposed:

- Mini-series
- Detectives

Both use Shakespeare's *Romeo and Juliet* as their focus. Detailed instructions are written out for all the workshop leaders to follow, and these appear below.

Mini-series

Phase 1

- Split the students into groups of five. Hand out a full and detailed synopsis of *Romeo and Juliet* to each group.

- Explain that each group represents a small television company. Each television company is pitching for a million-pound contract with the BBC for a six-episode costume drama mini-series.

- The 'companies' should divide the story into six roughly equal parts, ensuring that at the end of each of the first five episodes there is a cliff-hanger. (Obviously, the aim is to ensure that the audience will tune in again the following week to see what has happened – and keep the ratings up!)

- The 'companies' should present their findings to the whole class with one of the workshop leaders taking on the role of the chief executive who will eventually award the contract.

The aim of this exercise is to explore the narrative structure of the play, and to find the moments of dramatic climax or suspense.

Phase 2

Extend this exercise after the contract has been awarded by asking each group to create a tableau, to be used for the front cover of the *Radio Times*, depicting the essence of a particular episode.

Phase 3

Now set up a mock audition procedure. First, decide what the director, producer and/or casting director want from a particular character. Select appropriate audition speeches for different characters. Individuals could then audition for certain parts and, as part of the audition/interview, explain how they would imagine the character being portrayed.

Detectives

In this activity, the pupils will eventually end up with their own synopsis of *Romeo and Juliet*.

Phase 1

- Explain that the pupils are detectives who have been employed to piece together the events of the play and give their 'superintendent' – the workshop leader – a clear chronological account of the events surrounding the deaths of Romeo and Juliet.

- Use a photocopy of the whole play, which you have divided into many scenes or smaller extracts.

- Divide the students into groups, giving each group one short extract.

- Ask them to work in role as detectives, finding key points in the extract.

- Once they have exhausted their enquiries, they should present their findings to the 'superintendent' in role. These findings can be in the form of key questions. The slant of their questioning and the quotations offered as evidence will prompt the workshop leader to give out another piece of text.

An example of an initial extract might be Act III, Scene 5, lines 1–57. This covers the exit of Romeo after the wedding night. Juliet tries to persuade Romeo it is not yet dawn, and not time for him to leave her, but finally she accepts that it is morning and time to part. The Nurse warns the lovers that Lady Capulet is coming. As Romeo leaves, Juliet's words are full of foreboding. Possible key questions arising from this extract might be:

i) If they have just got married, why does Romeo have to leave via the window?
ii) Why does Romeo say: 'I must be gone and live, or stay and die'?
iii) Romeo and Juliet seem to be very much in love with each other, but is there something wrong?
iv) Why is there something very ominous in the words Juliet speaks:

'O, God, I have an ill-divining soul!
Methinks I see thee now, thou art so low,
As dead in the bottom of a tomb.
Either my eyesight fails, or thou look'st pale.'

v) Why would Juliet not want to meet her mother, Lady Capulet, at this stage?
vi) How and why is the Nurse implicated in this intrigue?

Phase 2
The detectives are then allocated another extract to help them develop their investigations. Possible scenes might be:

● where Romeo first meets Juliet at the ball, which would give an insight into how their love started and has dangerously and secretly developed;
● where Juliet takes poison in order to pretend to die;
● where Juliet is told by her father she must marry Paris;
● before Romeo has met Juliet, where he talks about his love for Rosaline.

Each will take the detectives in different directions, enabling them slowly to piece the story together.

Phase 3
Extend the activity by interrupting the whole proceedings and allowing the detectives to 'overhear' or 'eavesdrop on' a scene which is acted out in front of them by the workshop leaders in role. This could be a scene from another part of the text or an imagined final scene between some of the characters. The detectives may now wish to question these characters about their history and their reasons for doing what they are doing. An interactive workshop has developed.

Carrying out the project

Allow time to rehearse.

Once the nature of the workshop or project has been decided, it has to be rehearsed before it is ready to go into the school. However, only when it is finally tried out with the students will it become clear whether the product is enjoyable, successful and useful for all the participants. It is also important to consider evaluation mechanisms: how can the students' work be successfully evaluated? Discuss this with the class teacher.

Find a way to evaluate the students' work.

Establish a code of practice.

By following a set code of practice, the workshop is likely to be successful. This should include:

● setting clear aims;
● structured planning;
● detailed and well-resourced preparation;
● a simple and workable activity or process;
● monitoring and evaluation based on clear criteria agreed by all those involved.

A CASE STUDY: POP-UP AND *IRON DREAMS*

This study gives an account of a professional children's theatre company, Pop-Up, and how its philosophies are realised in one of its productions, *Iron Dreams*.

On pp.250–251, Michael Dalton, artistic director of the London-based Pop-Up, talks in detail about children's theatre. Along with other practitioners, he strives 'to make shows that are not just non-patronising to the child, but are also relevant to children'. This philosophy underpins Pop-Up's work.

The structure of the company

Pop-Up is an established children's theatre company.

Pop-Up was founded in 1982, and is funded by the Arts Council of England. The company presents more than 200 performances each year to over 25,000 people around the United Kingdom and overseas. Pop-Up's administrative base is at 95 Southgate Road, London N1 3JS (tel: 0171 275 8376).

Pop-Up has just three permanent staff: the artistic director, Michael Dalton, the administrative director, Jackie Eley, and the producer, Jane Wolfson. During production periods, they employ many freelance professionals, from a stage manager to costume- and prop-makers. The company's productions usually last between 45 minutes and one hour, without an interval, and require a performing space of six metres by six metres, with a height of three metres. On tour, the acting company travels around the country in a five-seater van.

The artistic director has overall responsibility for the productions. He commissions new work, leads research, and directs and oversees the designer, composer, choreographer and so on.

The administrative director deals with all aspects of tour booking, fundraising, contracts and deals, marketing and publicity. She deals with the unions, principally Equity for the actors and BECTU for the stage or technical staff. She liaises carefully with sponsors and funding bodies to ensure that they are fully updated about the company's work.

The producer is the link between the two senior staff. She takes an active role in the creative process of the rehearsals, and takes rehearsals when the director is required to spend time with the designer or composer. She will often visit the company on tour, reporting back on how the production is developing or how venues or schools receive the play. At Pop-Up, the producer has specific responsibility for writing the Teacher's Resource Pack. This is distributed free to all school groups which attend the show; it provides teachers with factual resources and practical activities, and offers guidance on how best to use the production as a stimulus for curriculum needs. The pack for *Iron Dreams* was 20 pages long and could be photocopied for the teacher to use easily.

261

Like all companies funded by the Arts Council, Pop-Up is a registered charity, and it is also a non-profit-making limited company. It has a board of directors, who serve on a voluntary basis and are mostly teachers, artists, business people and representatives of the communities the company serves. The board acts as an advisory group, but it also has the legal responsibility to ensure that Pop-Up works professionally in all areas of its activity. Pop-Up is a member of the Independent Theatre Council and a leading member of the umbrella organisation, the Association of Professional Theatre for Children and Young People (APT).

Iron Dreams

In the summer of 1996, Michael Dalton directed a specially commissioned new play by the young playwright Tim Newton, which went on a national tour. Its popularity was such that the company agreed to re-mount the production for another national tour during the autumn of 1997.

Iron Dreams is a play for anyone over six years old. It revolves around the life of the famous 19th-century Victorian engineer Isambard Kingdom Brunel, best remembered for his work on the first tunnel under the Thames in London, the Clifton Suspension Bridge in Bristol, the design and construction of the Great Western Railway between Paddington, London, and Bristol, and many great ships, including the first iron-hulled vessel, the SS *Great Britain*, launched in 1858. Many of these feature in the play. The launch of the SS *Great Britain*, the opening of the Thames Tunnel and the breaking of the land speed record by a steam train are all dramatically recreated by what Dalton calls 'an innovative blend of visual imagery, physical performance and an atmospheric original musical score'.

Iron Dreams *provides a new slant on an old story.*

Dalton asked the playwright to offer a new perspective upon this pioneer of the industrial age. By seeing his great achievements though the eyes of his children, the play explores unorthodox family relationships in the Victorian period. (The younger Isambard did not wish to follow his father, and had been born with a physical impairment to his leg which restricted his ability to move quickly like other children; his sister Florence, however, was interested in being an engineer, an unlikely career for a Victorian female.)

Iron Dreams *was part of Pop-Up's wider artistic and education policy.*

For Pop-Up, this story offered an opportunity to continue developing its artistic policy of producing original plays which explore important issues in young people's lives. *Iron Dreams* offered an opportunity to use theatre as a way of addressing:

- the expectations placed upon young people by others, particularly parents;
- the pressure that young people are under when trying to fulfil others' ambitions for them;
- aspirations and dreams;

262

● how society labels people because of their gender or physical appearance.

Iron Dreams was popular with schools, because the production was based within the Victorian period, which their pupils needed to study. Specifically, *Iron Dreams* was an exciting, live, dramatic stimulus for teachers and pupils studying Key Stage 2 History Unit 3A, which states that pupils should be taught about the changes in industry and transport during the Victorian period, with specific reference to Brunel and the growth of the railways. In addition, schools could relate the play to the Channel 4 schools' programme *How We Used to Live: The Victorians*, screened during the same term as the original tour took place. As one teacher said, it fired 'an imaginative response to the Victorian world of Brunel beyond the demands of the curriculum, making young people think about themselves as people who can make choices, however hard this may be'.

Minor characters are important in the play.

The play was written to be performed by four actors: Brunel, his son Isambard the Third, Florence and one actor playing four minor parts of characters from the period. Although only minor, these four additional characters have an important role in the dramatic structure of the play, helping it to move beyond the story of Brunel's life. These interludes enrich key thematic and dramatic moments, or reveal important character traits. For example, in Scene 5, the children have been distracted by the fairground and stalls that have been set up in anticipation of the opening of the Thames Tunnel. They meet the character Tommy Hopper:

A scene from Pop-Up's Iron Dreams, *by Tim Newton*

Tommy: What an honour. The children of this country's greatest engineer have seen my show! 'Tommy Hopper's celebrated Cosmoramic Flea Circus as Witnessed by the Family Brunel, on the occasion of the opening of the Thames Tunnel, Rotherhithe.' That's a hell of a title, pardon my French. (*As an aside*) I'll have to get a bigger banner. Madam, Sir, I thank you. The Brunels have made my day.

Isambard: I'd rather be a Hopper.

Tommy: What? You, sir, a humble Hopper? Oh no, no, no, believe you me, you're better off a Brunel.

Isambard: But you *wanted* to do what your father did.

Tommy: It's true, I did. Don't you?

(*Isambard looks anxiously at Florence for a moment, then shakes his head.*)

Tommy: (*To Florence*) Have I said something wrong?

Florence: Isambard likes horses.

Tommy: Horses more in the blood, eh? Oh, I see. Have you told him?

Isambard: He wouldn't understand.

Tommy: A clever man like him?

Florence: Could you have told your father if you did not like the circus?

Tommy: (*Pondering*) I see what you mean. It is not easy, but the longer you leave it, the harder it gets. Give it a try, you never know.

Isambard: I'm afraid to.

Tommy: Pick the right moment, it won't be as bad as you think.

Isambard: You haven't met him.

(Newton, T., *Iron Dreams*, Pop-Up, 1996, pp.42–3)

The process of creating the play was collaborative.

As part of the process of developing the text, Dalton held several practical workshop sessions with actors he knew and trusted, workshopping storylines and scenarios given to him by the writer. He used improvisation, hot-seating and rough drafts of scenes already written to explore the story and the characters suggested for the play. Tim Newton went away from the sessions inspired to write new dialogue, to flesh out each character or to focus on a particular moment in order to allow the audience to reflect upon a key theme with greater clarity. Even when the script was finally finished, Tim sat in on rehearsals, and would rewrite speeches or scenes if something new and exciting had been discovered through the process of the day's rehearsal. As Dalton says:

Everyone involved in the production is part of the creative team. In as much as the designer brought to his designs an excitement at discovering great Victorian etchings and photographs, or Joe Young, the composer, sampled a whole range of industrial sounds into his original score, so the actors can influence the dramatic development of scenes as they engage in rehearsals with the text given to them by Tim. A good production is a result of this collective creativity.

This creative process influenced the inclusion of the longest single speech in the play. The writer senses that it is the right moment for Isambard finally to speak out, as the play enters its closing stages. It is a dramatic and powerful moment, as he literally and symbolically casts aside his metal leg brace and demands to be listened to.

Isambard: Stop talking about dreams. That's all I ever hear about, your dreams. What about mine? What about Flo's? And everybody else's? I don't dream about the things you do, I dream about horses, riding, flying horses through the sky, I know I'll never do it, I know that – but that's my dream. Not steam engines or bridges; and especially not iron. You dream about it all you want, I never will, I hate it. It's cold and it's hard and it's heavy. Every day you make me put this iron on my leg because *you* say it's best for me. I can't keep up with Flo, or you, or anyone – I dream that I can, but I never will, never, and this just makes it worse. And all that everybody ever says is that it's best for me. I wish someone would listen to what I think is best for me. I'd like someone to listen. All you ever do is talk. Well, I don't like this heavy iron thing I have to wear, and I'm not an engineer! (*Isambard begins to unfasten the straps on his leg calliper.*) I'll walk with a stick if I have to, I won't mind, but please, please, father, don't make me wear this anymore. (*He holds the calliper out in front of him defiantly.*) It hurts. (*There is a pause. Brunel looks at his son for a long time. The Palomino horse canters past the train.*)

(Newton, T., *Iron Dreams*, pp.74–5)

Theatre has a place within the wider school context.

Dalton invests a lot of time in a personal belief that young people should speak up or be given an opportunity to voice their opinions. They should be able to shape their own lives on the basis of real and informed choices, and talk of their aspirations and fears. *Iron Dreams* is a theatre education product which he hopes will achieve this aim. It is based on his experience of young people and on research undertaken in schools.

Another scene from Iron Dreams

Assessment and evaluation

Iron Dreams, like any professional theatre production, has been reviewed by the press. This is a formal way for a company to receive feedback. The critic will often influence a potential audience's opinions of the play, and a good review will draw a large audience. Pop-Up particularly encourages reviews in specialist publications. For example, *Iron Dreams* received the following reviews from the leading newspaper for teachers, *The Times Educational Supplement*, and the highly popular London listings magazine *Time Out*.

Heavy Metal

Isambard Kingdom Brunel, the pioneering engineer remembered and honoured for some of the most outstanding and innovative achievements of the 19th century, was a fanatical genius ahead of his time.

Seen through the eyes of his two children, Florence and Isambard, Tim Newton's play *Iron Dreams*, for Pop-Up charts the life and work of Brunel, as its affects their lives and dreams.

Newton makes young Isambard a romantic dreamer, while Florence shares her father's passion for engineering. The emotional conflict of Isambard who tries to become the engineer his father assumes he's destined to be and second, to tell him he never will be, is weighed against Florence's own agony of being a girl with a 'man's' talents.

The play is as much about being true to one's self as it is an historical piece on the finest engineer of the last century. Tightly written and excellently acted, it shows not just Brunel's success as an engineer but how that success made him something of a failure as a father. Terence Frisch is a convincingly bombastic but kindly Brunel whose obsession with his own vision of the future blinds him to the emotional needs of his children.

It is this sort of theatre which fires imaginations, brings history to life and makes children want to learn.

Helen Rose

Above:
The Times Educational Supplement (5th July 1996)

Right: Time Out

Children

Shows & Activities 'Iron Dreams'

Tim Newton's play about nineteenth-century engineer Isambard Kingdom Brunel, directed by Michael Dalton, packs in masses of history, geography and technology yet does so in a manner that is emotionally and dramatically satisfying.

Against Matt Edward's appropriately innovative set, constructed in metal and lacquered wood and augmented by a couple of exquisite models which most children (and this adult), would give their eye teeth for, Brunel's life and achievements are recounted in flashback, recalled by his children for the benefit of a journalist. Jeremy Killick, as the son expected by his charismatic father (played by Terence Frisch) to become an engineer, is a cowed, dreamy boy, trapped in a leg brace designed by pa and desperately trying to tell his father that his dreams are of real horses, not iron ones. Florence (Nicola Blackwell), bright and aggressive, has inherited her father's talents but suffers the frustration of seeing his ambitions channelled into her unreceptive brother. In this short, rich play we also encounter a handful of other nineteenth-century characters – all played by the versatile Richard Oldham, notably showman and flea-circus owner Tommy Hopper, and Dr Dionysius Lardner, a contemporary of Brunel's who considered his achievements unhealthy and unnatural. In a scene reminiscent of Selwyn Gummer feeding his daughter a beefburger, Brunel, determined to silence the opponent who heckles at all his openings, sends his children into the Thames Tunnel – where seven labourers have died – to prove its safety. Pop-Up have pulled off a trick few children's theatre companies could achieve so successfully.

Sara O'Reilly

However, it is the responses from children that are more valued. Letters received are circulated among all the actors and staff, and Pop-Up always writes in response to these letters. Such feedback is important, and also usefully summarises the impact of good-quality children's theatre.

I know how the boy felt. I don't like to be what my Dad wants me to be. I'd like to go on a flying horse one day.

(Stewart, aged eight, Enniskillen, Northern Ireland)

I liked the bit when the music came on and the actors did funny movements. It was like they were not in Victorian times just for a second.

(Annaliese, aged eight, Saltash, Cornwall)

There was one bit I didn't understand. But my friend Ben told me afterwards. But I didn't tell him why the boy cried. Sometimes I don't want to tell anyone that.

(Serdar, aged seven, Birmingham)

And, my oh my, what a name! Isambard Kingdom Brunel! That is definitely a posh name. If I was him, I might not know how to spell it.

(Jenny, aged nine, Crewe)

Resource Activities

1. THE ROLE OF THE EDUCATION OFFICER

Aim
To gain an overview of the role of an education officer in theatres and companies in the UK.

Objectives
● To establish an understanding of the work practices of an education officer.
● To devise education-in-theatre activities appropriate for a variety of audiences, using the resources of a theatre as the focus.
● To write a job description for an education officer.
● To prepare for a mock interview for an education officer post.

Activity A: Background
● You work for the Manchester Royalty Theatre as their education officer. During the autumn term, your theatre will be presenting a production of Shakespeare's *Macbeth*. (Choose another well-known text if you wish.) A teacher from one of your local schools approaches you with the idea of working with her and four other schools. She suggests using the production as a stimulus for some curriculum work with 15-year-olds following GCSE courses.
● Read pp.246–249 about the role of an education officer and pp.255–260, where there are sample workshops on *Romeo and Juliet* that may be useful for guidance.
● Read sections of an appropriate GCSE syllabus.

Tasks
● Draw up in writing the agenda for a short meeting with the five teachers. What questions would need to be raised? For example, how much time is available for the project? Are they looking for a one-off workshop? Which of the theatre's resources will be available? How many actors will be present? What role would you want the teachers to play?

● Role-play this meeting with a small group.

● Devise a potential workshop activity, based on the information from the meeting.

● When the workshop activities have been devised, answer the following questions:

i) What briefing will you need to give the actors and teachers involved?
ii) Give specific examples of how you will physically manage the young people through the experience.
iii) How does this explore the needs of the curriculum they are following? (Refer to the appropriate GCSE syllabus for this.)
iv) What suggestions would you make to the teachers for follow-up

activities?

v) How would you assess the workshop?

Activity B: Background

- You are the artistic director of Appletown Theatre. You have been to the Manchester Royalty Theatre and have seen the benefits of employing an education officer. Below is a description of the venue.
- Read the background information above, and in particular the material on the role of an education officer on pp.246–249.

Appletown Theatre

Appletown Theatre is funded and exists to provide 'different things to different people'. It functions as an arts centre serving a 400 square kilometre rural area in Cumbria. The centre is a multifunctional building containing a flexible 550-seat performance space, a foyer space doubling as an art gallery and a café open from 10am until 11pm daily. The programme of events offered is drawn from professional companies across all art forms, but principally comprises theatre. Programming includes the Royal National Theatre's mobile (touring) productions, Paines Plough (a new writing company), English Touring Theatre and Tara Arts (a London-based Asian theatre company: see pp.88–92). The centre's published mission is:

To provide a range of first-class facilities and events to foster and promote all forms of arts activity and an appreciation of the arts.

At present, the centre wishes to develop new audiences, to commission new work and to strengthen links with local resources and agencies (schools, youth groups, Age Concern centres, women's refuges).

Tasks

- Using the venue description as a resource, draft a job description for a potential new officer. This job description will be sent to candidates interested in applying for the job when it is advertised nationally. Consider the following:

  i) What points would you wish particularly to highlight in a job description?
  ii) What skills would you want from such an officer?
  iii) What specific experience or knowledge would be required?
  iv) Is it useful if an officer has worked with community groups?
  v) Does the officer need experience of office management, or knowledge of writing applications for funding from local or national bodies such as the Arts Council?

- Imagine you have applied for the job of education officer and are invited for an interview. At the interview, you are required to make a five-minute presentation on your priorities in the first six months as the education officer. Prepare this presentation, using a series of headings to focus your thoughts. You may wish to choose: liaising

269

with local communities; looking for skills and enthusiasms among the arts centre's staff; key events to be planned. (For further help with this activity, see the section on presentation skills in Chapter 1, pp.20–22.)

2. EXPLORING YOUTH THEATRE

Aim
To gain an understanding of the place of youth theatre in the UK.

Objective
To devise a youth theatre programme appropriate for an established youth theatre.

Background
- The Arts Council of England is offering £5,000 for the development of a three-month rolling programme of activity in the youth theatre attached to your venue, the Theatre Royal in Exeter. You are the part-time co-ordinator of the youth theatre. Traditionally, the youth theatre meets in the theatre's rehearsal room on a Saturday morning, and you run workshops, which are improvisation-based. The participants pay for this.
- Read pp.254–255 about youth theatre. In addition, if you have time, you may wish to contact the National Association of Youth Theatres for general information; contact details are on p.23.
- Below is a description of the venue.

The Theatre Royal, Exeter

Reopened in 1986 after a major refurbishment, the Theatre Royal in Exeter is a large, 1,200-seat theatre, which presents a wide range of large- and middle-scale productions drawn from the subsidised and commercial sectors. The programming during the autumn 1999 season includes:

- a traditional family pantomime, *Snow White*, starring a number of personalities with a high television profile;
- a production of a Rodgers and Hammerstein musical, *Annie Get Your Gun*;
- runs of dramas produced by the Royal National Theatre and the Chichester Festival Theatre (*The Alchemist* and *The Doll's House*);
- a physical theatre production of *Animal Farm*.

The theatre aims at all times, given economic restraints, to work towards achieving its published mission:

. . . to lead its community towards a full appreciation of the theatrical arts by providing as varied as possible a range of productions of excellence in a high-quality context and environment. It must seek to: entertain whilst educating, serve whilst leading, and listen whilst stating.

The theatre is the home of the flourishing Exeter Theatre Royal Youth Theatre.

Task

Using all the information, devise an extensive programme of youth theatre 'activities' which will maximise the resources of the theatre and establish firm footings for future work when the £5,000 grant has been spent. You may consider the following questions:

i) Would you wish to use visiting professionals?
ii) Would you want to commission work?
iii) Would you consider taking the youth theatre out of Exeter – on tour, perhaps?
iv) Is there a programme of activity that could be devised in connection with the main house activities?

Present your findings as a document to be circulated among staff at the theatre.

3. CREATING A THEATRE EDUCATION PRODUCT

This activity can be extended into a full-length theatre education piece; it is intended to act as a trial run for later projects.

Aim
To consider the processes involved in the creation of a theatre education project.

Objectives
- To undertake research in preparation for a theatre education project.
- To experience the methodologies usefully employed when devising a piece of children's theatre or a simple theatre-in-education product.
- To write script extracts for a piece of theatre education.

Background
Read the sections on TIE and Pop-Up on pp.243–246 and 261–267. In addition, it would also be useful to read pp.255–260, which contain suggestions about an education project, and pp.132–150 in Chapter 4 about devising theatre.

Tasks
- Undertake some initial research into finding a topic for a potential devised theatre education product. You will need to investigate the likely audience and its interests. The following are some ideas:

  i) Talk to local community leaders; young people; retired people at a community day centre.
  ii) Read tales and fables; reports published by specialists (e.g. on drug or substance abuse or HIV); published theatre scripts.
  iii) Look at newspaper or magazine articles; photographs; exhibitions at a local museum or gallery.
  iv) Listen to pop songs; traditional music or music from other cultures; the radio evening news.

271

- Start to identify the age group of your target audience, potential performance venues and so on.

- Once you have completed your research, decide what your audience will be, and based on that what the content and form of your piece will be.

- Undertake further research into the subject matter and, if appropriate, the form of the piece. (See pp.142–144 of Chapter 4 for suggestions about further research.)

- Create a scenario or storyline for the theatre piece you wish to devise, making use of your research. What might happen? When is it set? Who might be the main characters? The scenario should be about 150 words long at this stage, and should contain a simple narrative which will be fleshed out in the devising and writing period.

Example: You have decided that the content will address the issue of prejudice surrounding HIV/AIDS, and will be aimed at 14-year-olds. Your scenario might read:

Peter lives with his mum in a village. He is 14 years old and goes every day to the local High School in the nearest town on a school bus. He likes football, but isn't very keen on studying. One day, his mum tells him that his uncle is coming to stay with them. His uncle is ill and needs time to rest. She believes the village would provide an ideal environment for him to recuperate. Peter is excited at the prospect. This uncle is much younger than his mum, and lives an exciting life in London. One day, Peter wants to work in London and earn lots of money in the City like his uncle. Rumours circulate in the village that Uncle Charlie is dying of an HIV-related illness. Suddenly, no-one wants to sit by Peter on the bus. His best friend John tells him why. Peter can't believe that he and his mum are going to die too.

- Using improvisation or similar techniques, start to flesh out one of the characters in the scenario you have written. Create a personal history by outlining the type of thing that the character might do every day. Ask yourself this kind of question:

  i) What are the character's private desires, hopes and ambitions?
  ii) What might the character like doing in his or her leisure time?
  iii) What about relationships with others in the story?

  You might like to hot-seat the character in focus at this stage. Record your findings.

- Use actors to play two characters from your story and improvise an imaginary conversation. Consider the choice of words. What might they talk about? What might be alluded to? Remember, people do not always mean what they say, or want to tell the truth. Record your findings: a tape recorder is useful. Draft a potential scene based on the improvised conversations. Use this as a draft script, to be reworked during the devising period. An example is given below to help guide your work. The final line is useful, as it starts to build a dilemma that needs to be resolved or tackled. Peter is obviously not happy, but his mum is not going to ask him, 'What's up?' at this point. This would not be dramatically interesting. Remember, theatre is often based on *conflicts*, creating a dramatic tension which drives the drama of the play.

Mum:	Peter, you're late. Football practice?
Peter:	Yeah.
Mum:	I thought that was on Tuesdays.
Peter:	No, we had to have an extra one.
Mum:	Are you OK? You look a bit down.
Peter:	Do I? Maybe I'm just tired. I'll go up and do my homework now.
Mum:	Really? (*Pause*) Just a minute, love. Why don't you have a Coke or something? I haven't sat down to chat for ages. I've been busy looking after Uncle Charlie. (*Silence*) Why don't you go up and see him? He's just having a rest before we eat.
Peter:	No, thanks.
Mum:	He'd like to see you; he's a bit low today, and . . .
Peter:	No, I don't want to see Charlie, OK?

● Look again at pp.243–244 on the techniques of Boal. Consider the appropriateness of using his forum theatre, with 'spect-actors', for the scene you have written. Imagine you are to take on the task of the Joker, the facilitator of the forum theatre. Devise questions that might usefully be asked of the audience if the action was stopped at the end of the scene above. The example that follows shows the range of questions the Joker might want to raise. Develop your own questions based on your own emerging theatre product.

- Why wouldn't Peter want to see Charlie?
- How does his mum feel?
- Is Peter's behaviour related to his treatment on the school bus?
- Does Peter believe his friend John? Will he catch AIDS from his uncle?
- Does Peter feel that because he aspired to be like his uncle that he might be accused of being gay?
- Peter's mum always said that Charlie was a real 'womaniser'. Peter can't believe he is gay. What might be really wrong with Charlie?
- Do you have to be gay to contract the HIV virus?

● If you are familiar with forum theatre and the extension to it in which the spect-actors intervene and take over actual roles in the performance, brainstorm possible interventions, trying out several amongst yourselves.

ANNOTATED BIBLIOGRAPHY

This bibliography includes volumes relevant to this chapter which are considered suitable for student reference. See also the general bibliography on p.380.

Arts Council of Great Britain, *Drama in Schools,* Arts Council of Great Britain, 1992
> A comprehensive overview of the role of drama and theatre within the school curriculum. Very useful. See also the companion publication, *Dance in Schools* (ACGB, 1993).

Arts Council of England, *Disability and the Arts: Get It Right*, ACE, 1996
> A guide to providing access and opportunities through arts practice to the disabled communities. Offers some useful examples of good practice. Easy to read. See also: Vine, C., *Graeae: Setting the Scene* (ACGB, 1992).

Boal, A. (trans. Jackson, A.), *Games for Actors and Non-Actors*, Routledge, 1992
> The most accessible of Boal's texts. Particularly useful for forum theatre.

Brinson, P. (ed.), *Arts and Communities: The Report of the National Enquiry into Arts in the Community*, Community Development Foundation, 1992
> A detailed and influential publication, which traces the role of the arts within the community, including youth arts activities.

Department of National Heritage, *Setting the Scene: The Arts and Young People*, DNH, 1996
> A hugely influential publication tracing the anticipated development of arts provision for young people into the 21st century, in response to government policy and particularly the National Lottery. The appendix contains several case studies. Very readable.

Dodgson, E., *Motherland*, Unwin, 1987
> The documentation of a theatre education project which recorded the memories of the West Indian community in London. This influential theatre project inspired many other drama educators to use the oral histories of communities, localities and workplaces in the creation of new community dramas and more general theatre education products. Excellent.

Downing, D. and Jones, T. (eds), *Special Theatre: The Work of Interplay Community Theatre for People with Severe Learning Difficulties – 1970 to 1985*, Calouste Gulbenkian Foundation, 1989
> A detailed account of the development and practices of one of the UK's leading theatre companies specialising in work for disabled people. Excellent.

Dunne, N., *Acting for Health, Acting Against HIV: A Report on the Effectiveness of Theatre in Health Education in HIV & AIDS Education,* The Theatre in Health Education Trust Publications, 1993
> A detailed report about present practices in the health education industry and the appropriation of theatre education practices. Very useful on the debate surrounding the use of TIE methodologies. Excellent.

Elwell, C., *Interface I: The Report of a Seminar on Education in Presenting Venues,* Arts Council of England, 1995
> The first report commissioned by the Arts Council of England as part of its Interface Initiative. Interface looks at the developments and growth that have occurred since 1990 in education work presented by both companies and venues. Interface provides a forum for venues and companies from across the country to debate issues of effective practice. The report cites a series of recommendations for future practice and development. The questions raised by the study are very useful when assessing the function, role and variety of education-in-theatre activity taking place in the UK. See also Elwell, C., I*nterface II: Report of a Seminar on Education for Touring Companies* (Arts Council of England, 1996) and *Interface III: Report on Five Education and Community Programmes in Presenting Venues in England* (ACE, 1996).

Holland, J., Hartley, K. and Kinder, K. (eds), *Arts in Their View: A Study of Youth Participation in the Arts,* National Foundation for Educational Research, 1995
> This publication presents evidence on young people's leisure activities, their attitudes to the arts, their participation in specific arts activities in schools and youth clubs, and their perceptions of the effects of arts involvement. Clear and precise.

Jackson, T. (ed.), *Learning Through Theatre: New Perspectives on Theatre and Education* (2nd Edition), Routledge, 1993
> An edited collection of essays tracing a historical and theoretical overview of the developments in the theatre education industry and the methodologies employed by a variety of practitioners. The book also places British work within an international context. The chapters address some of the key issues that are directly influencing theatre education practice in the late 1990s. The only text of its kind, and an essential reader.

Kempe, A., *The GCSE Drama Coursebook,* Stanley Thornes, 1990
> A quality GCSE textbook, which makes useful reading prior to work at post-16 level. The sections 'Means to an End: Tackling Issues Through Drama' and 'Forum Theatre' provide a useful introduction to many of the styles of theatre education activity described in this chapter.

Manser, S. and Wilmot, H., *Artists in Residence: A Teacher's Handbook*, London Arts Board/St Katherine and Shadwell Trust, 1995

> A very user-friendly guide to setting up arts education residencies, offering lots of examples of good practices. Suggests a code of practice.

Reddington, C., *Can Theatre Teach? An Evaluative Analysis of TIE*, Pergamon, 1983

> This book, together with the introduction to her collection *Six TIE Programmes* (Methuen, 1987) covers many of the issues surrounding TIE, and gives very useful examples of working TIE programmes.

Winser, K. (ed.), *Arts Professionals in Schools – A Step-by-Step Guide to Artists-in-Schools Projects*, Norfolk Educational Press, 1995

> A practical guide to setting up a residency programme, particularly with schools. Offers examples of good practice. Clear and useful.

See the bibliography of Chapter 4 (p.162) for books on devising theatre.

There are many printed texts of TIE programmes and children's theatre plays. It is worth contacting Samuel French (tel: 0171 387 9373), Offstage mail order (tel: 0171 485 4996) or other good theatre bookshops and asking for appropriate lists, such as *Plays for Young People*.

Periodicals

There are a number of periodical publications available which document current practices in theatre education activity. They are a useful resource, as well as offering insights into the changes taking place within the theatre education industry as a result of public policy or innovation among leading practitioners.

Arts Management Weekly

Rheingold Publishing, Freepost, Gravesend, Kent DA12 3BR (tel: 01474 334500)

> Weekly newspaper-style magazine for the arts industry, particularly aimed at managers and administrators.

95 percent: The Voice of Youth

Youth Arts Network, Youth Clubs UK, 11 St Bride Street, London EC4A 4AS (tel: 0171 353 2369)

> Quarterly magazine focusing upon youth concerns. Regularly offers accounts of youth arts projects.

Mailout: Arts Work for People

Kirklees Media Centre, 7 Northumberland Street, Huddersfield HD1 1RL (tel: 01484 469009)

> Bi-monthly independent magazine focusing upon arts practices

and current trends in arts education provision. Excellent.

National Campaign for the Arts News
National Campaign for the Arts, Francis House, Francis Street, London SW1P 1DE (tel: 0171 828 4448)
> Quarterly magazine for the UK's leading arts lobbying organisation.

Arts Education Magazine
National Foundation for Arts Education, Westminster College, Oxford OX2 9AT (tel: 01865 247 644)
> Quarterly magazine documenting arts education projects, with a particular emphasis on schools.

SCYPT Journals
From libraries, or Greenwich and Lewisham Young People's Theatre, Burrage Road, London SE18 7JZ (tel: 0181 854 1316)
> Variable publishing dates. These journals are influential in the documentation of the TIE industry. Useful as a resource for research documenting the historical development of TIE.

Design and Stage Management

David Wood

In this chapter, we are concerned with some of the supporting elements of stage production: design, lighting and stage management. It includes the following sections:

● Theatre design
● Stage lighting and its design
● The role of stage management

Of course, other elements go to make up the realisation of a production on stage. However, the principles outlined here can apply to costume, sound and other areas of theatre design.

THEATRE DESIGN

The purpose of theatre design

An example of a modern and successful production may help to illustrate why theatre is often enriched by stage design in its various forms.

The set of An Inspector Calls *at the Royal National Theatre, 1993. At the end of the play, the house on stilts has collapsed*

J.B. Priestley's play *An Inspector Calls*, written in 1945, is a modern morality play. In it, a smug and self-satisfied middle-class family is visited by a detective who is investigating the death of a young woman.

Gradually, the detective implicates each member of the family in the death of the woman. The play's dialogue and form had become rather dated, until Stephen Daldry directed a revival in London in 1993. The success of the play was partly owing to its startling scenic design. The designer, Ian MacNeil, placed the action in a little house elevated on stilts, which collapsed as the family began to blame one another for the woman's death towards the end of the play.

The set brilliantly illustrated the themes of the play: the family has cut itself off, creating a comfortable but brittle structure for itself above the ugly realities of life. Inevitably, this home, like the family's smug existence, must come crashing down. This is theatre design at its best, both serving the performers and the production and also adding a unique layer to the overall impression gained by the audience.

Theatre design encompasses set, costume, make-up and lighting design, as well as the props which dress the set and are carried and used by the characters. More recently, even sound has been categorised as a form of design for the theatre.

There are a range of functions for design.

Design for the theatre has been used throughout the ages for several purposes:

- to convey a sense of mood, atmosphere and theme, as in the example above;
- to focus the audience's attention on the stage. This is also one reason why lighting is used in a darkened auditorium;
- to help the audience to believe in the play, for example by dressing the cast in authentic costume in a period play;
- to give a sense of the location of scenes, for example by using lighting to simulate dappled sunlight in an outdoor scene;
- to give a sense of the period during which a play is set, for example by placing Roman columns on stage in *Julius Caesar*.

Design can be lavish or minimal.

Approaches to theatre design have altered over time.

Sometimes a production uses a large, complicated set, with period costumes and props. On other occasions, directors and designers take a 'minimalist' approach and use a bare stage, a little furniture or a few props. Such a minimalist design may be an ideal solution when there is a small design budget. Equally, fashions in design can change. The evidence suggests that plays in the 16th century were performed on a bare stage, with a few simple chairs or stools. By the 18th century, designers were using beautifully painted landscapes as backdrops, with cleverly calculated perspectives to give depth to the set. Early 19th-century theatre astonished its audiences with elaborate special effects, such as trapdoor disappearances. Nowadays, we accept both realistic and more abstract or minimalist theatre design. In every case, design is there to serve and enhance the work of the performers, and to support the production.

An interview with stage designer Keith Orton

A theatre designer describes his work.

Keith Orton trained as a stage designer after following a different career in design. In his first few years in the theatre, he has been very successful. He works as a self-employed freelance designer at such places as the Lyric Theatre in Hammersmith, and has been employed as resident designer at the Oldham Coliseum. Here he talks about his work.

I was initially trained as a graphic designer, and worked in that profession for 10 or 11 years. During that time, I was involved in amateur theatre, and I became more and more involved as a designer. I was asked to work at the Oldham Coliseum three to four months after completing a course in theatre design. It was a great experience working there, but I decided to go freelance. Oldham has a low proscenium stage, so you cannot design anything with height. I'm excited by the prospect of designing for other stage shapes and not just for the proscenium.

Some directors have very set ideas about what they want, but on the other hand some give virtually no input to the design of the play. What I do first is read the text very thoroughly; I spend a long time reading the play, going through the text between four and six times, before I think about what it's going to look like visually. This is so that when I do start thinking visually about it, I don't fall into the traps of the things that aren't going to work for the whole piece.

Sometimes I'll then do a flow chart which breaks it all up into pages of the script, including entrances and exits for the performers, so that, for instance, when I come to do costume I can see when people are on and off stage and I know when there are going to be problems with costume changes.

I get a lot of visual reference around the particular location, period or subject of the play. Because of my graphics background, you sort a lot of things out in your mind before you put anything down on paper. I like to do a lot of preparatory work before I sit down and start designing. I tend to get ideas very quickly, then I turn to the reference material to make sure that the idea is actually valid. Sometimes I suddenly get inspiration, when everything fits into place, but I would never class myself as a fine artist, so I don't sketch very much. Because of my background, I don't think that way. I'm much more inclined to think about shape and boldness. I prefer to get the model box and cut out lots of bits of white card and balsa wood and play around in the space to get height etc., because to me it doesn't help to use two dimensions when you are going to create something in three dimensions. You get a much stronger feel for space, you can check things like sightlines, and as you are designing in three dimensions you get a much more cohesive design.

In my personal approach to designing, a certain amount of humour plays a part. You have to catch people's attention in graphic design, and I've carried that into stage design. My designs often have a quirky sense of humour about them.

I start work on the design about four to six weeks before the design deadline. By this time, you have had all the discussions with the director. That's when you have the dimensions of the 1:25 scale for the set. In a big project, set and costume design are split right away,

Working with one stage shape and in one venue can be constricting.

Study the text or scenario thoroughly.

Sometimes a flow chart may help.

Gather reference material.

Designers differ in their approaches to the task.

Sometimes they have a personal style.

280

but in a smaller project it's one individual who designs both. This can be better, because you get a more cohesive feel. The whole thing gels together; your ideas for the set carry through to the costume. Once you have finished the model set, there is a production meeting. This is when all departments at a theatre get to see the model and the costume sketches. That's one of the worst days in the whole process. Departments like wardrobe are so busy working out what they have got to achieve in their little bit of the project that you get almost no feedback. While you are designing, you bear in mind what the budget is, but this is when it is costed, and departments have to get those costings in very rapidly. You also have to give the lighting designer things to work with. Sometimes you can even make design decisions with the lighting designer.

The first production meeting is vital.

Then of course there's a presentation of the costumes and set to the actors. In a lot of ways, you have to persuade people like actors that the decisions you have made are the right ones. You are seeing the whole thing, but they have only a personal angle.

During the making period you are continually making design decisions – you are out buying fabrics or buying props with the stage manager. You have to bear the available budget in mind and consider whether you compromise on your original ideas to keep within budget. There is a lot of 'having to get on' with all people in all departments. Some of the best productions are when everyone gets on well together.

Here we have selected two of Keith Orton's designs for closer study. The first design was done for an Oldham Coliseum production of Willy Russell's play *Educating Rita*. (You can see Keith Orton's design plans on pages 288–89.)

If you look at *Educating Rita* from a textual point of view, you could say it's basically a room setting – a 'box set'. But the director didn't want a completely realistic set, he wanted realistic elements. I did a bit of research into university rooms, but I didn't feel it was right for what we wanted to do with it. I woke up one morning and decided I wanted the whole idea of education portrayed, so I came up with the idea of using a page from the dictionary on education, and this became the set. It was a very strong image, because the whole thing was about Rita entering the world of education and being frightened and intimidated.

The director was very dubious about it at first, because he hates it when the audience comes in and reads the set! So I had to re-think. By breaking the bookcases through the scenic backdrop, you could get a sense of the whole idea of the set, but you couldn't actually read it. That's one of the few occasions when I've worked with a director who's said, 'I don't think I'm going to like this idea, but you carry on and you show me otherwise.' So when I did the model I tried to incorporate the negative things he was saying, to try and make the model sell the idea. The use of colour was important as well. I made the text grey, not black, and the background colour was sepia, so it made the room look smoky as well. So it didn't dominate.

Keith Orton's set for Educating Rita

The design carries some of the theme of the show. It's quite simple staging, but it still works completely well as a room. I'm very keen on designing the floor. It's so much an important part of the set, because when you're in the upper circle of a theatre you see so much of that. So we carried on the lettering to cover the floor. We were extremely worried about the time it would take to do the lettering, so we got in touch with a signwriter and said, 'How would you like to do a complete backcloth for a set?', and we got them very excited about it, because it was something they had never done. They ended up doing all that lettering for next to nothing!

The second example is Dario Fo and Franca Rame's play *Female Parts*. This production was in the studio theatre at Oldham Coliseum.

This is very simple: we had a £500 budget. I talked with the director about lots of Italian ideas. The one thing that screams out at me in depicting working-class Italian life is washing hanging up across the streets. We started then discussing actually painting everything onto the washing line, and carrying that whole theme through the play. The woman is ironing anyway through the first part. I carried it through by using the Italian colours of green, red and white, and the tiles on the floor were in the shape of the map of Italy, as well.

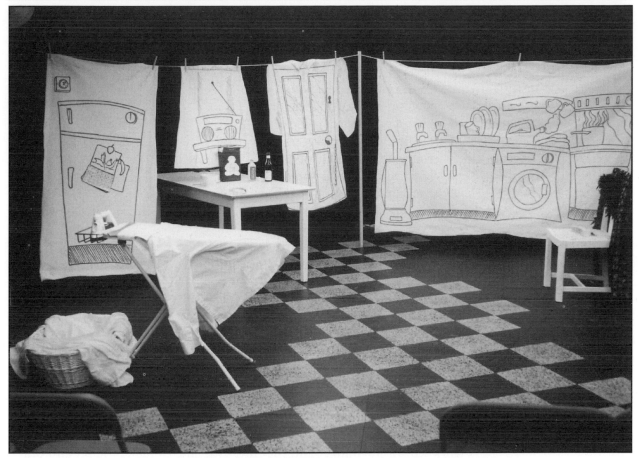

Keith Orton's set for Female Parts

The design process

A process for design can be determined.

Keith Orton's description of his work helps us to put the process of designing into a structure. With some variations, depending on the theatre space or the budget, there is always a structured process of designing for the theatre.

Getting to know the play or piece

This will involve careful reading of the text, noting exits and entrances, the location and period in which the play is set, the way in which the performers use elements of the design, such as doors, and the way in which locations change, scene by scene (this is considered further in Activity 8 on p.316). It will also involve talking creatively with the director about his or her approach to the play and ideas for the design.

Generating ideas

This might involve:

- getting ideas through looking at books, posters and pictures;
- sketching;
- talking to the director or other people involved in the play or in a past production of it;
- simply thinking until you get inspiration.

Researching the period or location in which the play is set

This might mean:

- conducting visual research, such as finding postcards and pictures;
- perhaps talking to experts, such as people who have lived in the country where the play is set;
- reading books and articles;
- visiting a particular location;
- visiting museums;
- using information stored on CD-ROM;
- obtaining recordings and videos;
- reading descriptions of life at the time the play is set;
- reading other books which might yield visual information or ideas.

Researching can be an inspiring or a stifling process, and it will probably be useful to make progress on the next stage at the same time.

Experimenting with ideas and materials

This might involve sketching, arranging a model set or small bricks to get an idea of stage shapes, trying out soft scenery such as cloth, or finding out if certain materials can be used effectively in the design. This is covered in Activity 2 below (see p.307).

Working within the design brief

A designer never has unlimited resources available. There are always constraints of time, money, personnel and materials. The designer must work within the budget and the time available to make the set and other elements of the design, and the deadlines for various stages of the design process must be carefully considered. He or she must work within the space available in the performance venue, and bear in mind the people and resources available for making the set. The design may even involve recycling materials from past productions.

All these things must be done in collaboration with other members of the team, such as lighting or costume designers, stage managers and the director. The design process will involve several meetings and demonstrations of the prototype designs, in order to ensure that they are in sympathy with the ideas of the director and that they work with the lighting and on the stage. Draft or experimental ideas will usually be modified in response to the reactions of the production team.

Developing prototype designs

See below (pp.286–290) for an explanation of how to make scale drawings and models.

The designer will usually make a model of the set design at a scale of 1:25. Using this model and other scale plans, the people who are going to construct the set can estimate how much in the way of materials they will need, and how the set should eventually look. (See Activity 3 on p.308 for more information on this.)

Making up the designs

In an amateur or fringe theatre show, a designer might make the set or costumes him or herself. In professional theatre, scenic carpenters and wardrobe take over and make up the designs. The design must be finished in sufficient time for the construction of the set to be completed and for adjustments to be made.

Making final adjustments

The design will be realised and perfected during technical and dress rehearsals and possibly the first performances. It may be necessary to make last-minute changes or even to discard a much-cherished idea because it simply does not work on stage.

The elements of theatre design

Having looked at the role of the designer, it is now useful to consider the ingredients or elements of a design. When working on a design, you will need to make a conscious effort to consider the following elements.

Size and shape

The designer will experiment with the shape of the set. One of the most straightforward shapes comprises three sides of a square, with the invisible fourth side being where the audience sits. However, this shape only suits a proscenium stage. It is also quite limited, and more often than not the designer will try to create a more interesting shape around the floor area and at the top of the scenery line.

Proportion

The size of the scenery in proportion to the performers is also something to bear in mind. Most notably, tall columns and wide staircases add to the grandeur of a scene, but can dwarf the characters. Designers must therefore make considered decisions about the relationship between the size of the scenery, the height of the average person and the number of people on stage.

Colour

The language of colour is well known to designers and visual artists in all fields. On the one hand, we associate various emotions and moods with different colours, but in addition colours can create optical effects, which may be useful: for example, lighter colours can make an area seem larger. Tones and shades are important, since a flat colour painted on a backdrop gives no impression of depth or texture. The designer will need to decide on appropriate colour schemes for the set, and these will need to work well with the costumes.

Texture

The surfaces of materials – rough, smooth, shiny, silky – also carry important visual messages. Rough-cast bricks, for example, could convey a sense of decaying surroundings, whereas smooth textures can give a feel of palatial richness. Keith Orton describes a versatile material for creating textures in stage design:

You do find that certain materials have surprising qualities for model designs and actual sets. One example of that is plastic padding [the material used for filling holes and dents in the bodywork of cars]. If you spread it onto a surface and then heavily sand it down, and then rub dye and paint into it, you get incredible textured surfaces like stone floors, and you can score into it to get pavements, floors and so on. So it's quite a nice way of getting textures that you want.

An illusion of textured surfaces can also be created by using certain scene-painting techniques, such as stippling (dotting the scenery with the end of the brush).

Line

Optical illusions are often created by the clever use of line. Vertical lines, such as columns, can give the impression of height, but this also narrows the look of the set. Horizontal lines on scenery flats make rooms look wider, and any parallel vertical lines that become farther apart do the same. Imaginary lines running through scenery, or actual lines in a floor pattern, can converge to create particularly strong points on the stage, such as a central place for speeches by important characters. A line at the top of a straight run of scenery flats can draw attention to the break between set and stage, which is often undesirable. Using angles and different levels at the top of the flats, on the other hand, breaks up this line and creates interest.

Materials for designing and set construction

A model set is important.

In order to experiment with design, it is necessary to work in three dimensions. From a scale drawing of the theatre space being used, designers create a 'model box' of the stage area, and sometimes of the auditorium, to the same scale. Within this, they can then use materials such as card to create model sets. Balsa wood is one of the most versatile materials for making model sets, and is available in a wide range of shapes. Another material obtainable from model-making and art supply shops, kappa board, is suitably light and strong for making model box stages. (Activity 3 on p.308 asks you to make a model box.)

The standard scale used for ground plans of theatres and for models is 1:25. Thus 1cm on the model represents 25cm on the actual stage, and 4cm represents every metre on the stage. It is important to write what is known as a 'legend' in one corner of the plan or model, stating the scale used, the name of the play the design is for and the name of the theatre in which the production will be staged. On pages 287–289 there are examples of professional plans drawn by Keith Orton for *Educating Rita*.

A number of materials are used in set construction.

All manner of materials are available for set construction, but some are more commonly used than others. Scenery flats are made from wooden frames and covered with a material such as hardboard or tightly stretched hessian. This can then be painted or textured for scenery of different styles.

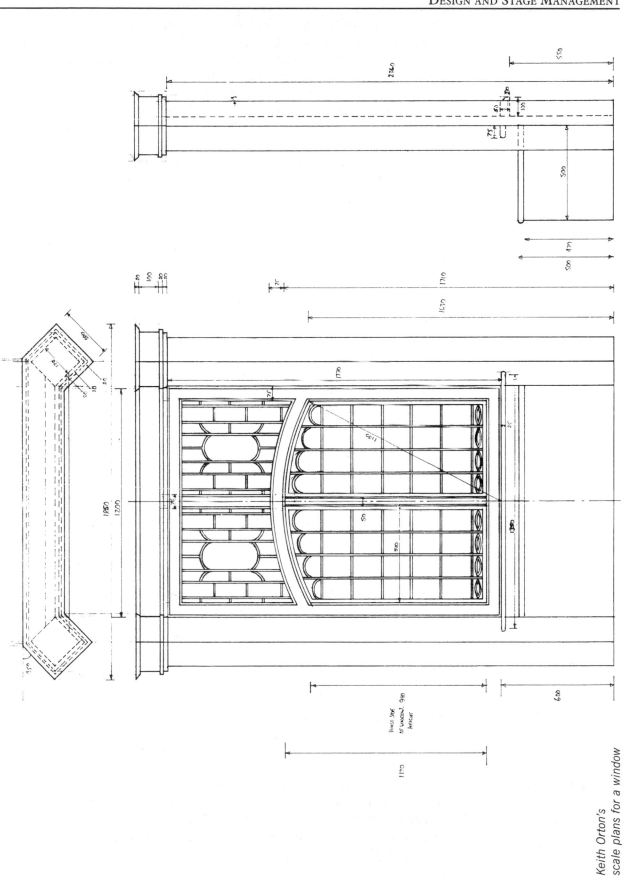

*Keith Orton's
scale plans for a window*

A stage floor plan

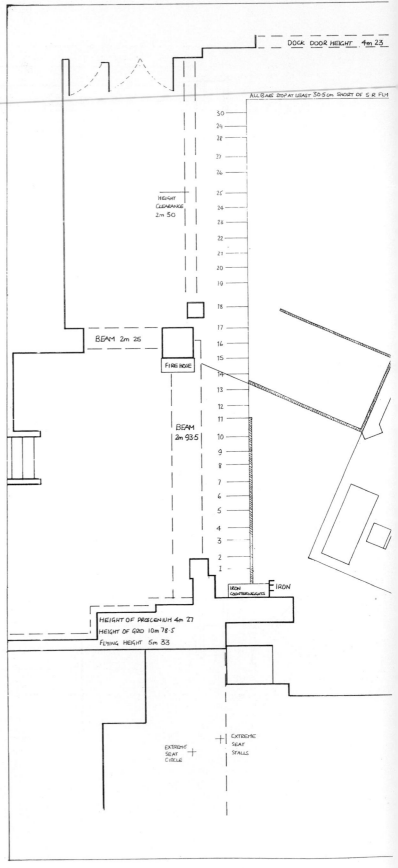

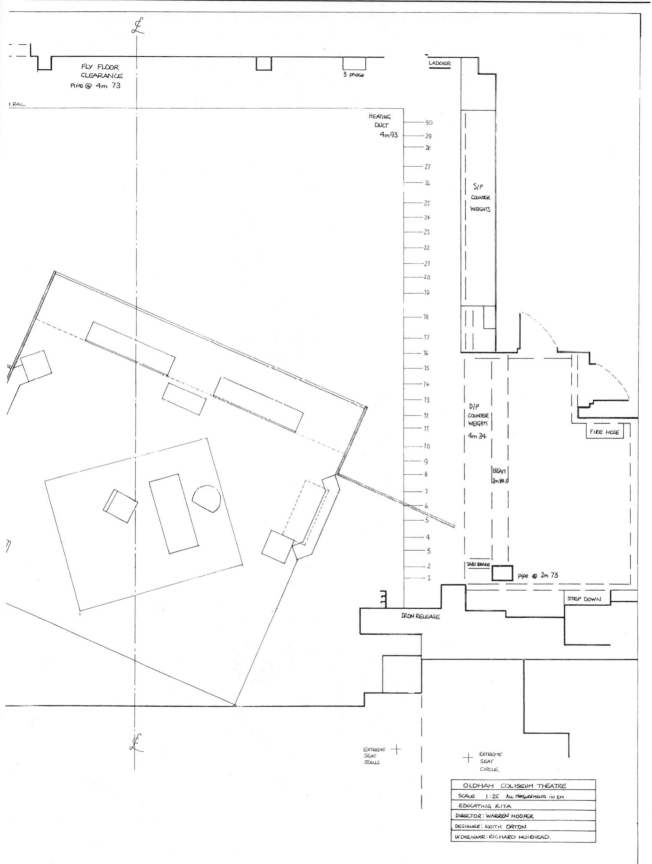

FLY FLOOR
CLEARANCE
PIPE @ 4m 73

3 phase

LADDER

1 RAIL

HEATING
DUCT
4m 93

30
29
28
27
26
25
24
23
22
21
20
19
18
17
16
15
14
13
12
11
10
9
8
7
6
5
4
3
2
1

S/P
COUNTER
WEIGHTS

D/P
COUNTER
WEIGHTS
4m 34

BEAM
2m 84·5

FIRE HOSE

TABS BRAKE

pipe @ 2m 73

STEP DOWN

IRON RELEASE

EXTREME
SEAT
STALLS

EXTREME
SEAT
CIRCLE

OLDHAM COLISEUM THEATRE
SCALE 1:25 ALL MEASUREMENTS IN CM
EDUCATING RITA
DIRECTOR: WARREN HOOPER
DESIGNER: KEITH ORTON
LX DESIGNER: RICHARD MUIRHEAD.

Painted backdrops are less commonly used now, because painted scenery can never equal the realistic impression given by scenery for television and film. Nevertheless, a coloured or plain cyclorama at the back of the stage can be used for projecting images or coloured lighting. (The 'cyclorama' is the term used for the rear of the stage as seen by the audience. It can be either the back wall of the stage area or a large suspended stage cloth covering the whole of the upstage field of vision.)

Many productions employ rostra blocks, which are often available in theatre spaces, to create levels, stairs and architectural interest in a scene. These blocks can be adapted, painted or covered in a range of ways. It is helpful to pack the underneath of rostra with material to deaden or damp the sound of people walking on them.

Soft scenery is used for several purposes. To mask the sides of the stage, narrow, angled 'legs' of material are placed on both wings. Suspended soft scenery can be stiffened with size (a form of diluted glue for sealing materials) and painted, and then cuts can be made in it to represent abstract or natural images. Gauze can be used to give the audience a partial view of aspects of the set. It can be lit from the front to mask what is behind it, or from behind to allow the audience to see through. It is thus ideal for unusual effects.

(There is an opportunity to design for these scenery materials in Activity 8 on p.316. Books on technical aspects of set design are included in the bibliography at the end of this chapter, p.317.)

STAGE LIGHTING AND ITS DESIGN

In 1545, the Italian artist and architect Sebastiano Serlio first advocated the use of candles and lamps behind coloured glass to light stages. The idea of stage lighting quickly spread around Europe, and probably influenced some of the sinister scenes in later Shakespeare plays and in Jacobean theatre.

The purposes of stage lighting are:

- to help the audience to see the performers better from a distance;
- to focus attention on the stage in a dark auditorium;
- to create the effect of natural lighting in different locations and at different times of the day, for example yellow light through a window on a sunny day, grey/blue for moonlight;
- to create special effects and atmosphere on stage, for example by using lighting angles to create heavy shadows in a melodrama;
- to enhance the themes which the director is emphasising and to support the overall design concept.

The role of the lighting designer

The lighting designer will work closely with the set designer in order to complement the elements of the set. Perhaps most importantly, he or she will try to enhance the directorial and design concept, conveying the key images or themes from the textual interpretation.

The lighting designer works closely with the set designer.

Having studied the script in some detail, taking note of references to lighting in the stage directions and clues about lighting in the text, a lighting designer will use his or her knowledge of the elements of lighting (angles and directions, colour, intensity and special effects) to create a scale plan of the lighting design. In the same way as for scenic design, this means a 1:25 ratio diagram showing the position of the lanterns from above. The plan details what sort of lanterns will be used, and where they will be fixed and angled on the lighting bars. An example of a plan is shown on pages 292–293.

Finally, a team of people, working from the plan, will rig the lighting up, and the lighting designer will experiment with the actual effects created. Scene by scene, he or she will work through the text, plotting the changes of lighting effects and recording the lighting intensity, the duration of fades and cross-fades and any other changes.

Types of lantern or lighting instrument

There are several popular types of lantern.

Three major types of lantern are in common use, though there are many variations on these types. They are shown below and on p.294 with the symbols that represent them on lighting plans.

The profile spotlight is so called because it casts a sharp, round beam. Its adjustable lens means that it can be focused. It throws a narrow beam of light, and is useful for special effects, as we shall see.

A profile spotlight

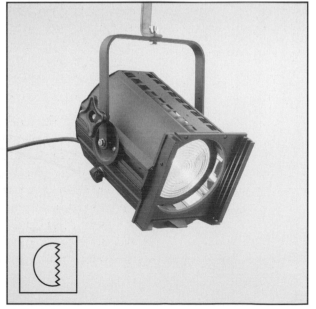

A fresnel

A lighting design plan by Vivien Loh for Land of the Forgotten Tide at the Minack Theatre, Cornwall

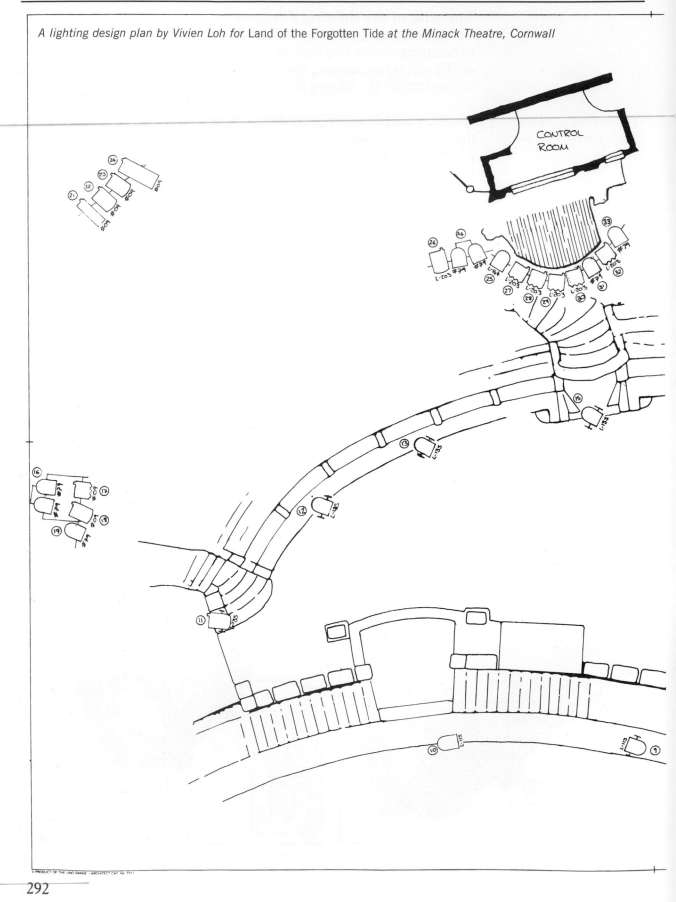

A PRODUCT OF THE UNO RANGE · ARCHITECT CAT. No 7311

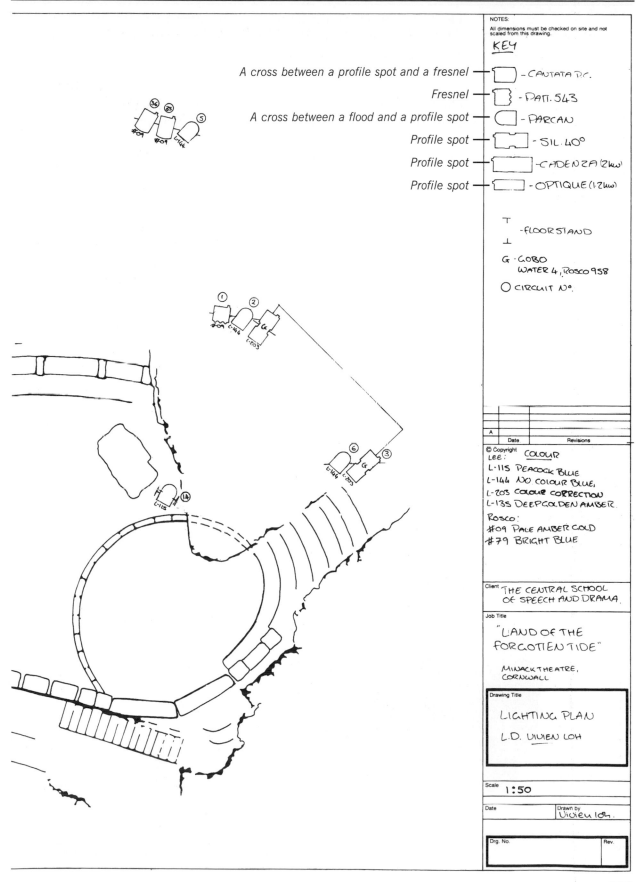

NOTES:
All dimensions must be checked on site and not scaled from this drawing.

KEY

A cross between a profile spot and a fresnel — ▢ – CANTATA P.C.

Fresnel — ▢ – PATT. 543

A cross between a flood and a profile spot — ◖ – PARCAN

Profile spot — ▢ – SIL. 40°

Profile spot — ▭ – CADENZA (2KW)

Profile spot — ▭ – OPTIQUE (1.2KW)

⊤ – FLOORSTAND
⊥

G – GOBO
   WATER 4, ROSCO 958

○ CIRCUIT Nº.

A		
	Date	Revisions

© Copyright

COLOUR
LEE:
L-115 PEACOCK BLUE
L-144 NO COLOUR BLUE
L-203 COLOUR CORRECTION
L-135 DEEP GOLDEN AMBER.

ROSCO:
#09 PALE AMBER GOLD
#79 BRIGHT BLUE

Client THE CENTRAL SCHOOL
OF SPEECH AND DRAMA.

Job Title
"LAND OF THE
FORGOTTEN TIDE"

MINACK THEATRE,
CORNWALL

Drawing Title

LIGHTING PLAN

L.D. VIVIEN LOH

Scale 1:50

Date | Drawn by Vivien Loh.

Drg. No. | Rev.

293

The fresnel is a versatile lantern, named after its inventor: it has a ridged lens, cleverly designed to diffuse the beam and so produce a softer-edged, wider area of light. This is the lantern which is most useful for the general lighting of the stage.

The floodlight, as the name suggests, throws a wide beam, which is useful for lighting a large area at close range. Though a flood will spill light over a stage and will not project light over a long distance, it is ideal for distributing, for example, a blue colour over a cyclorama.

Beyond these main types of lantern, there are more specialised versions designed for particular purposes: symmetric and asymmetric floods, conical beam spotlights and parcans, for example (see Reid, *Stage Lighting*, in the bibliography). Lanterns also come in a variety of strengths: 500 or 650 watts, or 1 or 2 kilowatts. Clearly the strongest of these will throw light farther. Each type of lantern has particular qualities, and a designer must experiment on stage with the lanterns available to see their capabilities at first hand.

Angles

To light effectively, a 45-degree angle is best.

If you direct light horizontally into the face of an actor, the audience will see a strange, flat face, with no shadows. Natural lighting usually falls onto people from above, and this creates the shadows and contours we see naturally. In order to light an area of the stage naturally, two lanterns need to be directed from 45 degrees above and 45 degrees to each side of the performers. If you also shine a lantern onto the performer from behind, you create depth and dimension in what the audience sees. This is often called 'sculpting' the performer, as the audience gets a three-dimensional impression of the stage.

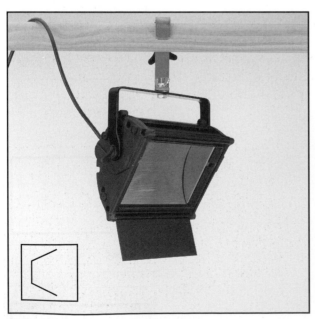

A floodlight

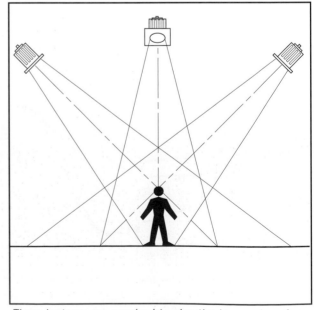

Three lanterns are required to give the impression of natural lighting

Fan setting in blocks ensures complete coverage.

One of the first tasks of the lighting designer is to ensure that all areas of the stage are lit in this way. This can be done by dividing the stage into squares of, say, three metres, and by setting lanterns so that as far as possible each square is lit by lanterns from these angles, with no dark spots. This is often called fan setting. Usually, fan setting the stage is the first task, because once the stage is lit you can see how many lanterns remain for other purposes, such as 'specials' (see below). In some unusual venues it may be difficult to fan set. The lighting design plan on pp.292–293 was done for an outdoor theatre where this was the case.

The stage settings can be enhanced by particular effects.

A good lighting designer is able to simulate natural light sources, if this is appropriate, to enhance a scene. Shadows of tree branches, moonlight through shutters or sunlight through open doors create realism in a scene; windows can be illuminated, pillars can throw vast shadows. Lighting can also be used in more abstract ways. For example, monologues may be delivered in sharp, square lighting shapes; an underpinning theme of dislocation could be emphasised by harsh, cold lighting and unsettling jagged shapes formed by gobos (see below, p.296).

Colour

Polycarbonate colour filters can be fitted over all types of lantern. (These are often called 'gels', because gelatine filters were used in the past.) There is a wide range of colours available, and many lighting designers use filters even for natural light, because plain 'white' lighting can be stark and cold on stage. It is useful to use a range of colours in lighting a scene. If you look at the sky, sea or countryside, it is clear that there is a variety of colours present in most surfaces. Single flat colours look unrealistic in all visual art. For this reason, a lighting designer using gels to create a sky effect on the cyclorama may well select a range of colours, from grey through blue to yellow.

Colour theory is a complex and exact science, which it is essential for a lighting designer to understand. Mixing colours can produce new colours, and a gel can produce an unexpected effect when the light hits the surface of coloured scenery or costumes. This is why lighting designers need to work closely with set and costume designers.

Intensity

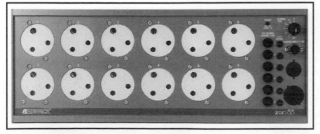

A standard thyrister dimmer pack (left) and manual control board (right). These are examples of simple equipment; most professional and some amateur venues have fully computerised boards

Control of the lanterns occurs through a thyrister dimmer and a control board.

When a lantern is plugged into a circuit on the lighting bar it is then controlled by a thyrister dimmer pack, into which at least 12 lanterns can be plugged. The dimmer pack is connected to a control board, which operates lanterns in groups, pairs or individually, using a slider to control the intensity of the light. This means that lanterns can be faded out at the end of a scene, or dimmed when appropriate. Virtually every coloured gel reduces light intensity, which is why lighting designers tend to err on the side of caution, using paler rather than darker gels.

Control boards have a series of channels, usually in multiples of six. There are always at least two sets of identical controls, to allow lighting operators to pre-set the lights for the next cue or scene. As the scene changes, the lighting operator can cross-fade between one lighting set-up, or state, and another, simply by changing the master. These days, most larger lighting boards are computerised. Each individual lighting state is entered and recorded as a number – the cue number – so that at each change of scene the operator can simply enter the number, rather than pre-setting each scene. The computerised boards can also store information about how long it should take to change from one lighting state to another. The light could fade during a scene at dusk over a period of, say, ten minutes, or a cross-fade could be programmed to occur over 20 seconds.

Although computerised boards are now the normal form of lighting control, it is important to remember that computerisation only simplifies mechanical tasks. Effective lighting is still dependent on the expertise of the designer, and the skill of the lighting operator and/or programmer.

Special effects and accessories

There is not enough space here to cover the full range of special effects and accessories available to the designer. Instead, we have given one or two examples to show the potential of special effects.

A 'gobo' is a wafer of steel with a cut-out pattern, which is inserted into a profile spot. The pattern can then be projected onto the scenery, the stage floor or the cyclorama. A range of gobo shapes is available. You

Examples of gobo patterns

could project a leaf pattern, prison bars, venetian blinds, a landscape or abstract shapes onto any of these surfaces, adjusting the image into sharp or soft focus. The gobo is a useful effect: it can indicate a location more simply than the use of scenery, or can add texture and depth to a less naturalistic scene.

'Barndoors' fit onto the front of lanterns, usually fresnels. As the name suggests, they are metal doors, which can be adjusted to narrow or shape a beam of light, and so reduce 'spill'. They can also define a place on the floor of the stage, such as the edge of a room.

Health and Safety

Health and Safety is extremely important.

Once lighting is being rigged, a number of safety precautions *must* be taken to avoid accidents or injury:

- The tallescope is a wheeled aluminium scaffolding on which riggers stand to hang lanterns on lighting bars. It is essential to use 'outriggers', or legs, to steady the tallescope. These should be just off the floor when moving it and adjusted and braked while lanterns are being rigged. If a tallescope is moved sharply, especially if a brake is accidentally left on, it will topple over. To be completely safe, a rigger should get off the tallescope when it is being moved. No tools should be left on a tallescope, since they could fall and cause injury.

- All lanterns should be screwed firmly to lighting bars and doubly secured using safety chains. This is a safety regulation set by local authorities.

- The riggers should work with thick, padded gloves. When focusing and final adjustments are made, lanterns become very hot.

- Electricity demands the greatest respect. Switch off the thyrister dimmer when plugging it into a lighting board or when plugging circuits from the board into the dimmer. Ensure that no lantern is moved in such a way that the cable is strained at any point.

- Any trailing cables must be taped up so that nothing can catch on them and nobody will trip over them.

(See also the bibliography on p.317.)

THE ROLE OF STAGE MANAGEMENT

This section briefly summarises the role of stage management, and gives an insight into the work of Peter Maccoy, who was an assistant stage manager at the Royal National Theatre in London for five years.

Stage management can often be done by a large team of people.

We use the term 'stage management', rather than 'stage manager', deliberately: many performances are so complex that one person on his or her own could not ensure that all elements of a production go to plan. Rather, it is usually the case that a stage management *team* is responsible for this, with different people having different jobs to do, while the stage manager supervises and takes ultimate responsibility for ensuring that performances of a play run smoothly.

The responsibilities of this team can be varied and diverse. For example, in Keith Dewhurst's promenade play *Candleford* (1979), there is a scene where a complete meal is eaten. Before each performance of *Candleford*, the stage management team would be responsible for preparing the meal which the performers eat.

The role of the stage manager is ultimately that of a co-ordinator.

For this reason, it is difficult to define the role of the stage manager, or to make any firm statements about the scope of this role. Ultimately, the stage manager is the co-ordinator of all the elements of the play in production, and ensures that the performance takes place successfully. His or her copy of the script will contain a complete record of everything that is to happen during performances. The stage manager's key role is to keep the production running smoothly, through cueing performers and effects during the show, setting the scenery and props on stage, and preparing personal props off stage for performers to carry on. The stage manager will run the technical and dress rehearsals of the play to ensure that everything is in place when and where the performers expect it. Before we look at the role in more detail, let us consider what an experienced stage manager, Peter Maccoy, has to say.

An interview with stage manager Peter Maccoy

Peter Maccoy has worked with a number of well-known directors. He spent five years at the Royal National Theatre, and has been Company and Stage Manager for seasons with the Chichester Festival Theatre and the Peter Hall Company and on tour with the Almeida Theatre Company.

The stage manager needs a broad knowledge of all areas of the production.

I got interested in drama at school, as a way of avoiding rugby! I went to university and spent most of my time doing student theatre, and then went to RADA and did the stage management course there. I worked as a stage hand and as a stage carpenter for some time. I was assistant stage manager and then deputy stage manager at the Mercury Theatre at Colchester, which gave me experience of a true repertory season. We did rigging and flying, we obtained the props, as well as stage managing. That was an excellent grounding in the job. Then I did five years as an ASM at the Royal National Theatre, working on some incredible productions. After that, I felt prepared to work on almost any level.

It is essential to know the script you are working with, or, if there is no script, the ideas behind a piece. You also need an understanding of what the creative team are planning, in terms of the design of the show and the creative concept behind it. You need to know what budget you've got to play with. You need to know the relevant Health and Safety regulations – i.e. what you can and can't do legally. The first thing I do is to read the script and do an in-depth analysis of everything it can tell me about the play technically.

The stage manager needs to be methodical and to question constantly.

It is your job to ensure that everything is thought of and that nothing is forgotten in a production. Every possible question about the staging of a show must be predicted. Before you meet the director, you need to have an armament of questions, so you can say, for instance, 'How are we going to do the sword fight in *Romeo and Juliet* if you are setting it in the 21st century?' You have to be quite methodical about your work. Before I know how it is going to be directed, I would have compiled lists containing breakdowns of the number of characters, the number of costumes they are likely to have, and any quick changes, props, scene changes, special effects etc., so that I am armed with that before I find out about the actual production I am doing. At this stage, you need to keep a very open mind, in case the director has unconventional ideas about the play. For example, the director may want to stage a traditional play with no set and no props.

Setting and running documents are vital.

You have to keep very clear lists, forms and charts that you update all the time and tick off. This is why stage managers love computers and databases now. Your lists eventually form a document which tells you where everything is and where it goes, and also tells people what to do with, for example, props. It would tell you where props are set, and how the scenery is set at the beginning of the show. This document, which is called a setting document, can be simple or complicated; you tailor it to the needs of the production.

As well as setting documents, you also have running documents, which tell you what happens throughout the show and what stage management can expect to do during each moment in it. Running documents evolve throughout the rehearsals, the technical rehearsals and up to the first night – sometimes beyond the first night. As a stage manager, you have to keep running documents up to date constantly. You need to know what everybody else is doing, because if someone is ill or is late you are the person who has to brief the replacement and tell them what to do. So you need to know what has changed along the way. More often than not, you have a team of people with you. In a big show it might be five, and each one will have a defined job.

Running technical rehearsals needs a firm hand.

Eventually the production gets into its venue, and scenery and lights are set, so that you can have technical rehearsals. During the technical rehearsals, it is of paramount importance to keep the show moving. When it grinds to a halt, you have to find out why, and estimate how long it is going to take to sort out a problem; you also have to be able to go back to run elements of the technical moments of the show again. You sometimes have to be quite firm with directors, because not everything has to be sorted out at the 'tech'. If the director says, 'The colour of that costume is wrong', it's the stage manager's job to say, 'Let's make a note of it and talk about it later – we don't need to talk about it now.'

So stage management exists to make sure that everything happens according to the needs of the production and the desires of the director. It's there to make sure it happens, from start of rehearsals to finish of production. Once the creative work with performers starts, that's when the stage manager gets involved.

Peter Maccoy's setting document for The Rose Tattoo

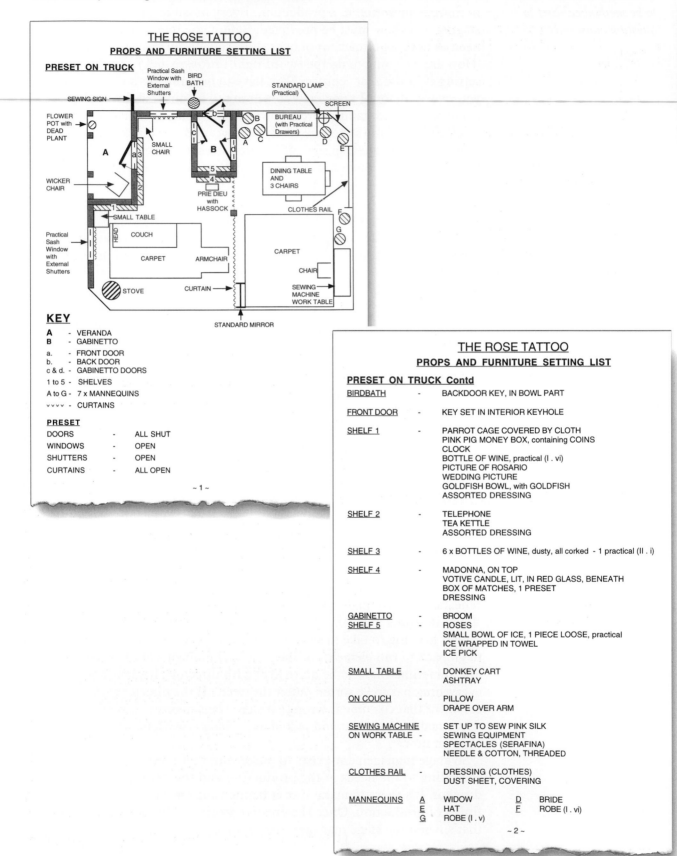

THE ROSE TATTOO

PROPS AND FURNITURE SETTING LIST

PRESET ON TRUCK

SEWING SIGN
Practical Sash Window with External Shutters
BIRD BATH
STANDARD LAMP (Practical)
SCREEN
FLOWER POT with DEAD PLANT
WICKER CHAIR
SMALL CHAIR
BUREAU (with Practical Drawers)
DINING TABLE AND 3 CHAIRS
PRIE DIEU with HASSOCK
CLOTHES RAIL
Practical Sash Window with External Shutters
SMALL TABLE
COUCH
CARPET
ARMCHAIR
CARPET
CHAIR
STOVE
CURTAIN
SEWING MACHINE WORK TABLE
STANDARD MIRROR

KEY

A	-	VERANDA
B	-	GABINETTO
a.	-	FRONT DOOR
b.	-	BACK DOOR
c & d.	-	GABINETTO DOORS
1 to 5	-	SHELVES
A to G	-	7 x MANNEQUINS
v v v v	-	CURTAINS

PRESET

DOORS	-	ALL SHUT
WINDOWS	-	OPEN
SHUTTERS	-	OPEN
CURTAINS	-	ALL OPEN

~ 1 ~

THE ROSE TATTOO

PROPS AND FURNITURE SETTING LIST

PRESET ON TRUCK Contd

BIRDBATH	-	BACKDOOR KEY, IN BOWL PART
FRONT DOOR	-	KEY SET IN INTERIOR KEYHOLE
SHELF 1	-	PARROT CAGE COVERED BY CLOTH PINK PIG MONEY BOX, containing COINS CLOCK BOTTLE OF WINE, practical (I . vi) PICTURE OF ROSARIO WEDDING PICTURE GOLDFISH BOWL, with GOLDFISH ASSORTED DRESSING
SHELF 2	-	TELEPHONE TEA KETTLE ASSORTED DRESSING
SHELF 3	-	6 x BOTTLES OF WINE, dusty, all corked - 1 practical (II . i)
SHELF 4	-	MADONNA, ON TOP VOTIVE CANDLE, LIT, IN RED GLASS, BENEATH BOX OF MATCHES, 1 PRESET DRESSING
GABINETTO	-	BROOM
SHELF 5	-	ROSES SMALL BOWL OF ICE, 1 PIECE LOOSE, practical ICE WRAPPED IN TOWEL ICE PICK
SMALL TABLE	-	DONKEY CART ASHTRAY
ON COUCH	-	PILLOW DRAPE OVER ARM
SEWING MACHINE ON WORK TABLE	-	SET UP TO SEW PINK SILK SEWING EQUIPMENT SPECTACLES (SERAFINA) NEEDLE & COTTON, THREADED
CLOTHES RAIL	-	DRESSING (CLOTHES) DUST SHEET, COVERING

MANNEQUINS	A	WIDOW	D	BRIDE
	E	HAT	F	ROBE (I . vi)
	G	ROBE (I . v)		

~ 2 ~

Peter Maccoy's running document for The Rose Tattoo

'THE ROSE TATTOO'
STAGE MANAGEMENT RUNNING PLOT - SR

PART 1
BEGINNERS

VIVI	-	DOLL
SALVATORE	-	HOOP
PEPPINA		
ASSUNTA	-	BASKET OF HERBS
STREGA	-	BESOM
GIUSEPPINA		

PRESET - PLACE PINK SILK IN PAPER BAG - PIN ON TOP

Q	ACTION		
1.	TAKE DOLL FROM VIVI DS & HOOP FROM SALVATORE US		
2.	PAGE BESOM FROM STREGA DS & RESET SL		
	RESET URN FROM SL PROPS SHELF TO SR		
3.	**ON S/By DSR**	-	PAGE ROPE TO STREGA (BEFORE GOAT)
4.	**1st GO DSR**	-	STREGA SHOUTS DS
	2nd GO DSR	-	SEND VIVI ON DSR
	3rd GO DSR	-	SEND STREGA ON DSR
5.	**ON B/O DSR**	-	FIELD GOAT FROM STREGA & PASS TO HANDLER
			GUIDE STREGA OFF
6.	**ON B/O DSR**	-	PAGE WREATH TO ASSUNTA
			TORCH OFF SERAFINA INTO WING
7.	**SCENE CHANGE**	USC (FROM R)	
	SET	-	URN ON SHELF
	STRIKE	- FROM SHELF -	2 STATUETTES
			SMALL VASE
		- FROM TABLE -	CHRYSANTHS
			PAPER BAG
			CORK SCREW
			MEASUREMENTS
8.	RESET SHAWL & APRON FROM PROPS TABLE CSR TO USR Q/C AREA		
9.	TAKE BALL FROM BRUNO DSR		
	ESCORT BRUNO TO CHAPERONE IN DRESSING ROOM AREA		
10.	CHECK ALVARO'S PERSONALS	-	ZIPPO LIGHTER
			LUCKY STRIKE PACKET & CIG/

11.	**AFTER 'INKY DINKY'**		
	ON GO USR	-	SHAKE, THEN DROP, CRASH BOX (from DSR)

12.	**AFTER 'BOOKS'** (JACK / ROSA / SERAFINA SCENE)		
	ON CALL	-	COLLECT STREGA
			SET BUCKET DSR
13.	**B/O AT END OF PART 1**		
	GUIDE STREGA OFF DSR		

'The Rose Tattoo' SM Ru[...]

INTERVAL

SET	-	CORKSCREW FROM OFF SR TO BOWL ON SIDEBOARD
RESET	-	KITE TO USR, ATTACH TO FLAT

PART 2
BEGINNERS

USR

BRUNO	-	KITE
SALVATORE		
PEPPINA	-	BASKET
GIUSEPPINA	-	BASKET

DSR
Fr. LEO

ON STAGE (FROM SR)

SERAFINA	-	BOTTLE, STRAP, KNICKERS (CHECK)

14.	LICORICE STICK FROM VIVI DSR		
15.	SET SALESMAN'S BAG ON FLOOR BY FIRE HOSE DSR		
16.	STRIKE KITE FROM BRUNO DSR & RESET USR		
17.	PAGE BASKET FROM CHAPERONE SR		
18.	**ON GO DSR**	-	SEND TWO BOYS ON
(19.	STRIKE SIGN FROM STAGE CSR, IF ACTRESS FAILS TO DO SO AS EXITS)		
20.	ESCORT TWO BOYS TO CHAPERONE SL		
21.	PAGE BRIEFCASE FROM SALESMAN DSR		

22.	**AFTER WINE POPPING** - WARN STREGA OF IMMINENT CALL		
23.	**ON GO DSR**	-	VIVI SCREAM
24.	**1st GO DSR**	-	3 CHILDREN ENTER
	2nd GO DSR	-	STREGA ENTERS
25.	TAKE GOAT FROM ALVARO DSR, GIVE TO HANDLER		
	WHEN ALVARO RE-ENTERS - CUE CHILD TO STOP BANGING LIDS		
26.	TAKE LARGE BUNCH OF BANANAS USR & GIVE TO CHILDREN US OF TRUCK		
	ON GO USR	-	Q ON CHILDREN
27.	PAGE 3 BANANAS & LARGE & SMALL BUNCHES FROM CHILDREN DSR		
28.	**ON GO DSR**	-	ALL 3 CHILDREN SCREAM
			GIVE 3 BANANAS BACK TO CHILDREN

29.	**ON CALL**	-	FETCH STREGA (during final JACK & ROSA scene)
30.	**ON GO DSR**	-	Q ON ASSUNTA CSR
31.	**ON FINAL B/O DSR**		WAVE TO ASSUNTA & HELP OFF
32.	**ON GO DSR**	-	Q ON ASSUNTA FOR CALL

'The Rose Tattoo' SM Running SR p.2

The emphasis is on 'management'.

It's more about management than stage, and the stage is the tool of the trade. You are managing performance. You are making sure it happens safely; you are making sure it always happens the same way; you are making sure that when there are problems you can solve them. You're trying to think of all the things that the others haven't thought of, and it's the performance which is central to it.

Communication is the key to stage management. You are communicating information, and if you are working as stage manager at the National Theatre that forms a large proportion of what you are doing. You are communicating information to do with props, scenery, sound and so on. Other people perform most of the tasks which keep the show moving, under the guidance of the stage management team. A good communicator would never have a conversation about the show and not put it down on paper, and similarly you should not put anything down on paper and not have a conversation with the people affected. If you have a note, you have to make sure that the person you are giving the note to understands it, by talking to them. Unless a conversation is backed up with paper, you can expect to forget things. The *ABC* of stage management is that information has to be Accurate, Brief and Clear. That goes for all information, whether it's information about a new prop, a change in scenery, or when a cue happens or where actors move.

Accurate and clear information and records are vital.

You are also there to keep the morale going, and keep positive. Never admit to not knowing anything, but say, 'I'll find out.' It gives people confidence. If people have confidence that the stage manager is on top of everything, when things do go wrong people will believe you can sort it out.

Be especially vigilant about Health and Safety.

Health and Safety is common sense. You have to feel sure that everything is safe. If something is unsafe, it is imperative that you say so. Health and Safety regulations are becoming less precise, because it is clear that you can't have a regulation for everything, for screwing a screw or hitting a hammer, so the onus now is on management, and what is called 'risk assessment'. For any activity which might be potentially dangerous, you have to do a risk assessment on it. It can take a long time. You are saying, 'What could go wrong, what could the risk be, and how can I stop it?' The local authorities take the lead in this. They are very strict. For example, a mock firearm, which I can order through the post, they would require me to keep under lock and key. The fire brigade and the police wouldn't.

The Mysteries at the National is the most inspiring and exciting show that I've worked on. Everybody loved it; there was an incredible atmosphere. The show ended with a dance, and everybody joined in – electricians, dressers. Bill Bryden, who directed it, is a remarkable director: if you are in a rehearsal room you are involved. If a stage hand says to him, 'Why don't you try it like this?', he will, and if it works he'll acknowledge them and thank them. You get used to sitting there as a stage manager, and not saying anything, but when you are working with such a director you feel important to the creative process.

Stage managers can contribute to the creative process.

(See pp.350–351 for more about stage management at the Royal National Theatre.)

The responsibilities of the stage management team

Stage management is a most responsible and diverse job, involving management techniques, technical expertise and a commitment to detail.

Large companies, amateurs and youth theatres may be able to use a stage manager earlier in the production process than smaller professional touring companies with tight budgets. In such a case, the stage manager will liaise with the designer on what is feasible in the theatre space and what is not. For example, he or she may know the view (the sight lines) obtained by the audience at the edges of the auditorium very well, and so might advise on how much masking scenery may be needed in front of the wings.

Rehearsals

Stage managers can be involved from an early stage.

The stage manager may set up the rehearsal room, marking out the stage dimensions and set on the floor with masking tape and placing furniture in a roughly accurate plan of the set, so that the performers and director can gain a feel for the stage.

The book

Keeping a book is a principal responsibility.

The 'book' is the accurate playing text of the production, including all stage business and the cues for the lighting, sound and other effects. It normally consists of a loose-leaf folder, with the text pasted on one side of a sheet of paper and a blank page for notes on the facing page. It is normally kept and updated by the stage manager. It is likely that the director will change elements of the production during rehearsals, so the book is usually completed in pencil. It is also necessary to work in a form of shorthand when entering the many notes needed in the book. There is an accepted shorthand for many stage terms. For example:

- SFX – sound effect
- LFX – lighting effect
- DS – downstage (from the actor's point of view)
- US – upstage
- SL – stage left
- SR – stage right

Preparing equipment

As Keith Orton mentions on p.281, the stage manager may spend time obtaining props, perhaps liaising with the designer to ensure that each prop is exactly what he or she had intended. The stage manager will also organise the hire of specialist equipment and obtain other essentials during the rehearsal period.

The stage manager will supervise the 'get-in' – the assembly of set, lights and other equipment on the stage prior to the technical and dress rehearsals. During this time, he or she will check the safety of all equipment and scenery, and ensure that no damage is done to the theatre or the equipment.

Dressing the set

Once the set is in place, the stage manager will often need to 'dress' it. This means placing and plotting all the items that are needed on stage at the start of the performance. It may need to be re-dressed for subsequent scenes, or during an interval. Some items must be prepared for the performers to use: bottles might have to be filled with coloured liquid to represent alcohol, a ringing telephone may have to be checked, and money may need to be placed in a drawer or a newspaper on a table.

Fire safety

The stage manager will probably have to conduct fire officers round the building, and so will have to be satisfied that the fire precautions meet the regulation standards. All scenery fabric must be treated with fire-retardant solution, for example. He or she must be familiar with this and with all other fire regulations for both the stage and the auditorium: the size of gangways, the audience capacity and, most importantly, the operation of illuminated fire exit signs. (See pp.366–371 for additional information.)

Props

The stage manager will maintain strict discipline over the use of personal props, which can easily be mislaid unless there is a system for their use. Commonly, a props table is prepared. Each prop to be carried on stage is placed on a labelled spot on a table next to the appropriate entrance onto the stage.

Scene changes

The stage manager will normally ensure that a team is ready to change scenery if necessary between or during scenes. A scene change must be carefully rehearsed so that:

● it takes the shortest possible time;
● it is safely carried out;
● everyone knows their role in the scene change;
● everything is placed accurately.

Technical rehearsals

The stage manager will run the technical rehearsals, or 'techs'. The technical effects, scenery changes, LFX, SFX and sometimes the positioning of props will be rehearsed, at first without the performers but with the director. Working systematically through the text, each cue will be rehearsed, starting with the signals and announcement for the audience to take its seats. Each effect will be considered for impact: is an SFX long and loud enough, is an LFX bright enough, is a scene change too long? When all the details have been fixed, they may be rehearsed with performers in a 'walk through'. The full text is not acted, but all the technical cues are run with performers in place. The stage manager takes charge of all these processes. (See pp.148–149 for further details on technical and dress rehearsals.)

Performance discipline
Finally, the stage manager is the manager of the show in performance. He or she takes ultimate responsibility for the discipline of performance and ensures that the performance runs exactly as it was rehearsed.

Resource Activities

1. CONSIDERING A STAGE DESIGN

Aim
To understand the idea of a design concept.

Objective
To create and present to others an initial design conception, with sketches and visual references, for a production of a classic text.

Background
The texts of Elizabethan and Jacobean plays make almost no reference to staging and scenery, and there is no evidence to suggest that elaborate scenery was created for productions at that time. In the 20th century, this has allowed designers and directors to conceive new productions of these classic texts with imaginative visual impact. The plays of Shakespeare, Marlowe, Ford and Webster have therefore been set in a range of locations, and in periods of time other than their own. There have been modern-dress and Victorian productions of these plays, and they have been transported to such places as India and Russia. Clearly, for a production to have integrity, its visual conception and design should be in tune with the themes of the play, the treatment offered by the director, and/or the play's significance in the modern world. Directors and designers are criticised when they offer design concepts of a classic play merely as a gimmick.

● You have been asked to design a production of John Webster's play *The Duchess of Malfi* (c.1614). The play is a revenge tragedy about jealousy, obsession and cruelty, and some of its most famous scenes – such as when the Duchess grasps and kisses a severed dead man's hand – were probably written for the newly designed and torchlit Blackfriars theatre. If this text is not available to you, use another text by one of the playwrights mentioned above.

● Read pp.278–286 about stage design.

Tasks
For this task, you will need to work closely with a director, or with your lecturer or teacher in the role of the director. Make yourself familiar with the text and read a supporting commentary about the play, possibly from one of the scholarly editions. Establish and make notes on:
i) when the play was written;
ii) when it was set;
iii) where it was set;
iv) when and where scenes take place.

● Discuss the themes of the play with your 'director', and establish what visual ideas and treatment he or she has in mind.

- Start researching for visual inspiration and sketching, as suggested on pp.283–284.

- Once you have spent a while collecting material and creating draft design ideas, go back to your director and present them, in order to get some feedback. In your presentation try to cover:
  i) how the set will be used by the actors;
  ii) how the design conception matches the treatment planned by the director;
  iii) how the set might be moved and adapted in different acts;
  iv) the architecture, style or fashion which influenced your choice.

  (For assistance with presentation skills, see Chapter 1, pp.20–22.)

2. EXPERIMENTING WITH DESIGN

Aim
To provide an opportunity for thinking about the elements of a design.

Objective
To create an initial design conception for the play you select, using set and lighting design materials.

Background
This task will involve you in considering the elements of design: space, levels, shape, proportion, light and line, texture, colour and tone.

You will need:

- some small modelling bricks;
- some torches or little spotlights, such as anglepoise lamps;
- some little cardboard figures about 7cm high;
- some scraps of material, especially black, and string or thread;
- if possible, little pieces of balsa wood and some paint colour sample cards from hardware shops.

Tasks
- First, select a play or story to design for. It should have an abstract setting, rather than a realistic room setting. Shakespeare's plays are ideal for this. Alternatively, do this task for a production based on the legends of King Arthur.

- List the locations needed in the production: for example, Camelot, the lake at Avalon, the sword in the stone at Westminster.

- Use the bricks to represent the stage shapes. (You could use full-sized rostra in a large space to experiment with settings for the production.) Consider:
  i) exits and entrances;
  ii) levels and staircases;
  iii) height, depth and width;
  iv) proportion.

- What do the performers (represented by the little figures) look like in relation to the design? (For example, columns and wide staircases can create an atmosphere of grandeur.) Make notes on your findings and sketches.

- Now darken the room and experiment with lighting effects using the anglepoise lamps or torches. How does the angle from which the light is coming change the feel of the scene? Make notes on your findings and sketches.

- Hang some of the material at the back of the 'stage' as a backdrop or cyclorama, or spread it across the floor. What signals about the setting are given by different types of texture? What do rough, smooth, silky or velvety textures denote? How could they be moved around on stage to change the atmosphere? Make notes on your findings and sketches.

- Choose some groups of colours from the colour cards or the material as the colour scheme for the production. Consider how we associate colours with certain moods, and the contrasts that might be used to suit comic, tragic, sinister or climactic scenes. Make notes on your findings and sketches.

3. MAKING A MODEL BOX

Aim
To understand the importance of creating a scale model box.

Objective
To complete a robust and re-usable model box of the principal performance space used.

Background
You will need a number of items usually obtained from an artist's supplier: thick black card, kappa board, masking tape, and a ruler or scale ruler, which specialist suppliers sell for architectural and other design work (this makes the job of creating a 1:25 scale plan very easy, since the scale is marked on one edge of the ruler). Balsa wood is easy to cut and also fairly light and strong: in particular, you will need long square sectioning to strengthen the model. You will find it helpful to use a long tape measure, such as the ones used on athletics fields, to measure the dimensions of your stage. Among the ordinary materials you will need are pencils, drawing instruments such as a protractor and set square, A3 or A2 plain paper, black paint, erasers and glue.

Read pp.283–290 for details.

Tasks
- Start by taking the measurements of the floor area of your stage, including the backstage area, in order to make a scale plan (i.e. a bird's-eye view of it). If it is a proscenium shape, you may later

find it useful to record the position of the front row of seating. If it is a thrust stage or a theatre-in-the-round, you will probably need to include all or part of the seating area in your measurements, because there are entries onto the stage through the audience.

● Record all these dimensions on a rough piece of paper first, and then make an exact scale copy using the 1:25 ratio. Show all the architectural features, including pillars, the exact width of doors, whether they open outwards or inwards, and any steps or different levels. Dimensions such as the width of the doors backstage may become critical when it comes to getting the set onto the stage.

● You will then need to sketch an elevation, or worm's-eye, view of the stage from downstage, making an accurate record of the height of door openings and walls and the height under the lighting bars. Once again, dimensions such as these could be critical for moving high scenery.

● Once you have the accurate dimensions, you can begin to make a model box. Start by cutting out a base board from strong material such as plywood or kappa board, which will not bend when you lift the eventual box with a set on it. Draw the plan on it, but ensure the board is a few centimetres larger. Often, model stages are made as neutral black boxes, so you could either cover it with black card or paint it for a matt black finish.

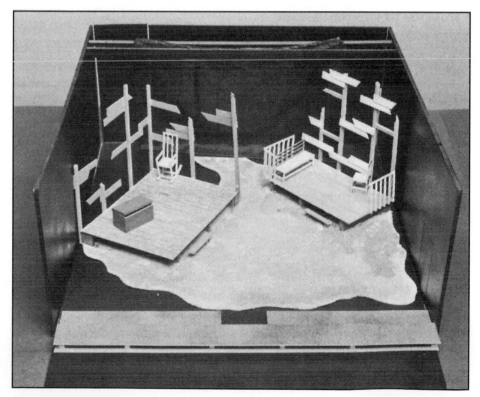

A typical model box

- Next, cut out and fit the walls, working from your elevation diagram. They can be fitted using masking tape and/or glue, and, importantly, should be strengthened using balsa wood sectioning on the rear side. This is why the floor board should be larger than the stage area. If right-angled joints are strengthened with balsa wood whenever possible, the model box will be more robust, and therefore can be used for longer. Cut out and fold the doors from the card, ensuring that they open in the right direction.

- The finished article should be strong, accurate, painted in a neutral colour, and of course recognisable as your stage!

4. SETTING THE STAGE

Aim
To experience the process of setting the stage and dressing the set.

Objective
To create setting documents and plans and to select visually appropriate props.

Background
- Mustapha Matura's play *The Playboy of the West Indies* is a reworking of J.M. Synge's earlier play *The Playboy of the Western World*. Both plays are set in isolated rural communities – Synge's in Mayo, Ireland, Matura's in eastern Trinidad. The plot concerns the arrival of a stranger who claims he has killed his father, but the play concentrates on the fascination he exerts over the rural community and the amoral reaction of the people, who take the stranger for a hero and clearly find him very attractive.
- The highly distinctive local dialect used in both plays implies that the set and props should look visually authentic.
- See p.300 for an example of a setting document, and Activity 3 for instructions for making a stage plan.

Tasks
- Using the extracts from the Matura play printed here, prepare a setting document, noting the positions of the scenery, furniture and props which are to be placed on stage at the start. Mark these on a plan of your own stage. Use this stage direction:

August 1950. A fishing village in Mayaro on the east coast of Trinidad – a rum shop. Evening. A counter. Tables. Chairs. Bags of rice stacked on one side. A door leading to room inside. Large, main, propped up window. Shelves of bottles on wall behind counter.

Further clues about what props are needed are scattered throughout the text, as these short extracts show:

PEGGY: *You sit down dey an cut yer bread an cheese and play sleepy . . .*

MIKEY: *Peggy, a bottle a White Label an . . . Stanley, yer firing [drinking]?*

310

STANLEY: *No tanks Mikey, Saterday fer me.*

MIKEY: *Tree glasses then . . .*

STANLEY: *Look, a new flannel shirt! Brand new! Take it. See if it fit!*

● Next, conduct some visual research to find out what sort of bottles and labels will look authentic. What fabric should be used for the rice bags? A character sleeps on them. What should they look like? What style should the chairs be? What items might be placed behind the counter? You will need to find pictures of this part of the world in about the 1950s.

● Finally, obtain a copy of the whole play, or the original version by Synge, and read an act, scanning the indications in the text of personal props used by characters or those which clearly dress the set. Mark them on the plan and list them. You will end up with the sort of setting document which stage managers use to prepare the stage for performance.

5. MAKING A LIGHTING PLAN

Aim
To experiment with lighting design.

Objective
To create an experimental lighting scale plan for your own theatre space, for selected scenes from *Our Country's Good* by Timberlake Wertenbaker.

Background
● *Our Country's Good* is a play about the theatre itself. It is based on a true account, and set in 1788, when an early group of convicts arrive in Australia to serve their sentences. Despite the brutal regime of punishment, the convicts gain much dignity when an enlightened officer decides to direct them in a production of *The Recruiting Officer*. A strong theme is that art can have a civilising effect.

● A production of the play is being staged in your theatre space. The director wishes to stage the exterior scenes, near the shore of Botany Bay, downstage, and the interior scenes upstage at a higher level. There are scenes in semi-darkness in the hold of the convict ship, a dream sequence when an aborigine describes the arrival of the convict ship and interior scenes at night in officers' tents. Finally, there are scenes on the shoreline.

● You will need paper, at least A3 size, a pencil, rulers and drawing instruments, and access to your theatre and its lighting control room.
● Read pp.290–297 on lighting design.

Tasks
You are asked to draw a lighting plan to discuss with the director, using about 30 lanterns in a smallish thrust-shaped stage.

- If possible, start by reading the play, or reading about it, in order to familiarise yourself with the themes.

- Draw a plan showing the lighting facilities in your own theatre, to the standard scale for theatre design: first make an accurate plan of the dimensions of the playing area (see pp.288–289), then draw in the exact positions of the lighting bars (and booms, if you have vertically fixed lighting).

- Using the tallescope, find out the circuit number of each of the sockets on the bars, which should be displayed on the sockets. Plot these numbers on the plan.

- Now start to plot the lighting, using the standard symbols for the types of lanterns you are using (see pp.291–294). Remember that fan setting the playing area is the first job (see p.295). Record the power of the lamps you are using. Use dotted lines to plot the angles of the lanterns if this is not clear.

- Consider what coloured gels you might use for the scenes mentioned above. Do you have spare lanterns after fan setting and could they be used for any special effects? What accessories might be needed: for example, gobos, barndoors or irises (which allow you to limit the circumference of a spotlight)?

- Attach notes to the plan with any an extra information about your ideas. Remember to include the legend (see p.293). When the plan is complete and accurate, you will be able to discuss it with other people in the context of the play.

6. EXPERIMENTING WITH LIGHTING SPECIALS

Aim
To experiment with the atmospheric special effects of lighting.

Objective
To create and note the effects of light projected from various angles and with various gels and lighting intensities.

Background
- Read pp.290–297 on lighting design.
- Select three pieces of scenery or large pieces of furniture on the basis of their shape and the visual interest they attract; for example, a park bench, a large cane chair, a scenic column, a tree, a scenery flat with a door or window in it. At least one of the objects should be tall, and they should be well spaced out on your stage.
- You will also need three or four lanterns, a tallescope and a range of gels. Ensure that you have all the safety equipment described on p.297 before you begin.

Tasks
- Use the lanterns to project onto the objects from a range of angles, and light them using different-coloured gels.

- Experiment with the sliders on your control board to achieve different intensities of light, but ensure that the audience is always able to pick out the objects.

- As you progress, note the mood and other information suggested by the lighting effect you have created, and record and sketch how you achieved the effect.

- Finally, light the objects so that they convey something of the following stage directions:
  i) a hot, still summer's day;
  ii) a clear, cold, moonlit night;
  iii) an uneasy menacing atmosphere;
  iv) evening – the sun is close to setting;
  v) light streaming into a dingy room from an open door or window.

- Make notes and sketches on your findings, recording them for future reference. This exercise should have demonstrated that planning a design on paper can be done much more effectively once you have hands-on experience of manipulating lanterns and seeing the effects they create.

7. WORKING WITH A RUNNING DOCUMENT

Aim
To learn about the process of creating running documents and running a technical rehearsal.

Objective
To create a running document and to walk it through in a mock tech.

Background
Read pp.297–305 on the role of stage management, and see in particular the sample running document on p.301.

You will eventually need to work in the performance space, using some lighting, a keyboard with some sound effects facilities and a tape recorder with some rock-and-roll music on cassette. A video camera and screen would be useful.

Bob Carlton's spoof musical *Return to the Forbidden Planet* is derived from 1950s science fiction films and the plot of Shakespeare's *The Tempest*. It was staged successfully in the West End of London and in Liverpool, and has been on tour. The following is an extract from the start of the musical. We have omitted a small section of dialogue which does not require any effects.

As the audience enter the theatre, pre-recorded 1950s rock-and-roll music plays over the ship's audio system. When front-of-house clearance is given, Captain Tempest brings the crew to their launch positions, i.e. they all go onto the stage and pick up their instruments. He then motions to the control desk and the front-of-house music fades.

CAPTAIN TEMPEST: Friends, crewmen, passengers, lend me your ears. I, Captain Tempest, welcome you aboard this routine survey flight. We hope you have a very pleasant trip. But any questions that should come to mind, just ask our Science Officer.

SCIENCE OFFICER: That's me.

CAPTAIN TEMPEST: Bosun?

BOSUN ARRAS: Yes, sir.

CAPTAIN TEMPEST: Commence the pre-flight checks.

BOSUN ARRAS: Check matrix.

Synthesiser effect.

NAVIGATION OFFICER: Check.

BOSUN ARRAS: Check all the photon shields.

Another synthesiser effect.

NAVIGATION OFFICER: Check.

BOSUN ARRAS: Check the Dilithian Crystal rods.

Synthesiser effect.

NAVIGATION OFFICER: Check.

BOSUN ARRAS: Check the gravitational resistors.

Synthesiser effect.

NAVIGATION OFFICER: Check.

BOSUN ARRAS: And now check all the audio-visual screens.

Blackout and the on-stage TV monitors come on.

NEWSREADER: *(on video screen):*

Two parents, both alike in dignity,
In outer space, where we our play locate,
From ancient grudge break to new mutiny
And on Forbidden Planet meet their fate.
From forth the fatal loins of these two foes
A lovely star-borne daughter takes her life,
Whose teenage crush and adolescent woes
Do drive her father mad and end his life.
The fearful passage of his death-marked love
And the continuance of her mother's rage,
Which, but a monstrous end, naught could remove,
Is now the two hours' traffic of our stage,
The which, if you with patient ears attend,
What here shall miss, our toil shall strive to mend.

The video screen goes off.

BOSUN ARRAS: We have completed all the pre-flight checks.

NAVIGATION OFFICER: 10, 9, 8, 7, 6, 5, 4, 3, 2, 1, 0. Ignition. We have lift off.

The drummer begins the drum solo opening of Wipeout *by the Surfaris and as the guitars and synthesiser join him the lights come up, giving the effect of the ship in action, and on the video screens we see the ship lift off from Earth and then its flight through the stars. The band continue to play* Wipeout, *but increasingly on each drum break we get the impression that the ship is becoming more unstable – much 'Star Trek' running from side to side and red lights*

flashing. Eventually the NAVIGATION OFFICER speaks although
Wipeout continues to play under the dialogue.

NAVIGATION OFFICER: Our sensors sir are picking up a storm
Of asteroids approaching very fast.
Evasive action should be taken now,
Or else we'll hit them.

CREW: Look out!

CAPTAIN TEMPEST: Holy cow!

Wipeout segue into – Great Balls of Fire *by Jerry Lee Lewis.*

SCIENCE OFFICER (*sings*): They shake my nerves and they rattle my
brain!

CAPTAIN TEMPEST (*sings*): These asteroids can drive a man insane!

NAVIGATION OFFICER (*sings*): They've broke the wheel.

SCIENCE OFFICER (*sings*): We'll all be killed!

ALL (*sing*): Goodness gracious great balls of fire!

The number continues as an instrumental under the following dialogue which is
spoken.

CAPTAIN TEMPEST: Bosun.

BOSUN ARRAS: Here master. What cheer?

CAPTAIN TEMPEST: Fall to it smartly, put up the photon shields, or
else our cause is lost. Bestir, Bestir!

CREW (*sings*): Goodness Gracious, Great Balls of Fire!

BOSUN ARRAS (*spoken*): Hey my hearts,
Cheerly cheerly my hearts,
Quick, quick, put up the force field –
Tend to the Captain's orders!

SCIENCE OFFICER: Good Captain have a care, let's use the Shuttle-
craft. Play the man.

CAPTAIN TEMPEST: I pray you keep below.

She doesn't move.

BOSUN ARRAS: Do you not hear him? You mar our labour. Keep your
cabin. You do assist the storm!

SCIENCE OFFICER (*sings*): I chew my nails and I twiddle my thumbs.
I'm really nervous and it ain't no fun.
Come on baby, I'm going crazy!

ALL (*sing*): Goodness gracious great balls of fire!

There is an explosion. The crew fall over. Silence. Then strange eerie music is heard:
synthesiser effect as a tractor beam hits the space ship and all becomes calm. On the
video screen we see a gradual descent from space to the surface of a planet . . .

Tasks

● Annotate this text as described on p.303, using shorthand and/or
symbols for lighting, sound and music effects. You will also need to
number them as cues. You may decide that extra effects, in addition
to the ones referred to in the text, are needed, and these must be
marked too.

● Once you have a running document which can be understood by
others, work as a small group to run through the effects on stage. Use

315

a few lanterns for the lighting, a tape recorder (clearly it will be ideal if you can obtain the actual music referred to), a keyboard for the electrical sound effects and a video screen. Assign each group member a role, i.e. lighting, sound, music, stage manager; it is useful to experience all the roles by rotating them in each run-through.

● Once you have practised this short stage management exercise, you may like to look at the whole musical, which not only has a unique mix of 1950s rock lyrics and adapted Shakespearean verse, but also contains a vast range of technical requirements.

8. DESIGNING FOR AN OPEN STAGE

Aim
To address the problems posed by designing for a multiple-location play.

Objective
To create a design in which the scenery can suggest a number of locations and can be moved between scenes.

Background
● Peter Flannery's play *Singer* has been described as an epic, charting the fortunes of Peter Singer from prisoner in a Nazi concentration camp to slum landlord in London to campaigner for the homeless. It poses particular problems for a designer. A realistic box set would not be feasible for this sweeping tale, whose action begins in Auschwitz and moves to Southampton docks, London streets, offices, painting studios and even 10 Downing Street.

● Read pp.278–290 on the role of the designer, and in particular pp.286–290 on materials.

● For guidance on making scenery, see the bibliography on p.317.

Tasks
● Obtain a copy of the play, or a similar play which has a spread of locations. Begin by charting the sequence of locations scene by scene.

● Consider what sort of materials and design might allow the scenery to be changed smoothly and quickly. Clearly, a full set would not have sufficient flexibility to work, so consider what simple scenery might suggest each location. In particular, this could be an opportunity to experiment with materials. Scenery flats, moveable trucks on wheels, gobos and rostra might be used, and you might also try to manipulate certain materials, such as paint on canvas or plastic padding to simulate brickwork or plaster (see p.286). It will be most important for you to use models to try out the moving of scenery between scenes, so this will be an opportunity to use a model box.

● Once you feel you have a flexible design solution, you might experiment with the materials chosen, for example by making a small scenic flat to paint on, or using a small piece of hardboard to create brickwork, plaster or wood effects.

ANNOTATED BIBLIOGRAPHY

This bibliography includes volumes relevant to this chapter which are considered suitable for student reference. See also the general bibliography on p.380.

Bond, D., *Stage Management: A Gentle Art*, A & C Black, 1991
> The most important book on stage management. It works at a professional level, yet is accessible.

Griffiths D., *Backstagers – A Teacher's Guide to Practical Backstage Skills*, Collins, 1996
> A wide-ranging book in ring-binder format, for schools and colleges.

Hoggett C., *Stage Crafts*, A & C Black, 1979
> The classic technical 'how to do it' text.

Holt M., *Stage Design and Properties*, Phaidon, 1988
> A very well-designed and informative book.

Kimber, K. and Wood, D., *Stages in Design: Assignments for the Performing Arts*, Hodder & Stoughton, 1994
> An excellent book for practical design activities.

Reid F., *Stage Lighting*, Focal Press, 1993
> A good contemporary book, with activities to try.

Reid F., *Designing for the Theatre*, A & C Black, 1989
> An informative book on principles and practice.

Reid F., *The Staging Handbook*, A & C Black, 1978
> A wide-ranging technical book.

9 Masks

Aurora Simpson and Vishni Velada Billson

The mask is a traditional theatre symbol

This chapter describes a diversity of masks and masking practice. It is divided up into the following sections:

- World masks
- Perceptions of the mask today
- Practical mask making

It is important to recognise that we have used certain masking practices as examples; clearly, this has led to the exclusion of many others. The list of further reading provided (on p.346) will extend your knowledge and understanding.

WORLD MASKS

'Mask' can be defined in various ways.

Mask (i) *covering, usu. of velvet or silk, for concealing face at balls etc., or of wire, gauze, etc., for protection e.g. of fencer, or worn by surgeon to prevent infection of patient, etc., or of any material as disguise or for grotesque appearance to amuse or terrify; respirator used to filter inhaled air or to supply gas for inhalation; hollow figure of human head worn by ancient Greek and Roman actors; likeness of person's face esp. one made by taking mould from face; disguise; masked person; screen used to exclude part of image . . .*

Mask (ii) *1. cover with mask; be disguised with mask. 2. Conceal from enemy's view, hinder from action by observing with adequate force, hinder by standing in its line of fire. 3. Disguise, conceal; protect from some process. 4. –ed ball.* (The Concise Oxford Dictionary of Current English, 1988)

Mask; blind, camouflage, cloak, concealment, cover, cover-up, disguise, domino, facade, false face, front, guise, pretence, screen, semblance, show, veil, veneer, visard-mask, visor, vizard.
(*Chambers Thesaurus*)

These dictionary definitions and thesaurus entries give a sense of the extensive use of masks. Forms of mask have been used for some 15,000 years, all over the world. The origins of masking are found deeply embedded in early ritual, and its function is as diverse as the masks themselves. Masks are used:

Masks have different uses.

- in a wide variety of theatre, dance and opera performances;
- at ceremonies;
- during initiation rites;
- at carnivals, festivals or parties;
- for protection;
- for disguise;
- as works of art in themselves.

In order to illustrate the diversity of the mask and its many uses and functions, there follows an account of masks from across the world and the theatrical or ritualistic context in which they were used. Clearly, the account given here can include only aspects of the lengthy and complex history of masking.

The mask in Asia

We begin with Japan, which has a rich history of masking:

The masks of Noh are generally neutral in expression, and it is the skill of the actor which brings the mask to life through subtle changes in his physical attitude. The art of the mask carver lies in creating an inanimate object which can be imbued with life. The masks themselves are small and only cover the front of the face, with small eyeholes. After donning his sumptuous costume the actor seats himself before a mirror and studies the mask, becoming one with the character he is about to perform. (Mack, *Masks: The Art of Expression*, p.145)

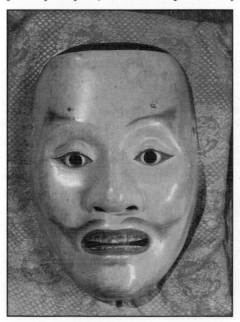

A Noh Theatre mask representing a Samurai

During the 11th century, Japan had two different theatre styles; Dengaku and Sarugaku. These eventually merged and became known as Noh Theatre. Still an art form in Japan, it is one of the oldest of the performing arts. Around 100 varieties of mask are used in this theatre, symbolising virtues such as honesty, nobility and weakness and representing

Noh Theatre is the oldest performing art form.

people, gods, demons and animals. The painting of these masks is significant: each colour represents a character type. For example, white symbolises a corrupt ruler, a red mask depicts righteousness and a black mask denotes a violent villain. In the sixth century, these masks were usually made of wood or cloth, and the actors bit on a strip of leather attached to the inside of the mask to hold it in place.

Whilst the Japanese mask is the most famous, there is a strong masking tradition across Asia. In China, the mask has been significant in rites and theatre since the time of the Chou dynasty (1122–221BC), when bronze masks were used in both secular and religious drama. Masks have also been used by witch doctors as part of their costume and in rituals. Chinese children would wear measle masks when appropriate, in order to frighten away demons who they believed brought this disease. For several centuries, from the 9th to the 15th century AD, death masks were made from gold or copper, and features were soldered on. These masks were then painted and covered with turquoise beads. The amount of gold used on the mask determined the status of the deceased.

For thousands of years, healing ceremonies commonly known as Shamanism have taken place throughout India, Ceylon, Java and Tibet. The ceremony includes the use of a set of ten masks, each representing a different disease; it takes the form of a dance or theatrical performance, consisting of a series of rituals which remove and capture the evil spirit causing illness to the patient. The illness is 'absorbed' into the mask of the devil dancer who exorcises the spirit. Versions of this ceremony still exist today all over the world.

The mask in Africa

The head was regarded as sacred by the Egyptians.

As in Asia, there are many examples of masking in Africa. The ancient Egyptians used mummy masks, which they believed aided a safe journey from death to the afterlife. (The earliest of these is thought to have existed

during the 21st century BC.) The head was regarded by the Egyptians as holding a person's soul; the death mask became a physical representation of this belief. Because the head was masked, the soul would be protected, and resurrection on a higher plane was ensured. Also, the mask preserved the personality of the deceased: these death masks became a record of appearance, like a portrait or photograph.

Tutankhamun's death mask, which was made of solid gold

320

Our desire [outwardly to preserve our soul] is a natural one for we subconsciously believe that personalities and emotions, while kept in memory, continue to live for us.
(The Royal Ontario Museum, *Masks: The Many Faces of Man*, an exhibition presented by the division of art and archaeology, 1959, Foreword)

Egyptian masking was not only connected with death. Religious masked dramas were performed at temples during festivals, and magicians used masks in rituals to cure the ill; these were made of linen, wood or plaster, and painted or gilded.

There are similarities between the Egyptian mummy masks and the gold death masks found in Ghana. The latter date back to the 18th century BC and are thought to have belonged to the Ashanti kings.

The earliest recorded African rock paintings were found in the mountains of Tassali in the Hoggar (Sahara) region and provide evidence of prehistoric masked ritual. The ancient Bushman rock paintings of South Africa show people wearing animal skins and heads whilst hunting. These are similar to early European paintings, which also show the mask being used as a disguise when hunting prey. Anthropologists suggest that these paintings show that the mask clearly originated in the human need for disguise in order to hunt successfully. However, an alternative view suggests that these masks were more than a mere disguise; rather, they also served to placate the hunted prey's spirit. The animal's role in the hunt was simulated by the villagers in a subsequent celebratory ritual, where the celebrants would 'wear' the animal.

Africa is cited as the continent of masking tradition.

A mask from Zaire

In Zambia, masks are often worn by the elders of a tribe or village during initiation ceremonies, in which young boys of seven or eight are circumcised. In these initiation ceremonies, the youth, too, wears a mask, representing a ghost of a past life. He physically casts aside the mask to symbolise the death of childhood. After the ceremony, he receives a miniature ivory mask to wear on his wrist or neck for good luck.

Africa is often hailed as the centre of mask-making traditions, and its masks are of several distinct and diverse types. These have influenced many societies across the centuries. For example,

321

African 'cubist' and distorted masks are important in the work of French artists such as Pablo Picasso and Henri Matisse. On the whole, it seems that African masks have a deep symbolic significance and are never used *purely* to entertain, as in some Western societies:

Masking performances can without discrepancy be both serious ritual and captivating entertainment.
(Mack, *Masks: The Art of Expression*, p.35)

A Nigerian mask used in masquerades of men's society

The mask in America

. . . something of the meaning behind the mask and the ritual mask-dances [of North America] may be conveyed by the following transcription of some chants recited at mask festivals:
'Wa! Everybody shakes with terror before the winter-mask of the man-eater-spirit-in-the-north!
'Wa! Everybody shakes with terror before the man-eater-mask-of-the raven!
'His hooked-beak-mask makes the heart beat faster!
'His bird's-head-mask makes the head beat faster!'
(Lommel, *Masks: Their Meaning and Function*, p.141)

A dual mask from North America

Masks are widespread throughout North America, and can generally be divided into two distinct types: the mask used to depict a 'spirit' and the mask used to represent an animal. A significant area for masks is the north-west coast of North America, where masks are carved from wood and painted with bright colours. They are commonly known as dual masks, and are in effect two masks, one behind the other. For example, as in the photographs here, the outside mask may depict an animal or bird, such as a raven; with the pull of a string this splits open to reveal a human mask, or vice versa.

As in other continents, the American mask was highly symbolic.

In the east and south-west regions of the United States lies the land of Iroquois. In around 400AD, masks from this region were made of plaited maize straw or painted carved wood, with hugely distorted features. The masks were used for the exorcism of demon spirits and to heal the sick. The maskers would don masks representing 'sickness demons', who would transform into healers and remove the sickness. Certain North American tribes would carve their masks from living trees: the mask would be carved into the tree and separated once a ritual had been performed. In around 1000AD the Zuni tribe would create their 'war god' mask only from a tree which had been struck by lightning, either because they believed the wood of the tree absorbed the power of the lightning and was therefore magical, or because the war god had specifically chosen this tree above all others, and thus the bark became sacred.

The Navaho tribe living in the southern part of North America in around 900–1200AD used masks during religious ceremonies to represent the gods. Certain 'god' masks were to remain completely silent throughout the ceremony, except to recite holy chants. If the masker were to speak, it was widely believed that he or she would become instantly blind, or become sick and die soon after.

In the Andes, during the fifth century BC, masks were made from dyed red or brown cloth. These are thought to have been put over the faces of the dead during funeral services. In northern Peru, some small grey masks dating from around 1200–1500AD have been discovered; these are thought to have represented animals, and were probably used during religious, initiation and burial ceremonies.

Pieces of ceramic masks discovered in the western Mexican states are believed to have represented the different gods. Some Mexican masks

An Aztec jade mosaic mask from Mexico

were decorated with jade, as in the photograph. Another type of Mexican mask is flattened, with minimal features, and made from stone. These masks were in the main used for funeral services, for the impersonation of deities, as trophies, as warriors' headdresses and for entertainment.

Clearly, the masks used throughout North and South American culture have had great significance. They were generally believed to have supernatural and curative powers.

The mask in Europe

In Europe, ancient cave paintings depict images of masked dancers and of hunting scenes dating back to around 30,000BC (see also p.321). Masks made the transition from early ritual to theatre during the ancient Greek civilisation.

The mask in Greek theatre

In ancient Greece, masks had a dual function. They were used both as physical protection during battle and for theatre performance.

During the seventh century BC, the Greeks established a large trained army, whose soldiers wore helmets and protective masks. These masks were usually made of bronze metal and covered most of the face. The Corinthian type was considered the most effective, having an additional long nose piece which gave extra protection.

The origins of Greek theatre are interwoven with religious ritual and festival. During early ritualistic ceremonies, a form of choral worship known as the *dithyramb* took place in honour of the god Dionysus. This ritual became the basis for Greek tragedy. As it developed, the *dithyramb* widened to embrace other gods and heroes, reflecting their stories in the form of choral song and speech. This opened up the possibility of more complex modes of storytelling, shifting the emphasis from religious worship, with a congregation, to theatre as an art form, watched by an audience.

Thespis became the figurehead of this natural transition. He challenged the traditional concept of the *dithyramb* by introducing dialogue between an actor and the chorus. Despite this significant change, however, the performances still maintained a religious and moral content.

The ancient Greeks were the first Europeans to use masks specifically for performance. Traditionally, these masks were large, with stylistic features, and covered the whole face. Early Greek masks basically fell into two categories, tragic and comic, as seen now in the classic and universal symbol for theatre. In time, these masks became more diverse; it has been suggested that there were approximately 30 different types. They were made mainly of natural materials such as cork, light wood and linen.

Greek theatres were vast (Epidauros seats around 2,000 people), so the characters had to be instantly recognisable from a substantial distance. Thus the masks were made with highly exaggerated features, which served the important functions of distinguishing status, age, sex and emotion. Men dominated theatre throughout this period: 'female' masks were worn by the all-male casts. The masks also enabled one actor to play several parts; this was particularly important in traditional Greek tragedy, where all the parts were played by one, two or three main actors (excluding the chorus). A further function of the mask was to unify the

A Greek comic theatre mask

chorus; this is clearly illustrated in the plays of Aristophanes, such as *The Frogs* and *The Birds*, where the actors/chorus took on the role of a group of animals.

Ancient Greek theatre masks covered the entire face, leaving a large opening for the mouth. There are two main theories for this. It has been suggested that the shape of the mouthpiece helped to project the actor's voice. Other historians believe that this was not in fact necessary, because of the excellent theatre acoustics, and that the exaggerated mouth was intended simply to determine the character's emotion, such as rage or sadness.

Andreas Lommel states in his book:

. . . the Latin word 'personare' means to sound through, referring to the voice of the actor 'sounding through' the mask. The 'person' or 'persona' is the mask itself, which represents something; it is not the real human being, the actor behind the mask.
(Lommel, *Masks: Their Meaning and Function*, p.198)

This suggestion of the mask having its own identity or persona has influenced theatre over two millenia. The Greek word for an actor was *hupocrites*; the word 'hypocrite' clearly has its origin here. All ancient Greek actors wore masks and were therefore literally 'two-faced': the face of the actor and the face of the mask character.

For further information on Greek theatre, see pp.26–27.

The mask in Roman theatre
Almost all Roman theatre was based on that of the ancient Greeks. This included not only the staging, text and characters, but also the costumes and masks. However, Roman amphitheatres, unlike Greek ones, were often also used as circus arenas. Within this space, vicious combats occurred, involving humans or animals or, at times, both. The barbaric displays eventually became entangled with theatrical performances.

Roman amphitheatres were not used exclusively for theatre performance.

Huge amphitheatres, the first of which was built by Julius Caesar in 46BC, were erected throughout the Roman Empire, but their purpose was that of displaying power and control rather than celebrating the arts. The most famous was the Coliseum in Rome, completed in 80AD and capable of seating 80,000.

Although Roman theatre clearly took on many traditionally Greek

325

theatrical devices, it established a different focus as it developed. The Romans were far more concerned with theatre being popular and enjoyable, preferring the Greek comedies and neglecting the tragedies.

There were significant differences in the architecture of Greek and Roman theatres.

Roman theatres were different in construction to those of ancient Greece. They were built on flat ground, encircled by a high stone wall and often ornately decorated. Higher stages were built, and curtains were later introduced; a large canopy was erected to protect the audience from the harsh sunlight. However, these added luxuries failed to retain audiences: theatre became distasteful as the Romans moved away from the Greek comic style and developed a vulgar, bawdy and exaggerated form. The acting became offensive and degrading to both actor and audience.

Plautus and Terence were two of the most widely recognised Roman comic playwrights. They were influenced by the original Greek texts, but incorporated many Roman details. Their works combine the style of Menanda, a Greek dramatist (342–292BC), with that of the *Fabula Atellana*, a form of improvised entertainment. (The *Fabula* is significant because certain of its characters, such as Marcus and Bucco, probably provided the basis for many of the *Commedia dell' Arte* characters of the Middle Ages onwards: see pp.115–116.)

The Romans adopted the Greek tragic masks, but made them of pewter, adding a higher peak over the forehead known as the *onkos*. The few tragedies that were staged were characterised by lavish costumes and set effects and long processions of animals. Theatre was fast becoming an

A relief from Pompeii showing typical Roman theatre masks

elaborate display of meaningless grandeur. This was later acknowledged by the more serious thespians of the time, which led to a new custom of reading tragedies aloud. In fact, Seneca wrote his plays solely to be spoken aloud, rather than acted.

The Romans also used masks in battle; they served as protection and disguise.

Like the Greeks, the Romans also used masks for battle, although some of these masks possessed female features, thought to be an 'amazon' disguise. The Roman gladiators wore masks for some 650 years. These had the dual function of protection and decoration.

The mask in Renaissance theatre

Commedia dell' Arte masks are probably the most famous in European theatre history.

The most significant genre in the history of theatre masks is *Commedia dell' Arte* (otherwise known as the theatre of the professionals) in the late feudal and early Renaissance period (15th–17th century). It is unknown exactly how *Commedia dell' Arte* as an art form was established. There is some debate as to whether it derived from the Greek comedies or the *Fabula Atellana*. There are definite links between all three performance styles in terms of bawdiness, farce and the appearance of 'stock' characters.

Commedia concentrated exclusively on the actor, as opposed to the textual implications of performance; all the actors improvised their own dialogue. They used techniques similar to those of the Romans, such as song and acrobatics; *Commedia* was based on gesture and movement. The innovative and revolutionary influence of this form of theatre is reflected by the first appearance of women as performers. Isabella Andreini, a leading actor in a company called Gelosi, became the first woman to tour with an Italian theatre company. This was despite a ban by Pope Sixtus V in 1558 denying all women throughout the Christian world the right to perform on the stage. However, because of the success and popularity of Andreini and her company, several Italian states lifted this ban.

During this period, theatre became portable.

Performances of *Commedia* were toured throughout Europe: theatres became portable. Simple stages were built on high platforms to enable the audience to see the action from afar. Curtains were used, and served many purposes: to cover the stage edge, to provide a storage space for props, to divide the backstage area from the front, to create a changing area and to form a backdrop. This backdrop was painted with basic street scenes and had several slits which served as exits and entrances. Ladders were erected on either side of the stage, and once actors had performed their scene they would stand on these and watch the play.

There was a lack of great playwrights in *Commedia dell' Arte* during this time, because the primary focus was on the actor and his or her physicalised character: all the plays were based on improvisation, which reached a highly developed level. (See also Chapter 4, pp.115–116.) Although this form represented an exciting and new style of performance, it limited actors to one particular character. However, these were studied in depth, and the actors honed the skills needed to portray the part.

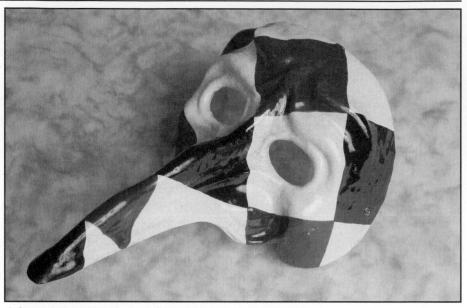

A Commedia dell' Arte *mask (see also the picture on p.116)*

Acting in masks became a recognised art form.

The masks of *Commedia dell' Arte* have their origins within both Greek and Roman comedies. There was a core group of characters, each with his or her own particular and easily recognisable mask. The audience therefore became familiar with the characters, and eagerly watched the different stories unfold. The identification with this familiar set of 'people' made *Commedia dell' Arte* hugely popular; it is possible to draw connections here with modern-day soap operas.

Commedia *masks are always half masks.*

The masks themselves were made of thin leather or straw and were lined with cloth. Unlike the masks of ancient Greece and Rome, they were crafted with delicate expressions and did not show any strong emotions. Features such as the nose were exaggerated, but as the mask covered only half the face it was left to the actor to convey the appropriate emotion. This allowed the acting to take on a different dimension. The actors no longer portrayed a single emotion, but a *character,* with a whole range of expressions and feelings. Whereas during the Greek and Roman periods the actors had literally 'acted out' the story, now the actor had to be responsible for interpreting the character and conveying this to the audience. The actors' movements became integral to this interpretation, and particular gestures were associated with individual characters. The actor had to '*jouer du masque*', that is 'play the mask', and this became an art form in itself, as indicated in this comment by Goldoni in his memoirs:

In those times [Greek and Roman], actors did not interpret the 'nuances' of passion and sentiment that are in vogue at present [16th century] . . . nowadays the actor is required to have 'soul', and the soul beneath the mask is as fire beneath ashes.
(Duchartre, *The Italian Comedy*, pp.46–48)

Commedia masks are the most prominent of the Renaissance period. However, during the early 1600s intricate and beautiful metal masks were crafted to protect hunters' faces from branches; masks were also used for royal and courtly functions such as masked balls, and in the ballet, where they survived until the late 18th century.

Masks and religion

As we have seen, the mask played an important role in the theatre of ancient Greece; in turn, theatre was closely connected with religion. Similarly, the mask was used in the rituals and festivals of the early Christian religion in Europe, connecting Christianity with its religious predecessor, paganism.

Hallowe'en is a traditional festival, which holds strong masking practices.

An example of the mask being used within a religious ritual that has both pagan and Christian characteristics is Hallowe'en. This was originally a Celtic new year festival, which became christianised in the Middle Ages and was retitled the feast of All Saints and All Souls. (Today, Hallowe'en has reclaimed something of its original pagan function, and is still celebrated in Europe and America.) During the Middle Ages, children would go from door to door 'trick-or-treating', wearing masks that portrayed the spirits of their long-dead ancestors, 'all souls'. Giving a 'treat' to the children represented a peace offering to these ancestors, enabling them to return peacefully to the afterlife.

The children's use of masks to represent 'souls' is more or less innocent and harmless. However, there are less innocent associations for the Hallowe'en 'witch' mask and its connection with the Christian religion. The irrational and bigoted persecution of witches until the 18th century is well known; while the stereotypical hag-like toys, puppets and masks bear no resemblance to the human originals, of course, they serve to reinforce the underlying concept of the 'evil witch'.

Witches are often depicted through mask.

The complete 'perversion' of the mask in Europe came with the so-called 'masks of shame'. Women who had been accused of being witches were forced to wear these masks at their trial, so that they already personified the evil of which they were being accused.
(Lommel, *Masks: Their Meaning and Function*, p.200)

Most carnivals use masks.

There are further examples of a pagan/Christian use of masks. The Slavs had a tradition of holding masked festivals for the Winter Solstice; these were later adapted into a form of Christian celebration. The strong association of masks with carnivals is also based on both Christian and pagan religion. The traditional Shrove Tuesday or Mardi Gras carnival was a time for wearing extravagant and colourful masks; this festival also celebrated spring fertility. Whilst the word 'carnival' originated from an event in the Christian (and pagan) calendar, it now embraces many different cultural festivals, both religious and non-religious. For example, in Britain today the Caribbean community in Notting Hill, London, celebrates carnival for two days in August. Thousands of people attend each year and a huge variety of masks are paraded in the street.

A carnival mask from the Notting Hill Carnival

Christmas, Carnival, Lent, Whitsuntide and Hallowe'en among others, are times of European masking. Like all traditions, these times are crucial. Life is no longer what it was and not yet what it will become.
(Mack, *Masks: The Art of Expression*, p.201)

Masks in contemporary Europe do not have a strong religious significance.

In Europe today, masks are no longer used to appease the dead or to ease the transition from childhood to adulthood. Masks are mostly used as fancy dress, to keep old myths alive, in theatre or to establish a form of communal pride, as in the Notting Hill Carnival. Masks do not have the same current cultural significance in Europe as they do in other areas of the world. However, Europe has a strong tradition of masks in religious ritual, festival and particularly theatre.

PERCEPTIONS OF THE MASK TODAY

Mask making is a tradition and its history continues to evolve.
(Frank and Jaffe, *Making Masks*, p.13)

The origins of the mask and its diverse development have led to complex perceptions regarding its use, function, identity and power. European theatre masks are commonly thought to be used for character disguise (as in *Commedia dell' Arte* during the Renaissance period) or for dramatic effect (in modern mask theatre companies such as Trestle Theatre Company). These masks are not thought to embody a 'spirit'. However, there is an argument that all masks 'transform' the wearer, whether in a spiritual sense (as in African ritual) or in a psychological sense (as in the modern theories of Keith Johnstone, a highly respected theatre practitioner who used masks in his improvisation work at the

Royal Court in the 1970s. See the Chapter 'Masks and Trance' in his book *Impro*.).

Here we address some recent and contemporary thoughts on masks and their use. Michael Chase (founder of the Mask Studio: see p.333) illustrates the significance of the mask within contemporary theatre in the following statement:

Masks enhance dramatic effect in theatre.

Most theatre today is deadened by the banality of bleak naturalism or by empty technological extravagance. When used consciously, the simple power of the mask brings a quality of magic, a dynamic relationship between the actor and audience and a vibrancy that can transform theatre into the living experience. (Chase, 'Tools for Transformation', *Total Theatre*, Volume VII no. 3, p.7)

Masked theatre is unusual today.

Sadly, masks are no longer widely used by theatre companies; mask making and masking have become specialised art forms. In fact, theatre companies such as Trestle and Ophaboom are known specifically as mask companies, because their productions use masks exclusively. Ophaboom's work has its roots primarily within the techniques of *Commedia dell' Arte*. Geoff Beale and Howard Gayton of Ophaboom Theatre, in an article entitled 'Madness of the Mask' state:

Some theatre practitioners believe that a masked performer can interact with the audience in a unique way.

. . . fundamental to our mask work is the state we call 'the madness of the mask' – where the character operates with a different logic to everyday thought . . . since masks live in the 'here and now', the concept of fourth wall theatre is an anathema to them. Whilst performing they make direct contact with, and often comment on, the audience's world.
(*Total Theatre*, Volume VII no. 3, autumn 1995, p.8)

When Ophaboom refer to the 'masks' as the performers, they are not suggesting that the actor is 'possessed' by the mask, but rather that the actor is directing the mask. Toby Wilshire of Trestle Theatre Company maintains that the mask is a theatrical device and a tool used by actors in performance for dramatic effect. In a recent interview, he said: 'There is a magic surrounding masks, but I believe it is in the audience's perception of the mask, not the mask itself . . . Yes, the mask has a magic; so does a Beatles song!'

Wilshire goes on to develop this parallel: 'Music and masks work on the brain in much the same way. They both conjure up thoughts in your mind, that is, your *own* thoughts.' Like Michael Chase, he believes that conscious transformation is at the heart of positive and clear mask work: 'To gain the optimum clarity of the masks, the actor must be in control. In modern theatre, if we use a "trance-like" state, the actor is not in control and then it becomes dangerous.'

Others hold a different view, and see masking as metamorphosis rather than the inhabiting of an inanimate object:

Once a student understands the immense difference between controlling a mask and being controlled by a mask, then he can be taught.
(Johnstone, *Impro*, p.172)

Here, Johnstone is refering to his well-developed technique of masked actors entering a trance-like state and becoming 'possessed' by their mask. In contrast to Wilshire, Johnstone firmly believes that the mask, when given an appropriate space, will 'take over' the performer. Susan Brooks, a dance theatre practitioner from Mid-Kent College, recently completed a mask project with her BTEC First Performing Arts students. She expresses a similar view to Johnstone, describing the students as 'waiting for the mask to lead them' and '. . . letting the mask take over enough to *become* the mask'. Brooks explains how the students became increasingly engrossed in this project, which was leading towards a performance. Throughout the eight-week module, the students responded in the form of poetry and prose:

The Mask
The main forces within my life.
The culture of which I am a part
The need for acceptance by friends.
The hatred and pity for those who look up to me.
The need to be loved.
The turmoil within.
This is my mask.

(BTEC First Performing Arts student, Mid-Kent College, 1996)

The view that the mask has metamorphic properties has a substantial history. The wearing of masks for rituals in the earliest civilisations was generally believed to metamorphose the wearer into a supernatural entity, and there are many examples of this. Indeed, some maskers believe that masks continue to hold power after they have been removed:

. . . such a situation is found among the Bangwa of Cameroon, where masks are carried on the shoulder by members of the night society. They have become too potent magically or mystically for them to be placed over the heads of humans.
(Mack, *Masks: The Art of Expression*, p.31)

Some practitioners believe mask work is essential for the training of actors.

Stanislavski said, 'Actors can be possessed by the characters they play, just as they can be possessed by masks.' Some practitioners believe that mask work is central to an understanding of the role of the actor within theatre. Former director of Trickster Theatre Company Nigel Jamieson feels that mask work is insufficient in Britain. He says that mask work is '. . . noticeably lacking in British theatrical training' (quoted in the *Guardian*, 1988). Michael Chase agrees:

Until actors training for the stage have had experience within the mask, they won't be using their full potential. Actors trained in masks have a special precision, a strong sense of ease of timing and presence, an awareness of what they are saying with their bodies.
(Chase, 'Tools for Transformation', p.7)

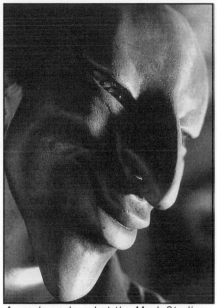

A mask produced at the Mask Studio

There has been a recent rise in the popularity of masks.

The recent increased interest in masks has had practical outcomes. Michael Chase's Mask Studio, in London, is a useful resource for anyone interested in masking practices. When asked to describe the Mask Studio, Chase said: 'The Mask Studio creates masks for use in theatre training, performance and self-development. We run workshops and courses in the creation and use of masks and provide information and exhibitions for educational purposes.'

The term 'mask' itself has evolved into a tidy metaphor for aspects of society. Reviewing a mask exhibition in 1977, Caroline Tisdall made the following observation in the *Guardian*:

The mask is once more becoming a regular feature of the news pages. Rapists, murderers, and terrorists are all represented, begging the question: what lies beneath the surface of our society?

Segy identifies another use of the metaphor:

Although people are apt to talk today of the 'image' of a man [or woman], a corporation, a public figure, still they do not fully realise what is presented to them is not 'real' but an image fabricated by professionals using techniques to make them believe in it. The image of personality, like any consumer good, is fabricated, packaged for merchandising, and projected for the effect or result it may produce . . . [the image is] . . . a non-material mask.
(Segy, *Masks of Black Africa*, p.56)

The word 'mask' has negative connotations today: it implies that something is 'hidden'.

The word 'mask' is a term often used in the context of negative aspects of our society and identity. Yet, in the theatre, mask work continues to build on a long and successful tradition of experimentation and the development of creative and expressive theatrical performances.

At its best, positive mask work allows actors to perform worldwide, crossing all language barriers and accessing a wide spectrum of cultural diversity. It engages with a mixed-ability and multicultural audience, and links people of all ages. Mask work enables performers and non-performers to explore issues in both a global and a personal context. Mask exploration can be used to tell stories in a dramatic form, to understand and engage with different cultures, to recreate ritualistic forms of expression through poetry, movement and dance, and to study particular theatre history periods. Perhaps more importantly, masks can provide us with a whole new understanding of our own everyday lives. When using masks, we are forced to focus on our own unconscious gestures and body language, and on the way we communicate our thought processes. When speech and facial expressions are removed, we begin to realise the full significance of masking, something that has been recognised throughout the world since masking began.

Mask work has far-reaching implications when used appropriately.

PRACTICAL MASK WORK

Making masks

Below are instructions for making two different types of mask: the first is a half mask made of brown paper tape, and the other is a full mask made of paper and based on a clay mould.

A brown paper tape half mask

Materials
- A hair band
- Short strips of gummed brown paper tape, available from stationers
- A bowl of water
- A sponge
- Paints (water based)
- White emulsion paint
- Brushes
- Scissors
- Ribbon or elastic (to tie)

Method
- Put on the head band, ensuring the hair is scraped back away from the face.
- Dampen the gummed side of the tape with a sponge and place it on the upper face area, leaving the eyes and nostril area free (so you can breathe). Completely cover the upper face with three to four layers, ensuring the mask shape is as you want it. Leave to dry on the face for 10 to 15 minutes.
- Carefully remove the mask from the face and give the mask a base coat of white emulsion paint.
- Pierce the mask with two holes just above the ears and thread elastic or ribbon through, tying it on the inside.
- Decorate the mask as desired with paint and any other materials, such as leaves, beads, feathers or string etc.

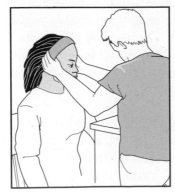

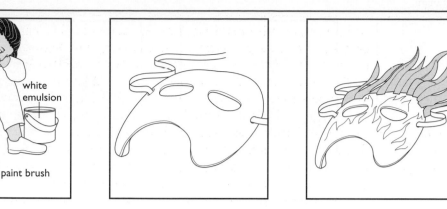

A clay mould whole mask

Materials
- Plasticine
- Modelling tools
- Clay board
- Clay
- Vaseline
- PVA glue
- Tissue paper (white)
- Brown paper
- Scalpel
- Cling film
- Muslin
- White emulsion paint
- Coloured paints (water-based)
- Brushes
- Waste material bits
- Scissors
- Elastic

Method
- Collect illustrations of masks and decide on a design.
- Mould your design from Plasticine, creating a mini-model.
- When you are satisfied with this, create a large version in clay. Allow for shrinkage. Remember that you are effectively creating the 'inside' of a face mask. Exaggerate all the features. If you have not finished, store the clay in a sealed bag.
- Once you are happy with the mould, allow it to dry over a couple of days.
- Grease the clay with Vaseline.
- Cover with a layer of cling film, piercing any air bubbles.
- Stick on three layers of tissue paper. This will form the inside of the face mask.
- Then add three layers of brown paper: use plenty of PVA. Add one layer of muslin. Continue with the brown paper. The more layers you use, the stronger your mask will be.
- Wait until all the layers are dry, then completely coat the outside with PVA.
- When this is completely dry (it is best left overnight), remove it from the mould. If this is difficult, break the clay mould with a hammer.
- Cut off any excess paper around the edge.

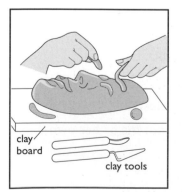

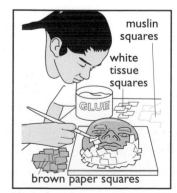

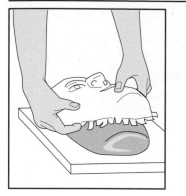
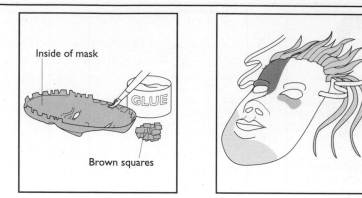

- Paste strips of brown paper over the edges of the mask to prevent it scratching.
- Paint the finished mask with a half-and-half mixture of PVA and white emulsion paint.
- Allow this to dry.
- Paint as desired and stick on additional materials, for example hair.
- Make holes in either side using scissors, and attach elastic.

Practical activities using masks

The following activities can be undertaken by groups using masks made by the above methods.

Emotional see-saw

- Choose two contrasting emotions, such as fear and love. As individuals, form still images of each of these.
- Using movement and mime, move from one emotion to the other, without your masks.
- Repeat this exercise with your own mask.
- Divide into two groups: one group does the exercise while the other group watches. Then swap over. Focus on body language.
- Discuss this process as a group. This audience input is essential for you to gain a variety of perceptions about the physical portrayal of such emotions with and without a mask. What happens when the mask is on?

Neutral?

- With a mask, stand in a *neutral* position in a space.
- Try this without the mask.
- Discuss what neutral *is*. Can we be truly neutral?

Responding in mask

- All the students face a wall with their eyes closed.
- The facilitator hands each student a mask (not his or her own), which the student puts on.
- Get into pairs and open your eyes.

- Respond spontaneously and appropriately to the other mask.

- As each of you becomes aware through the other's improvised mime who you are, find gestures which allow interaction with the other mask. Music can be very helpful here.

- Watch some of each other's improvisation work and discuss it.

Choral movement

- Without masks, in large groups, the students learn a series of synchronised movements: for example, walking through a forest, hearing a strange sound, reacting as if alarmed, hiding as a whole group.

- Repeat the same sequence wearing the masks.

- Watch (or video) each other and discuss the theatrical effect of this work.

Interview with Toby Wilshire of Trestle Theatre Company

Background

Toby Wilshire is the artistic director and co-founder of Trestle Theatre Company. This established company (founded in 1981) has developed its own unique style of masks, which have become the company's trademark. Trestle is a touring company, which combines comedy with visual and physical theatre to create original, dynamic devised performances. It performs to over 40,000 people a year. For every piece of work, new masks are designed and created. Since 1981, the company has experimented with various mask-making materials. Today, all its masks are made using a vacu-form technique. Trestle's devised piece *Passionfish* was first produced in 1996 (see also pp.342–344).

Q How was the company set up?

In 1981, the final year of my degree at Middlesex Polytechnic, myself and two others, Sally Cook and Alan Riley, collaborated on our honours piece, using masks . . . this was the start of Trestle. [In association with John Wright, see pp.79–85.]

Q What inspired you to work with masks?

At 17, I saw the Moving Picture Mime Show, a production called *The Examination*. They were basically the first British mime company. They used 'Basle' masks, which were all white. They were Swiss masks for festival. When I got into college our mime tutor, John Wright, used masks with us, and I went from there.

Q How are the masks designed and created?

Initially, we get a lump of Plasticine and clay and play around with it. When we've made something we like, we use it as a mould. We used to cover them with papier mâché; nowadays we've become a bit more sophisticated. In 1987, we started using Cellastic, and in 1995 began using a technique called vacu-form . . . we used to use stage make-up on them, but now we use acrylic paints and varnish them.

Q **What rehearsal techniques do you use with the masks?**

Basically improvisation, with and without masks. We actually audition the 'masks' for each part . . . one of the exercises we do is for the masked actor to get on stage and do nothing. By doing this it's like looking at the actor's actions and reactions under a microscope. We do a lot of rehearsals without masks, just focusing on gesture and movement, and also the mask can become hot and uncomfortable to wear. One of our golden rules is to make sure the actors perform at least six feet away from the audience.

Q **Why?**

If the mask comes closer than this, the audience know it's an actor.

Q **Why did you call your production *Passionfish*?**

Because it's the combination of two opposites: the fish is slimy, cold and wet, the passion hot and fiery.

Q **Who made the set?**

My brother makes all our sets. We have to be able to dismantle it and put it back quickly, because we're touring all the time, we're never based in one venue . . . you have to be able to put it up in an hour.

Q **How many masks are used in the play?**

There are seven different masks. We always use full masks, because they work by suspending disbelief. Actually, our masks go much further back than the face, and with the wig the actors can turn their backs to the audience without breaking the fantasy.

Q **Is there a script for *Passionfish*?**

Actually, this is the first time we've produced a synopsis script before rehearsals. Most of our shows are completely improvised, but all are scripted after the initial performance tour.

Resource Activities

1. THE HISTORY OF MASKS AND MASKING

Aim
To familiarise students with the history of masks and their role within society.

Objective
To gain an understanding of masks within theatre.

Background
- Read pp.324–329 on Greek, Roman and Renaissance theatre.
- Read pp.20–22 on presentation techniques.

Tasks
- Divide into three groups. Each group should research theatre in a different historical period: Greek, Roman or Renaissance. Complete a research package, using additional resources such as photos, diagrams and information from other sources.

- Each of the groups should present its findings, with the others taking notes.

- Discuss and identify links and common features of masking across the three periods.

2. PRACTICAL MASK WORK

Aims
- To gain an understanding of masks in relation to text, space, movement, language and staging.
- To demonstrate an awareness of newly acquired knowledge and process in both a practical and a theoretical form.

Objectives
- To research, design and create a functional mask for use in performance.
- To develop a clear understanding of the mask and masking techniques.

Background
- Read the mask-making guidelines and the practical exercises on pp.334–337.
- Read pp.20–22 on presentation techniques.
- You may wish to keep a record of this project for evaluation. Read pp.17–20 for advice on making a personal and group record, and pp.150–154 for further guidance on evaluation.

Tasks

- Take a simple text such as the fable of the three little pigs or a poem. Choose a story with strong dramatic potential. Read through as a whole group and discuss the potential for masks: character, atmosphere, themes and imagery. An appropriate poem might be:

Summer Fires of Mulanje Mountain

Your matronly face is blood-red like the flesh of a water-melon;
Smoke is rising ascension-like
through your hair . . . you have
become a burning field of neon

Skin to skin bonfires to
awaken mountain shrines? No, for
these are fires lit by angry heat
power generated by summer

Unfailing reminder of
age-long lomwe* *tribal icons,*
the fires paint veins of dried rivers
and sculpt faces of dead relatives
as they burn every summer.

* lomwe: *communal name of people who live around Mount Mulanje*

(Edison Mpina, quoted in Calder et al, *New Poetry of Africa*, p.1)

- In small groups, find a fairytale, anansi or folk story, a poem or a similar textual stimulus for a masked performance.

- Make notes on themes, movement and space.

- In pairs, make half masks using the method shown on pp.334–335. Decorate the masks as appropriate for the different characters. Add papier mâché features if appropriate.

- Using your masks, undertake a number of the practical activities on pp.336–337.

- Start drawing together your story outline, emphasising the strong emotions in the narrative. Limit speech and dialogue: concentrate on the physical aspects of the storytelling.

- Rehearse and perform the work.

- Evaluate your work. Discuss how the masks worked; the strengths and weaknesses of the masks; the audience reaction; any historical influences on your mask work.

- Complete personal and/or group records and evaluation, if appropriate. Display your masks as part of this record.

3. A MASKED PRODUCTION

This activity can be used as an alternative or an extension to the previous activity.

Aim
To develop advanced theatrical mask work.

Objectives
- To make a clay mould mask.
- To use clay masks within a full masked piece.
- To gain an insight into texts that are appropriate for masked work.

Background
- Read pp.318–334.
- Read the mask-making guidelines and the practical exercises on pp.334–337.
- You may wish to keep a record of this project for evaluation. Read pp.17–20 for advice on making a personal and group record, and pp.150–154 for further guidance on evaluation.

Tasks
- In discussion, identify key aspects of masked theatre that the group believes are essential for any masked work. When a list has been drawn up, keep this visible as you progress with your project. Refer back to it regularly, to ensure that your work is in line with these key features.

- Choose a text which has extensive possibilities for masked work, such as *Animal Farm* by George Orwell or *Alice in Wonderland* by Lewis Carroll.

- Read the text and cast it appropriately.

- Analyse the text as a group, looking specifically at themes, mask potential, movement and imagery.

- Sketch and make notes of ideas for your mask, based on your character.

- Working in pairs, make clay mould masks as shown on pp.335–336. Decorate the mask with materials appropriate for your character. Add papier mâché features if appropriate.

- Using your masks, undertake a number of the practical activities on pp.336–337.

- Start drawing together your story outline, emphasising the strong emotions and simple, key moments in the narrative. Because these are full masks, how are you going to deliver a narrative without voices? Do you need a voiceover at all? Will you wear masks throughout the piece or remove them occasionally?

- Rehearse and perform the work.

- Evaluate your work. Discuss how the masks worked; the strengths and weaknesses of the masks; the audience reaction; how your mask work related to the key points that you originally identified; any historical influences on your mask work; the delivery of the narrative; the freedoms or limitations of mask work.

● Complete personal and/or group records and evaluation, if appropriate. Display your masks as part of this record.

4. INTERVIEWING

Aims
● To develop a further understanding of contemporary mask theatre.
● To understand techniques of questioning.

Objectives
● To compile an individual set of appropriate interview questions.
● Throughout the interview, to show an awareness of mask work.

Background
Read the interview with Toby Wilshire on pp.337–338. This interview was conducted after seeing a performance of the company's production *Passionfish*. We devised nine questions, which can be loosely divided into three categories: Wilshire's background and inspiration, his mask philosophy, and the performance of *Passionfish*.

Tasks
● Discuss the interview with Toby Wilshire.

● Devise a series of five questions for interviewing each of the following people:
  i) the director of a masked piece;
  ii) an actor in a masked piece;
  iii) a mask maker.

● Having done some practical mask work (using the exercises in Activities 2 and 3), interview each other in pairs, paying particular attention to how the mask feels, whether it is comfortable, how it works in relation to your character, and what you need to improve upon to make your mask work more effectively. Base your interview on the questions you devised above.

● Tape or make notes on one interview. Transcribe this accurately. Discuss these transcriptions, identifying where the questions or answers needed expanding or clarifying.

● If you have access to professionals, interview them using your revised list of questions.

5. REVIEWING

Aims
● To further an understanding of masked theatre.
● To analyse a review of a masked production and develop a review technique.
● To utilise research, resources and experience appropriately.

Objectives
● To watch and review a masked production.
● To put mask work in a contemporary theatrical context.

Background
Read the interview with Toby Wilshire on pp.337–338 and the synopsis and reviews below.

Passionfish *is a piece of experimental visual theatre, using masks, text and choreography to tell of six people, all of whom are suspended in time, caught in a rut, or poised on the edge of their future . . . it is the tale of six people at different stages of their lives, spanning different time frames but shown simultaneously.*
(Toby Wilshire and Joff Chafer, *Passionfish* Education Pack, 1996)

Passionfish *is a darkly comic, passionate play that speaks directly of the 1990s. It explores themes of time, being adrift and rites of passage, combining masks, text and choreography with music from Bach to Bacharach. It is a show that spans two hours, one day or one year. It lasts as long as it takes to bake a loaf of bread, fall in and out of love or live an entire life. It is Easter, Christmas, the summer holidays. It is another day of darkness and laughter. It is the first day of many . . . The choices and uncertainties of the late 20th century are scrutinised as six characters confront their expectations of the future, a future they can see but have trouble reaching. Only one man, Mr. Mayfly, as old as the century, carries with him the memories of order and certainty in an increasingly uncertain and uncaring world.*
(Trestle Theatre Company, *Passionfish* programme, 1996)

The following is a sample review that might be written by a student:

Passionfish *explores the theme of time and is a piece of abstract theatre carefully choreographed to show a colourful array of different relationships. One is aware of time passing at different speeds for different characters, but in*

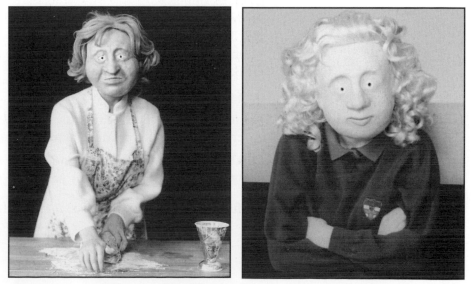

'Grace' (left) and 'Schoolgirl' from Passionfish

343

reality the play lasts for as long as it takes Grace to make and bake a loaf of bread . . .

. . . The larger-than-life masks used for Passionfish evoke many different emotions. In the opening scene, one is struck by the calm and overpowering simplicity of the masks. Grace, played by Jilly Dickens, enters the stage area and pauses for a minute or two: the stillness is filled with a sadness which soon becomes a feeling of anticipation as she begins to knead the dough. In contrast, Schoolgirl, played by Mary Stockley, depicted a comical representation of adolescence. Her movements and gesture spoke through the mask, enabling the audience to identify fully with the character . . .

. . . There were two unmasked characters in the play, known as Night and Day. They were a young couple in love and were the only ones who used dialogue, speaking exclusively to one another. Ironically, although they had the power of speech it served only to reflect their inability to communicate. Hence, the masks became even more significant and the mimed communication more compelling . . .

. . . the performers demonstrated powerful and expressive mask work. This unified approach held the audience in a suspension of disbelief, drawn in at different times by the masks, the performers and the combination of the two . . .

. . . The witty plot and sub-plots combined with the extravagant technical devices captivated the audience until the loaf was cooked (this happens live on stage in a functional oven, the glass door providing a full view of the bread baking) . . .

Tasks

● Discuss the information on pp.337–338 and the synopsis and review extracts of *Passionfish* above.

● What do you now know about *Passionfish*? Write lists under these headings:
i) Themes
ii) Types of mask
iii) Narrative plot
iv) Characterisation
v) Impact on the audience
vi) Background of the company

Add other headings if appropriate.

● What else would you like to know about *Passionfish* that is not covered in the reviews? Make a note of these things.

● Combine these two lists. Visit and review a masked production, using these notes as a guide for your own review.

USEFUL ADDRESSES

The following are London-based institutions and contacts which offer mask-related resources.

Kazzum Arts Project
Selby Centre
Selby Road
Tottenham
London
N17 8JN
Tel: 0181 808 6793

The Commonwealth Institute
Kensington High Street
London
W8 6NQ
Tel: 0171 6034 335

The Horniman Museum &
Gardens
London Road
Forest Hill
London
SE23 3PQ
Tel: 0181 699 1872

The Theatre Museum
1c Tavistock Street
London
WC2E 7PA
Tel: 0171 836 7891

Schools Library Service
62 Sherland Road
London
W9 2EH
Tel: 0171 798 3820

Pictorial Charts Educational Trust
27 Kirchen Road
London
W13 OUD

Trestle Theatre Company
47–49 Wood Street
Barnet
Herts
EN5 4BS
Tel: 0181 441 0349

The British Museum
Great Russell Street
London
WC1B 3DG
Tel: 0171 636 1555

The Museum of Mankind
6 Burlington Gardens
London
W1X 2EX
Tel: 0171 437 2224

The Mask Studio
(currently moving premises)
Tel: 0171 387 8549
Fax: 0171 387 1808
e-mail: 101606.775@
compuserve.com

ANNOTATED BIBLIOGRAPHY

This bibliography includes volumes relevant to this chapter which are considered suitable for student reference. See also the general bibliography on p.380.

Frank, V. and Jaffe, D., *Making Masks*, The Apple Press, 1992
Offers very basic, colourful, easy-to-follow, step-by-step masking techniques. An excellent introduction, which provides a clear and brief historical overview of masks.

Hartnoll, P., *The Theatre: A Concise History*, Thames and Hudson, 1985
Dated but still useful, as it gives a clear insight into the progression of European theatre, with specific reference to masks.

Horniman Mask Education Pack, Horniman Museum Education Centre, 1991
This pack is worth having, as it refers to masks stored in the Horniman Museum. It contains simple illustrations and a short summary of masks from around the world.

Johnstone, K., *Impro: Improvisation and the Theatre*, Eyre Methuen Ltd., 1981
Johnstone explores in detail the relationship between the actor and the mask. He discusses at length the concept of the 'trance' and gives a unique perspective into the power of the mask. Perhaps dated, but gives some excellent student activities for mask work.

Lommel, A., *Masks: Their Meaning and Function*, Ferndale Editions, 1981
Although several years old, this book offers an excellent insight into the psychological background and development of masks across the world. It has inspired and influenced much work over the years. A must for all mask practitioners.

Mack, J., *Masks: The Art of Expresssion*, The British Museum Press, 1994
This is the most contemporary text. Full of excellent photographs of masks that can be found at the British Museum. Mack's style is both descriptive and accessible. He examines in detail the varied functions of the mask worldwide, placing it within a historical context.

Rudlin, J., *Commedia dell' Arte: An Actor's Handbook*, Routledge, 1994
Focuses on the practice of *Commedia*. Accessible for practical work, containing details of each mask's characterisation and short scenarios which could be used.

Segy, L., *Masks of Black Africa*, Dover Publications Inc., 1976
An interesting contrast between African and Western masking concepts. Offers a variety of definitions of the mask and their implications on society.

10 Arts Management and Administration

Stephen Leib (with assistance from Pippa Bound)

Arts management and administration underpin the creative aspects of the arts in society. Administrative responsibilities range from finding private sponsors for a new art exhibition to marketing a new 'hit musical', from developing a newly built theatre's safety policy to promoting an overall artistic policy, and from the seasonal programming of productions to the hiring of actors.

Such activities operate within a structured management system in the arts and entertainment industry. This chapter will explore some of the roles and function of arts management and administration, in the following sections:

- Relationships and responsibilities in arts management
- Audience profiling: marketing and targeting
- Funding and finance
- Legal requirements and legislation applicable to performance art

RELATIONSHIPS AND RESPONSIBILITIES IN ARTS MANAGEMENT

In Chapter 5, there is a brief description of many of the key roles in arts administration within the theatre industry (see pp.170–180). This section builds on those descriptions by giving specific examples of administrative roles in the theatre industry. Here, we delineate and compare professional relationships in two different hierarchy models within the arts industry, and examine the roles of some of the key figures. This material is based on interviews given by the company manager at the Royal National Theatre, London, and the production manager at the Palace Theatre, Watford.

The Royal National Theatre
The National Theatre is a great building in every sense. The architect, Sir Denys Lasdun, incorporated not only three auditoriums, but eight bars and a restaurant, modern workshops, paint rooms, wardrobes, property shops, rehearsal rooms and advanced technical facilities the like of which had never been seen in a British theatre, where cramped and difficult positions were usually the norm backstage.

The Royal National Theatre

The building on London's South Bank now stands as a lasting reminder of the vision of its founding Director, Lord Olivier, and all who work in it and visit it are reminded of his enormous contribution to theatre in Britain and in particular, the Royal National Theatre.
(Elms, *The London Theatre Scene*, p.75)

At the Royal National Theatre, as with most arts institutions in the 1990s, the artistic policy is closely linked to the business policy. Both of these policies are the responsibility of the artistic director (formerly Richard Eyre, now Trevor Nunn) and the board of management.

The Royal National Theatre has a complex hierarchical structure.

As in the hypothetical diagram opposite, the board lies at the centre of the communication network at the National; it controls the hiring of all staff, including the acting company. In addition, it is responsible for the general running, maintenance and management of the building itself. It is a top-down model of management. All personnel report to a head of department, who in turn has to report to either the general manager, the head of finance, the artistic director or the executive director, and they report to the board. The board of the Royal National Theatre comprises the executive director, the artistic director and the financial director, together with additional peripheral business managers who do not work for the theatre directly, but take an interest in its funding, programming and mission. There is also a representative from the local council, who addresses the legal, safety and licensing requirements of the theatre. In order to examine the relationship between artistic direction and the management structure at the Royal

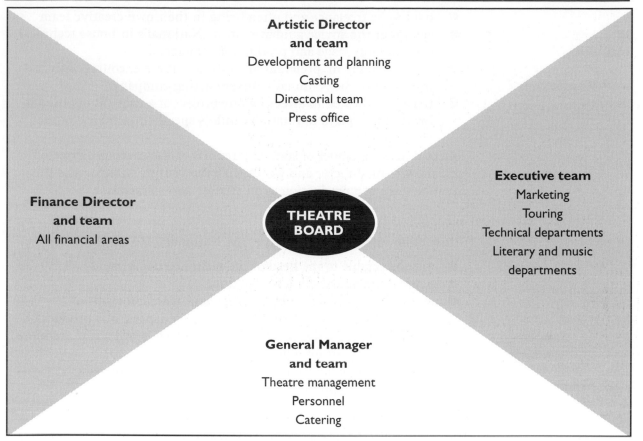

A typical staff structure for a large-scale theatre. (See also p.168.)

National Theatre, it is useful to identify certain key figures in the artistic process. (General descriptions of these roles are on pp.170–180.)

Artistic director

The artistic director:

- is answerable to the board of management and the finance committee;
- is responsible for the hiring and firing of staff within his sector and the acting company (under the direction of the board);
- devises an artistic policy statement for the theatre;
- produces a schedule of plays to be presented in a rotational order, with 'blocks' of performances for each theatre;
- liaises with all heads of department within his sector;
- occasionally directs plays;
- has a say in the hiring of directors and creative teams, such as lighting and set designers;
- has some responsibility for strategic planning and income generation.

Directors

Directors working at the National:

- are answerable to the artistic director;

- tend to be freelance and often bring in their own creative team;
- act under the advice/guidance of the National's in-house technical staff, notably stage and production managers;
- have some say in 'preferential' casting, but are encouraged to cast from within the National's current acting company;
- remain dedicated to directing one project at a time (as opposed to two or three plays in rotation), unless specified in their contract.

There is also a member of staff who reports to the executive director and the artistic director and works with the visiting director and the creative team of a production as an adviser and assistant.

Production managers
Production managers employed at the National:

- are answerable to the head of the technical department;
- control the budget for a production;
- act as advisers to the stage management teams in terms of availability of capital to finance particular aspects of a production; may liaise indirectly with the board to put forward a case for more financial support for a project;
- are responsible for seeing that all technical elements of a production are produced on time and on budget.

Choreographers
Choreographers who work at the National are answerable to the director, company manager and often the musical director. However, this is not a permanent job in the theatre: choreographers are usually contracted in from outside, especially if the National is staging one of its rare large-scale musicals. The choreographer will then come in as part of a 'packaged' creative team. There is one permanent member of staff who is responsible for general movement if a production calls for this.

Musical directors
Musical directors who work at the National are answerable to the music manager (a permanent member of staff). However, like choreographers, musical directors are freelance workers who are hired from production to production, along with musicians and composers.

Stage management teams
The Royal National Theatre's stage management team consists of 24 people, divided into six teams. Each team has a stage manager, a deputy stage manager and two assistant stage managers. They are all answerable to the head of the technical department. Stage management teams almost always remain dedicated to individual projects, in one particular theatre, and are responsible for the frequent overnight get-in and fit-up arrangements, alongside others such as costumes and props staff and set designers. The company manager, who answers to the head of planning, allocates the dressing-rooms to the acting company. If she is away, then the stage managers assume this role. (For further information on stage management

teams at the RNT, see the interview with Peter Maccoy on pp.298–302.)

Relationships between performers and administrators

Actors at the National are cast in various ways. It may happen that a particular actor is chosen by a director because he or she has always wanted that actor to play that particular role. However, whilst working at the National, freelance directors are encouraged to use actors in the current company.

The head of casting is closely involved in hiring actors for productions, and makes final casting arrangements between actors and their agents, where necessary. It is also her responsibility to hire understudies for every production (except for the Cottesloe Theatre, where it is too expensive to hire understudies).

It is the job of the head of planning to ensure that when actors are hired for more than one production there are no clashes between performance and rehearsal times. The policy for hiring actors on this basis is that a performer must have a 12-hour (overnight) rest before coming to rehearsals the next morning. However, if the actor is in a play that same evening, he or she must, by law, be allowed a two-hour break between rehearsal and performance. If a play has been out of the 'revolving block' repertory system for more than a week, the actor is required to do an afternoon line run before the evening's performance. Out of a six-week rehearsal period, therefore, the director might realistically have only a four-week period of concentrated rehearsal. At the National (as in any other professional or amateur company), the actors are answerable to the director, the stage management teams, the production manager and the company manager.

Methods of communication

It is important to make sure departments and individuals are kept informed.

The Royal National Theatre is a large and potentially unwieldy institution, both physically and hierarchically. A 'green paper' has been developed within the technical and artistic departments which details who is doing what and where, week by week and production by production, throughout the building. In addition, there are weekly production meetings between all the heads of department so that everyone involved with a particular production knows the schedule to which he or she is expected to work and can share the latest rehearsal developments.

Artistic policy

The Artistic Policy at the National is diverse, pluralistic and popularist. Our work is intended to be popular and accessible, even if its contents are complex and disturbing. Our ambition is to achieve the very highest standards. In the words of the 'spiritual father' of the National Theatre, Harley Granville Barker, to be 'Better than the theatre around the corner'.
(Artistic Policy Statement, The Royal National Theatre Publications Department, 1995)

The policy [for the National Theatre] has to be to try and present to the highest standards possible, a varied amount of theatre . . . so that people who come to the National Theatre would come to see more than one play. In other words, we are offering them a lot of different shows in a week, and that was always the aim; that people would keep coming back.
(Rosemary Beattie, Company Manager, Royal National Theatre, 1995)

The Palace Theatre, Watford

The Watford Palace of Varieties was opened in December 1908, featuring music hall. The many famous artists who appeared during this era included George Robey, Charlie Chaplin, Little Tich, the Seymour Hicks Company, Stan Laurel, Fred Karno's Company, Marie Lloyd and Dan Leno Jr.
The building itself has undergone many changes from the basic music hall shell that it originally was, and as recently as 1984 a new wing was opened consisting of new rehearsal facilities and an elegant new bar and bistro. It was during World War I that plays were first produced at the Palace. Famous names who appeared during the 1920s and 1930s included Bob Hope, Gracie Fields, Anton Dolin, Wendy Toye, Ian Flemming and Helen Vayne.

Weekly rep continued throughout the war period, with companies formed by Andrew Melville and Jimmy Perry [who] approached the Corporation with the idea of transferring the theatre lease into civic hands. The Corporation readily agreed, and formed the Watford Civic Theatre Trust Ltd.
(Watford Palace Theatre publicity, 1995)

In 1987, the artistic director Lou Stein took over the Palace Theatre; during his time there, he was responsible for 72 productions, for introducing several new policies, including the development of a new education department, and for commissioning a wide variety of new, nearly new and multicultural programmes within the growing arts community in Watford. Giles Croft, a former production manager at the Royal National Theatre, has recently taken up residence in the role of artistic director, and the Eastern Arts Board continues to be one of the major investors in productions, in conjunction with Lloyds Bank plc. (See pp.359–366 for information about funding and finance.)

Roles and relationships
As you can see from the diagram opposite, the Watford Palace's system of organisation shares many features with that of the Royal National Theatre. The artistic director liaises with the board and the finance manager to find funding for projects, and also spends some time directing productions. The board comprises local councillors and some key members of the theatre staff.

The Palace Theatre is a receiving house, with fewer staff.

However, the management structures within the Palace Theatre are much more condensed than at the National. The clear difference between the Royal National Theatre and the Palace Theatre is that the National is a production house which can afford to finance a constant rotation of plays in its three theatres, whereas the Palace Theatre is a receiving house for touring productions, with only occasional 'home-grown' productions.

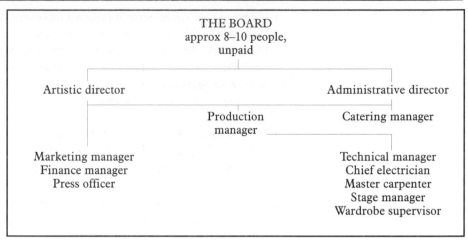

The Palace Theatre's system of communication

The result of this is that there are far fewer full-time staff working at the Palace Theatre.

Methods of communication
A weekly meeting is attended by the head of each technical department; this is similar to the Royal National Theatre's stage management team meetings. The timescale for a major production is four to five months, and weekly schedules are drawn up to keep all departments informed.

Artistic policy
Local reaction to plays is observed very closely, to ensure that the theatre is meeting its goals and aims within the community. These are as follows:

To provide a stimulating and challenging programme of artistic activity in a welcoming and accessible environment, for the enjoyment of the community.

Aims
1) As a subsidised regional repertory theatre, to present an artistic programme of the highest national standards in terms of what we present and how we present it, by:

- *striving to constantly challenge and extend the artistic boundaries of our organisation and its practice through innovation, education, new work and an international perspective.*
- *seeking to involve artists (actors, writers, designers, directors and other practitioners) of a high calibre in the theatre's work, encouraging those who are up and coming as well as those already established in their field.*
- *aiming as a centre of cultural activity in the region to provide a variety of theatre of the highest quality.*
- *taking the work of the Palace Theatre to as wide an audience as possible through touring regionally, nationally – where appropriate – and internationally through Watford's twin town network.*

2) To encourage and enable the community both locally and regionally to make full use of the theatre and its resources, by:

- *creating positive links with the community through which information and*

353

ideas can be exchanged to promote an understanding of the different needs that exist.

● *recognising that the community consists of many different people and responding in our programming, information and pricing.*

● *enabling the community to participate and play an active part in the work of the theatre.*

● *fostering links with local businesses to ensure that they are aware of the opportunities the theatre is able to offer them with their own commercial aims through supporting its work.*

● *ensuring the theatre and its facilities provide a friendly and welcoming atmosphere.*

(Artistic Policy Statement, Watford Palace Theatre, 1996)

AUDIENCE PROFILING, MARKETING AND TARGETING

The marketing team sells the production.

One of the most important aspects of arts administration lies in the hands of a company's marketing and publicity team. It is their job to ensure that as many people as possible are made aware of a production's strengths, its dates and its venue, and to retain that audience for future productions through mailing lists and promotional material.

This job is made that much harder by the constant competition in the media marketplace for other 'products' intent on gaining an audience's attention. Helen Sharman writes:

Catching an audience is like catching a fish – a mixture of planning, patience and good luck. Choose your bait, cast your line, hook your target, then reel it in and, most important, hang on to it – audiences, like fish, are slippery customers.
(Sharman, *Bums on Seats*, p.2)

Professional theatre marketing

Marketing means making the theatre attractive and accessible.

The first link in the publicity chain for a production company is the marketing manager (sometimes called the marketing officer). This person needs to know every 'selling point' about the show: the dates, times and venue for posters, programmes, press releases and leaflets; the names of director, designers and key cast members; and details about the style, plot and related issues of the production. A marketing manager represents the public face of a production before it is seen. Brian Gilmour, one of the marketing officers at the Royal National Theatre, summarises his job as follows:

The job of marketing is to make the theatre – both building and productions – attractive and accessible to as many people as possible, from distributing leaflets to administering a team of sales representatives. Advance information and exclusive priority booking are offered to mailing list members. At many theatres the marketing officer will write leaflet copy, organise posters, place advertising, and edit programmes and other publications (though the larger companies have separate departments to do this.). Marketing is also to do with the theatre's seat pricing structure.
(cited in Cohen, *Theatre Works*, p.45)

In a company as large and as busy as the National, the marketing manager leads a large department. There is a team of graphic designers, artists and photographers, a box-office manager and staff, an education department, and the press and publicity team:

The press office generates free publicity in newspapers and magazines, and on television and radio; organises editorial coverage, preview radio/TV extracts before the first night, interviews and photo calls with actors and production team; and invites critics to review plays. The office also deals with calls from the press about arts policies, funding and censorship. Small theatres may not even have a full-time press office, the work being covered by the house manager or other member of the administration.
(ibid. p.44)

Posters and leaflets for individual Royal National Theatre productions are designed in-house. The print and publications department provides the graphics, and commissions photographs and paintings if required; it is also responsible for purchasing copyright images. As well as leaflets on individual productions, 250,000 repertory leaflets are produced every seven to eight weeks, which outline all the productions that the theatre is presenting, both in-house and on tour. The leaflets are sent to all 35,000 names on the mailing list, and distributed to other venues by distribution companies such as Brochure Display and Theatre Dispatch. In order to market the productions effectively, the theatre often uses postal questionnaires to gauge the composition of the audience in terms of age, race, gender and so on.

Marketing student and amateur theatre

Marketing amateur theatre is done locally.

The general principles of marketing theatre remain the same whether it is professional or amateur. Attracting people to the theatre to see productions is the top priority. If you are involved in student or amateur theatre, the scale is naturally smaller, and the marketing will be localised. The following points are worth considering if you are involved with marketing student or amateur shows.

General points
At the outset of the project, production or season, ensure that the choice of piece(s) is appropriate in style, content, range and so on for both the company and the target audience. Populist theatre such as musicals can be balanced by more innovative work. Consider the time of year and date of your production: for example, certain religious holidays or school holidays might restrict or swell audience numbers. Maintain a watching brief on other local productions, in an attempt to avoid overlap.

Check that you have the performance rights to the piece, if it is a published text. If you are in any doubt, Samuel French Ltd can give you the name of the performance rights holder for any theatrical show (see p.377).

Ensure you budget appropriately for marketing. Obtaining quotes from printers or designers is important. Clarify what should be included in your budget. Do you have to pay for the performing rights, for example?

Start marketing your show some months before the production dates. Use posters, leaflets ('fliers'), local radio advertisement, local newspaper listings and mailing lists. Professional and personable contact is invaluable when approaching the media and public. Aim for an immediate impact:

Publicity is about advertising and selling. To sell anything successfully, the product – in your case a theatre group – must have a clear identity, an image that is easily remembered. Think of yourselves as a packet of cornflakes, or a washing powder. You recognise your favourite brand a mile off, you buy it because you like it and, if this time it has a free plastic widget for the kids, or a money saving offer for you, then that is a bonus.
(Sharman, *Bums on Seats*, p.3)

Remember that there is a captive market in the family and friends of the company. These can be approached through the members of the company. Consider also targeting a relevant audience: for example, if the show has a connection with a local industry, you may be able to sell an evening to that company. If there is a regular audience for your productions, your marketing might include reference to past popular productions.

Posters and fliers

Do not design these by committee. The director and/or the designer alone should make any decisions. Bright, clear visuals help, particularly pictures; be original, if costs allow, in colour, shape and so on. Generally, however, posters will be A3 in size and fliers will be A5.

Posters may include the following information:

- the name of the company, show, author, venue and any sponsor(s);
- dates and times;
- the box-office telephone number and/or address;
- the price of tickets (including concessions);
- any other details that the performance rights company states need to be on publicity material, such as 'Presented by special arrangement with . . .';
- perhaps a sentence or two that give an idea about the production, or reviews about the play if it has been previously performed.

Fliers should include all of the above, but much of the relevant information can be put on the reverse. Ensure that the text is proofread several times for errors, by different people.

When the posters are printed, make sure that there are enough for a wide circulation to as many outlets as possible: do not waste money paying for unnecessary advertising space.

Media coverage

Media coverage is a useful means of bringing a production to the notice of a mass audience; you might want to consider some of these points:

- Ensure that press and radio publicity gives all the necessary

There is no need to pay for advertising.

information in a concise, original and exciting way.

- Do not waste money paying for radio or television coverage; many local newspapers or radio stations offer a free service.
- Write to all newspaper and magazine listings services with details of your production.
- Invite the press to photo calls with the cast.
- Send complimentary tickets to the press and invite them to review your production.
- Advertise competitions and special discounts on tickets.
- Use contacts to get details of your production on the Internet or even on Ceefax/Oracle.

Further publicity

Other forms of publicity may include:

- using a mailing list to contact your audience;
- open days and social occasions which can be used to promote your next production;
- using fetes, carnivals and other events to advertise shows, for example by performing extracts from the show or having cast members on a carnival float.

Box office and tickets

The box office should always begin selling tickets several weeks before the show is due to be presented. Ticket prices should be agreed by the director, and the tickets should be printed in good time; they need to show all relevant details such as the date, time and venue of the performance.

The ticket itself can have a three- or four-part format:

Three-part tickets are probably the most useful. The stubs left in the book give you the number of tickets that are 'out on the street' before the show, the section surrendered at the door gives you an accurate audience figure on the night, and the third section [is] retained by the public . . . Four-part tickets can be very useful for giving your audience a form of currency on those occasions when you include a 'free drink' or a meal, or even a raffle.
(Sharman, *Bums on Seats*, p.49)

It is helpful to use a theatre seating plan which records how many tickets have been sold, how many are left before the start of each performance, and how many are sold on the door.

Front-of-house organisation and tasks

Other than the actors, the only members of staff with whom the public might come into contact once inside the theatre are the theatre stewards, the front-of-house manager and the theatre manager.

Theatre manager

The theatre manager maintains the vital link between the public and the show's producer. He or she is responsible for booking the show into the theatre, and thus has a vested interest in its success, without playing any direct part in its preparation or production.

Front-of-house manager

The front-of-house manager:

- holds the licence for the run of a show from the local authority;
- is responsible for seeing to the needs of the audience and organising their safe entrance into the theatre, their comfort and safety during the performance and their safe departure after it;
- deals with any problems or complaints from the public;
- oversees the box office and ticket sales;
- organises the ushers and programme sellers;
- is responsible for the pre-show and interval refreshments (where applicable);
- ensures the correct use of the 'No Smoking' and 'Fire Exit' signs;
- is responsible for any special guests, such as VIPs or the press;
- organises a balance sheet showing the settlement of all accounts debited against all the takings for ticket sales, programmes and refreshments;
- is responsible for making the foyer look as inviting and attractive as possible, often using previous production photographs, photos of the cast and cast lists.

Theatre stewards

Theatre stewards report to the front-of-house manager, but are often employed by agencies such as the Stoll Moss Theatre Group plc. Their responsibilities include:

- arriving one hour before curtain-up to check that the auditorium is clean before the audience is admitted;
- checking that rows and seats are clearly numbered;
- ensuring that the audience is admitted to the auditorium on time (usually half an hour before curtain-up);
- showing the audience members to their seats;
- selling programmes;
- dealing with latecomers in a discreet way (usually admitting them at a natural 'break' in the performance);
- looking after any charity collections that the theatre may have organised with an external party.

On-the-job training is required to be a theatre steward, especially since the Hillsborough football disaster in 1989 and the subsequent Taylor Report (1990), which stated that all stewards at any public entertainment should have some basic first-aid training in case of such emergencies (such as a First-Aid at Work certificate from the Red Cross or St John Ambulance Brigade), and also that they should be easily identifiable in the event of an evacuation of the venue. They should know all escape routes from the venue and the venue's evacuation procedures, and should always carry torches with them.

FUNDING AND FINANCE

Preparing for any type of performance in today's market is financially challenging. Successful and reputable professional West End producers such as Cameron Mackintosh or Michael White are able to go to 'backers' or 'angels', people who risk money by funding professional productions. Outside the West End, small professional companies and amateurs need to consider financial outlay alongside many other factors. Theatre productions can be prohibitively expensive, and government funding can be difficult to obtain.

Government funding: the Arts Council and the National Lottery

Since 1946, all government funding of the arts industry has been channelled via the Arts Council of Great Britain. In 1994, this became the Arts Council of England (ACE), with regional councils for Scotland and Wales. (See pp.240 and 242 for further details.) The Arts Council receives public money from the government to ensure that the industry is protected and supported financially and legally. The basic cash grant for 1996–7 was £191.1 million; from these funds the Arts Council continues to provide regular grants to arts organisations. One-off grants are also available in the form of Development Funds.

In addition to major grants to national institutions such as the Royal Shakespeare Company, the Royal National Theatre and the Royal Opera House, a number of fringe companies receive annual grants from the Arts Council. Examples of such companies include:

Fixed-term funded organisations

Black Mime Theatre Company:	£102,500
Cheek by Jowl Theatre Company:	£106,700
Red Shift Theatre Company:	£114,800
Shared Experience:	£153,200
Theatre de Complicité:	£135,700
Trestle Theatre Company:	£127,000

(Figures published by the Arts Council of England Publications Department, November 1995)

Regional Arts Boards and the National Lottery are sources of finance.

The Arts Council of England devolves its funds to smaller Regional Arts Boards (RABs), providing around 90 per cent of the RABs' total income. Each RAB is responsible for the management of its own financial affairs; its accountability to the ACE centres on the publication of annual reports and accounts and the appraisal by ACE of two RABs a year, on a five-year cycle.

In addition to the government funding disseminated by the Arts Council, money to help fund the arts comes from the National Lottery:

The National Lottery was launched in November 1994. The Department of National Heritage (DNH) was responsible for the introduction of the legislation which established the Lottery, and for the setting up of the National Lottery Distribution Fund (NLDF) . . . Camelot Group, who operate the Lottery, pay 28 per cent of their income into the NLDF. The fund is divided equally between the five 'good causes': the arts, sports, heritage, charities and projects to celebrate the year 2000 and the third millennium. The DNH issued directions in June 1994 that the money from the Lottery should fund capital projects and that these projects should have a significant element of partnership funding . . .
(The Arts Council of England Publications Department, November 1995)

By definition, capital projects are large financial projects such as the construction of new buildings, the improvement of old buildings, the purchase of equipment, the carrying out of feasibility studies or design competitions, and the commissioning of new works of public art. However, the NLDF has now changed its policy of only funding capital projects, and will consider various types of scheme. In the first year of the Lottery, 78 per cent of awards were made to community-based projects. The beneficiaries of these awards included:

● schools;
● amateur musicians;
● sports clubs;
● local theatres;
● museums;
● woodlands;
● local conservation groups;
● the unemployed;
● community arts;
● pensioners' groups;
● disabled people;
● caring charities, particularly those assisting the disadvantaged.

This is just a small sample of the types of organisation that have approached the Lottery for funding so far. For more information on grants and National Lottery funding, write to the Arts Council of England (see p.377), and ask for the relevant information pack. If your company is interested in applying for a National Lottery grant, this means working in a partnership. The Lottery provides half of the capital for your project, whilst your company has to find the other half.

Sponsorship and further funding for student and amateur companies

Many student and amateur theatre companies are self-financing. There are various methods of funding work. For example, box-office income may cover the cost of the production, either in retrospect or through receipts from the previous production. However, bear in mind the following point:

Every budget must take account of the possible income from the audience, but do not work back from that. Calculate what the production will cost and see how you can meet it. If you cannot meet it re-think your production values rather than doing a cut-rate version. Cheap theatre cannot be disguised, but economical theatre is much better than extravagant theatre.
(McCafferey, *Directing a Play*, p.30)

Education establishments sometimes provide funding for curriculum work within their overall budget. Post-16 arts courses may have access to such funding, and in addition performance spaces and other facilities such as lighting or wardrobe are often in place. For example, a college would have an equipped studio or theatre space and possibly a wardrobe store. This is a form of hidden funding.

Alternatively, productions may be self-financed by the company members and their friends and family, who provide money or goods for the production.

Groups may also seek additional funding. The Arts Council produces useful documentation about its own funding mechanisms, including the National Lottery, and several books are available which give information about other grants, charity funding and sponsorship (see bibliography, p.378). There are also a number of organisations with relevant expertise which are willing to answer enquiries on funding and fundraising (see useful addresses, pp.205–206 and p.377).

Many organisations have systems for dealing with sponsorship applications.

If you are applying for sponsorship, many organisations will require you to complete specific forms with particular details about your application. It is inadvisable to write without checking whether such information is available. However, if you are not asked to follow any specific format, you may consider the following checklist for any application for funding, whether this is from arts bodies or local businesses.

● Prepare your application thoroughly and rigorously.

● Outline the company's selling points, such as its artistic policy and other types of associated community or charity work it might do.

● Include details about previous productions and statements from external parties on their success and the role of your company in the local community.

● Provide clear details about the reason for the application. For example, provide details about new equipment that would be purchased.

● If you are applying for sponsorship from larger corporations, be aware that major banks, building societies and insurance companies tend to divide their sponsorship money up annually among 'favourite charities' or donate lump sums towards designated projects. For example, large productions at the Watford

Palace Theatre have been sponsored by Lloyd's Bank plc. This allocation of funds always takes place at the beginning of the financial year, 1 April, so any applications for money should be submitted a year before this date, or six months beforehand at the very latest.

It is not easy to find a willing sponsor. Do not be disheartened if you fail to strike lucky on your first attempt. Draw up a list of at least a dozen likely prospects and be prepared to work through them all.

A word of warning: don't attempt to contact them all at once . . . Compromise and target prospects in batches of three or four.

It is worth aiming for local companies, or at least local branches of national organisations. Your offer of an advertising opportunity will be that much more attractive if your catchment area for publicity matches theirs.

The first thing you need is the right contact. A letter that is vaguely addressed to the managing director is not enough. If you do not have a name, telephone the company and find out. Check the person's title, name and initials, and also confirm that you have the correct address.

Then write a brief letter, outlining the nature of your group, explaining that you are seeking sponsorship for the next production, and giving an indication of what is in it for them.

Ask for a meeting in the near future, and make sure you give clear instructions on how you can be contacted.
(Sharman, *Bums on Seats*, pp.63–4)

● Offer your sponsors something in return. Find as many ways of promoting your sponsors as possible: advertising their name in the programme, in press releases and on posters, fliers and T-shirts; offering them free tickets; encouraging them to meet the cast and/or attend rehearsals; ensuring that a member of the front-of-house team takes care of them at performances.

Budgets
The details concerning income and expenditure in professional theatres are complex and daunting. On pp.363–364 are balance sheets for the Palace Theatre, Watford and a typical large-scale theatre.

For smaller companies, the need for budgeting is still important. The form on p.365 is useful for setting up such a budget. The second column on the form would need to be constantly updated, but the basic list gives a clear idea of the likely areas of expenditure.

Allow for performance rights fees in your budget.

Items such as 'Licence/Royalties' (performance rights) for published plays can be expensive and need to be worked out at the outset of a project. Performance rights fees are generally calculated either at somewhere between 15 and 20 per cent of total box-office sales or as a fixed total per performance (with a guaranteed minimum of at least

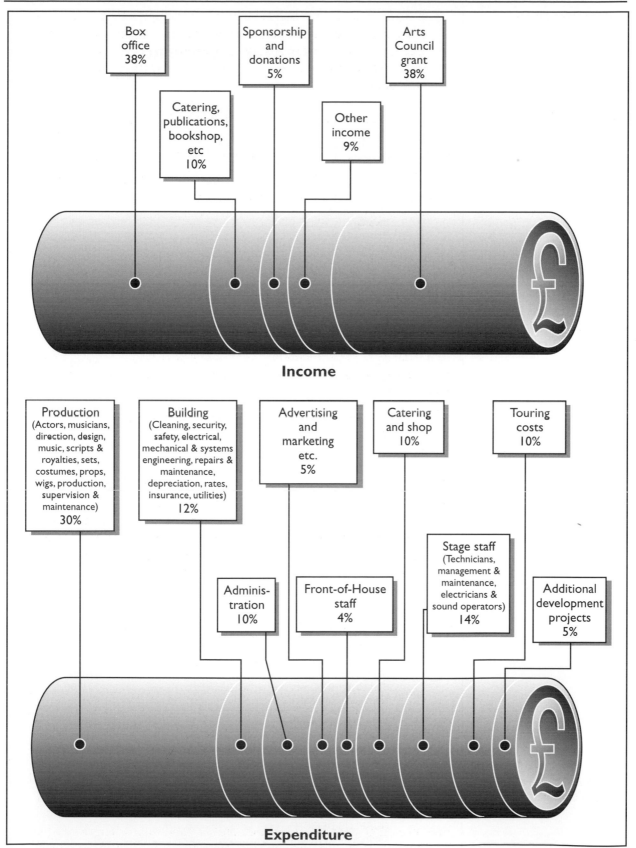

Income and expenditure for a typical large-scale theatre.

PALACE THEATRE – WATFORD
1996/97

Annual
Budget
£
1996/97

THEATRE PROGRAMME

Own Productions
Income 477576
Expenditure 465834
Contribution 11741

Touring Work
Income 45585
Expenditure 51562
Contribution .... -5977

Pantomime
Income 177504
Expenditure 148870
Contribution 28634

Single Performances
Income 26860
Expenditure 24083
Contribution 2777

Lettings
Income 24000
Expenditure 14411
Contribution 9589

Green Room
Income 33000
Expenditure
Contribution 33000

Miscellaneous Income 2000
Miscellaneous Costs
Contribution 2000

TOTAL CONTRIBUTION TO FIXED COSTS 81764

Box office 69951
Admin/Management 180296
Cleaning Maintenance 22391
Staff Costs Subtotal 272538
Administration 55326
Marketing and Box Office 94000
Establishment Costs 131700
Education Programme 36874

TOTAL FIXED COSTS 590438

OPERATING DEFICIT PLUS REVENUE GRANTS .... –508674
Watford Council 267300
Eastern Arts Board 204500
herts County Council 36874
Revenue Grant Subtotal 508674

SURPLUS/DEFICIT
Council Intervention 0

BUDGET

PRODUCTION: Circulation: Dir/Des/PM/SM/
DATE: Props/Tech

Expenditure		Budget	To Date

Administration Costs
Stationary ....
Photocopying ....
Postage ....
Insurance ....
Telephone ....
Bank Charges ....
Audit Fee ....

Venue Costs
Hire Fee ....
Display Costs ....
Publicity Contract ....
Staff Contract ....

Marketing Costs
Design Costs ....
Posters ....
Leaflets ....
Other Print ....
Newspapers ....
Postage ....
Merchandising ....
Reserve ....

Production Costs
Fees (Director ....
(Designer ....
(Other ....
Set ....
Costumes ....
Wigs ....
Make up ....
Props ....
Furniture ....
Weapons ....
Transport ....
Lighting/Sound ....
Musical Instruments/Scores ....
Hire of Rehearsal Room ....
License/Royalties ....
Scripts ....
....

Total Expenditure
....
....

A production budget's expenditure sheet from A Phaidon Theatre Manual – Directing a Play *by M. McCafferey, Phaidon Press Ltd., 1988)*

£50.00 per performance), plus VAT. These are paid to the performance copyright holders. If the production is a musical, and band parts have been hired, the cost of this hire is charged at the same time, as well as hire charges for scripts and any other production material the copyright holders might have supplied. For example, in a production of *Oh What a Lovely War,* an essential part of the show is the use of slides and sound effects, which are supplied by the rights holders. (See pp.234–235 for activities on *Oh What A Lovely War.*) All payments for copyright should be paid within two weeks of the final performance.

In addition to forecasting expenditure, all companies have to account for all actual expenditure. Detailed records of expenditure are important for any production. The production manager or director is likely to be the budget holder in smaller-scale productions, and may devise his or her own record system. However, there are several computer programmes on the market which can provide balance sheets to assist in the keeping of such records.

LEGAL REQUIREMENTS AND LEGISLATION APPLICABLE TO PERFORMANCE ART

Whenever and wherever a production is presented, by an amateur or professional company, it must always be organised with the highest regard for Health and Safety working practices.

A venue must have a performance licence covering a production.

To this end, a performance licence is required, which lays down all the legal requirements pertaining to the venue and other key aspects of the production. This will usually cover the entire run of the show, from fit-up to get-out. This section briefly summarises some of these legal requirements and their relevance to live theatrical performances, including both indoor performances and outdoor events such as pop concerts.

Local legislation
Public entertainments are licensed both in and outside London. There is a presumption in law that licences should only be granted subject to such conditions as may be necessary. They may be issued either annually or occasionally for one or more occasions. Local authorities are empowered to attach technical conditions to licences which must be met by the licensee. Failure to meet these conditions is a criminal offence.

The authorities may refuse to issue licences, but in doing so, they must be seen to be acting reasonably. Also, in setting conditions for the licence, they must only require that which is reasonable and practical. Applicants who have been refused a licence, or who feel that the conditions are unreasonable or impractical, may appeal firstly to a Magistrates Court, and subsequently to a Crown Court against the local authorities' decision . . .

Premises such as football grounds are subject to special legal requirements, and Safety Certificates are issued under the 'Safety at Sports Grounds' Act (1975). Usually these do not cover pop concerts, and the local authority will issue a

Special Safety Certificate for such events.
(Thompson, *Focal Guide to Safety in Live Performance*, p.10)

In assessing the elements of a live performance which will be relevant for the licence, the following areas should be taken into consideration:

- means of access and escape;
- public address installation;
- the staging arrangements;
- sight lines;
- production details;
- barriers and fencing;
- the evacuation plan;
- mixers, delay towers and temporary towers;
- policing, security and stewarding, first aid and emergency service provision.

The photograph below gives an idea of the importance of safety at live events.

Safety measures at a large-scale concert

The use of firearms and chemicals is closely monitored.

In theatrical productions, there are also laws and separate licences which govern the use of firearms on stage. These must be fully supervised and checked by a representative of the local authority and the stage manager prior to a run of performances. The same applies to hazardous chemicals such as dry ice, under the 'Control of Substances Hazardous to Health' (COSHH) Regulations (1988). In professional theatre, there must be a COSHH certificate (see p.368) clearly located on a wall, which covers any members of the workforce who come into contact with hazardous chemicals, whether solid, liquid or gaseous, as part of their full-time job. For example, production departments such as

COSHH – What YOU need to know

In order to comply with the Control of Substances hazardous to health Regulations 1988, you must be aware of the following information. Make sure you are – it could save your life one day!

Department

Product Name

Uses

Composition

Physical and chemical properties

Risks to health

Factors which increase risks

Maximum/occupational exposure limits

Symptoms of overexposure

Storage precautions

Transport precautions

Handling/use precautions – including advice on personal protective equipment

Disposal precautions

Emergency action - fire, spillage, first aid

☐ Fire Officer   ☐ Health & Safety Officer

Additional information – ecological hazards, relevant regulations, advice to occupational medical officers, references

Name, address and telephone number of supplier

Reference number, date of issue

Symbols to note

Toxic/ Very Toxic — A substance which if it is inhaled or ingested or it penetrates the skin, may involve serious acute or chronic health risks and even death

Harmful — A substance which if it is inhaled or ingested or it penetrates the skin, may involve limited health risks

Irritant — A non-corrosive substance which, through immediate, prolonged or repeated contact with the skin or mucous membrane can cause inflammation

Corrosive — A substance which may on contact with living tissues destroy them

A COSHH certificate

368

wardrobe or set design might regularly come into contact with wood, metal, paints, dyes and solvents, which may produce fumes or dust in the working atmosphere. These may subsequently affect workers, actors and visitors to these areas. The working conditions in such places are constantly reviewed, and safety certification is constantly updated to keep theatres and other venues in line with other workplaces. Theatres which have public bars must also have a licence to serve alcohol, and must keep within the licensing requirements, including not serving alcohol to patrons under 16 years of age. A production company can be taken to court and heavily fined if it is found to be in breach of the bar licence issued by the local council.

Audience seating capacity

The safety of the audience is paramount.

It is usually the local authority which plays a large part in deciding what is the appropriate seating capacity for a performance venue, but in fact common sense (and reference to the venue's own safety policy handbook) should tell a box-office manager not to sell more tickets than permitted. Sometimes a venue will display a 'Standing Room Only' sign outside its doors, but it is in fact both dangerous and unlawful to have audience members sitting in the aisles, as they block emergency escape routes, becoming a major hazard if an evacuation of the venue is necessary. All seating should be as comfortable as possible, and should allow clear sight lines to the acting area. If the venue has no seating and the audience has to stand (as in a promenade performance), there should be careful assessment of the floor capacity to prevent overcrowding.

The holding capacity for any space occupied by the audience should be based on the following:

1. The number of seats where seating accommodation is provided
2. One person for each 450 mm (1' 6") length of seating where bench seating is provided
3. One person per 0.5m² (5ft²) on stepped terraces (This standard is reasonable for one day events or evening performances)
4. One person per 0.75m² (8ft²) on sloping terraces and arenas, whether indoor or outdoor. This is more of a comfort standard, and is probably excessive for the average short event.
(Thompson, *Focal Guide to Safety*, pp.17–18)

Another area that needs to be taken into consideration is quick and easy access for disabled patrons, who must also be catered for. Usually, in theatres, a limited amount of space is reserved for wheelchairs, with access into and around the theatre by lifts or ramps. At concerts, a similar principle is operated, but a reserved wheelchair bay is constructed, so that the wheelchair user and accompanying friends and relatives can watch the concert from the same location.

Requirements of the chief fire officer

All aspects of a production must be checked by the fire officer.

For any public performance, the regulations concerning fire safety procedures are of paramount importance. These not only cover the safe handling and use of pyrotechnics, but also require the flammability of every item of furniture, set, costumes, props, curtains, lighting and sound equipment, both on stage and in the auditorium, to be checked by means of a flame test. This must be carried out by the local fire officer, together with the stage/production manager(s), before the beginning of a run of performances. Any element of the production found to be flammable, and therefore dangerous – even if it is vital to the production – can be legally removed by the fire officer until it is made safe. This can be done by chemically flameproofing as many flammable items as is both practical and reasonable. Just as many provisions must be made to protect the audience from the causes and effects of fire as to ensure the safety of the backstage areas. At every performance, an 'iron' or safety curtain (usually made out of iron sheets) must be lowered and raised in the audience's presence to reassure people of their safety in the event of a fire. This curtain shuts the auditorium off from the backstage area, and is normally tested during the interval.

Once these checks are completed, the fire officer will the give the stage manager the 'all clear' certificate, which provides a checklist of procedures to be carried out before every performance.

Fire precautions must be followed.

The other responsibilities of the fire officer are to ensure that all fire extinguishers are full and functional and have not been tampered with, and to check the fire alarms, sprinklers and smoke-detector system. Access to and signs for the fire exits must be functioning and not obscured, before, during and after the performance. The fire officer must also make sure that all full-time staff are familiar with the venue's fire evacuation procedures, and there should be periodic drills for them.

All areas within the building, both front-of-house and backstage, should have clearly displayed notices instructing people what to do in the event of discovering a fire. These should read as follows:

> *In the event of discovering a fire,*
> *DO NOT ATTEMPT TO TACKLE THE FIRE YOURSELF.*
> *Operate the nearest fire alarm and alert the stage manager or another member of staff. In the event of evacuation, help all children and disabled patrons to leave the theatre in an orderly manner. Contact the emergency services by dialling 999 and asking for the fire service. Tell them the address of the venue and provide as much detail as possible, leaving your name and telephone number in case you are cut off.*

The fire instruction sheet should be accompanied by a detailed map of a 'meeting point' where all audience members, cast and theatre staff will assemble in case of a fire.

If a fire occurs during a performance, the stage manager will stop the performance with an announcement such as: 'Ladies and gentlemen, because of unforeseen circumstances, we are unable to finish this performance. We would appreciate it if you could leave the building as quickly and as quietly as possible by the nearest route indicated by the theatre stewards/ushers/staff. We apologise for any inconvenience caused.' The safety curtain is then dropped in order to contain the fire.

If evacuation of the backstage area is necessary, it is the stage manager's responsibility to ensure that all doors and windows are shut and preferably locked. It is also his or her duty to ensure that all performers and members of staff sign in as they arrive. This will then form a register to check that they can all be accounted for.

Performance licence checks

In the front of most scripts today, it is common to find the following notice: 'Warning: publication of this play does not mean it is available for performance. Please do not consider a production before permission is granted . . . Performance without permission is an infringement of copyright.'

Copyright permission must be granted.

It is the production manager's responsibility to ensure that all licences have been obtained and checks carried out, and that copyright permission has been granted by the holders of the copyright material (for example, Samuel French Ltd: see p.377) before a production goes ahead. Copyright laws exist in the United Kingdom on all plays whose authors are still alive or have been dead for less than 70 years. In some cases, the deceased playwright's copyright will be passed on to an estate after this time, and it then becomes the property of the estate. Most authors also tend to stipulate as part of their copyright that only limited (if any) cuts may be made to their original work by the director. Similarly, severe restrictions can be placed on video or sound recordings taken during a production, and on '. . . reproducing by any other mechanical means any part of the text [which is] strictly forbidden without the written consent of the copyright holders'.

If these legalities are not adhered to, the copyright holders are well within their rights to have a production closed and to sue the company for infringement of copyright.

Resource Activities

1. RELATIONSHIPS AND RESPONSIBILITIES IN ARTS MANAGEMENT

Aim
For students to take on some of the roles within a successful administration hierarchy.

Objectives
- To show an awareness of the working procedures and means of communication of administrative roles.
- To develop an artistic policy for a particular venue.
- To evaluate the effectiveness of contributions to these tasks.

Background
- Read pp.347–354.
- Read pp.150–154 on evaluating your own work, and pp.20–22 on presentation skills

Tasks
- Choose one administrative role from the following list and prepare a short presentation explaining the responsibilities implicit in that role and how it affects the function of other administrative jobs.
  i) producer
  ii) artistic director
  iii) company manager
  iv) stage manager
  v) director, choreographer or musical director
  vi) sound, lighting, costume or prop designer
  vii) finance manager

- In small groups, draw a diagram to explain the hierarchy of these roles within a company, with a very brief explanation of each person's function next to the job title.

- In a large group, plan an artistic policy for your school, college or company. This should include:
  i) details on how the venue is used (for example, it might be used for drama, dance and musical entertainment, and for social occasions);
  ii) policies for multicultural entertainment;
  iii) the possibility of introducing a theatre education department into the venue;
  iv) which audience the venue is supposed to appeal to;
  v) how the use of the venue might be extended to include the local community.

  You may need to do some market research.

- Take on appropriate administrative roles and set up a pre-production meeting, at which a production should be chosen and the venue details discussed. (The purpose of this exercise is to see whose job it is to co-ordinate the various 'departmental roles' and to identify the communication structure between them).

● Imagine it is now five weeks into the rehearsal period. As a group, out of role, brainstorm a potential agenda for a production meeting to be held at this time.

● You are likely to overspend your production budget by £3,000. Discuss what cutbacks each department might be able to make to rectify this situation.

● Try a role-playing scenario in which a professional actor has some complaint to make about his or her conditions of work, such as clashing rehearsal times, problems with dressing-room allocation or a larger problem. The first person the actor will go to is the company manager. How will this person sort the problem out, and if he or she cannot, who will be asked to look at the problem next? Work the solution out within your small group. Try a similar scenario where the director or some other member of the creative team has come across a problem. For both these exercises, note down who made decisions and why.

● In the role of artistic director, you are going to face a board of directors or a local funding body to supplement the budget for your next big show. How are you going to convince the body that this is a worthwhile project? How can you match your show to its needs? This exercise may be brainstormed within a group, or may be developed into a more formal presentation or document.

● Orally evaluate your effectiveness in your chosen role(s), stating what you think the key parts of the job involve and what part it has to play in the communication structure between departments.

2. MARKETING

Aim
To undertake various marketing and promotional tasks, which will involve finding 'contacts' and creating a professional image for a production.

Objectives
● To try out a number of marketing strategies to generate interest in a 'real' production.
● To produce a range of publicity material and run a box office.
● To evaluate the effectiveness of contributions to these tasks.

Background
There is a range of jobs associated with marketing a production and targeting an audience. All the tasks should be done with a common production in mind. If you have undertaken Activity 1 in Chapter 5, pp.199–200, base this production on the arts venue that you have studied. You should attempt to show some evidence of wider research.

Read pp.354–358 for more help with these tasks.

Tasks

- Choose a production which you can market to a family audience. In large groups, write down as many of the key 'marketable' points about the production as possible. Include details such as potential 'star names', the image or logo to use on publicity material, where the best venue would be to stage this production and when it should occur. You might also consider special offers you could make to the public regarding ticket prices (party bookings, free prize draws, etc.).

- Consider the budget implications. Refer to the budget breakdowns on pp.363–365 for guidance. Allocate a certain amount for marketing.

- Design a poster or leaflet for this production. Remember that pictures and colour are the first aspects that the public will notice. What other important information do you have to communicate? You might include a booking form on a leaflet. You might also try producing car stickers or badges to promote your show. Make enquiries about printing and designing costs at local printing firms. Add these costs to your portfolio of material.

- Write a press release about this production, in the form of a general 'introductory' letter to the local free press. Tape record a press release or advertisement which you might send to a local radio station.

- Arrange a mock photo call for this production. Using rough drawings, arrange all the poses that the photographer would take. This photo call might take place in an interesting or appropriate location other than your immediate environment. Take these photos, using members of your group. Write a couple of brief sentences underneath each photograph which might be appropriate for a press release.

- Set up a mock box office for the evening of your performance. Try out different scenarios, in which you have to deal with customers collecting tickets, or with complaints and problems. How effective are the staff in dealing with these? What sort of training might they need?

- Evaluate the effectiveness of your publicity campaign.

3. FUNDING AND FINANCE

Aim

To plan and budget for a full-scale performance, and to find all appropriate sources of income through sponsorship and grant funding.

Objectives

- To create a show budget on paper and explain how the income and expenditure will operate.
- To try out strategies for generating income.

- To deal with post-show finances, including performing rights fees.
- To evaluate the effectiveness of contributions to these tasks.

Background

These tasks can be carried out either in the order in which they appear, as a mini-project, or as discrete activities. Each member of the group should take on an administrative role that might be performed in a small production company. Some of the tasks will involve actual contact with an external authority, so make sure that you have whatever information you need to hand before you progress.

Read pp.359–366 to help you with these tasks.

Tasks

- Hold a production meeting, at which each person should outline in detail his or her total budgetary needs for a year and how this money will be spent. (It may be appropriate to use the Watford Palace figures as a guide, and scale down from there: see p.364.)

- Design a budget income/expenditure sheet based on these figures. You will have to guess the income figures, but they must be balanced at the end of the production.

- Write an introductory letter which you would send to a potential sponsor, detailing your company's needs and what you can offer the company in terms of advertising opportunities.

- Contact your Regional Arts Board to see how you would apply for government grants and funding.

- Set up a computer programme such as 'Quicken' or 'Bank book' (where available) to show records of income and expenditure for the show.

- Make a list of events that could be held to raise more funds for your production. You might try to run one of these to raise money for your next production.

- Imagine that your production is over. Discuss with a small group the responsibilities of the finance officer at this stage. What other expenses might still be outstanding?

4. LEGAL REQUIREMENTS AND LEGISLATION

Aim

To address the legal requirements of putting on a production.

Objectives

- To apply for copyright permission to perform a production.
- To agree the terms and conditions for a performance with the local licensing authority.
- To design a safe and appropriate seating plan.
- To run practice fire drills, explain the venue's evacuation and fire

procedures and obtain appropriate certification for the venue regarding health and safety policy.
- To evaluate the effectiveness of contributions to these tasks.

Background
- It would be advisable to carry out these tasks for a *real* production. This might just as easily relate to an outside venue as to a theatre.
- Read pp. 366–371 to help you with these tasks.

Tasks
- Apply in writing or by phone to Samuel French Ltd (see p.377) for performing rights to a play of your choice.

- Contact your local licensing authority and apply for a public entertainment licence. It may be that your venue already has one of these, but contact the authority anyway to find out what this covers. You will have to send specific details about any special licensing requirements of your venue, such as a bar or the performing of live music. If the production has any special licensing requirements, such as the use of firearms or dry ice, these must also be detailed.

- Write out a fire instruction sheet and make sure that all students are aware of where these are placed and what to do in the event of discovering a fire. Ensure that all students are aware of fire, safety and evacuation procedures for your venue. At an appropriate time, organise a fire drill, and check that a register is kept by the person in charge.

- Design an 'ideal' seating plan. Consider the shape and size of the stage. Decide what sort of seating would be preferable: for example, chairs placed on rostra blocks, seating on floor level, seating fixed to the floor so that it does not tip over, and so on. Check for visibility sight lines and comfort. Allow for wheelchair facilities, wide aisles and quick access to fire escapes. Check that there are illuminated fire exit signs.

- Contact your local fire department to see whether someone will come to talk about fire safety in theatres.

- Write a list of checks that must be carried out by a stage management team before a performance is given an 'all clear' certificate by the chief fire officer.

- Write a Health and Safety policy which covers all full-time employees in a theatre. This will require further reading and research.

- Evaluate the importance of the Health and Safety policies you have devised, and say how effective you think they would be. Are there any areas of the theatre you may have forgotten, such as the fly tower, the dressing rooms or the administration offices? Also evaluate your success in gaining a performing copyright licence (where appropriate) and a public entertainments licence. Was this harder to do than you expected? If you had to do this again, what would you do differently?

USEFUL ADDRESSES

The list below is intended to be representative of a general cross-section of contacts relevant to this chapter. They are all correct at the time of going to press.

Samuel French Theatre Bookshop
52 Fitzroy Street
London W1P 6JR
Tel: 0171 387 9373

The Royal National Theatre
Upper Ground
South Bank
London SE1 9PX
Tel (general information):
0171 633 0880
Tel (bookshop):
0171 928 2033 ext 600
Tel (education dept):
0171 928 5214

The National Operatic and
Dramatic Association
NODA House
1 Crestfield Street
London WC1H 8AU
Tel: 0171 837 5655

Independent Theatre Council
12 Leathermarket
Weston Street
London SE1 3ER
Tel: 0171 403 1727

ITC is a membership organisation offering guidance on approaching funders and making applications. ITC's 'Starting a performing arts company' course has a fundraising section.

The Arts Council of England,
14 Great Peter Street,
London SW1P 3NQ,
Tel: 0171 312 0123

The Theatre Museum
Russell Street
Covent Garden
London WC2E 7PE
Tel: 0171 836 7891

Equity
Guild House
Upper St Martin's Lane
London WC2H 9EG
Tel: 0171 379 6000

Directory of Social Change (DSC)
24 Stephenson Way
London NW1 2DP
Tel: 0171 209 5151
Fax: 0171 209 5049

DSC runs a varied range of courses, including ones on developing a fundraising strategy and raising money from statutory groups and trusts.

ANNOTATED BIBLIOGRAPHY

This bibliography includes volumes relevant to this chapter which are considered suitable for student reference. See also the general bibliography on p.380.

Cohen, N., *Theatre Works: A Guide to Working in the Theatre*, Education and Publications Department, Royal National Theatre, 1992

> A practical step-by-step book which introduces the various aspects of administration and technical work behind the scenes at the Royal National Theatre. It gives personal accounts of career paths that one can take in order to attain a similar job in a regional or professional theatre, and has a useful section on how to apply for further education in these areas.

Cook, P., *How to Enjoy Theatre* (series editor Melvyn Bragg), Piatkus Ltd, 1983

> A helpful handbook which gives the historical background to theatre (very similar to *Theatre Arts* by R.A. Banks); it also has some interesting chapters on the process of staging live theatre, and breaks down the hierarchy system in theatre, explaining who does what job. There are also extensive Theatre Terms and Further Reading sections at the back.

Elms, S. (et al), *The London Theatre Scene*, Frank Cook Travel Guides, 1979

> Primarily a seating guide to most of the big West End theatres, so that you can see where you will be sitting when you order your tickets. However, it also provides some historical information about these theatres and details about annual live theatrical events.

McCafferey, M., *A Phaidon Theatre Manual: Directing a Play* (series editor, David Mayer), Phaidon Press Ltd, 1988

> A useful reference book for the first-time director, which gives a detailed breakdown of the pre-production, rehearsal/staging and post-production processes. It includes many useful charts, diagrams and pictures and offers sound working knowledge and advice from a professional director. This book is one of a series, and cross-references occur throughout.

Sharman, H., *Bums on Seats: How to Publicise Your Show*, A & C Black Ltd, 1992

> Again, a useful book aimed solely at a show's marketing team. It offers very practical suggestions on how a publicity team might approach marketing (all based on the author's first-hand experience), as well as giving useful contacts for poster, ticket and leaflet printing, merchandising and other publicity tradespeople.

Stuart, P., *Theatre Procedure and Practice, or Who Does What in the Theatre?*, Kemble Press Ltd, 1982

> A *very* detailed look at the roles of the administration and artistic staff in the running of a theatre, giving a full breakdown of what these jobs entail. It has colour-coded pages for each section, and other chapters deal with the practical aspects of working in and running a theatre, ranging from basic electricity for the stage manager to costume and make-up. Also contains useful diagrams, a glossary of theatre terms and a helpful contacts list.

Thompson, G., *Focal Guide to Safety in Live Performance*, Butterworth Heinemann Ltd, 1993

> Contains a lot of hefty theoretical knowledge on the legal aspects of safe working practices at different live performance venues, such as sports arenas, theatres and outdoor concerts. Occasionally offers some practical/legal advice for those who wish to pursue a career in this field, but does so in a rather unwieldy style. Its main practical use is for brief references and photographs.

Additional reading

Clarke, S., *The Complete Fundraising Handbook*, Directory of Social Change, London, 1993

Doulton, A.M., *The Arts Funding Guide*, Directory of Social Change (DSC), London, 1994

Hayman, R., *The Set Up*, Methuen (Publications) Ltd, 1973

Jones, S. (ed.), *Fundraising: The Artist's Guide to Planning and Financial Work*, AN Publications, Sunderland, 1993

McFarlane, G., *Copyright: The Development and the Exercise of the Performance Right*, Offord Press, 1981

Rosenberg, H., *How to Apply for Grants, Loans and Other Sources of Finance*, Gee Publishing Ltd, London, 1994

Scottish Arts Council, *Advice: Applying to Charitable Trusts and Foundations*, Edinburgh, 1995

Sweeting, E., *Theatre Administration*, Pitman, 1969 (out of print, but available in libraries or the Theatre Museum library)

Villemur, A. (ed.), *The Directory of Grant Making Trusts*, 13th Edition, 1993–94, Charities Aid Foundation, 1993

General Bibliography

ABSA/WH Smith Sponsorship Manual, ABSA, 1986

Allen, John, *A History of Theatre in Europe*, Heinemann Educational, 1983

Annett, M. and Simmonds, N., *Actor's Guide to Auditions and Interviews*, A & C Black, 1995

Ansorge, P., *Disrupting the Spectacle*, Pitman, 1975

Arden, J., *Pretend the Pretence*, Eyre Methuen, 1977

Arnott, Peter D., *Public and Performance in the Greek Theatre*, Routledge,London 1989

Arts Council of England, *Disability and the Arts: Get It Right*, ACE, 1996

Arts Council of England, *The Policy for Drama of the English Arts Funding System*, ACE, 1996

Arts Council of Great Britain, *Drama in Schools*, ACGB, 1992

Arts Council of Great Britain, *The Glory of the Garden: The Developments of the Arts in England*, ACGB, 1983

Baker, Michael, *The Rise of the Victorian Actor*, Croom Helm Ltd, 1978

Barlow, Wilfred, *The Alexander Principle*, Victor Gollancz Ltd, 1973

Barry, C., Dean, A., Norrish, K., Poynton, K., Wheeler, M. (eds), *Contacts No. 85*, Spotlight, 1995/96

Beale, G. and Gayton, H., 'Madness of the Mask', *Total Theatre*, Volume VII no. 3, Autumn 1995

Bentley, Eric (ed.), *The Theory of the Modern Stage*, Penguin Books Ltd, 1968

Berkshire Education Department, *Awards and Grants*, Berkshire LEA, 1996

Berry, Cicely, *The Actor and his Text*, Virgin Books, 1992 (first published by Harrap, 1987)

Berry, Cicely, *Voice and the Actor*, Virgin Books, 1993 (first published by Harrap, 1973)

Boal, A. (trans. Jackson, A.), *Games for Actors and Non-Actors*, Routledge, 1992

Boal, A.,*The Rainbow of Desire: The Boal Method of Theatre and Therapy*, Routledge, 1995

Boal, A., *Theatre of the Oppressed*, Pluto Press, 1979

Bolton, G., *New Perspectives on Classroom Drama*, Simon & Schuster, 1992

Bond, D., *Stage Management: A Gentle Art*, A & C Black, 1991

Bostock, L., *Speaking in Public*, HarperCollins, 1994

Bradby, D. and Williams, D., *Directors' Theatre*, Macmillan Modern Dramatist, 1988

Braun E., *The Director and the Stage*, Methuen, 1987

Brinson, P. (ed.), *Arts and Communities: The Report of the National Enquiry into Arts in the Community*, Community Development Foundation, 1992

Brook, P., *The Empty Space*, Penguin, 1968

Bull, J., *New British Political Dramatists*, Macmillan, 1984

Calder, A., Mapanje, J., Pieterse, C., *New Poetry of Africa*, Heinemann Educational, 1983

Calouste Gulbenkian Foundation, *The Arts in Schools: Principles, Practice and Provision*, CGF, 1982

Carlton, B., *Return to the Forbidden Planet*, Methuen, 1985

Carnegie UK Trust, *Arts and Disabled People: The Attenborough Report*, Bedford Square Press, 1985

Cassady, M., *The Book of Cuttings for Acting and Directing*, National Textbook Company, 1991

Chambers, C., *Playwrights' Progress: Patterns of Postwar British Drama*, Oxford, 1987

Chapman, G. and Robson, P., *Making Masks for Children*, Macdonald Young Books Ltd, 1995

Chase, M., 'Tools for Transformation', *Total Theatre* Volume VII no. 3, 1995

Clarke, S., *The Complete Fundraising Handbook*, Directory of Social Change, London, 1993

Clements, Paul, *The Improvised Play: The Work of Mike Leigh*, Methuen, 1983

Cohen, N., *Theatre Works: A Guide to Working in the Theatre*, Royal National Theatre Publications Department and Theatre Museum Education Department, 1992

Cook, P., *How to Enjoy Theatre* (series editor Melvyn Bragg), Piatkus Ltd, 1983

Cooper, S. and Mackey, S., *Theatre Studies: An Approach for Advanced Level*, Stanley Thornes, 1995

Cordry, D., *Mexican Masks*, Austin: University of Texas Press, 1980

Cote, H. M. (ed.), *I Am Not Myself: The Art of African Masquerade*, University Art Museum at University of California Santa Barbara, 1985

Coult, T. and Kershaw, B., *Engineers of the Imagination*, Methuen, 1983

Courtney, R., *The Dramatic Curriculum*, Heinemann, 1980

Craig, S., *Dreams and Reconstructions*, Amberlane Press, 1980

Dahl, D., *Residencies in Education*, AN Publications, 1990

Davies, A., *Other Theatres*, Barnes and Noble, 1987

Department for Education and Employment, *Career Development Loans Application Pack*, Crown Copyright, 1995

Department of National Heritage, *A Creative Future: Ways Forward for the Arts, Crafts and Media in England*, Her Majesty's Stationery Office, 1993

Dodgson, E., *Motherland*, Unwin, 1987

Dodgson, T., *The Arts in Society*, 1993 (unpublished)

Doney, M., *World Crafts: Masks*, Watts Books, 1995

Doulton, A.M., *The Arts Funding Guide*, Directory of Social Change (DSC), London, 1994

Downing, D. and Jones, T. (eds), *Special Theatre: The Work of Interplay Community Theatre for People with Severe Learning Difficulties 1970 to 1985*

Duchatre, P. L., *The Italian Comedy*, Dover Publications, 1966

Duncan, S., *The Guide to Careers and Training in the Performing Arts*, The Cheverell Press, 1993

Dunne, N., *Acting for Health, Acting Against HIV: A Report on the Effectiveness of Theatre in Health Education in HIV and AIDS Education*, The Theatre in Health Education Trust Publication, 1993

Elms, S. (et al), *The London Theatre Scene*, Frank Cook Travel Guides, 1979

Elsom, J., *Post-War British Theatre*, Routledge & Kegan Paul, 1979

Elwell, C., *Interface I: The Report of a Seminar on Education in Presenting Venue*, Arts Council of England, 1995

Elwell, C., *Interface II: Report of a Seminar on Education for Touring Companies*, Arts Council of England, 1996

Encyclopaedia Britannica, *The History of Western Theatre*, Encyclopaedia Britannica Inc, 1994

England, A., *Theatre for the Young*, Macmillan, 1990

Festival Fringe Society, *How to Do a Show on the Fringe*, Festival Fringe Society, 1996

Findlater, R. (ed.), *25 Years of the English Stage Company*, Amber Press, 1981

Fo, D., *The Tricks of the Trade*, Methuen, 1991

Frank, V. and Jaffe, D., *Making Masks*, The Apple Press, 1992

Frost, A. and Yarrow, R., *Improvisation in Drama*, Methuen, 1992

Garnham, N., 'The Political Economy and the Production of Culture' in
Inglis, F., *Capitalism and Communication*, Sage, 1990

Gauntlett, M and O'Connor, B., *Drama Studies*, Longman Australia Pty Ltd, 1995

Goonatilleka, M. H., *Masks and Mask Systems of Sri Lanka*, Tamarind Books. 1978

Goorney, H., *The Theatre Workshop Story*, Eyre Methuen, 1981

Griffiths, D., *Backstagers: A Teacher's Guide to Practical Backstage Skills*, Collins, 1996

Gross, R.D., *Psychology: The Science of Mind and Behaviour*, Hodder & Stoughton, 1987

Gurr, Andrew, *The Shakespearean Stage, 1574–1642*, Cambridge University
Press, 1992

Harris, S. and Shaw, P., *The Report for the Arts Council of Great Britain's Touring
Department on the Work of Touring Companies and Venues in the Field of
Education and Audience Development*, Arts Council of Great Britain, 1993

Hartnoll, P. (ed), *The Concise Oxford Companion to the Theatre*, Oxford University
Press. 1990

Hartnoll, P., *The Theatre: A Concise History*, Thames and Hudson, 1985

Hayes, R. and Reason J., *Voluntary But Not Amateur*, London Voluntary Service
Council, 1985

Hayman, R., *The Set Up*, Methuen, 1973

Hickson, A., *Creative Action Methods in Groupwork*, Winslow Press, 1995

Hodgson, J. and Richards, E., *Improvisation*, Eyre Methuen, 1967

Hoggett, C., *Stage Crafts*, A & C Black, 1991

Holland, J., Hartley, K. and Kinder, K., (eds), *Arts in Their View: A Study of
Youth Participation in the Arts*, National Foundation for Educational
Research, 1995

Holt M., *Stage Design and Properties*, Phaidon, 1988

Horniman Mask Education Pack, Horniman Museum Education Centre, 1991

Itzin, C. (ed.), *Alternative Theatre Handbook*, Theatre Quarterly Publications, 1980

Itzin, C., *Stages in the Revolution*, Eyre Methuen, 1980

Jackson, T. (ed.), *Learning Through Theatre: New Perspectives on Theatre and
Education (2nd Edition)*, Routledge, 1993

Janner, G., *Janner on Presentation*, Business Books (Hutchinson) Ltd, 1984

Johnstone, K., *Impro: Improvisation and the Theatre*, Eyre Methuen Ltd, 1981

Jones, S. (ed.), *Fundraising: The Artist's Guide to Planning and Financial Work*,
AN Publications, 1993

Kempe, A., *The GCSE Drama Coursebook*, Stanley Thornes, 1990

Kershaw, B., *The Politics of Performance: Radical Theatre as Cultural Intervention*,
Routledge, 1992

Kimber, K. and Wood, D., *Stages in Design: Assignments for the Performing Arts*,
Hodder & Stoughton, 1994

King, J. C. H., *Portrait Masks From the North West Coast of America*, Thames &
Hudson, 1979

Lees, Sarah (ed.), *Disability Arts and Culture Papers*, Shape Publications, 1992

Lewis, J., *Arts Culture and Enterprise: The Politics of Art and the Cultural Industries*

Ley, G., 'The Rhetoric of Theory: The Role of Metaphor in Brook's Empty
Space' in *New Theatre Quarterly*, August 1993

Lommel, A., *Masks: Their Meaning and Function*, Ferndale Editions, 1981

London Arts Board, *Bringing Out the Artist in the Child: Practice of Artists in
Schools*, London Arts Board, 1992

Mack, J., *Masks: The Art of Expression*, The British Museum Press, 1994

MacLennan, E., *The Moon Belongs to Everyone: Making Theatre with 7:84*,
Methuen, 1990

Manser, S. and Wilmot, H., *Artists in Residence: A Teacher's Handbook*, London Arts Board/St. Katherine and Shadwell Trust, 1995

Marowitz C., *Prospero's Staff*, Indiana Studies in Theatre and Drama, 1986

Marowitz, C. et al (eds), *The Encore Reader*, Methuen, 1965

Mason, B., *Street Theatre and Other Outdoor Performance*, Routledge, 1992

Matura, M., *Playboy of the West Indies*, Broadway Play Publishing Inc., 1988

McCafferey, M., *A Phaidon Theatre Manual: Directing A Play* (series editor, David Mayer), Phaidon Press Ltd, 1988

McFarlane, G., Copyright: *The Development and the Exercise of the Performance Right*, Offord Press, 1981

McGrath, J., *A Good Night Out*, Methuen, 1981

Mechanical and Copyright Protection Society, *On the Right Track*, MCPS Ltd, 1995

Microsoft Corporation, *Mask*, Microsoft®, Encarta®, 96, Encylopaedia © 1993–1995

Miller, Arthur, *Death of a Salesman*, Penguin Books Ltd, 1985

NCVQ, *GNVQ Mandatory Units for Advanced Performing Arts and Entertainment Industries*, NCVQ, 1996

Neelands, J., *Structuring Drama Work*, CUP, 1990

Newton, T., *Iron Dreams*, Pop-Up, 1996 (unpublished)

Norton, M., *Writing Better Fund-raising Applications: A Practical Guide*, Directory of Social Change Publications, 1992

Nuttall, J., *Bomb Culture*, Paladin, 1969

O'Toole, J., *The Process of Drama*, Routledge, 1992

Oddey, A., *Devising Theatre: A Practical and Theoretical Handbook*, Routledge, 1994

Onyx Consultancy/Arts Council of Great Britain, *Black Artists in Schools: A Report on Training Needs*, ACGB, 1993

Oreglia, G., *The Commedia dell' Arte*, Methuen, 1968

Owusu, K., *The Struggle for Black Arts in Britain*, Comedia, 1986

Ratcliffe, M., *Platform Papers: Directors*, The Royal National Theatre, 1993

Rea, K., *A Better Direction*, Calouste Gulbenkian Foundation, 1989

Reddington, C., *Can Theatre Teach? An Evaluative Analysis of TIE*, Pergamon, 1983

Rees, R., *Fringe First: Pioneers of Fringe Theatre on Record*, Oberon Books, 1992

Reid, F., *Designing for the Theatre*, A & C Black, 1989

Reid, F., *Stage Lighting*, Focal Press, 1993

Reid, F., *The Staging Handbook*, A & C Black, 1978

Richardson, J., *Careers in the Theatre*, Kogan Page Ltd, 1995

Richie, R. (ed.), *The Joint Stock Book*, Methuen, 1987

Robinson, K., *Exploring Theatre and Education*, Heinemann, 1980

Roose-Evans, James, *Experimental Theatre from Stanislavski to Peter Brook*, Routledge, 1991

Rosenberg, H., *How to Apply for Grants, Loans and Other Sources of Finance*, Gee Publishing Ltd, 1994

Royal Ontario Museum, *Masks: The Many Faces of Man*, an exhibition presented by the Division of Art and Archaeology, 1959

Rudlin, J., *Commedia dell' Arte: An Actor's Handbook*, Routledge, 1994

Saint-Denis, Suria (ed.), *Training for the Theatre: Michel Saint-Denis*, Heinemann, 1982

Scottish Arts Council, *Advice: Applying to Charitable Trusts and Foundations*, 1995

Seaton, A., Davidson, G., Schwarz, C., Simpson, J. (eds), *Chambers Thesaurus*, W & R Chambers Ltd, 1990

Segy, I., *Masks of Black Africa*, Dover Publications Inc, 1976

Semple, M., 'Arts Education and Cultural Diversity' in Fyfe, A. and Figueroa, P. (eds), *Education for Cultural Diversity: The Challenge of a New Era*, Routledge, 1993

Sharman, H., *Bums on Seats: How to Publicise Your Show*, A & C Black Ltd, 1992

Sharp, C. and Dust, K., *Artists in Schools*, Bedford Square Press, 1990

Spolin, V., *Improvisation for the Theatre: Including Two Hundred and Twenty Theatre Games*, Pitman and Sons, 1963

Stafford-Clark, M., *Letters to George*, Nick Hern Books, 1990

Stanislavksi, C., *An Actor Prepares*, Methuen, 1991

Stanislavski, C., *Building a Character*, Methuen, 1991

Stratton, D., 'Mystery and Magic Under the Mask' in *The Sunday Telegraph*, 8 October 1989

Stuart, P., *Theatre Procedure And Practice, or Who Does What In The Theatre?* Kemble Press Ltd, 1982

Suffolk, L., 'Theatre, Memory and Learning: The Long-Term Impact of Theatre-in-Education' in Tickle, L. (ed.), *The Arts in Education: Some Research Studies*

Sweeting, E., *Theatre Administration*, Pitman, 1969

Sykes, J. B. (ed), *The Concise Oxford Dictionary of Current English*, Oxford University Press, 1988

Talbot, L., 'Masks for Bald Italians' in the *Ham & High*, 10 August 1990

The Arts Council of Great Britain, *Dance in Schools*, ACGB, 1993

The Arts Council of Great Britain, *Looking Over the Edge: Advisory Structures for Theatre in Education*, ACGB, 1994

The National Curriculum Council, *Arts in Schools Project: 5–16, The Arts 5–16: Practice and Innovation*, and *The Arts 5–16: A Curriculum Framework*, Oliver & Boyd/NCC, 1989 (three books)

The Royal Society of Arts, *Guaranteeing an Entitlement to the Arts in Schools*, Royal Society of Arts, 1995

Theatre Papers, Volume III, nos 2 and 8, Dartington, 1979

Thompson, G., *Focal Guide to Safety in Live Performance*, Butterworth Heinemann Ltd, 1993

Thurston, J., *The Prop Builder's Mask Making Handbook*, Betterway Books, F & W Publications Inc, 1990

Tisdall, C., 'Masquerade', in the *Guardian*, 8 December 1977

Tomlinson, R., *Disability, Theatre and Education*, Souvenir Press Ltd, 1982

Trestle Theatre Company, Programme and Education Pack for *Passionfish*, 1996

Tydeman, William, *The Theatre in the Middle Ages*, Cambridge University Press, 1978

Vidal, J., 'Opening Moves', the *Guardian*, 21 March 1988

Villemur, A. (ed), *The Directory of Grant Making Trusts, 13th Edition, 1993–94*, Charities Aid Foundation, 1993

Vine, C., *Graeae: Setting the Scene*, ACGB, 1992

Whitley, A., *Look Before You Leap: An Advice and Rights Guide for Choreographers*, Dance UK, 1995

Willet, John, (ed.), *Brecht on Theatre*, Methuen, 1957

Willet, John, *The Theatre of Bertholt Brecht*, Methuen, 1977

Williams, David, *Peter Brook: A Theatrical Casebook*, Methuen, 1988

Williams, R., *Keywords: A Vocabulary of Culture and Society*, Fontana, 1976

Winser, K. (ed.), *Arts Professionals in Schools:A Step-by-Step Guide to Artists-in-Schools Projects*, Norfolk Educational Press, 1995

Wright, L., *Masks*, Franklin Watts, 1989

INDEX

Page numbers in bold indicate a main reference to the subject.